The Sociology-Philosophy Connection

The Sociology-Philosophy Connection

Dr. Mahesh Kumar Singh

RANDOM PUBLICATIONS

NEW DELHI - 110 002 (INDIA)

The Sociology-Philosophy Connection

ISBN 978-93-51114-53-6

Published in 2014 in India by

RANDOM PUBLICATIONS

4376-A/4B, Gali Murari Lal, Ansari Road

New Delhi-110 002

Phone: +9111-43580356, 23289044

E-mail: randomexports@gmail.com; sales@randompublications.com; info@randompublications.com

Reprinted 2025

Type Setting by: Friends Media, Delhi-110089

Digitally Printed at: Replika Press Pvt. Ltd.

Preface

Sociology is the scientific study of human social behavior and its origins, development, organizations, and institutions. It is a social science that uses various methods of empirical investigation and critical analysis to develop a body of knowledge about human social actions, social structure and functions. A goal for many sociologists is to conduct research which may be applied directly to social policy and welfare, while others focus primarily on refining the theoretical understanding of social processes. Subject matter ranges from the micro level of individual agency and interaction to the macro level of systems and the social structure. Sociological reasoning predates the foundation of the discipline. Social analysis has origins in the common stock of Western knowledge and philosophy, and has been carried out from as far back as the time of ancient Greek philosopher Plato if not before. The origin of the survey, i.e., the collection of information from a sample of individuals, can be traced back to at least the Domesday Book in 1086, while ancient philosophers such as Confucius wrote on the importance of social roles. There is evidence of early sociology in medieval Islam.

Sociology overlaps with a variety of disciplines that study society, in particular anthropology, political science, economics, and social philosophy. Many comparatively new fields such as communication studies, cultural studies, demography and literary theory, draw upon methods that originated in sociology. The terms "social science" and "social research" have both gained a degree of autonomy since their origination in classical sociology. The distinct field of social psychology emerged from the many intersections of sociological and psychological interests, and is further distinguished in terms of sociological or psychological emphasis. Philosophy is the study of general and fundamental problems, such as those connected with reality, existence, knowledge, values, reason, mind, and language. Philosophy is distinguished from other ways of addressing such problems by its critical, generally systematic approach and its reliance on rational argument. Social philosophers place new emphasis on understanding the social contexts for political, legal, moral, and cultural questions, and to the development of novel theoretical frameworks, from social ontology to care ethics to cosmopolitan theories of democracy, human rights, gender equity and global justice. There is often a considerable overlap between the questions addressed by social philosophy and ethics or value theory. Other forms of social philosophy include political philosophy and jurisprudence, which are largely concerned with the societies of state and government and their functioning. Social philosophy, ethics, and political philosophy all share intimate connections with other disciplines in the social sciences. In turn, the social sciences themselves are of focal interest to the philosophy of social science. Most social scientists and philosophers claim that sociology and philosophy are disjointed fields of inquiry. Some have wondered how to trace the precise boundary between them. In fact, sociological research has demonstrably philosophical presuppositions. In turn, some findings of sociology are bound to correct or enrich the philosophical theories that deal with the world, our knowledge of it, or the ways of acting upon it.

This important book will prove to be a very useful tool for researchers and students across the social sciences.

I thank all members of my team who have helped in the preparation of the book. My special thanks go to "Random Publications" who have published the book.

— Dr. Mahesh Kumar Singh

Contents

1

Introduction

Sociology

Sociology is the study of human social behaviour and its origins, development, organizations, and institutions. It is a social science which uses various methods of empirical investigation and critical analysis to develop a body of knowledge about human social actions, social structure and functions. A goal for many sociologists is to conduct research which may be applied directly to social policy and welfare, while others focus primarily on refining the theoretical understanding of social processes. Subject matter ranges from the micro level of individual agency and interaction to the macro level of systems and the social structure.

The traditional focuses of sociology include social stratification, social class, social mobility, religion, secularization, law, and deviance. As all spheres of human activity are affected by the interplay between social structure and individual agency, sociology has gradually expanded its focus to further subjects, such as health, medical, military and penalinstitutions, the Internet, and the role of social activity in the development of scientific knowledge.

The range of social scientific methods has also expanded. Social researchers draw upon a variety of qualitative and quantitative techniques. The linguistic and cultural turns of the mid-twentieth century led to increasingly interpretative, hermeneutic, and philosophic approaches to the analysis of society. Conversely, recent decades have seen the rise of new analytically, mathematically and computationally rigorous techniques, such as agent-based modelling and social network analysis.

Classification

Sociology should not be confused with various general social studies courses which bear little relation to sociological theory or social science research methodology. The US National Science Foundation, classifies Sociology as a STEM Field.

History

Origins: Sociological reasoning predates the foundation of the discipline. Social analysis has origins in the common stock of Western knowledge and philosophy, and has been carried out from as far back as the time of ancient Greek philosopher Plato if not before. The origin of the survey, i.e., the collection of information from a sample of individuals, can be traced back to at least the Domesday Book in 1086, while ancient philosophers such as Confucius wrote on the importance of social roles. There is evidence of early sociology in medieval Islam. Some consider Ibn Khaldun, a 14th-century Arab Islamic scholar from North Africa, to have been the first sociologist; his *Muqaddimah* was perhaps the first work to advance social-scientific reasoning on social cohesion and social conflict. Most sociological concepts were used in English prior to their adoption as the technical language of sociology.

The word *sociology* (or *"sociologie"*) is derived from both Latin and Greek origins. The Latin word: *socius*, "companion"; the suffix *-logy*, "the study of" from Greek-ëïãßá from ëüãïò, *lógos*, "word", "knowledge". It was first coined in 1780 by the French essayist Emmanuel-Joseph Sieyès (1748–1836) in an unpublished manuscript. Sociology was later defined independently by the French philosopher of science, Auguste Comte (1798–1857), in 1838. Comte used this term to describe a new way of looking at society. Comte had earlier used the term "social physics", but that had subsequently been appropriated by others, most notably the Belgian statistician Adolphe Quetelet. Comte endeavoured to unify history, psychology and economics through the scientific understanding of the social realm. Writing shortly after the malaise of the French Revolution, he proposed that social ills could be remedied through sociological positivism, an epistemological approach outlined in *The Course in Positive Philosophy* [1830–1842] and *A General View of Positivism* (1848). Comte believed a positivist stage would mark the final era, after conjectural theological and metaphysical phases, in the progression of human understanding. In observing the circular dependence of theory and observation in science, and having classified the sciences, Comte may be regarded as the first philosopher of science in the modern sense of the term.

Comte gave a powerful impetus to the development of sociology, an impetus which bore fruit in the later decades of the nineteenth century. To say this is certainly not to claim that French sociologists such as Durkheim were devoted disciples of the high priest of positivism. But by insisting on the irreducibility of each of his basic sciences to the particular science of sciences which it presupposed in the hierarchy and by emphasizing the nature of sociology as the scientific study of social phenomena Comte put sociology on the map. To be sure, [its] beginnings can be traced back well beyond Montesquieu, for example, and to Condorcet, not to speak of Saint-Simon, Comte's immediate predecessor. But Comte's clear recognition of sociology as a particular science, with a character of its own, justified Durkheim in regarding him as the father or founder of this science, in spite of the fact that Durkheim did not accept the idea of the three states and criticized Comte's approach to sociology.

— Frederick Copleston A *History of Philosophy: IX Modern Philosophy* 1974,

Both Auguste Comte and Karl Marx (1818-1883) set out to develop scientifically justified systems in the wake of European industrialization and secularization, informed by various key movements in the philosophies of history and science. Marx rejected Comtean positivism but in attempting to develop a *science of society* nevertheless came to be recognized as a founder of sociology as the word gained wider meaning. For Isaiah Berlin, Marx may be regarded as the "true father" of modern sociology, "in so far as anyone can claim the title."

To have given clear and unified answers in familiar empirical terms to those theoretical questions which most occupied men's minds at the time, and to have deduced from them clear practical directives without creating obviously artificial links between the two, was the principle achievement of Marx's theory. The sociological treatment of historical and moral problems, which Comte and after him, Spencer and Taine, had discussed and mapped, became a precise and concrete study only when the attack of militant Marxism made its conclusions a burning issue, and so made the search for evidence more zealous and the attention to method more intense.

— Isaiah Berlin *Karl Marx: His Life and Environment* 1937,

Herbert Spencer (27 April 1820 – 8 December 1903) was one of the most popular and influential 19th century sociologists. It is estimated that he sold one million books in his lifetime, far more than any other sociologist at the time. So strong was his influence that many other 19th century thinkers, including Émile Durkheim, defined their ideas in relation to his. Durkheim's *Division of Labour in Society* is to a large extent an extended debate with Spencer from whose sociology, many commentators now agree, Durkheim borrowed extensively. Also a notable biologist, Spencer coined the term "survival of the fittest". Whilst Marxian ideas defined one strand of sociology, Spencer was a critic of socialism as well as strong advocate for a laissez-faire style of government. His ideas were highly observed by conservative political circles, especially in the United States and England.

Foundations of the Academic Discipline

Formal academic sociology was established by Émile Durkheim (1858–1917), who developed positivism as a foundation to practical social research. While Durkheim rejected much of the detail of Comte's philosophy, he retained and refined its method, maintaining that the social sciences are a logical continuation of the natural ones into the realm of human activity, and insisting that they may retain the same objectivity, rationalism, and approach to causality. Durkheim set up the first European department of sociology at the University of Bordeaux in 1895, publishing his *Rules of the Sociological Method* (1895).

For Durkheim, sociology could be described as the "science of institutions, their genesis and their functioning".

Durkheim's seminal monograph, *Suicide* (1897), a case study of suicide rates amongst Catholic and Protestant populations, distinguished sociological analysis from psychology or philosophy. It also marked a major contribution to the theoretical concept of structural functionalism. By carefully examining suicide statistics in different police districts, he attempted to demonstrate that Catholic communities have a lower suicide rate than that of Protestants, something he attributed to social (as opposed to individual or psychological) causes. He developed the notion of objective *sui generis* "social facts" to delineate a unique empirical object for the science of sociology to study. Through such studies he posited that sociology would be able to determine whether any given society is 'healthy' or 'pathological', and seek social reform to negate organic breakdown or "social anomie".

Sociology quickly evolved as an academic response to the perceived challenges of modernity, such as industrialization, urbanization, secularization, and the process of "rationalization". The field predominated in continental Europe, with British anthropology and statistics generally following on a separate trajectory. By the turn of the 20th century, however, many theorists were active in the Anglo-Saxon world. Few early sociologists were confined strictly to the subject, interacting also with economics, jurisprudence, psychology and philosophy, with theories being appropriated in a variety of different fields. Since its inception, sociological epistemologies, methods, and frames of inquiry, have significantly expanded and diverged.

Durkheim, Marx, and the German theorist Max Weber (1864-1920) are typically cited as the three principal architects of social science. Herbert Spencer, William Graham Sumner, Lester F. Ward, Vilfredo Pareto, Alexis de Tocqueville, Werner Sombart, Thorstein Veblen, Ferdinand Tönnies, Georg Simmel and Karl Mannheim are occasionally included on academic curricula as founding theorists. Each key figure is associated with a particular theoretical perspective and orientation.

Marx and Engels associated the emergence of modern society above all with the development of capitalism; for Durkheim it was connected in particular with industrialization and the new social division of labour which this brought about; for Weber it had to do with the emergence of a distinctive way of thinking, the rational calculation which he associated with the Protestant Ethic (more or less what Marx and Engels speak of in terms of those 'icy waves of egotistical calculation'). Together the works of these great classical sociologists suggest what Giddens has recently described as 'a multidimensional view of institutions of modernity' and which emphasizes not only capitalism and industrialism as key institutions of modernity, but also 'surveillance' (meaning 'control of information and social supervision') and 'military power' (control of the means of violence in the context of the industrialization of war).

— John Harriss *The Second Great Transformation? Capitalism at the End of the Twentieth Century* 1992,

Other Developments

The first college course entitled "Sociology" was taught in the United States at Yale in 1875 by William Graham Sumner. In 1883 Lester F. Ward, the first president of the American Sociological Association, published *Dynamic Sociology—Or Applied social science as based upon statical sociology and the less complex sciences* and attacked the laissez-faire sociology of Herbert Spencer and Sumner. Ward's 1200 page book was used as core material in many early American sociology courses. In 1890, the oldest continuing American course in the modern tradition began at the University of Kansas, lectured by Frank W. Blackmar. The Department of Sociology at the University of Chicago was established in 1892 by Albion Small, who also published the first sociology textbook: An introduction to the study of society 1894. George Herbert Mead and Charles Cooley, who had met at the University of Michigan in 1891 (along with John Dewey), would move to Chicago in 1894.

Their influence gave rise to social psychology and the symbolic interactionism of the modern Chicago School. The *American Journal of Sociology* was founded in 1895, followed by the *American Sociological Association* (ASA) in 1905. The sociological "canon of classics" with Durkheim and Max Weber at the top owes in part to Talcott Parsons, who is largely credited with introducing both to American audiences. Parsons consolidated the sociological tradition and set the agenda for American sociology at the point of its fastest disciplinary growth. Sociology in the United States was less historically influenced by Marxism than its European counterpart, and to this day broadly remains more statistical in its approach.

The first sociology department to be established in the United Kingdom was at the London School of Economics and Political Science (home of the *British Journal of Sociology*) in 1904. Leonard Trelawny Hobhouse and Edvard Westermarck became the lecturers in the discipline at the University of London in 1907. Harriet Martineau, an English translator of Comte, has been cited as the first female sociologist. In 1909 the *Deutsche Gesellschaft für Soziologie* (German Sociological Association) was founded by Ferdinand Tönnies and Max Weber, among others. Weber established the first department in Germany at the Ludwig Maximilian University of Munich in 1919, having presented an influential new antipositivist sociology. In 1920, Florian Znaniecki set up the first department in Poland. The *Institute for Social Research* at the University of Frankfurt (later to become the Frankfurt School of critical theory) was founded in 1923. International co-operation in sociology began in 1893, when René Worms founded the *Institut International de Sociologie*, an institution later eclipsed by the much larger International Sociological Association (ISA), founded in 1949.

Positivism and Anti-Positivism

Positivism: The overarching methodological principle of positivism is to conduct sociology in broadly the same manner as natural science. An emphasis on empiricism and the scientific method is sought to provide a tested foundation for sociological research based on the assumption that the only authentic knowledge is scientific knowledge, and that such knowledge can only arrive by positive affirmation through scientific methodology.

"Our main goal is to extend scientific rationalism to human conduct... What has been called our positivism is but a consequence of this rationalism."

— Émile Durkheim, *The Rules of Sociological Method* (1895),

The term has long since ceased to carry this meaning; there are no fewer than twelve distinct epistemologies that are referred to as positivism. Many of these approaches do not self-identify as "positivist", some because they themselves arose in opposition to older forms of positivism, and some because the label has over time become a term of abuse by being mistakenly linked with a theoretical empiricism. The extent of antipositivist criticism has also diverged, with many rejecting the scientific method and others only seeking to amend it to reflect 20th century developments in the philosophy of science. However, positivism (broadly understood as a scientific approach to the study of society) remains dominant in contemporary sociology, especially in the United States.

Loïc Wacquant distinguishes three major strains of positivism: Durkheimian, Logical, and Instrumental. None of these are the same as that set forth by Comte, who was unique in advocating such a rigid (and perhaps optimistic) version. While Émile Durkheim rejected much of the detail of Comte's philosophy, he retained and refined its method. Durkheim maintained that the social sciences are a logical continuation of the natural ones into the realm of human activity, and insisted that they should retain the same objectivity, rationalism, and approach to causality. He developed the notion of objective *sui generis* "social facts" to delineate a unique empirical object for the science of sociology to study.

The variety of positivism that remains dominant today is termed *instrumental positivism*. This approach eschews epistemological and metaphysical concerns (such as the nature of social facts) in favour of methodological clarity, replicability, reliability and validity. This positivism is more or less synonymous with quantitative research, and so only resembles older positivism in practice. Since it carries no explicit philosophical commitment, its practitioners may not belong to any particular school of thought. Modern sociology of this type is often credited to Paul Lazarsfeld, who pioneered large-scale survey studies and developed statistical techniques for analyzing them. This approach lends itself to what Robert K. Merton called middle-range theory: abstract statements that generalize from segregated hypotheses and empirical regularities rather than starting with an abstract idea of a social whole.

Anti-Positivism

Reactions against social empiricism began when German philosopher Hegel voiced opposition to both empiricism, which he rejected as uncritical, and determinism, which he viewed as overly mechanistic. Karl Marx's methodology borrowed from Hegelian dialecticism but also a rejection of positivism in favour of critical analysis, seeking to supplement the empirical acquisition of "facts" with the elimination of illusions. He maintained that appearances need to be critiqued rather than simply documented. Early hermeneuticians such as Wilhelm Dilthey pioneered the distinction between natural and social science ('Geisteswissenschaft'). Various neo-Kantian philosophers, phenomenologists and human scientists further theorized how the analysis of the social world differs to that of the natural world due to the irreducibly complex aspects of human society, culture, and being.

At the turn of the 20th century the first generation of German sociologists formally introduced methodological anti-positivism, proposing that research should concentrate on human cultural norms, values, symbols, and social processes viewed from a resolutely subjective perspective. Max Weber argued that sociology may be loosely described as a science as it is able to identify causal relationships of human "social action"—especially among "ideal types", or hypothetical simplifications of complex social phenomena. As a non-positivist, however, Weber sought relationships that are not as "historical, invariant, or generalizable" as those pursued by natural scientists. Fellow German sociologist, Ferdinand Tönnies, theorized on two crucial abstract concepts with his work on "Gemeinschaft and Gesellschaft" (lit. *community* and *society*). Tönnies marked a sharp line between the realm of concepts and the reality of social action: the first must be treated axiomatically and in a deductive way ("pure sociology"), whereas the second empirically and inductively ("applied sociology").

[Sociology is] ... the science whose object is to interpret *the meaning of social action* and thereby give a *causal explanation* of the way in which the *action proceeds* and the *effects which it produces*. By 'action' in this definition is meant the human behaviour when and to the extent that the agent or agents see it as *subjectively meaningful* ... the meaning to which we refer may be either (a) the meaning actually intended either by an individual agent on a particular historical

occasion or by a number of agents on an approximate average in a given set of cases, or (b) the meaning attributed to the agent or agents, as types, in a pure type constructed in the abstract. In neither case is the 'meaning' to be thought of as somehow objectively 'correct' or 'true' by some metaphysical criterion. This is the difference between the empirical sciences of action, such as sociology and history, and any kind of *prior* discipline, such as jurisprudence, logic, ethics, or aesthetics whose aim is to extract from their subject-matter 'correct' or 'valid' meaning.

— Max Weber *The Nature of Social Action* 1922,

Both Weber and Georg Simmel pioneered the "*Verstehen*" (or 'interpretative') method in social science; a systematic process by which an outside observer attempts to relate to a particular cultural group, or indigenous people, on their own terms and from their own point-of-view. Through the work of Simmel, in particular, sociology acquired a possible character beyond positivist data-collection or grand, deterministic systems of structural law. Relatively isolated from the sociological academy throughout his lifetime, Simmel presented idiosyncratic analyses of modernity more reminiscent of the phenomenological and existential writers than of Comte or Durkheim, paying particular concern to the forms of, and possibilities for, social individuality. His sociology engaged in a neo-Kantian inquiry into the limits of perception, asking 'What is society?' in a direct allusion to Kant's question 'What is nature?'

The deepest problems of modern life flow from the attempt of the individual to maintain the independence and individuality of his existence against the sovereign powers of society, against the weight of the historical heritage and the external culture and technique of life. The antagonism represents the most modern form of the conflict which primitive man must carry on with nature for his own bodily existence. The eighteenth century may have called for liberation from all the ties which grew up historically in politics, in religion, in morality and in economics in order to permit the original natural virtue of man, which is equal in everyone, to develop without inhibition; the nineteenth century may have sought to promote, in addition to man's freedom, his individuality (which is connected with the division of labour) and his achievements which make him unique and indispensable but which at the same time make him so much the more dependent on the complementary activity of others; Nietzsche may have seen the relentless struggle of the individual as the prerequisite for his full development, while socialism found the same thing in the suppression of all competition – but in each of these the same fundamental motive was at work, namely the resistance of the individual to being leveled, swallowed up in the social-technological mechanism.

— Georg Simmel *The Metropolis and Mental Life* 1903,

Theoretical Frameworks

The contemporary discipline of sociology is theoretically multi-paradigmatic. Modern sociological theory descends from the historical foundations of functionalist (Durkheim) and conflict-centred (Marx) accounts of social structure, as well as the micro-scale structural (Simmel) and pragmatist (Mead) theories of social interaction. Contemporary sociological theory retains traces of these approaches.

Presently, sociological theories lack a single overarching foundation, and there is little consensus about what such a framework should consist of. However, a number of broad paradigms cover much present sociological theorizing. In the humanistic parts of the discipline, these paradigms are referred to as *social* theory, and are often shared with the humanities. The discipline's dominant scientifically-oriented areas generally focus on a different set of theoretical perspectives, which by contrast are generally referred to as *sociological* theory. These include sociological field theory, new institutionalism, social networks, social identity, social and cultural capital, toolkit and cognitive theories of culture, and resource mobilization. Analytical sociology is an ongoing effort to systematize many of these middle-range theories.

Functionalism

A broad historical paradigm in both sociology and anthropology, functionalism addresses the social structure as a whole and in terms of the necessary function of its constituent elements. A common analogy (popularized by Herbert Spencer) is to regard norms and institutions as 'organs' that work toward the proper-functioning of the entire 'body' of society. The perspective was implicit in the original sociological positivism of Comte, but was theorized in full by Durkheim, again with respect to observable, structural laws. Functionalism also has an anthropological basis in the work of theorists such as Marcel Mauss, Bronis³aw Malinowski and Radcliffe-Brown. It is in Radcliffe-Brown's specific usage that the prefix 'structural' emerged. Classical functionalist theory is generally united by its tendency towards biological analogy and notions of social evolutionism. As Giddens states: "Functionalist thought, from Comte onwards, has looked particularly towards biology as the science providing the closest and most compatible model for social science. Biology has been taken to provide a guide to conceptualizing the structure and the function of social systems and to analyzing processes of evolution via mechanisms of adaptation ... functionalism strongly emphasizes the pre-eminence of the social world over its individual parts (i.e. its constituent actors, human subjects)."

Conflict Theory

Functionalism aims only toward a general perspective from which to conduct social science. Methodologically, its principles generally contrast those approaches that emphasize the "micro", such as interpretivism or symbolic interactionism. Its emphasis on "cohesive systems", however, also holds political ramifications. Functionalist theories are often therefore contrasted with "conflict theories" which critique the overarching socio-political system or emphasize the inequality of particular groups. The works of Durkheim and Marx epitomize the political, as well as theoretical, disparities, between functionalist and conflict thought respectively:

To aim for a civilization beyond that made possible by the nexus of the surrounding environment will result in unloosing sickness into the very society we live in. Collective activity cannot be encouraged beyond the point set by the condition of the social organism without undermining health.

— Émile Durkheim *The Division of Labour in Society* 1893,

The history of all hitherto existing society is the history of class struggles.

Freeman and slave, patrician and plebeian, lord and serf, guild-master and journeyman, in a word, oppressor and oppressed, stood in constant opposition to one another, carried on an uninterrupted, now hidden, now open fight, a fight that each time ended, either in a revolutionary re-constitution of society at large, or in the common ruin of the contending classes.

— Karl Marx&Friedrich Engels *The Communist Manifesto* 1848,

20th Century Social Theory

The functionalist movement reached its crescendo in the 1940s and 1950s, and by the 1960s was in rapid decline. By the 1980s, functionalism in Europe had broadly been replaced by conflict-oriented approaches. While some of the critical approaches also gained popularity in the United States, the mainstream of the discipline instead shifted to a variety of empirically-oriented middle-range theories with no single overarching theoretical orientation. To many in the discipline, functionalism is now considered "as dead as a dodo."

As the influence of both functionalism and Marxism in the 1960s began to wane, the linguistic and cultural turns led to myriad new movements in the social sciences: "According to Giddens, the orthodox consensus terminated in the late 1960s and 1970s as the middle ground shared by otherwise competing perspectives gave way and was replaced by a baffling variety of competing perspectives. This third 'generation' of social theory includes phenomenologically inspired approaches, critical theory, ethnomethodology, symbolic interactionism, structuralism, post-structuralism, and theories written in the tradition of hermeneutics and ordinary language philosophy."

The structuralist movement originated from the linguistic theory of Ferdinand de Saussure and was later expanded to the social sciences by theorists such as Claude Lévi-Strauss. In this context, 'structure' refers not to 'social structure' but to the semiotic understanding of human culture as a system of signs. One may delineate four central tenets of structuralism: First, structure is what determines the structure of a whole. Second, structuralists believe that every system has a structure. Third, structuralists are interested in 'structural' laws that deal with coexistence rather than changes. Finally, structures are the 'real things' beneath the surface or the appearance of meaning.

Post-structuralist thought has tended to reject 'humanist' assumptions in the conduct of socialtheory. Michel Foucault provides a potent critique in his *archaeology of the human sciences*, though Habermas and Rorty have both argued that Foucault merely replaces one such system of thought with another. The dialogue between these intellectuals highlights a trend in recent years for certain schools of sociology and philosophy to intersect. The anti-humanist position has been associated with "postmodernism," a term used in specific contexts to describe an *era* or *phenomena*, but occasionally construed as a *method*.

Structure and Agency

Structure and agency form an enduring ontological debate in social theory: "Do social structures determine an individual's behaviour or does human agency?" In this context 'agency' refers to the capacity of individuals to act independently and make free choices, whereas 'structure' relates to factors which limit or affect the choices and actions of individuals (such as social class, religion, gender, ethnicity, and so on). Discussions over the primacy of either structure and agency relate to the core of sociological epistemology ("What is the social world made of?", "What is a cause in the social world, and what is an effect?"). A general outcome of incredulity toward structural or agential thought has been the development of multidimensional theories, most notably the action theory of Talcott Parsons and Anthony Giddens's theory of structuration.

Research Methodology

Sociological research methods may be divided into two broad categories:

- Quantitative designs approach social phenomena through quantifiable evidence, and often rely on statistical analysis of many cases (or across intentionally designed treatments in an experiment) to create valid and reliable general claims
- Qualitative designs emphasize understanding of social phenomena through direct observation, communication with participants, or analysis of texts, and may stress contextual and subjective accuracy over generality

Sociologists are divided into camps of support for particular research techniques. These disputes relate to the epistemological debates at the historical core of social theory. While very different in many aspects, both qualitative and quantitative approaches involve a systematic interaction between theory and data. Quantitative methodologies hold the dominant position in sociology, especially in the United States. In the discipline's two most cited journals, quantitative articles have historically outnumbered qualitative ones by a factor of two. (Most articles published in the largest British journal, on the other hand, are qualitative.) Most textbooks on the methodology of social research are written from the quantitative perspective, and the very term "methodology" is often used synonymously with "statistics." Practically all sociology PhD program in the United States require training in statistical methods. The work produced by quantitative researchers is also deemed more 'trustworthy' and 'unbiased' by the greater public, though this judgment continues to be challenged by antipositivists.

The choice of method often depends largely on what the researcher intends to investigate. For example, a researcher concerned with drawing a statistical generalization across an entire population may administer a survey questionnaire to a representative sample population. By contrast, a researcher who seeks full contextual understanding of an individual's social actions may choose ethnographic participant observation or open-ended interviews. Studies will commonly combine, or 'triangulate', quantitative *and* qualitative methods as part of a 'multi-strategy' design. For instance, a quantitative study may be performed to gain statistical patterns or a target sample, and then combined with a qualitative interview to determine the play of agency.

Sampling

Quantitative methods are often used to ask questions about a population that is very large, making a census or a complete enumeration of all the members in that population infeasible. A 'sample' then forms a manageable subset of a population. In quantitative research, statistics are used to draw inferences from this sample regarding the population as a whole. The process of selecting a sample is referred to as 'sampling'. While it is usually best to sample randomly, concern with differences between specific subpopulations sometimes calls for stratified sampling. Conversely, the impossibility of random sampling sometimes necessitates nonprobability sampling, such as convenience sampling or snowball sampling.

Methods

The following list of research methods is neither exclusive nor exhaustive:

- Archival research or the Historical method: draws upon the secondary data located in historical archives and records, such as biographies, memoirs, journals, and so on.
- Content analysis: The content of interviews and other texts is systematically analyzed. Often data is 'coded' as a part of the 'grounded theory' approach using qualitative data analysis (QDA) software, such as NVivo, Atlas.ti, or QDA Miner.
- Experimental research: The researcher isolates a single social process and reproduces it in a laboratory (for example, by creating a situation where unconscious sexist judgments are possible), seeking to determine whether or not certain social variables can cause, or depend upon, other variables (for instance, seeing if people's feelings about traditional gender roles can be manipulated by the activation of contrasting gender stereotypes). Participants are randomly assigned to different groups which either serve as controls—acting as reference points because they are tested with regard to the dependent

variable, albeit without having been exposed to any independent variables of interest—or receive one or more treatments. Randomization allows the researcher to be sure that any resulting differences between groups are the result of the treatment.

- Longitudinal study: An extensive examination of a specific person or group over a long period of time.
- Observation: Using data from the senses, the researcher records information about social phenomenon or behaviour. Observation techniques may or may not feature participation. In participant observation, the researcher goes into the field (such as a community or a place of work), and participates in the activities of the field for a prolonged period of time in order to acquire a deep understanding of it. Data acquired through these techniques may be analyzed either quantitatively or qualitatively.
- Survey research: The researcher gathers data using interviews, questionnaires, or similar feedback from a set of people sampled from a particular population of interest. Survey items from an interview or questionnaire may be open-ended or closed-ended. Data from surveys is usually analyzed statistically on a computer.

Computational Sociology

Sociologists increasingly draw upon computationally intensive methods to analyze and model social phenomena. Using computer simulations, artificial intelligence, text mining, complex statistical methods, and new analytic approaches like social network analysis and social sequence analysis, computational sociology develops and tests theories of complex social processes through bottom-up modelling of social interactions.

Although the subject matter and methodologies in social science differ from those in natural science or computer science, several of the approaches used in contemporary social simulation originated from fields such as physics and artificial intelligence. By the same token, some of the approaches that originated in computational sociology have been imported into the natural sciences, such as measures of network centrality from the fields of social network analysis and network science. In relevant literature, computational sociology is often related to the study of social complexity. Social complexity concepts such as complex systems, non-linear interconnection among macro and micro process, and emergence, have entered the vocabulary of computational sociology. A practical and well-known example is the construction of a computational model in the form of an "artificial society", by which researchers can analyze the structure of a social system.

Practical Applications of Social Research

Social research informs politicians and policy makers, educators, planners, lawmakers, administrators, developers, business magnates, managers, social workers, non-governmental organizations, non-profit organizations, and people interested in resolving social issues in general. There is often a great deal of crossover between social research, market research, and other statistical fields.

Areas of Sociology

- Social organization is the study of the various institutions, social groups, social stratification, social mobility, bureaucracy, ethnic groups and relations, and other similar subjects such as education, politics, religion, economy and so forth.
- Social psychology is the study of human nature as an outcome of group life, social attitudes, collective behaviour, and personality formation. It deals with group life and the individual's traits, attitudes, beliefs as influenced by group life, and it views man with reference to group life.
- Social change and disorganization is the study of the change in culture and social relations and the disruption that may occur in society, and it deals with the study of such current problems in society such as juvenile delinquency, criminality, drug addiction, family conflicts, divorce, population problems, and other similar subjects.
- Human ecology deals with the nature and behaviour of a given population and its relationships to the group's present social institutions. For instance, studies of this kind have shown the prevalence of mental illness, criminality, delinquencies, prostitution, and drug addiction in urban centres and other highly developed places.
- Population or demography is the study of population number, composition, change, and quality as they influence the economic, political, and social system.
- Sociological theory and method is concerned with the applicability and usefulness of the principles and theories of

group life as bases for the regulation of man's environment, and includes theory building and testing as bases for the prediction and control of man's social environment.

- Applied sociology utilizes the findings of pure sociological research in various fields such as criminology, social work, community development, education, industrial relations, marriage, ethnic relations, family counselling, and other aspects and problems of daily life.

Scope and Topics

Culture: For Simmel, culture referred to "the cultivation of individuals through the agency of external forms which have been objectified in the course of history". Whilst early theorists such as Durkheim and Mauss were influential in cultural anthropology, sociologists of culture are generally distinguished by their concern for modern (rather than primitive or ancient) society. Cultural sociology is seldom empirical, preferring instead the hermeneutic analysis of words, artifacts and symbols. The field is closely allied with critical theory in the vein of Theodor W. Adorno, Walter Benjamin, and other members of the Frankfurt School. Loosely distinct to sociology is the field of cultural studies. Birmingham School theorists such as Richard Hoggart and Stuart Hall questioned the division between "producers" and "consumers" evident in earlier theory, emphasizing the reciprocity in the production of texts. Cultural Studies aims to examine its subject matter in terms of cultural practices and their relation to power. For example, a study of a subculture (such as white working class youth in London) would consider the social practices of the group as they relate to the dominant class. The "cultural turn" of the 1960s ushered in structuralist and so-called postmodern approaches to social science and placed culture much higher on the sociological agenda.

Criminality, Deviance, Law and Punishment

Criminologists analyze the nature, causes, and control of criminal activity, drawing upon methods across sociology, psychology, and the behavioural sciences. The sociology of deviance focuses on actions or behaviours that violate norms, including both formally enacted rules (e.g., crime) and informal violations of cultural norms. It is the remit of sociologists to study why these norms exist; how they change over time; and how they are enforced. The concept of deviance is central in contemporary structural functionalism and systems theory. Robert K. Merton produced a typology of deviance, and also established the terms "role model", "unintended consequences", and "self-fulfilling prophecy".

The study of law played a significant role in the formation of classical sociology. Durkheim famously described law as the "visible symbol" of social solidarity. The sociology of law refers to both a sub-discipline of sociology and an approach within the field of legal studies. Sociology of law is a diverse field of study which examines the interaction of law with other aspects of society, such as the development of legal institutions and the effect of laws on social change and vice versa. For example, an influential recent work in the field relies on statistical analyses to argue that the increase in incarceration in the US over the last 30 years is due to changes in law and policing and not to an increase in crime; and that this increase significantly contributes to maintaining racial stratification.

Economic Sociology

The term "economic sociology" was first used by William Stanley Jevons in 1879, later to be coined in the works of Durkheim, Weber and Simmel between 1890 and 1920. Economic sociology arose as a new approach to the analysis of economic phenomena, emphasizing class relations and modernity as a philosophical concept. The relationship between capitalism and modernity is a salient issue, perhaps best demonstrated in Weber's *The Protestant Ethic and the Spirit of Capitalism* (1905) and Simmel's *The Philosophy of Money* (1900). The contemporary period of economic sociology, also known as *new economic sociology*, was consolidated by the 1985 work of Mark Granovetter titled "Economic Action and Social Structure: The Problem of Embeddedness".

This work elaborated the concept of embeddedness, which states that economic relations between individuals or firms take place within existing social relations (and are thus structured by these relations as well as the greater social structures of which those relations are a part). Social network analysis has been the primary methodology for studying this phenomenon. Granovetter's theory of the strength of weak ties and Ronald Burt's concept of structural holes are two best known theoretical contributions of this field.

Environment

Environmental sociology is the study of human interactions with the natural environment, typically emphasizing human dimensions of environmental problems, social impacts of those problems, and efforts to resolve them. As with other subfields of sociology, scholarship in environmental sociology may be at one or multiple levels of analysis, from global (e.g. world-systems) to local, societal to individual. Attention is paid also to the processes by which environmental problems become *defined* and *known* to humans.

Education

The sociology of education is the study of how educational institutions determine social structures, experiences, and other outcomes. It is particularly concerned with the schooling systems of modern industrial societies. A classic 1966 study in this field by James Coleman, known as the "Coleman Report", analyzed the performance of over 150,000 students and found that student background and socioeconomic status are much more important in determining educational outcomes than are measured differences in school resources (*i.e.* per pupil spending). The controversy over "school effects" ignited by that study has continued to this day. The study also found that socially disadvantaged black students profited from schooling in racially mixed classrooms, and thus served as a catalyst for desegregation busing in American public schools.

Family, Gender, and Sexuality

Family, gender and sexuality form a broad area of inquiry studied in many subfields of sociology. The sociology of the family examines the family, as an institution and unit of socialization, with special concern for the comparatively modern historical emergence of the nuclear family and its distinct gender roles. The notion of "childhood" is also significant. As one of the more basic institutions to which one may apply sociological perspectives, the sociology of the family is a common component on introductory academic curricula. Feminist sociology, on the other hand, is a normative subfield that observes and critiques the cultural categories of gender and sexuality, particularly with respect to power and inequality.

The primary concern of feminist theory is the patriarchy and the systematic oppression of women apparent in many societies, both at the level of small-scale interaction and in terms of the broader social structure. Feminist sociology also analyses how gender interlocks with race and class to produce and perpetuate social inequalities. "How to account for the differences in definitions of femininity and masculinity and in sex role across different societies and historical periods" is also a concern. Social psychology of gender, on the other hand, uses experimental methods to uncover the microprocesses of gender stratification. For example, one recent study has shown that resume evaluators penalize women for motherhood while giving a boost to men for fatherhood. Another set of experiments showed that men whose sexuality is questioned compensate by expressing a greater desire for military intervention and sport utility vehicles as well as a greater opposition to gay marriage.

Health and Illness

The sociology of health and illness focuses on the social effects of, and public attitudes toward, illnesses, diseases, disabilities and the aging process. Medical sociology, by contrast, focuses on the inner-workings of medical organizations and clinical institutions. In Britain, sociology was introduced into the medical curriculum following the Goodenough Report (1944).

Internet

The Internet is of interest to sociologists in various ways; most practically as a tool for research and as a discussion platform. The sociology of the Internet in the broad sense regards the analysis of online communities (e.g. newsgroups, social networking sites) and virtual worlds. Online communities may be studied statistically through network analysis or interpreted qualitatively through virtual ethnography. Organizational change is catalyzed through new media, thereby influencing social change at-large, perhaps forming the framework for a transformation from an industrial to an informational society. One notable text is Manuel Castells' *The Internet Galaxy*—the title of which forms an inter-textual reference to Marshall McLuhan's *The Gutenberg Galaxy*.

Knowledge and Science

The sociology of knowledge is the study of the relationship between human thought and the social context within which it arises, and of the effects prevailing ideas have on societies. The term first came into widespread use in the 1920s, when a number of German-speaking theorists, most notably Max Scheler, and Karl Mannheim, wrote extensively on it. With the dominance of functionalism through the middle years of the 20th century, the sociology of knowledge tended to remain on the periphery of mainstream sociological thought.

It was largely reinvented and applied much more closely to everyday life in the 1960s, particularly by Peter L. Berger and Thomas Luckmann in *The Social Construction of Reality* (1966) and is still central for methods dealing with qualitative understanding of human society (compare *socially constructed reality*). The "archaeological" and "genealogical" studies of Michel Foucault are of considerable contemporary influence.

The sociology of science involves the study of science as a social activity, especially dealing "with the social conditions and effects of science, and with the social structures and processes of scientific activity." Important theorists in the sociology of science include Robert K. Merton and Bruno Latour. These branches of sociology have contributed to the formation of science and technology studies.

Literature

Sociology of literature is a subfield of sociology of culture. It studies the social production of literature and its social implications. A notable example is Pierre Bourdieu's 1992 *Les Règles de L'Art: Genèse et Structure du Champ Littéraire,* translated by Susan Emanuel as *Rules of Art: Genesis and Structure of the Literary Field* (1996). None of the founding fathers of sociology produced a detailed study of literature, but they did develop ideas that were subsequently applied to literature by others. Marx's theory of ideology was directed at literature by Pierre Macherey, Terry Eagleton and Fredric Jameson. Weber's theory of modernity as cultural rationalisation, which he applied to music, was later applied to all the arts, literature included, by Frankfurt School writers such as Adorno and Jürgen Habermas. Durkheim's view of sociology as the study of externally-defined social facts was redirected towards literature by Robert Escarpit. Bourdieu's own work is clearly indebted to Marx, Weber and Durkheim.

Media

As with cultural studies, media study is a distinct discipline which owes to the convergence of sociology and other social sciences and humanities, in particular, literary criticism and critical theory. Though the production process or the critique of aesthetic forms is not in the remit of sociologists, analyses of socialising factors, such as ideological effects and audience reception, stem from sociological theory and method. Thus the 'sociology of the media' is not a subdiscipline *per se*, but the media is a common and often-indispensable topic.

Military

Military sociology aims toward the systematic study of the military as a social group rather than as an organization. It is a highly specialized subfield which examines issues related to service personnel as a distinct group with coerced collective action based on shared interests linked to survival in vocation and combat, with purposes and values that are more defined and narrow than within civil society. Military sociology also concerns civilian-military relations and interactions between other groups or governmental agencies. Topics include the dominant assumptions held by those in the military, changes in military members' willingness to fight, military unionization, military professionalism, the increased utilization of women, the military industrial-academic complex, the military's dependence on research, and the institutional and organizational structure of military.

Political Sociology

Historically political sociology concerned the relations between political organization and society. A typical research question in this area might be: "Why do so few American citizens choose to vote?" In this respect questions of political opinion formation brought about some of the pioneering uses of statistical survey research by Paul Lazarsfeld. A major subfield of political sociology developed in relation to such questions, which draws on comparative history to analyze socio-political trends. The field developed from the work of Max Weber and Moisey Ostrogorsky.

Contemporary political sociology includes these areas of research, but it has been opened up to wider questions of power and politics. Today political sociologists are as likely to be concerned with how identities are formed that contribute to structural domination by one group over another; the politics of who knows how and with what authority; and questions of how power is contested in social interactions in such a way as to bring about widespread cultural and social change. Such questions are more likely to be studied qualitatively. The study of social movements and their effects has been especially important in relation to these wider definitions of politics and power.

Race and Ethnic Relations

The sociology of race and of ethnic relations is the area of the discipline that studies the social, political, and economic relations between races and ethnicities at all levels of society. This area encompasses the study of racism, residential segregation, and other complex social processes between different racial and ethnic groups. This research frequently interacts with other areas of sociology such as stratification and social psychology, as well as with postcolonial theory. At the level of political policy, ethnic relations are discussed in terms of either assimilationism or multiculturalism. Anti-racism forms another style of policy, particularly popular in the 1960s and 70s.

Religion

The sociology of religion concerns the practices, historical backgrounds, developments, universal themes and roles of religion in society. There is particular emphasis on the recurring role of religion in all societies and throughout recorded history. The sociology of religion is distinguished from the philosophy of religion in that sociologists do not set out to assess the validity of religious truth-claims, instead assuming what Peter L. Berger has described as a position of "methodological atheism". It may be said that the modern formal discipline of sociology *began* with the analysis of religion in Durkheim's 1897 study of suicide rates amongst Roman Catholic and Protestant populations. Max Weber published four major texts on religion in a context of economic sociology and social stratification: *The Protestant Ethic and the Spirit of Capitalism* (1905), *The Religion of China: Confucianism and Taoism* (1915), *The Religion of India: The Sociology of Hinduism and Buddhism* (1915), and *Ancient Judaism* (1920). Contemporary debates often centre on topics such as secularization, civil religion, and the role of religion in a context of globalization and multiculturalism.

Social Networks

A social network is a social structure composed of individuals (or organizations) called "nodes", which are tied (connected) by one or more specific types of interdependency, such as friendship, kinship, financial exchange, dislike, sexual relationships, or relationships of beliefs, knowledge or prestige. Social networks operate on many levels, from families up to the level of nations, and play a critical role in determining the way problems are solved, organizations are run, and the degree to which individuals succeed in achieving their goals. Social network analysis makes no assumption that groups are the building blocks of society: the approach is open to studying less-bounded social systems, from non-local communities to networks of exchange. Rather than treating individuals (persons, organizations, states) as discrete units of analysis, it focuses on how the structure of ties affects individuals and their relationships. In contrast to analyses that assume that socialization into norms determines behaviour, network analysis looks to see the extent to which the structure and composition of ties affect norms. Unlike most other areas of sociology, social network theory is usually defined in formal mathematics.

Social Psychology

Sociological social psychology focuses on micro-scale social actions. This area may be described as adhering to "sociological miniaturism", examining whole societies through the study of individual thoughts and emotions as well as behaviour of small groups. Of special concern to psychological sociologists is how to explain a variety of demographic, social, and cultural facts in terms of human social interaction. Some of the major topics in this field are social inequality, group dynamics, prejudice, aggression, social perception, group behaviour, social change, nonverbal behaviour, socialization, conformity, leadership, and social identity. Social psychology may be taught with psychological emphasis. In sociology, researchers in this field are the most prominent users of the experimental method (however, unlike their psychological counterparts, they also frequently employ other methodologies). Social psychology looks at social influences, as well as social perception and social interaction.

Stratification

Social stratification is the hierarchical arrangement of individuals into social classes, castes, and divisions within a society. Modern Western societies stratification traditionally relates to cultural and economic classes arranged in three main layers: upper class, middle class, and lower class, but each class may be further subdivided into smaller classes (e.g. occupational). Social stratification is interpreted in radically different ways within sociology. Proponents of structural functionalism suggest that, since the stratification of classes and castes is evident in all societies, hierarchy must be beneficial in stabilizing their existence. Conflict theorists, by contrast, critique the inaccessibility of resources and lack of social mobility in stratified societies.

Karl Marx distinguished social classes by their connection to the means of production in the capitalist system: the bourgeoisie own the means, but this effectively includes the proletariat itself as the workers can only sell their own labour power (forming the material base of the cultural superstructure). Max Weber critiqued Marxist economic determinism, arguing that social stratification is not based purely on economic inequalities, but on other status and power differentials (e.g. patriarchy). According to Weber, stratification may occur amongst at least three complex variables: (1) Property (class): A person's economic position in a society, based on birth and individual achievement. Weber differs from Marx in that he does not see this as the supreme factor in stratification. Weber noted how managers of corporations or industries control firms they do not own; Marx would have placed such a person in the proletariat. (2) Prestige (status): A person's prestige, or popularity in a society. This could be determined by the kind of job this person does or wealth, and (3) Power (political party): A person's ability to get their way despite the resistance of others. For example, individuals in state jobs, such as an employee of the

Federal Bureau of Investigation, or a member of the United States Congress, may hold little property or status but they still hold immense power. Pierre Bourdieu provides a modern example in the concepts of cultural and symbolic capital. Theorists such as Ralf Dahrendorf have noted the tendency toward an enlarged middle-class in modern Western societies, particularly in relation to the necessity of an educated work force in technological or service-based economies. Perspectives concerning globalization, such as dependency theory, suggest this effect owes to the shift of workers to the Third World.

Urban and Rural Sociology

Urban sociology involves the analysis of social life and human interaction in metropolitan areas. It is a discipline seeking to provide advice for planning and policy making. After the industrial revolution, works such as Georg Simmel's *The Metropolis and Mental Life* (1903) focused on urbanization and the effect it had on alienation and anonymity. In the 1920s and 1930s The Chicago School produced a major body of theory on the nature of the city, important to both urban sociology and criminology, utilising symbolic interactionism as a method of field research. Contemporary research is commonly placed in a context of globalization, for instance, in Saskia Sassen's study of the "Global city". Rural sociology, by contrast, is the analysis of non-metropolitan areas.

Work and Industry

The sociology of work, or industrial sociology, examines "the direction and implications of trends in technological change, globalization, labour markets, work organization, managerial practices and employment relations to the extent to which these trends are intimately related to changing patterns of inequality in modern societies and to the changing experiences of individuals and families the ways in which workers challenge, resist and make their own contributions to the patterning of work and shaping of work institutions."

Sociology and the Other Academic Disciplines

Sociology overlaps with a variety of disciplines that study society, in particular anthropology, political science, economics, and social philosophy. Many comparatively new fields such as communication studies, cultural studies, demography and literary theory, draw upon methods that originated in sociology. The terms "social science" and "social research" have both gained a degree of autonomy since their origination in classical sociology. The distinct field of social psychology emerged from the many intersections of sociological and psychological interests, and is further distinguished in terms of sociological or psychological emphasis.

Sociology and applied sociology are connected to the professional and academic discipline of social work. Both disciplines study social interactions, community and the effect of various systems (i.e. family, school, community, laws, political sphere) on the individual. However, social work is generally more focused on practical strategies to alleviate social dysfunctions; sociology in general provides a thorough examination of the root causes of these problems. For example, a sociologist might study *why* a community is plagued with poverty. The applied sociologist would be more focused on practical strategies on *what* needs to be done to alleviate this burden. The social worker would be focused on *action*; implementing theses strategies "directly" or "indirectly" by means of mental health therapy, counselling, advocacy, community organization or community mobilization.

Social anthropology is the branch of anthropology that studies how contemporary living human beings behave in social groups. Practitioners of social anthropology, like sociologists, investigate various facets of social organization. Traditionally, social anthropologists analysed non-industrial and non-Western societies, whereas sociologists focused on industrialized societies in the Western world. In recent years, however, social anthropology has expanded its focus to modern Western societies, meaning that the two disciplines increasingly converge.

Sociobiology is the study of how social behaviour and organization have been influenced by evolution and other biological process. The field blends sociology with a number of other sciences, such as anthropology, biology, and zoology. Sociobiology has generated controversy within the sociological academy for allegedly giving too much attention to gene expression over socialization and environmental factors in general. Entomologist E. O. Wilson is credited as having originally developed and described Sociobiology.

Irving Louis Horowitz, in his *The Decomposition of Sociology* (1994), has argued that the discipline, whilst arriving from a "distinguished lineage and tradition", is in decline due to deeply ideological theory and a lack of relevance to policy making: "The decomposition of sociology began when this great tradition became subject to ideological thinking, and an inferior tradition surfaced in the wake of totalitarian triumphs." Furthermore: "A problem yet unmentioned is that sociology's malaise has left all the social sciences vulnerable to pure positivism—to an empiricism lacking any theoretical basis. Talented individuals who might, in an earlier time, have gone into sociology are seeking intellectual stimulation in business, law, the natural sciences, and even creative writing; this drains sociology of much needed potential." Horowitz cites the lack of a 'core discipline' as exacerbating the problem. Randall Collins, the Dorothy Swaine Thomas Professor in Sociology at the University of Pennsylvania and a member of the Advisory Editors Council of the Social Evolution & History journal, has voiced similar sentiments: "we have lost all coherence as a discipline, we are breaking up into a conglomerate of specialities, each going on its own way and with none too high regard for each other."

In 2007, *The Times Higher Education Guide* published a list of 'The most cited authors of books in the Humanities' (including philosophy and psychology). Seven of the top ten are listed as sociologists: Michel Foucault (1), Pierre Bourdieu (2), Anthony Giddens (5), Erving Goffman (6), Jürgen Habermas (7), Max Weber (8), and Bruno Latour (10).

Philosophy

Philosophy is the study of general and fundamental problems, such as those connected with reality, existence, knowledge, values, reason, mind, and language. Philosophy is distinguished from other ways of addressing such problems by its critical, generally systematic approach and its reliance on rational argument. In more casual speech, by extension, "philosophy" can refer to "the most basic beliefs, concepts, and attitudes of an individual or group".

The word "philosophy" comes from the Ancient Greek öéëïóïößá (*philosophia*), which literally means "love of wisdom". The introduction of the terms "philosopher" and "philosophy" has been ascribed to the Greek thinker Pythagoras.

Areas of Inquiry

Philosophy is divided into many sub-fields. These include epistemology, logic, metaphysics, ethics, and aesthetics. Some of the major areas of study are considered individually below.

Epistemology

Epistemology is concerned with the nature and scope of knowledge, such as the relationships between truth, belief, and theories of justification.

Skepticism is the position which questions the possibility of completely justifying any truth. The regress argument, a fundamental problem in epistemology, occurs when, in order to completely prove any statement, its justification itself needs to be supported by another justification. This chain can do three possible options, all of which are unsatisfactory according to the Münchhausen trilemma. One option is infinitism, where this chain of justification can go on forever. Another option is foundationalism, where the chain of justifications eventually relies on basic beliefs or axioms that are left unproven. The last option, such as in coherentism, is making the chain circular so that a statement is included in its own chain of justification.

Rationalism is the emphasis on reasoning as a source of knowledge. Empiricism is the emphasis on observational evidence via sensory experience over other evidence as the source of knowledge. Rationalism claims that every possible object of knowledge can be deduced from coherent premises without observation. Empiricism claims that at least some knowledge is only a matter of observation. For this, Empiricism often cites the concept of tabula rasa, where individuals are not born with mental content and that knowledge builds from experience or perception. Epistemological solipsism is the idea that the existence of the world outside the mind is an unresolvable question.

Parmenides (fl. 500 BC) argued that it is impossible to doubt that thinking actually occurs. But thinking must have an object, therefore something *beyond* thinking really exists. Parmenides deduced that what really exists must have certain properties—for example, that it cannot come into existence or cease to exist, that it is a coherent whole, that it remains the same eternally (in fact, exists altogether outside time). This is known as the third man argument. Plato (427–347 BC) combined rationalism with a form of realism. The philosopher's work is to consider being, and the essence (ousia) of things. But the characteristic of essences is that they are universal. The nature of a man, a triangle, a tree, applies to all men, all triangles, all trees. Plato argued that these essences are mind-independent "forms", that humans (but particularly philosophers) can come to know by reason, and by ignoring the distractions of sense-perception.

Modern rationalism begins with Descartes. Reflection on the nature of perceptual experience, as well as scientific discoveries in physiology and optics, led Descartes (and also Locke) to the view that we are directly aware of ideas, rather than objects. This view gave rise to three questions:

1. Is an idea a true copy of the real thing that it represents? Sensation is not a direct interaction between bodily objects and our sense, but is a physiological process involving representation

(for example, an image on the retina). Locke thought that a "secondary quality" such as a sensation of green could in no way resemble the arrangement of particles in matter that go to produce this sensation, although he thought that "primary qualities" such as shape, size, number, were really in objects.

2. How can physical objects such as chairs and tables, or even physiological processes in the brain, give rise to mental items such as ideas? This is part of what became known as the mind-body problem.
3. If all the contents of awareness are ideas, how can we know that anything exists apart from ideas?

Descartes tried to address the last problem by reason. He began, echoing Parmenides, with a principle that he thought could not coherently be denied: I *think*, therefore I *am* (often given in his original Latin: *Cogito ergo sum*). From this principle, Descartes went on to construct a complete system of knowledge (which involves proving the existence of God, using, among other means, a version of the ontological argument). His view that reason alone could yield substantial truths about reality strongly influenced those philosophers usually considered modern rationalists (such as Baruch Spinoza, Gottfried Leibniz, and Christian Wolff), while provoking criticism from other philosophers who have retrospectively come to be grouped together as empiricists.

Logic

Logic is the study of the principles of correct reasoning. Arguments use either deductive reasoning or inductive reasoning. Deductive reasoning is when, given certain statements (called premises), other statements (called conclusions) are unavoidably implied. Rules of inferences from premises include the most popular method, modus ponens, where given "A" and "If A then B", then "B" must be concluded. A common convention for a deductive argument is the syllogism. An argument is termed valid if its conclusion does follow from its premises, whether the premises are true or not, while an argument is sound if its conclusion follows from premises that are true. Propositional logic uses premises that are propositions, which are declarations that are either true or false, while predicate logic uses more complex premises called formulae that contain variables. These can be assigned values or can be quantified as to when they apply with the universal quantifier (always apply) or the existential quantifier (applies at least once). Inductive reasoning makes conclusions or generalizations based on probabilistic reasoning. For example, if "90% of humans are right-handed" and "Joe is human" then "Joe is probably right-handed". Fields in logic include mathematical logic (formal symbolic logic) and philosophical logic.

Metaphysics

Metaphysics is the study of the most general features of reality, such as existence, time, the relationship between mind and body, objects and their properties, wholes and their parts, events, processes, and causation. Traditional branches of metaphysics include cosmology, the study of the world in its entirety, and ontology, the study of being.

Within metaphysics itself there are a wide range of differing philosophical theories. Idealism, for example, is the belief that reality is mentally constructed or otherwise immaterial while realism holds that reality, or at least some part of it, exists independently of the mind. Subjective idealism describes objects as no more than collections or "bundles" of sense data in the perceiver. The 18th-century philosopher George Berkeley contended that existence is fundamentally tied to perception with the phrase *Esse est aut percipi aut percipere* or "To be is to be perceived or to perceive".

In addition to the aforementioned views, however, there is also an ontological dichotomy within metaphysics between the concepts of particulars and universals as well. Particulars are those objects that are said to exist in space and time, as opposed to abstract objects, such as numbers. Universals are properties held by multiple particulars, such as redness or a gender. The type of existence, if any, of universals and abstract objects is an issue of serious debate within metaphysical philosophy. Realism is the philosophical position that universals do in fact exist, while nominalism is the negation, or denial of universals, abstract objects, or both.Conceptualism holds that universals exist, but only within the mind's perception.

The question of whether or not existence is a predicate has been discussed since the Early Modern period. Essence is the set of attributes that make an object what it fundamentally is and without which it loses its identity. Essence is contrasted with accident: a property that the substance has contingently, without which the substance can still retain its identity.

Ethics and Political Philosophy

Ethics, or "moral philosophy," is concerned primarily with the question of the best way to live, and secondarily, concerning the question of whether this question can be answered. The main branches of ethics are meta-ethics, normative ethics, and applied ethics. Meta-ethics concerns the nature of ethical thought, such as the origins of the words good and bad, and origins of other comparative words of various ethical systems, whether there are absolute ethical truths, and how such truths could be known. Normative ethics are more concerned with the questions of how one ought to act, and what the right course of action is. This is where most ethical theories are generated. Lastly, applied ethics go beyond theory and step into real world ethical practice, such as questions of whether or not abortion is correct. Ethics is also associated with the idea of morality, and the two are often interchangeable.

One debate that has commanded the attention of ethicists in the modern era has been between consequentialism (actions are to be morally evaluated solely by their *consequences*) and deontology (actions are to be morally evaluated solely by consideration of agents' *duties*, the *rights* of those whom the action concerns, or both). Jeremy Bentham and John Stuart Mill are famous for propagating utilitarianism, which is the idea that the fundamental moral rule is to strive toward the "greatest happiness for the greatest number".

However, in promoting this idea they also necessarily promoted the broader doctrine of consequentialism. Adopting a position opposed to consequentialism, Immanuel Kant argued that moral principles were simply products of reason. Kant believed that the incorporation of consequences into moral deliberation was a deep mistake, since it denies the necessity of practical maxims in governing the working of the will. According to Kant, reason requires that we conform our actions to the categorical imperative, which is an absolute duty. An important 20th-century deontologist, W.D. Ross, argued for weaker forms of duties called *prima facie* duties.

More recent works have emphasized the role of character in ethics, a movement known as the *aretaic turn* (that is, the *turn towards virtues*). One strain of this movement followed the work of Bernard Williams. Williams noted that rigid forms of consequentialism and deontology demanded that people behave impartially. This, Williams argued, requires that people abandon their personal projects, and hence their personal integrity, in order to be considered moral. G.E.M. Anscombe, in an influential paper, "Modern Moral Philosophy" (1958), revived virtue ethics as an alternative to what was seen as the entrenched positions of Kantianism and consequentialism. Aretaic perspectives have been inspired in part by research of ancient conceptions of virtue. For example, Aristotle's ethics demands that people follow the *Aristotelian mean*, or balance between two vices; and

Confucian ethics argues that virtue consists largely in striving for harmony with other people. Virtue ethics in general has since gained many adherents, and has been defended by such philosophers as Philippa Foot, Alasdair MacIntyre, and Rosalind Hursthouse.

Political philosophy is the study of government and the relationship of individuals (or families and clans) to communities including the state. It includes questions about justice, law, property, and the rights and obligations of the citizen. Politics and ethics are traditionally inter-linked subjects, as both discuss the question of what is good and how people should live. From ancient times, and well beyond them, the roots of justification for political authority were inescapably tied to outlooks on human nature. In *The Republic*, Plato presented the argument that the ideal society would be run by a council of philosopher-kings, since those best at philosophy are best able to realize the good. Even Plato, however, required philosophers to make their way in the world for many years before beginning their rule at the age of fifty.

For Aristotle, humans are political animals (i.e. social animals), and governments are set up to pursue good for the community. Aristotle reasoned that, since the state (*polis*) was the highest form of community, it has the purpose of pursuing the highest good. Aristotle viewed political power as the result of natural inequalities in skill and virtue. Because of these differences, he favoured an aristocracy of the able and virtuous. For Aristotle, the person cannot be complete unless he or she lives in a community. His *The Nicomachean Ethics* and *The Politics* are meant to be read in that order. The first book addresses virtues (or "excellences") in the person as a citizen; the second addresses the proper form of government to ensure that citizens will be virtuous, and therefore complete. Both books deal with the essential role of justice in civic life.

Nicolas of Cusa rekindled Platonic thought in the early 15th century. He promoted democracy in Medieval Europe, both in his writings and in his organization of the Council of Florence. Unlike Aristotle and the Hobbesian tradition to follow, Cusa saw human beings as equal and divine (that is, made in God's image), so democracy would be the only just form of government. Cusa's views are credited by some as sparking the Italian Renaissance, which gave rise to the notion of "Nation-States".

Later, Niccolò Machiavelli rejected the views of Aristotle and Thomas Aquinas as unrealistic. The ideal sovereign is not the embodiment of the moral virtues; rather the sovereign does whatever is successful and necessary, rather than what is morally praiseworthy.

Thomas Hobbes also contested many elements of Aristotle's views. For Hobbes, human nature is essentially anti-social: people are essentially egoistic, and this egoism makes life difficult in the natural state of things. Moreover, Hobbes argued, though people may have natural inequalities, these are trivial, since no particular talents or virtues that people may have will make them safe from harm inflicted by others. For these reasons, Hobbes concluded that the state arises from a common agreement to raise the community out of the state of nature. This can only be done by the establishment of a sovereign, in which (or whom) is vested complete control over the community, and is able to inspire awe and terror in its subjects.

Many in the Enlightenment were unsatisfied with existing doctrines in political philosophy, which seemed to marginalize or neglect the possibility of a democratic state. Jean-Jacques Rousseau was among those who attempted to overturn these doctrines: he responded to Hobbes by claiming that a human is by nature a kind of "noble savage", and that society and social contracts corrupt this nature. Another critic was John Locke. In *Second Treatise on Government* he agreed with Hobbes that the nation-state was an efficient tool for raising humanity out of a deplorable state, but he argued that the sovereign might become an abominable institution compared to the relatively benign unmodulated state of nature.

Following the doctrine of the fact-value distinction, due in part to the influence of David Hume and his student Adam Smith, appeals to human nature for political justification were weakened. Nevertheless, many political philosophers, especially moral realists, still make use of some essential human nature as a basis for their arguments.

Marxism is derived from the work of Karl Marx and Friedrich Engels. Their idea that capitalism is based on exploitation of workers and causes alienation of people from their human nature, the historical materialism, their view of social classes, etc., have influenced many fields of study, such as sociology, economics, and politics. Marxism inspired the Marxist school of communism, which brought a huge impact on the history of the 20th century.

Aesthetics

Aesthetics deals with beauty, art, enjoyment, sensory-emotional values, perception, and matters of taste and sentiment.

Specialized Branches

- Philosophy of language explores the nature, the origins, and the use of language.

- Philosophy of law (often called jurisprudence) explores the varying theories explaining the nature and the interpretations of the law in society.
- Philosophy of mind explores the nature of the mind, and its relationship to the body, and is typified by disputes between dualism and materialism. In recent years there has been increasing similarity between this branch of philosophy and cognitive science.
- Philosophy of religion
- Philosophy of science
- Metaphilosophy

Many academic disciplines have also generated philosophical inquiry. These include history, logic, and mathematics.

History

Many societies have considered philosophical questions and built philosophical traditions based upon each other's works.

Eastern philosophy is organized by the chronological periods of each region. Historians of western philosophy usually divide the subject into three or more periods, the most important being ancient philosophy, medieval philosophy, and modern philosophy.

Ancient Philosophy

Egypt and Babylon: There are authors who date the philosophical maxims of Ptahhotep before the 25th century. For instance, Pulitzer Prize winning historian Will Durant dates these writings as early as 2880 BCE within *The Story of Civilization: Our Oriental History*. Durant claims that Ptahhotep could be considered the very first philosopher in virtue of having the earliest and surviving fragments of moral philosophy (i.e., "The Maxims of Ptah-Hotep"). Ptahhotep's grandson, Ptahhotep Tshefi, is traditionally credited with being the author of the collection of wise sayings known as *The Maxims of Ptahhotep*, whose opening lines attribute authorship to the vizier Ptahhotep: *Instruction of the Mayor of the city, the Vizier Ptahhotep, under the Majesty of King Isesi.*

The origins of Babylonian philosophy can be traced back to the wisdom of early Mesopotamia, which embodied certain philosophies of life, particularly ethics, in the forms of dialectic, dialogues, epic poetry, folklore, hymns, lyrics, prose, and proverbs. The reasoning and rationality of the Babylonians developed beyond empirical observation. The Babylonian text *Dialog of Pessimism* contains similarities to the agnostic thought of the sophists, the Heraclitean doctrine of contrasts, and the dialogues of Plato, as well as a precursor to the maieutic Socratic method of Socrates and Plato. The Milesian philosopher Thales is also traditionally said to have studied philosophy in Mesopotamia.

Ancient Chinese

Philosophy has had a tremendous effect on Chinese civilization, and throughout East Asia. The majority of Chinese philosophy originates in the Spring and Autumn and Warring States era, during a period known as the “Hundred Schools of Thought”, which was characterized by significant intellectual and cultural developments. It was during this era that the major philosophies of China, Confucianism, Mohism, Legalism, and Taoism, arose, along with philosophies that later fell into obscurity, like Agriculturalism, Chinese Naturalism, and the Logicians. Of the many philosophical schools of China, only Confucianism and Taoism existed after the Qin Dynasty suppressed any Chinese philosophy that was opposed to Legalism.

Confucianism is humanistic, philosophy that believes that human beings are teachable, improvable and perfectible through personal and communal endeavour especially including self-cultivation and self-creation. Confucianism focuses on the cultivation of virtue and maintenance of ethics, the most basic of which are *ren*, *yi*, and *li*. *Ren* is an obligation of altruism and humaneness for other individuals within a community, *yi* is the upholding of righteousness and the moral disposition to do good, and *li* is a system of norms and propriety that determines how a person should properly act within a community.

Taoism focuses on establishing harmony with the Tao, which is origin of and the totality of everything that exists. The word “Tao” (or “Dao”, depending on the romanization scheme) is usually translated as “way”, “path” or “principle”. Taoist propriety and ethics emphasize the Three Jewels of the Tao: compassion, moderation, and humility, while Taoist thought generally focuses on nature, the relationship between humanity and the cosmos ()Y°Nøv”^); health and longevity; and wu wei, action through inaction. Harmony with the Universe, or the origin of it through the Tao, is the intended result of many Taoist rules and practices.

Ancient Graeco-Roman

Ancient Graeco-Roman philosophy is a period of Western philosophy, starting in the 6th century [c. 585] BC to the 6th century AD. It is usually divided into three periods: the pre-Socratic period, the Ancient Classical Greek period of Plato and Aristotle, and the post-Aristotelian (or Hellenistic) period. A fourth period that is sometimes added includes the Neoplatonic and Christian philosophers of Late Antiquity. The most important of the ancient philosophers (in terms of subsequent influence) are Plato and Aristotle. Plato specifically, is credited as the founder of Western philosophy. The philosopher Alfred North Whitehead said of Plato: "The safest general characterization of the European philosophical tradition is that it consists of a series of footnotes to Plato. I do not mean the systematic scheme of thought which scholars have doubtfully extracted from his writings. I allude to the wealth of general ideas scattered through them."

It was said in Roman Ancient history that Pythagoras was the first man to call himself a philosopher, or lover of wisdom, and Pythagorean ideas exercised a marked influence on Plato, and through him, all of Western philosophy. Plato and Aristotle, the first Classical Greek philosophers, did refer critically to other simple "wise men", which were called in Greek "sophists," and which were common before Pythagoras' time. From their critique it appears that a distinction was then established in their own Classical period between the more elevated and pure "lovers of wisdom" (the true Philosophers), and these other earlier and more common travelling teachers, who often also earned money from their craft.

The main subjects of ancient philosophy are: understanding the fundamental causes and principles of the universe; explaining it in an economical way; the epistemological problem of reconciling the diversity and change of the natural universe, with the possibility of obtaining fixed and certain knowledge about it; questions about things that cannot be perceived by the senses, such as numbers, elements, universals, and gods. Socrates is said to have been the initiator of more focused study upon the human things including the analysis of patterns of reasoning and argument and the nature of the good life and the importance of understanding and knowledge in order to pursue it; the explication of the concept of justice, and its relation to various political systems.

In this period the crucial features of the Western philosophical method were established: a critical approach to received or established views, and the appeal to reason and argumentation. This includes Socrates' dialectic method of inquiry, known as the Socratic method or method of "elenchus", which he largely applied to the examination of key moral concepts such as the Good and Justice. To solve a problem, it would be broken down into a series of questions, the answers to which gradually distill the answer a person would seek. The influence of this approach is most strongly felt today in the use of the scientific method, in which hypothesis is the first stage.

Ancient Indian

The term Indian philosophy (Sanskrit: *Darshanas*), refers to any of several schools of philosophical thought that originated in the Indian subcontinent, including Hindu philosophy, Buddhist philosophy, and Jain philosophy. Having the same or rather intertwined origins, all of these philosophies have a common underlying themes of Dharma and Karma, and similarly attempt to explain the attainment of emancipation. They have been formalized and promulgated chiefly between 1000 BC to a few centuries AD.

India's philosophical tradition dates back to the composition of the Upanisads in the later Vedic period (c. 1000-500 BCE). Subsequent schools (Skt: *Darshanas*) of Indian philosophy were identified as orthodox (Skt: *astika*) or non-orthodox (Skt: *nastika*) depending on whether they regarded the Vedas as an infallible source of knowledge. By some classifications, there are six schools of orthodox Hindu philosophy and three heterodox schools. The orthodox are Nyaya, Vaisesika, Samkhya, Yoga, Purva mimamsa and Vedanta. The Heterodox are Jain, Buddhist and materialist (Cârvâka). Other classifications also include Pashupata, Saiva, Raseœvara and PâGini Darœana with the other orthodox schools.

Competition and integration between the various schools was intense during their formative years, especially between 500 BC to 200 AD. Some like the Jain, Buddhist, Shaiva and Vedanta schools survived, while others like Samkhya and Ajivika did not, either being assimilated or going extinct. The Sanskrit term for "philosopher" is *dârúanika*, one who is familiar with the systems of philosophy, or *darœanas*.

In the history of the Indian subcontinent, following the establishment of a Vedic culture, the development of philosophical and religious thought over a period of two millennia gave rise to what came to be called the six schools of *astika*, or orthodox, Indian or Hindu philosophy. These schools have come to be synonymous with the greater religion of Hinduism, which was a development of the early Vedic religion.

Ancient Persian

Persian philosophy can be traced back as far as Old Iranian philosophical traditions and thoughts, with their ancient Indo-Iranian roots. These were considerably influenced by Zarathustra's teachings. Throughout Iranian history and due to remarkable political and social influences such as the Macedonian, the Arab, and the Mongol invasions of Persia, a wide spectrum of schools of thought arose.

These espoused a variety of views on philosophical questions, extending from Old Iranian and mainly Zoroastrianism-influenced traditions to schools appearing in the late pre-Islamic era, such as Manicheism and Mazdakism, as well as various post-Islamic schools. Iranian philosophy after Arab invasion of Persia is characterized by different interactions with the old Iranian philosophy, the Greek philosophy and with the development of Islamic philosophy. Illuminationism and the transcendent theosophy are regarded as two of the main philosophical traditions of that era in Persia. Zoroastrianism has been identified as one of the key early events in the development of philosophy.

5th–16th Centuries

Europe: Medieval Medieval philosophy is the philosophy of Western Europe and the Middle East during the Middle Ages, roughly extending from the Christianization of the Roman Empire until the Renaissance. Medieval philosophy is defined partly by the rediscovery and further development of classical Greek and Hellenistic philosophy, and partly by the need to address theological problems and to integrate the then widespread sacred doctrines of Abrahamic religion (Islam, Judaism, and Christianity) with secular learning.

The history of western European medieval philosophy is traditionally divided into two main periods: the period in the Latin West following the Early Middle Ages until the 12th century, when the works of Aristotle and Plato were preserved and cultivated; and the "golden age" of the 12th, 13th and 14th centuries in the Latin West, which witnessed the culmination of the recovery of ancient philosophy, and significant developments in the field of philosophy of religion, logic and metaphysics.

The medieval era was disparagingly treated by the Renaissance humanists, who saw it as a barbaric "middle" period between the classical age of Greek and Roman culture, and the "rebirth" or *renaissance* of classical culture. Yet this period of nearly a thousand years was the longest period of philosophical development in Europe, and possibly the richest. Jorge Gracia has argued that "in intensity, sophistication, and achievement, the philosophical flowering in the thirteenth century could be rightly said to rival the golden age of Greek philosophy in the fourth century B.C."

Some problems discussed throughout this period are the relation of faith to reason, the existence and unity of God, the object of theology and metaphysics, the problems of knowledge, of universals, and of individuation.

Philosophers from the Middle Ages include the Christian philosophers Augustine of Hippo, Boethius, Anselm, Gilbert of Poitiers, Peter Abelard, Roger Bacon, Bonaventure, Thomas Aquinas, Duns Scotus, William of Ockham and Jean Buridan; the Jewish philosophers Maimonides and Gersonides; and the Muslim philosophers Alkindus, Alfarabi, Alhazen, Avicenna, Algazel, Avempace, Abubacer, Ibn Khaldûn, and Averroes. The medieval tradition of Scholasticism continued to flourish as late as the 17th century, in figures such as Francisco Suarez and John of St. Thomas.

Aquinas, father of Thomism, was immensely influential in Catholic Europe, placed a great emphasis on reason and argumentation, and was one of the first to use the new translation of Aristotle's metaphysical and epistemological writing. His work was a significant departure from the Neoplatonic and Augustinian thinking that had dominated much of early Scholasticism.

Renaissance

The Renaissance ("rebirth") was a period of transition between the Middle Ages and modern thought, in which the recovery of classical texts helped shift philosophical interests away from technical studies in logic, metaphysics, and theology towards eclectic inquiries into morality, philology, and mysticism. The study of the classics and the humane arts generally, such as history and literature, enjoyed a scholarly interest hitherto unknown in Christendom, a tendency referred to as humanism. Displacing the medieval interest in metaphysics and logic, the humanists followed Petrarch in making man and his virtues the focus of philosophy.

The study of classical philosophy also developed in two new ways. On the one hand, the study of Aristotle was changed through the influence of Averroism. The disagreements between these Averroist Aristotelians, and more orthodox catholic Aristotelians such as Albertus Magnus and Thomas Aquinas eventually contributed to the development of a "humanist Aristotelianism" developed in the Renaissance, as exemplified in the thought of Pietro Pomponazzi and Giacomo Zabarella. Secondly, as an alternative to Aristotle, the study of Plato and the Neoplatonists became common. This was assisted by the rediscovery of works which had not been well known previously in Western Europe. Notable Renaissance Platonists include Nicholas of Cusa, and later Marsilio Ficino and Giovanni Pico della Mirandola.

The Renaissance also renewed interest in anti-Aristotelian theories of nature considered as an organic, living whole comprehensible independently of theology, as in the work of Nicholas of Cusa, Nicholas Copernicus, Giordano Bruno, Telesius, and Tommaso Campanella. Such movements in natural philosophy dovetailed with a revival of interest in occultism, magic, hermeticism, and astrology, which were thought to yield hidden ways of knowing and mastering nature (e.g., in Marsilio Ficino and Giovanni Pico della Mirandola).

These new movements in philosophy developed contemporaneously with larger religious and political transformations in Europe: the Reformation and the decline of feudalism. Though the theologians of the Protestant Reformation showed little direct interest in philosophy, their destruction of the traditional foundations of theological and intellectual authority harmonized with a revival of fideism and skepticism in thinkers such as Erasmus, Montaigne, and Francisco Sanches. Meanwhile, the gradual centralization of political power in nation-states was echoed by the emergence of secular political philosophies, as in the works of Niccolò Machiavelli (often described as the first modern political thinker, or a key turning point towards modern political thinking), Thomas More, Erasmus, Justus Lipsius, Jean Bodin, and Hugo Grotius.

East Asia

Mid-Imperial Chinese philosophy is primarily defined by the development of Neo-Confucianism. During the Tang Dynasty, Buddhism from Nepal also became a prominent philosophical and religious discipline. (It should be noted that philosophy and religion were clearly distinguished in the West, whilst these concepts were more continuous in the East due to, for example, the philosophical concepts of Buddhism.)

Neo-Confucianism is a philosophical movement that advocated a more rationalist and secular form of Confucianism by rejecting superstitious and mystical elements of Daoism and Buddhism that had influenced Confucianism during and after the Han Dynasty. Although the Neo-Confucianists were critical of Daoism and Buddhism, the two did have an influence on the philosophy, and the Neo-Confucianists borrowed terms and concepts from both. However, unlike the Buddhists and Daoists, who saw metaphysics as a catalyst for spiritual development, religious enlightenment, and immortality, the

Neo-Confucianists used metaphysics as a guide for developing a rationalist ethical philosophy.

Neo-Confucianism has its origins in the Tang Dynasty; the Confucianist scholars Han Yu and Li Ao are seen as forbears of the Neo-Confucianists of the Song Dynasty. The Song Dynasty philosopher Zhou Dunyi is seen as the first true "pioneer" of Neo-Confucianism, using Daoist metaphysics as a framework for his ethical philosophy.

Elsewhere in East Asia, Japanese Philosophy began to develop as indigenous Shinto beliefs fused with Buddhism, Confucianism and other schools of Chinese philosophy and Indian philosophy. Similar to Japan, in Korean philosophy the emotional content of Shamanism was integrated into the Neo-Confucianism imported from China.

India

The period between 5th and 9th centuries CE was the most brilliant epoch in the development of Indian philosophy as Hindu and Buddhist philosophies flourished side by side. Of these various schools of thought the non-dualistic Advaita Vedanta emerged as the most influential and most dominant school of philosophy. The major philosophers of this school were Gaudapada, Adi Shankara and Vidyaranya.

Advaita Vedanta rejects theism and dualism by insisting that "Brahman [ultimate reality] is without parts or attributes...one without a second." Since Brahman has no properties, contains no internal diversity and is identical with the whole reality, it cannot be understood as God. Brahman though being indescribable is at best described as Satchidananda (merging "Sat" + "Chit" + "Ananda", i.e., Existence, Consciousness and Bliss) by Shankara. Advaita ushered a new era in Indian philosophy and as a result, many new schools of thought arose in the medieval period. Some of them were Visishtadvaita (qualified monism), Dvaita (dualism), Dvaitadvaita (dualism-nondualism), Suddhadvaita (pure non-dualism), Achintya Bheda Abheda and Pratyabhijña (the recognitive school).

Middle East

In early Islamic thought, which refers to philosophy during the "Islamic Golden Age", traditionally dated between the 8th and 12th centuries, two main currents may be distinguished. The first is Kalam, that mainly dealt with Islamic theological questions. These include the Mu'tazili and Ash'ari. The other is Falsafa, that was founded on interpretations of Aristotelianism and Neoplatonism. There were attempts by later philosopher-theologians at harmonizing both trends, notably by Ibn Sina (Avicenna) who founded the school of Avicennism, Ibn Rushd (Averroës) who founded the school of Averroism, and others such as Ibn al-Haytham (Alhacen) and Abû Rayhân al-Bîrûnî.

17th–20th Centuries

Early Modern Philosophy

Chronologically, the early modern era of Western philosophy is usually identified with the 17th and 18th centuries, with the 18th century often being referred to as the Enlightenment. Modern philosophy is distinguished from its predecessors by its increasing independence from traditional authorities such as the Church, academia, and Aristotelianism; a new focus on the foundations of knowledge and metaphysical system-building; and the emergence of modern physics out of natural philosophy.

Other central topics of philosophy in this period include the nature of the mind and its relation to the body, the implications of the new natural sciences for traditional theological topics such as free will and God, and the emergence of a secular basis for moral and political philosophy. These trends first distinctively coalesce in Francis Bacon's call for a new, empirical program for expanding knowledge, and soon found massively influential form in the mechanical physics and rationalist metaphysics of René Descartes.

Thomas Hobbes was the first to apply this methodology systematically to political philosophy and is the originator of modern political philosophy, including the modern theory of a "social contract". The academic canon of early modern philosophy generally includes Descartes, Spinoza, Leibniz, Locke, Berkeley, Hume, and Kant, though influential contributions to philosophy were made by many thinkers in this period, such as Galileo Galilei, Pierre Gassendi, Blaise Pascal, Nicolas Malebranche, Isaac Newton, Christian Wolff, Montesquieu, Pierre Bayle, Thomas Reid, Jean d'Alembert, and Adam Smith. Jean-Jacques Rousseau was a seminal figure in initiating reaction against the Enlightenment. The approximate end of the early modern period is most often identified with Immanuel Kant's systematic attempt to limit metaphysics, justify scientific knowledge, and reconcile both of these with morality and freedom.

19th-Century Philosophy

Later modern philosophy is usually considered to begin after the philosophy of Immanuel Kant at the beginning of the 19th century.

German philosophy exercised broad influence in this century, owing in part to the dominance of the German university system. German idealists, such as Johann Gottlieb Fichte, Georg Wilhelm Friedrich Hegel, and Friedrich Wilhelm Joseph Schelling, transformed the work of Kant by maintaining that the world is constituted by a rational or mind-like process, and as such is entirely knowable. Arthur Schopenhauer's identification of this world-constituting process as an irrational will to live influenced later 19th- and early 20th-century thinking, such as the work of Friedrich Nietzsche and Sigmund Freud.

After Hegel's death in 1831, 19th-century philosophy largely turned against idealism in favour of varieties of philosophical naturalism, such as the positivism of Auguste Comte, the empiricism of John Stuart Mill, and the materialism of Karl Marx. Logic began a period of its most significant advances since the inception of the discipline, as increasing mathematical precision opened entire fields of inference to formalization in the work of George Boole and Gottlob Frege. Other philosophers who initiated lines of thought that would continue to shape philosophy into the 20th century include:

- Gottlob Frege and Henry Sidgwick, whose work in logic and ethics, respectively, provided the tools for early analytic philosophy.
- Charles Sanders Peirce and William James, who founded pragmatism.
- Søren Kierkegaard and Friedrich Nietzsche, who laid the groundwork for existentialism and post-structuralism.

20th-Century Philosophy

Within the last century, philosophy has increasingly become a professional discipline practiced within universities, like other academic disciplines. Accordingly, it has become less general and more specialized. In the view of one prominent recent historian: "Philosophy has become a highly organized discipline, done by specialists primarily for other specialists. The number of philosophers has exploded, the volume of publication has swelled, and the subfields of serious philosophical investigation have multiplied. Not only is the broad field of philosophy today far too vast to be embraced by one mind, something similar is true even of many highly specialized subfields."

In the English-speaking world, analytic philosophy became the dominant school for much of the 20th century. In the first half of the century, it was a cohesive school, shaped strongly by logical positivism, united by the notion that philosophical problems could and should be solved by attention to logic and language. The pioneering work of Bertrand Russell was a model for the early development of analytic philosophy, moving from a rejection of the idealism dominant in late 19th-century British philosophy to an neo-Humean empiricism, strengthened by the conceptual resources of modern mathematical logic.

In the latter half of the 20th century, analytic philosophy diffused into a wide variety of disparate philosophical views, only loosely united by historical lines of influence and a self-identified commitment to clarity and rigor. The post-war transformation of the analytic program led in two broad directions: on one hand, an interest in ordinary language as a way of avoiding or redescribing traditional philosophical problems, and on the other, a more thoroughgoing naturalism that sought to dissolve the puzzles of modern philosophy via the results of the natural sciences (such as cognitive psychology and evolutionary biology).

The shift in the work of Ludwig Wittgenstein, from a view congruent with logical positivism to a therapeutic dissolution of traditional philosophy as a linguistic misunderstanding of normal forms of life, was the most influential version of the first direction in analytic philosophy. The later work of Russell and the philosophy of W.V.O. Quine are influential exemplars of the naturalist approach dominant in the second half of the 20th century. But the diversity of analytic philosophy from the 1970s onward defies easy generalization: the naturalism of Quine and his epigoni was in some precincts superseded by a "new metaphysics" of possible worlds, as in the influential work of David Lewis. Recently, the experimental philosophy movement has sought to reappraise philosophical problems through social science research techniques.

On continental Europe, no single school or temperament enjoyed dominance. The flight of the logical positivists from central Europe during the 1930s and 1940s, however, diminished philosophical interest in natural science, and an emphasis on the humanities, broadly construed, figures prominently in what is usually called "continental philosophy". 20th-century movements such as phenomenology, existentialism, modern hermeneutics, critical theory, structuralism, and poststructuralism are included within this loose category. The founder of phenomenology, Edmund Husserl, sought to study consciousness as experienced from a first-person perspective, while Martin Heidegger drew on the ideas of Kierkegaard, Nietzsche, and Husserl to propose an unconventional existential approach to ontology.

In the Arab-speaking world Arab nationalist philosophy became the dominant school of thought, involving philosophers such as Michel Aflaq, Zaki al-Arsuzi, Salah al-Din al-Bitar of ba'athism and Sati' al-Husri. These people disregarded much of Marx's research, and were mostly concerned with the individual's spirituality which would, in the fight against imperialism and oppression, lead to a united Arab Nation.

Major Traditions

German Idealism: Forms of idealism were prevalent in philosophy from the 18th century to the early 20th century. Transcendental idealism, advocated by Immanuel Kant, is the view that there are limits on what can be understood, since there is much that cannot be brought under the conditions of objective judgment. Kant wrote his *Critique of Pure Reason* (1781–1787) in an attempt to reconcile the conflicting approaches of rationalism and empiricism, and to establish a new groundwork for studying metaphysics. Kant's intention with this work was to look at what we know and then consider what must be true about it, as a logical consequence of the *way* we know it. One major theme was that there are fundamental features of reality that escape our direct knowledge because of the natural limits of the human faculties. Although Kant held that objective knowledge of the world required the mind to impose a conceptual or categorical framework on the stream of pure sensory data—a framework including space and time themselves—he maintained that *things-in-themselves* existed independently of our perceptions and judgments; he was therefore not an idealist in any simple sense. Kant's account of *things-in-themselves* is both controversial and highly complex. Continuing his work, Johann Gottlieb Fichte and Friedrich Schelling dispensed with belief in the independent existence of the world, and created a thoroughgoing idealist philosophy.

The most notable work of this German idealism was G. W. F. Hegel's *Phenomenology of Spirit*, of 1807. Hegel admitted his ideas were not new, but that all the previous philosophies had been incomplete. His goal was to correctly finish their job. Hegel asserts that the twin aims of philosophy are to account for the contradictions apparent in human experience (which arise, for instance, out of the supposed contradictions between "being" and "not being"), and also simultaneously to resolve and preserve these contradictions by showing their compatibility at a higher level of examination ("being" and "not being" are resolved with "becoming"). This program of acceptance and reconciliation of contradictions is known as the "Hegelian dialectic".

Philosophers influenced by Hegel include Ludwig Andreas Feuerbach, who coined the term projection as pertaining to our inability to recognize anything in the external world without projecting qualities of ourselves upon those things; Karl Marx; Friedrich Engels; and the British idealists, notably T. H. Green, J. M. E. McTaggart and F. H. Bradley. Few 20th-century philosophers have embraced idealism. However, quite a few have embraced Hegelian dialectic. Immanuel Kant's "Copernican Turn" also remains an important philosophical concept today.

Pragmatism

Pragmatism was founded in the spirit of finding a scientific concept of truth that does not depend on personal insight (revelation) or reference to some metaphysical realm. The meaning or purport of a statement should be judged by the effect its acceptance would have on practice. Truth is that opinion which inquiry taken far enough would ultimately reach. For Charles Sanders Peirce these were principles of the inquirer's self-regulation, implied by the idea and hope that inquiry is not generally fruitless. The details of how these principles should be interpreted have been subject to discussion since Peirce first conceived them. Peirce's maxim of pragmatism is as follows: "Consider what effects, which might conceivably have practical bearings, we conceive the object of our conception to have. Then, our conception of these effects is the whole of our conception of the object." Like postmodern neo-pragmatist Richard Rorty, many are convinced that pragmatism asserts that the truth of beliefs does not consist in their correspondence with reality, but in their usefulness and efficacy.

The late 19th-century American philosophers Charles Sanders Peirce and William James were its co-founders, and it was later developed by John Dewey as instrumentalism. Since the usefulness of any belief at any time might be contingent on circumstance, Peirce and James conceptualised final truth as something only established by the future, final settlement of all opinion. Critics have accused pragmatism falling victim to a simple fallacy: because something that is true proves useful, that usefulness is the basis for its truth. Thinkers in the pragmatist tradition have included John Dewey, George Santayana, W. V. O. Quine and C. I. Lewis. Pragmatism has more recently been taken in new directions by Richard Rorty, John Lachs, Donald Davidson, Susan Haack, and Hilary Putnam.

Phenomenology

Edmund Husserl's phenomenology was an ambitious attempt to lay the foundations for an account of the structure of conscious experience in general. An important part of Husserl's phenomenological project was to show that all conscious acts are directed at or about objective content, a feature that Husserl called *intentionality*.

In the first part of his two-volume work, the *Logical Investigations* (1901), he launched an extended attack on psychologism. In the second part, he began to develop the technique of *descriptive phenomenology*, with the aim of showing how objective judgments are grounded in conscious experience—not, however, in the first-person experience of particular individuals, but in the properties essential to any experiences of the kind in question.

He also attempted to identify the essential properties of any act of meaning. He developed the method further in *Ideas* (1913) as *transcendental phenomenology*, proposing to ground actual experience, and thus all fields of human knowledge, in the structure of consciousness of an ideal, or transcendental, ego. Later, he attempted to reconcile his transcendental standpoint with an acknowledgement of the intersubjective life-world in which real individual subjects interact. Husserl published only a few works in his lifetime, which treat phenomenology mainly in abstract methodological terms; but he left an enormous quantity of unpublished concrete analyses.

Husserl's work was immediately influential in Germany, with the foundation of phenomenological schools in Munich and Göttingen. Phenomenology later achieved international fame through the work of such philosophers as Martin Heidegger (formerly Husserl's research assistant), Maurice Merleau-Ponty, and Jean-Paul Sartre. Through the work of Heidegger and Sartre, Husserl's focus on subjective experience influenced aspects of existentialism.

Existentialism

Existentialism is a term applied to the work of a number of late 19th- and 20th-century philosophers who, despite profound doctrinal differences, shared the belief that philosophical thinking begins with the human subject—not merely the thinking subject, but the acting, feeling, living human individual. In existentialism, the individual's starting point is characterized by what has been called "the existential attitude", or a sense of disorientation and confusion in the face of an apparently meaningless or absurd world. Many existentialists have also regarded traditional systematic or academic philosophy, in both style and content, as too abstract and remote from concrete human experience.

Although they did not use the term, the 19th-century philosophers Søren Kierkegaard and Friedrich Nietzsche are widely regarded as the fathers of existentialism. Their influence, however, has extended beyond existentialist thought.

The main target of Kierkegaard's writings was the idealist philosophical system of Hegel which, he thought, ignored or excluded the inner subjective life of living human beings. Kierkegaard, conversely, held that "truth is subjectivity", arguing that what is most important to an actual human being are questions dealing with an individual's inner relationship to existence. In particular, Kierkegaard, a Christian, believed that the truth of religious faith was a subjective question, and one to be wrestled with passionately.

Although Kierkegaard and Nietzsche were among his influences, the extent to which the German philosopher Martin Heidegger should be considered an existentialist is debatable. In *Being and Time* he presented a method of rooting philosophical explanations in human existence (*Dasein*) to be analysed in terms of existential categories (*existentiale*); and this has led many commentators to treat him as an important figure in the existentialist movement. However, in *The Letter on Humanism*, Heidegger explicitly rejected the existentialism of Jean-Paul Sartre.

Sartre became the best-known proponent of existentialism, exploring it not only in theoretical works such as *Being and Nothingness*, but also in plays and novels. Sartre, along with Simone de Beauvoir, represented an avowedly atheistic branch of existentialism, which is now more closely associated with their ideas of nausea, contingency, bad faith, and the absurd than with Kierkegaard's spiritual angst. Nevertheless, the focus on the individual human being, responsible before the universe for the authenticity of his or her existence, is common to all these thinkers.

Structuralism and Post-Structuralism

Inaugurated by the linguist Ferdinand de Saussure, structuralism sought to clarify systems of signs through analyzing the discourses they both limit and make possible. Saussure conceived of the sign as being delimited by all the other signs in the system, and ideas as being incapable of existence prior to linguistic structure, which articulates thought. This led continental thought away from humanism, and toward what was termed the decentreing of man: language is no longer spoken by man to express a true inner self, but language speaks man.

Structuralism sought the province of a hard science, but its positivism soon came under fire by poststructuralism, a wide field of thinkers, some of whom were once themselves structuralists, but later came to criticize it. Structuralists believed they could analyze systems from an external, objective standing, for example, but the poststructuralists argued that this is incorrect, that one cannot transcend structures and thus analysis is itself determined by what it examines, while the distinction between the signifier and signified was treated as crystalline by structuralists, poststructuralists asserted that every attempt to grasp the signified results in more signifiers, so meaning is always in a state of being deferred, making an ultimate interpretation impossible.

Structuralism came to dominate continental philosophy throughout the 1960s and early 1970s, encompassing thinkers as diverse as Claude Lévi-Strauss, Roland Barthes and Jacques Lacan. Post-structuralism came to predominate over the 1970s onwards, including thinkers such as Michel Foucault, Jacques Derrida, Gilles Deleuze and even Roland Barthes; it incorporated a critique of structuralism's limitations.

The Analytic Tradition

The term *analytic philosophy* roughly designates a group of philosophical methods that stress detailed argumentation, attention to semantics, use of classical logic and non-classical logics and clarity of meaning above all other criteria. Some have held that philosophical problems arise through misuse of language or because of misunderstandings of the logic of our language, while some maintain that there are genuine philosophical problems and that philosophy is continuous with science. Michael Dummett in his *Origins of Analytical Philosophy* makes the case for counting Gottlob Frege's *The Foundations of Arithmetic* as the first analytic work, on the grounds that in that book Frege took the linguistic turn, analyzing philosophical problems through language. Bertrand Russell and G.E. Moore are also often counted as founders of analytic philosophy, beginning with their rejection of British idealism, their defence of realism and the emphasis they laid on the legitimacy of analysis. Russell's classic works *The Principles of Mathematics,On Denoting* and *Principia Mathematica* with Alfred North Whitehead, aside from greatly promoting the use of mathematical logic in philosophy, set the ground for much of the research program in the early stages of the analytic tradition, emphasizing such problems as: the reference of proper names, whether 'existence' is a property, the nature of propositions, the analysis of definite descriptions, the discussions on the foundations of mathematics; as well as exploring issues of ontological commitment and even metaphysical problems regarding time, the nature of matter, mind, persistence and change, which Russell tackled often with the aid of mathematical logic. Russell and Moore's philosophy, in the beginning of the 20th century, developed as a critique of Hegel and his British followers in particular, and of grand systems of speculative philosophy in general, though by no means all analytic philosophers reject the philosophy of Hegel nor speculative philosophy. Some schools in the group include logical positivism, and ordinary language both markedly influenced by Russell and Wittgenstein's development of Logical Atomism the former positively and the latter negatively.

In 1921, Ludwig Wittgenstein, who studied under Russell at Cambridge, published his *Tractatus Logico-Philosophicus,* which gave a rigidly "logical" account of linguistic and philosophical issues. At the time, he understood most of the problems of philosophy as mere puzzles of language, which could be solved by investigating and then minding the logical structure of language. Years later, he reversed a number of the positions he set out in the *Tractatus*, in for example his second major work, *Philosophical Investigations* (1953). *Investigations* was influential in the development of "ordinary language philosophy," which was promoted by Gilbert Ryle, J.L. Austin, and a few others. In the United States, meanwhile, the philosophy of W.V.O. Quine was having a major influence, with such classics as Two Dogmas of Empiricism. In that paper Quine criticizes the distinction between analytic and synthetic statements, arguing that a clear conception of analyticity is unattainable. He argued for holism, the thesis that language, including scientific language, is a set of interconnected sentences, none of which can be verified on its own, rather, the sentences in the language depend on each other for their meaning and truth conditions. A consequence of Quine's approach is that language as a whole has only a thin relation to experience. Some sentences that refer directly to experience might be modified by sense impressions, but as the whole of language is theory-laden, for the whole language to be modified, more than this is required. However, most of the linguistic structure can in principle be revised, even logic, in order to better model the world. Notable students of Quine include Donald Davidson and Daniel Dennett. The former devised a program for giving a semantics to natural language and thereby answer the philosophical conundrum "what is meaning?". A crucial part of the program was the use of Alfred Tarski's semantic theory of truth. Dummett, among others, argued that truth conditions should be dispensed within the theory of meaning, and replaced by assertibility conditions. Some propositions, on this view, are neither true nor false, and thus such a theory of meaning entails a rejection of the law of the excluded middle. This, for Dummett, entails antirealism, as Russell himself pointed out in his *An Inquiry into Meaning and Truth.*

By the 1970s there was a renewed interest in many traditional philosophical problems by the younger generations of analytic philosophers. David Lewis, Saul Kripke, Derek Parfit and others took an interest in traditional metaphysical problems, which they began exploring by the use of logic and philosophy of language. Among those problems some distinguished ones were: free will, essentialism, the nature of personal identity, identity over time, the nature of the mind, the nature of causal laws, space-time, the properties of material beings, modality, etc. In those universities where analytic philosophy has spread, these problems are still being discussed passionately. Analytic philosophers are also interested in the methodology of analytic philosophy itself, with Timothy Williamson, Wykeham Professor of Logic at Oxford, publishing recently a book entitled *The Philosophy of Philosophy*. Some influential figures in contemporary analytic philosophy are: Timothy Williamson, David Lewis, John Searle, Thomas Nagel, Hilary Putnam, Michael Dummett, Peter van Inwagen and Saul Kripke. Analytic philosophy has sometimes been accused of not contributing to the political debate or to traditional questions in aesthetics. However, with the appearance of *A Theory of Justice* by John Rawls and *Anarchy, State and Utopia* by Robert Nozick, analytic political philosophy acquired respectability. Analytic philosophers have also shown depth in their investigations of aesthetics, with Roger Scruton, Nelson Goodman, Arthur Danto and others developing the subject to its current shape.

Applied Philosophy

The ideas conceived by a society have profound repercussions on what actions the society performs. The applied study of philosophy yields applications such as those in ethics—applied ethics in particular—and political philosophy. The political and economic philosophies of Confucius, Sun Zi, Chanakya, Ibn Khaldun, Ibn Rushd, Ibn Taimiyyah, Niccolò Machiavelli, Gottfried Wilhelm Leibniz, John Locke, Jean-Jacques Rousseau, Adam Smith, Karl Marx, John Stuart Mill, Mahatma Gandhi, Martin Luther King Jr., and others—all of these have been used to shape and justify governments and their actions.

In the field of philosophy of education, progressive education as championed by John Dewey has had a profound impact on educational practices in the United States in the 20th century. Descendants of this movement include the current efforts in philosophy for children, which are part of philosophy education. Carl von Clausewitz's political philosophy of war has had a profound effect on statecraft, international politics, and military strategy in the 20th century, especially in the years around World War II. Logic has become crucially important in mathematics, linguistics, psychology, computer science, and computer engineering.

Other important applications can be found in epistemology, which aid in understanding the requisites for knowledge, sound evidence, and justified belief (important in law, economics, decision theory, and a number of other disciplines). The philosophy of science discusses the underpinnings of the scientific method and has affected the nature of scientific investigation and argumentation. As such, philosophy has fundamental implications for science as a whole. For example, the strictly empirical approach of Skinner's behaviourism affected for decades the approach of the American psychological establishment. Deep ecology and animal rights examine the moral situation of humans as occupants of a world that has non-human occupants to consider also. Aesthetics can help to interpret discussions of music, literature, the plastic arts, and the whole artistic dimension of life. In general, the various philosophies strive to provide practical activities with a deeper understanding of the theoretical or conceptual underpinnings of their fields.

Often philosophy is seen as an investigation into an area not sufficiently well understood to be its own branch of knowledge. For example, what were once philosophical pursuits have evolved into the modern day fields such as psychology, sociology, linguistics, and economics.

Sociology and Philosophy

Sociology means the study of society on a generalized or abstract level. In an empirical science the generalizations concerning a specified field of inquiry are drawn from facts observed in that field or in closely related fields these generalizations are drawn. Without assuming any knowledge on a level of higher abstraction concerning reality as a whole. All propositions that constitute an empirical science from a self-sufficient system. No propositions are allowed to play a role in the system if it contains knowledge which is not empirical. In other words it is not formulated under the limitations just stated.

On the contrary philosophy is primarily an attempt to understand reality in its totality. From a multitude of observed facts the philosopher proceeds to certain ultimate principles which have taken together attempt to explain reality as a whole. Thus whereas the sociologist explains society in terms of acts observed in society and eventually in related fields of empirical knowledge, the social philosopher explains society in terms of the explanation he gives to total reality. The latter can speak of the first causes, supreme values and ultimate ends the sociologist is not entitled to do so. Modern philosophy and sociology came into existence during one time period to explain the social crisis of Europe in the 19th century. Sociology aimed to be in with to provide a social doctrine that would guide social policy. This aim has now been abandoned.

There exist some links between sociology and philosophy. There is a philosophy of sociology in the same sense as a philosophy of science that is an examination of the methods, concepts and arguments used in sociology. There is a close relationship between sociology and moral and social philosophy the subject matter of sociology is human social behaviour as guided by values: moral and social philosophy studies values and the sociologists study values and human valuation as facts. On occasions the sociologist is made to distinguish between fact and value. It is only by some training that social philosophy becomes competent to distinguish between fact and value. It can be said that the study of sociology leads to philosophical quest. Durkheim thought that sociology has to necessarily contribute to a renewal of philosophical questions. This made him indulge in some epistemological discussions a branch of philosophy. Karl Mannheim argued that sociology of knowledge had implications for epistemology. Both of them thought that sociology can make a direct contribution to philosophy.

While sociology leads to philosophical reflections much of it also begins there. Sociological research will become trivial if it ignores the larger problems of social life which are coordinated in philosophical world-views and in social doctrines.

Relationship between Sociology and Philosophy

Sociology was once called one of the branches of philosophy, i.e., at a time when philosophy was regarded as the mother of all the sciences. In the 19th century, psychology, or the science of human behaviour; and sociology, or the science of human society, emerged out of philosophy as independent sciences.

What had once been called the mental philosophy, or the philosophy of mind, became the science of sociology, and what had once been social philosophy, or the philosophy of history, became the science of sociology.

The word 'philosophy' is derived from Greek language and it literally means 'love of wisdom'. Philosophy is concerned with the task of acquiring knowledge regarding the causes and laws of all things.

Sociology can be said to have originated with some philosophical ambitions- to provide an account of the course of human history, to explain the social crisis of the (European) 19th century, to seek out the avenues for social welfare and social reform.

As Bottomore has pointed out whether the philosophical ambitions or aims of sociology are still alive or died out, one could find connections between sociology and philosophy in three respects which are explained below.

Three Connections between the Two Sciences:

Philosophy of Sociology: Any science has a philosophy of its own in the sense it is commit-ted to acquire knowledge relevant to its field in its own legitimate ways. Sociology is ever vigilant in its examination of the methods, concepts and arguments. This philosophical scrutiny is more ur-gently felt in sociology than in the natural sciences because of the very nature of sociology.

Sociology Entertains Philosophical Thoughts: More than any other social science, socio-logy raises to a greater extent philosophical problems in its studies. Hence a sociologist at studies is bound to consider the philosophical issues which are always in the background of sociological problem only a sociological theory but also a "Philosophical world view" and a "revolutionary doctrine".

"Both Durkheim and Manheim seemed to claim that sociology can make a direct contribution to philosophy, in the sense of settling philosophical questions. Durkheim, for instance, wrote- "I believe that sociology, more than any other science, has a contribution to make to the renewal of philosophical questions.

Sociological reflection is bound to prolong itself by a natural progress in the form of philosophical reflection". In his own study of religion Durkheim transgressed the field of sociological thought and stepped into epistemological discussion.

Intimate Relationship between Sociology and Social Philosophy: Social Philosophy seems to be the meeting point of sociology and philosophy. Its role in the social sciences is "the study of the fundamental principles and concepts of social life in their epistemological and axiological aspects..."

The epistemological aspect is concerned with the question of knowledge; and the axiological aspect deals with the questions of value. The former deals with the fundamental principles and concepts of social life such as man, society, justice, happiness, etc. It also delves deep into the validity of the assumptions, principles and inferences of the social sciences.

It also tries to synthesise its results with those of the other sciences that deal with man. The latter (i.e., the axiological aspect) deals with the ultimate values of social life and the means of attaining them. It thus tries to interpret and esti-mate the social phenomena in terms of ethical principles. The object of social philosophy is, therefore, the attainment of social good itself.

The study of society is inextricably mixed up with moral values. Because the subject-matter of sociology is human behaviour which is directed and guided by values on the one hand and impulses and interests, on the other.

Thus the sociologist is bound to study values and human valuations, as facts. To do this, he must have some knowledge of values in their own context, that is, in moral and social philosophy.

For example, he must know the role and influence of 'dharma' in the making of Indian institutions, and that of individualism and liberalism in the making of American institutions.

Here the concepts such as 'dharma', individualism and liberalism are mostly ethical in nature, but they are studied as objects of knowledge. Only a sociologist who is capable of distinguishing between questions of fact and value questions, can make such studies more objective.

As Bottomore writes, "Only by some training in social philosophy can the sociologist become competent to distinguish the different issues, and at the same time to see their relationships to each other".

In conclusion, we can say that a philosopher who is well acquainted with the social sciences and a sociologist who is sufficiently grounded in philosophy could become, more competent in their respective fields. As Vierkandt says, "Sociology is productive only when it has a philosophical basis".

In the absence of such a basis sociology can pile together facts and investigations and achieve no final meaning or end. Social sciences may deal with means, but social philosophy deals with ends without disregarding the means. As Ginsberg says, "Social philosophy is bound to be the golden crown of the social sciences."

What Distinguishes Philosophy from Sociology?

Philosophy Overview

- Philosophy is a very broad field that touches on many areas of study. Traditionally, philosophy strives for a systematic, logically consistent view of phenomena or concepts, although many anti-systematic philosophies also exist. Political philosophy examines the nature of political systems, and their underlying assumptions. Philosophy of mind tackles tough questions about consciousness, and the relationship between perception, reality and the self. Moral philosophy engages with questions of right and wrong, and explores how individuals and groups act under different circumstances.

Sociology Overview

- Unlike philosophy, sociology is a social science, and a relatively new field. It emerged in the 19th century, and developed as a full-fledged academic discipline in the 20th century. Sociology is the study of the dynamic relationship of individuals and groups to social structures, institutions and culture. On a practical level, it seeks to understand and improve how people live and interact within society.

Practical Applications of Philosophy

- Because it is often abstract and theoretical, some people accuse philosophy of being an impractical pursuit divorced from real-world applications. However, philosophy underpins or influences many fields that are firmly rooted in practical concerns. For example, philosophers who study and comment on politics and political systems may seek to improve the effectiveness of government and the administration of justice. Moral philosophy applies to the everyday ethical decisions of individuals, as well as to huge, national questions of moral action, like warfare or environmental problems. More recently, philosophy and experimental psychology have grown increasingly intertwined, as philosophers explore the deeper questions of consciousness. Philosophy, therefore, may help to answer crucial questions about how our minds and brains operate.

Practical Applications of Sociology

- Sociology applies scientific methods to the study of social phenomena and problems. As such, it offers an empirical and systematic method for addressing the most perplexing conundrums facing human civilization. For example, some sociologists study the effects of deprivation on children, and identify ways to break the cycle of poverty. Other sociologists study workplaces and other social institutions to observe and render conclusions about how people interact, for the sake of improving our relations with one another. Because we all live within a society, sociology is ultimately relevant to everyone, and can serve to demystify the fundamental workings of the social structures in which we spend our lives.

2

Philosophy of Social Science

The philosophy of social science is the study of the logic and method of the social sciences, such as sociology, anthropology, and political science. Philosophers of social science are concerned with the differences and similarities between the social and the natural sciences, causal relationships between social phenomena, the possible existence of social laws, and the ontological significance of structure and agency.

Auguste Comte and Positivism

Comte first described the epistemological perspective of positivism in *The Course in Positive Philosophy*, a series of texts published between 1830 and 1842. These texts were followed by the 1848 work, *A General View of Positivism* (published in English in 1865). The first three volumes of the *Course* dealt chiefly with the physical sciences already in existence (mathematics, astronomy, physics, chemistry, biology), whereas the latter two emphasised the inevitable coming of social science. Observing the circular dependence of theory and observation in science, and classifying the sciences in this way, Comte may be regarded as the first philosopher of science in the modern sense of the term. For him, the physical sciences had necessarily to arrive first, before humanity could adequately channel its efforts into the most challenging and complex "Queen science" of human society itself. His *View of Positivism* would therefore set-out to define, in more detail, the empirical goals of sociological method.

Comte offered an account of social evolution, proposing that society undergoes three phases in its quest for the truth according to a general 'law of three stages'. The idea bears some similarity to Marx's view that human society would progress toward a communist peak.

This is perhaps unsurprising as both were profoundly influenced by the early Utopian socialist, Henri de Saint-Simon, who was at one time Comte's teacher and mentor. Both Comte and Marx intended to develop, scientifically, a new secular ideology in the wake of European secularisation. The early sociology of Herbert Spencer came about broadly as a reaction to Comte; writing after various developments in evolutionary biology, Spencer attempted (in vain) to reformulate the discipline in what we might now describe as socially Darwinistic terms. (Spencer was in fact a proponent of Lamarckism rather than Darwinism).

The modern academic discipline of sociology began with the work of Émile Durkheim (1858–1917). While Durkheim rejected much of the detail of Comte's philosophy, he retained and refined its method, maintaining that the social sciences are a logical continuation of the natural ones into the realm of human activity, and insisting that they may retain the same objectivity, rationalism, and approach to causality. Durkheim set up the first European department of sociology at the University of Bordeaux in 1895, publishing his *Rules of the Sociological Method* (1895). In this text he argued: "our main goal is to extend scientific rationalism to human conduct... What has been called our positivism is but a consequence of this rationalism." Durkheim's seminal monograph, *Suicide* (1897), a case study of suicide rates amongst Catholic and Protestant populations, distinguished sociological analysis from psychology or philosophy.

The positivist perspective, however, has been associated with 'scientism'; the view that the methods of the natural sciences may be applied to all areas of investigation, be it philosophical, social scientific, or otherwise. Among most social scientists and historians, orthodox positivism has long since fallen out of favour. Today, practitioners of both social and physical sciences recognize the distorting effect of observer bias and structural limitations. This scepticism has been facilitated by a general weakening of deductivist accounts of science by philosophers such as Thomas Kuhn, and new philosophical movements such as critical realism and neopragmatism. Positivism has also been espoused by 'technocrats' who believe in the inevitability of social progress through science and technology. The philosopher-sociologist Jürgen Habermas has critiqued pure instrumental rationality as meaning that scientific-thinking becomes something akin to ideology itself.

Durkheim, Marx, and Weber are more typically cited as the fathers of contemporary social science. In psychology, a positivistic approach has historically been favoured in behaviourism.

Epistemology

In any discipline, there will always be a number of underlying philosophical predispositions in the projects of scientists. Some of these predispositions involve the nature of social knowledge itself, the nature of social reality, and the locus of human control in action. Intellectuals have disagreed about the extent to which the social sciences should mimic the methods used in the natural sciences. The founding positivists of the social sciences argued that social phenomena can and should be studied through conventional scientific methods. This position is closely allied with scientism, naturalism and physicalism; the doctrine that all phenomena are ultimately reducible to physical entities and physical laws. Opponents of naturalism, including advocates of the *verstehen* method, contended that there is a need for an interpretive approach to the study of human action, a technique radically different to natural science. The fundamental task for the philosophy of social science has thus been to question the extent to which positivism may be characterized as 'scientific' in relation to fundamental epistemological foundations. These debates also rage *within* contemporary social sciences with regard to subjectivity, objectivity, intersubjectivity and practicality in the conduct of theory and research. Philosophers of social science examine further epistemologies and methodologies, including realism, critical realism, instrumentalism, functionalism, structuralism, interpretivism, phenomenology, and post-structuralism.

Though essentially all major social scientists since the late 19th century have accepted that the discipline faces challenges that are different from those of the natural sciences, the ability to determine causal relationships invokes the same discussions held in science meta-theory. Positivism has sometimes met with caricature as a breed of naive empiricism, yet the word has a rich history of applications stretching from Comte to the work of the Vienna Circle and beyond. By the same token, if positivism is able to identify causality, then it is open to the same critical rationalist non-justificationism presented by Karl Popper, which may itself be disputed through Thomas Kuhn's conception of epistemic paradigm shift. Early German hermeneuticians such as Wilhelm Dilthey pioneered the distinction between natural and social science ('Geisteswissenschaft'). This tradition greatly informed Max Weber and Georg Simmel's antipositivism, and continued with critical theory. Since the 1960s, a general weakening of deductivist accounts of science has grown side-by-side with critiques of "scientism", or 'science *as ideology*'. Jürgen Habermas argues, in his *On the Logic of the Social Sciences* (1967), that "the positivist thesis of unified science, which assimilates all the sciences to a natural-scientific model, fails because of the intimate relationship between the social sciences and history, and the fact that they are based on a situation-specific understanding of meaning that can be explicated only hermeneutically ... access to a symbolically prestructured reality cannot be gained by observation alone." *Verstehende* social theory has been the concern of phenomenological works, such as Alfred Schütz *Phenomenology of the Social World* (1932) and Hans-Georg Gadamer's *Truth and Method* (1960). Phenomenology would later prove influential in the subject-centred theory of the post-structuralists.

The mid-20th century linguistic turn led to a rise in highly philosophical sociology, as well as so-called "postmodern" perspectives on the social acquisition of knowledge. One notable critique of social science is found in Peter Winch's Wittgensteinian text *The Idea of Social Science and its Relation to Philosophy* (1958). Michel Foucault provides a potent critique in his archaeology of the human sciences, though Habermas and Richard Rorty have both argued that Foucault merely replaces one such system of thought with another.

One underlying problem for the social psychologist is whether studies can or should ultimately be understood in terms of the meaning and consciousness behind social action, as with folk psychology, or whether more objective, natural, materialist, and behavioural facts are to be given exclusive study. This problem is especially important for those within the social sciences who study qualitative mental phenomena, such as consciousness, associative meanings, and mental representations, because a rejection of the study of meanings would lead to the reclassification of such research as non-scientific. Influential traditions like psychodynamic theory and symbolic interactionism may be the first victims of such a paradigm shift. The philosophical issues lying in wait behind these different positions have led to commitments to certain kinds of methodology which have sometimes bordered on the partisan. Still, many researchers have indicated a lack of patience for overly dogmatic proponents of one method or another.

Social research remains extremely common and effective *in practise* with respect to political institutions and businesses. Michael Burawoy has marked the difference between public sociology, which is focused firmly on practical applications, and *academic* or *professional* sociology, which involves dialogue amongst other social scientists and philosophers.

Ontology

Structure and agency forms an enduring debate in social theory: "Do social structures determine an individual's behaviour or does human agency?" In this context 'agency' refers to the capacity of individuals to act independently and make free choices, whereas 'structure' refers to factors which limit or affect the choices and actions of individuals (such as social class, religion, gender, ethnicity, and so on). Discussions over the primacy of structure or agency relate to the very core of social ontology ("What is the social world made of?", "What is a cause in the social world, and what is an effect?"). One attempt to reconcile postmodern critiques with the overarching project of social science has been the development, particularly in Britain, of critical realism. For critical realists such as Roy Bhaskar, traditional positivism commits an 'epistemic fallacy' by failing to address the ontological conditions which make science possible: that is, structure and agency itself.

Intercultural Philosophy

Intercultural philosophy (or sometimes world philosophy) is an approach to philosophy that had its precursors in the past but has started as a concept in the 1980s. It mostly emanates from the German-speaking parts of Europe and can be seen as a need to factor other cultures into one's own philosophical thinking and thus creating an intercultural perspective.

The Idea of Intercultural Philosophy

In the long history of philosophical thought there has always been a claim for universality although many great thinkers from the past see philosophical value only in the western tradition and oversee what other parts of the world have achieved on their own over the centuries. Eurocentric philosophers such as Georg Wilhelm Friedrich Hegel agree upon Greek being the only birthplace of philosophy and traditions such as the Chinese or Indian ones are only teachings of wisdom. Others speak of more than one birthplace and include Asian traditions.

Karl Jaspers, a German psychiatrist and philosopher, developed the theory of an axial age, referring to the period from 800 BCE to 200 BCE, during which philosophical thinking evolved in China, Indian and the Occident. Jasper's theory is widely accepted by those philosophising interculturally.

In contrast to any eurocentrism there are those philosophers who believe that there needs to be communication as well as collaboration between different traditions and cultures especially in today's global situation, given that intercultural interactions and encounters are a fact of human existence. The goal is to extend one's thinking into including other cultures, to not only consider one tradition but as many as possible such as Asian, Latin-American, Islamic, or African. It is no longer important to ask questions on your own for this would be a very regional approach. Intercultural philosophy shouldn't be an academic subject besides others but an attitude followed by everybody who philosophises. No matter what philosophical orientation, other culture's thoughts should be taken into consideration.

For Raimon Panikkar it is also important to connect religion and philosophy as they are both key elements of human reality and important to many cultures. When developing an approach to intercultural philosophy one has to abandon the idea of using only one's own ways of demonstration and description but has to include other forms such as dance, music, architecture, rituals, art, literature, myths, proverbs, folk tales and so on. A manner of meeting has to be found to allow a variety of exchange where one's own tradition can be preserved and not be forged into one big syncretism.

The only way to stop cultures from being absorbed by globalisation and becoming something of a world culture, which is monoculturally predetermined, according to Fornet-Betancort, is the project of an intercultural dialogue. Others view China and Japan as an example of intercultural practise that others could learn from as they have managed to integrate Buddhism without losing their own cultural identity. Philosophers such as Wimmer and Mall postulate forms of dialogue in which all parties are on the same level ('Ebene der Gleichheit') without having any other power but the better argument.

Main Thinkers

It is not possible to name any forefathers or -mothers of intercultural thought simply because there have always been individuals in the history of philosophy that have had an intercultural approach in their theories. Although nothing defined and without much impact. Since intercultural philosophy has become a concern to more than just a couple of philosophers there are quite a few names to be mentioned. Their concept of intercultural philosophy differs according to their personal background but what they all agree upon is the practical relevance this approach presents. They each have their own suggestions for how intercultural philosophy should respond to today's situation of globalisation.

Raúl Fornet-Betancourt

Fornet-Betancourt (* 1946) is a professor in the department for missiology in Aachen, Germany. He was born and raised in Cuba where he already came in contact with more than one culture, namely with the European or Hispanic and the African culture. His main interest lies with the Latin-American philosophy, though he has declared he doesn't research the Latin-American philosophy on his own but with help from philosophers native to this tradition. Fornet-Betancourt sees the importance of an intercultural approach in the overcoming of any eurocentrism still dominating the world. The history of philosophy shouldn't be reconstructed on the basis of the expansionary development but by means of the diversity of all cultures of humankind. But not only the past should be taken into consideration, the redesign of the present is of equal importance. Intercultural philosophy is a means for making variety heard.

Heinz Kimmerle

Kimmerle (* 1930) is professor emeritus at the Erasmus-university in Rotterdam. He intends to develop a way from colonial thinking towards a dialogue with the African philosophy based on complete equality in order to conceive of an intercultural concept of philosophy. For Kimmerle interculturality influences everything and therefore philosophy has to adapt itself to interculturality in all sub areas as to not lose its practical relevance. In his opinion philosophy of art plays an important role for it pioneers intercultural thinking.

Ram Adhar Mall

Mall (* 1937) is a professor of philosophy and teaches intercultural philosophy and hermeneutics at the university of Munich. He has systematically worked through Indian philosophy and sociology, and views himself to be an insider as well as an outsider due to his Indian heritage and Western education. For Mall interculturality derives from the overlapping of cultures that don't exist on their own. Intercultural philosophy is by no means a romantic notion for anything non-European but an attitude which has to precede philosophical thinking. Only then comparative philosophy becomes possible. Mall has worked out a hermeneutic he calls 'analogous', which moves between two hermeneutic extremes, namely radical difference and total identity. Working out overlappings despite differences enables to understand other cultures not identical to one's own. Mall pleads for abandonment of any claim to absolute right in theory as well as practice.

Franz Martin Wimmer

Wimmer (* 1942) is an associate professor at the university of Vienna. It is important to him to liberate the concept of philosophy from eurocentrism. He defines the contents of philosophy regarding to questions asked. Any tradition concerning themselves with either logic, ontology, epistemology or the justification of norms and values is indeed philosophical. Philosophy should be intercultural all the time even though it isn't yet so. It is quite a 'predicament of culturality' that philosophy claims to be universal but on the other hand will always be embedded in culture, certain means of expression and certain questions. Wimmer concerns himself with the history of philosophical thought which has to be rewritten in order to include other traditions beside the occidental. He also wants to develop ways to enable intercultural dialogues, or 'polylogues', as he calls them.

Approaches to an Intercultural Dialogue

When working with different cultures one can't just insist of one's own methods and ask everyone else to do so as well. Communications have to be adapted to this new situation. Many philosophers of intercultural thought suggest similar but nonetheless different rules or guidelines when approaching other traditions.

Polylogue

This is a concept of the Austrian philosopher Franz Martin Wimmer. He postulates that within interculturally orientated philosophy methods have to be found which disable any rash universalism or relativistic particularism. When making other voices heard, so to speak, not only should be asked what they say and why but also with what justification and due to what believes and convictions. Between radicalism and universalism there has to be a third way to carry out the program of philosophy with the help of other cultures. Wimmer calls this way polylogue, a dialogue of many. Answers to thematic questions should be worked out during such a polylogue. He drafts a 'minimal rule': never accept a philosophical thesis from an author of a single cultural tradition to be well founded. But how does a polylogue look like? Wimmer assumes an issue relevant in four traditions (A, B, C and D) for the sake of illustration. The can have one-sided influence (→) or reciprocal influence (↔). There are different models to be distinguished:

One-sided influence

A → B and A → C and A → D

In this model there is no dialogue possible. It is the goal the expansion of tradition A together with the extinction of cultures such as B, C and D. The reaction of those doesn't have to be the same. The may fiercely object or completely imitate tradition A. This is an example for eurocentrism.

One-sided and transitive influence

A → B and A → C and A → D and B → C

In this model dialogues aren't necessary as well. A continues to be the most influential culture, B ignores D, C ignores D. It may be due to the twofold influence upon C that comparative notions occur. 12

Partly reciprocal influence

There are many forms such as:

A ↔ B and A → C and A → D

or:

A ↔ B and A → C and A → D and B → C

up to:

A ↔ B and A ↔ C and A ↔ D and B ↔ C and B ↔ D and C → D

All forms here can be seen as selective acculturation. There are some dialogues or even polylogues possible, with the exception of D.

Complete reciprocal influence: the polylogue

A ↔ B and A ↔ C and A ↔ D and B ↔ C and B ↔ D and C ↔ D

For each tradition is the other quite interesting which is the consistent model for intercultural philosophy. Reciprocal influence happens based on complete equality. Of course in when it comes to practical use it might not be as carefully balanced. One tradition may be more interested in the second than the third which is a common difficulty regarding intercultural dialogue in general.

Rules of Thumb

Elmar Holenstein (* 1937) is a Swiss philosopher who concerns himself with questions regarding phenomenology and philosophy of language and culture. He observes a number of rules of thumb that make it possible to avoid intercultural misunderstandings for the most part. Rule of logical rationality – One has to assume that thoughts not logical to oneself do not make the culture or tradition a logical or prelogical but rather that one has misunderstood them. Rule of teleological rationality (functionality rule) – People pursue an end in what they do and don't only express themselves with logical rationality. It is easy to misunderstand if one cannot distinguish logical and teleological rationality, the literal meaning of a sentence and the goal pursued with it.

Humanity rule (naturalness rule) – Before meaningless, unnatural, non-human or immature behaviour and corresponding values are attributed to people of another culture, it is better to begin by doubting the adequacy of one's own judgement and knowledge.

Nos-quoque rule (we-do-it-too-rule) – If one encounters something in a foreign culture which one is completely unwilling to accept without contradiction, it is not unlikely that one will find comparable, if not worse occurrences in one's own culture, historical and contemporary.

Vos-quoque rule (you-do-it-too-rule) – Considering the former rule, it is no less probable that one will find persons in the foreign culture who reject the scandalous event as well.

Anti-crypto-racism rule – When people are frustrated, they are inclined to perceive their own shortcomings in magnified form in members of other groups. Crypto-racism, hidden racism, becomes manifest when one's own feeling of superiority is threatened. Foreign cultures have to be analysed to shed a revealing light on one's own culture.

Personality rule – It is possible to avoid misjudgements and tactlessness by never treating members of another culture as objects or means of research, but as research partners of equal right.

Subjectivity rule – A self-image is no more to be taken at face value than are the impressions of an outsider. According to their constitution and the kind of encounter, people tend to overestimate, super-elevate and embellish themselves, or to underestimate, diminish and denigrate themselves.

Ontology-deontology rule (›is‹ versus ›ought‹ rule) – Behaviour codes and constitutional texts do not represent conditions as they are, but as they should be according to the view of the group that have the say. Sometimes they manifest a mirror image of what is not the case but considered proper behaviour.

Depolarization rule (rule against cultural dualism) – Polarisation is an elementary means of reducing complexity and classifying things.

Its primary function is not to render things as they in fact are, but rather to represent them in a manner in which they are useful. Polarisations with their simplification, exaggeration, absolutism, and exclusivity are best prevented by comparing several cultures with each other, instead of restricting the comparison to two, and by paying attention to the circumstances under which such a polar relationship between two cultures can be maintained and under what conditions it can also be detected within the cultures that are contrasted with each other.

Non-homogeneity rule – The assumption that cultures are homogeneous is a temptation to place the various eras, trends and formations to be found in them in a uni-linear order as if they are only distinguished by their degree of development and none of them has its own originality and autonomy.

Agnosticism rule – There are mysteries that will remain unanswered in all cultures and across cultures. One has to be prepared for the fact that satisfactory answers might not be found.

Gregor Paul's Basic Rules for Intercultural Philosophy

Paul is an associate professor at the university of Karlsruhe. His concerns are epistemology, logic, aesthetics and comparative philosophy as well as human rights. He has formulated 16 methodological rules regarding intercultural philosophy.

1. Ascertain similarities and make them explicit
2. Identify differences, and to describe and explain them
3. Dispel prejudices
4. Avoid mystification and exoticism
5. Assume the existence of universal, logical laws
6. To only compare equalities and to avert category mistakes
7. Avoid generalisations
8. Not to mistake parts of a tradition for the whole (e.g. identify Zen as the Eastern philosophy)

Rules regarding comparative philosophy:

1. Accept the universal validity of the common and pragmatic principle of causality as at least heuristic and pragmatic principle
2. Orient oneself on the existence of anthropological constants
3. To justify the identification of certain issues regarding to similarities and differences, in particular regarding the relevance of those identifications

Comparative philosophy should furthermore meet certain demands:

1. To explicit the underlying and guiding concept of philosophy
2. Avoid ethnocentrism and eurocentrism
3. To use terms such as 'German philosophy' and 'East' and 'West' just as abbreviation for 'philosophy formulated or developed in Germany' and 'philosophy formulated and developed in Asia'

Further common rules:

1. Multidisciplinarity and
2. Contextualisation of important examples.

Those 16 rules shall help to enable an exchange between cultures on an equal level.

Intercultural Media

Beside the work of individual philosophers journals have been published to spread the intercultural thought and make as many voices heard as possible. Polylog is a journal for intercultural philosophising, published in Vienna, Austria since 1998 and offers articles mostly in the German language. Simplegadi is also a journal for intercultural philosophy, published in Padua, Italy since 1996.

The journal's language is Italian. Since 2010, the Centro Interculturale Dedicato a Raimon Panikkar (Intercultural Centre Dedicated to Raimon Panikkar) publishes Cirpit Review in print or in digital format, promoting and spreading cultural events inspired by Raimon Panikkar's thought.

Mechanism

Mechanism is the belief that natural wholes (principally living things) are like complicated machines or artifacts, composed of parts lacking any intrinsic relationship to each other. Thus, the source of an apparent thing's activities is not the whole itself, but its parts or an external influence on the parts.

The doctrine of mechanism in philosophy comes in two different flavours. They are both doctrines of metaphysics, but they are different in scope and ambitions: the first is a global doctrine about nature; the second is a local doctrine about humans and their minds, which is hotly contested. For clarity, we might distinguish these two doctrines as universal mechanism and anthropic mechanism.

There is no constant meaning in the history of philosophy for the word Mechanism. Originally, the term meant that cosmological theory which ascribes the motion and changes of the world to some external force. In this view material things are purely passive, while according to the opposite theory (i.e., Dynamism), they possess certain internal sources of energy which account for the activity of each and for its influence on the course of events; These meanings, however, soon underwent modification.

The question as to whether motion is an inherent property of bodies, or has been communicated to them by some external agency, was very often ignored. With a large number of cosmologists the essential feature of Mechanism is the attempt to reduce all the qualities and activities of bodies to quantitative realities, i.e. to mass and motion. But a further modification soon followed. Living bodies, as is well known, present at first sight certain characteristic properties which have no counterpart in lifeless matter. Mechanism aims to go beyond these appearances. It seeks to explain all "vital" phenomena as physical and chemical facts; whether or not these facts are in turn reducible to mass and motion becomes a secondary question, although Mechanists are generally inclined to favour such reduction. The theory opposed to this biological mechanism is no longer Dynamism, but Vitalism or Neo-vitalism, which maintains that vital activities cannot be explained, and never will be explained, by the laws which govern lifeless matter.

—"Mechanism" in *Catholic Encyclopedia* (1913)

Universal Mechanism

The older doctrine, here called universal mechanism, is the ancient philosophies closely linked with materialism and reductionism, especially that of the atomists and to a large extent, stoic physics. They held that the universe is reducible to completely mechanical principles—that is, the motion and collision of matter. Later mechanists believed the achievements of the scientific revolution had shown that all phenomenon could eventually be explained in terms of 'mechanical' laws, natural laws governing the motion and collision of matter that imply a thorough going determinism: if *all* phenomena can be explained *entirely* through the motion of matter under physical laws, then even more surely than the gears of a clock determine that it must strike 2:00 an hour after striking 1:00, *all* phenomena must be completely determined: whether past, present or future.

The French mechanist and determinist Pierre Simon de Laplace formulated the sweeping implications of this thesis by saying:

We may regard the present state of the universe as the effect of the past and the cause of the future. An intellect which at any given moment knew all of the forces that animate nature and the mutual positions of the beings that compose it, if this intellect were vast enough to submit the data to analysis, could condense into a single formula the movement of the greatest bodies of the universe and that of the lightest atom; for such an intellect nothing could be uncertain and the future just like the past would be present before its eyes.

—Pierre Simon Laplace, *A Philosophical Essay on Probabilities*

One of the first and most famous expositions of universal mechanism is found in the opening passages of *Leviathan* by Thomas Hobbes (1651). What is less frequently appreciated is that René Descartes was a staunch mechanist, though today, in Philosophy of Mind, he is remembered for introducing the mind-body problem in terms of dualism and physicalism.

Descartes was a substance dualist, and argued that reality was composed of two radically different types of substance: extended matter, on the one hand, and immaterial mind, on the other. Descartes argued that one cannot explain the conscious mind in terms of the spacial dynamics of mechanistic bits of matter cannoning off each other. Nevertheless, his understanding of biology was thoroughly mechanistic in nature:

"I should like you to consider that these functions (including passion, memory, and imagination) follow from the mere arrangement of the machine's organs every bit as naturally as the movements of a clock or other automaton follow from the arrangement of its counter-weights and wheels." (Descartes, Treatise on Man, p.108)

His scientific work was based on the traditional mechanistic understanding that animals and humans are completely mechanistic automata. Descartes' dualism was motivated by the seeming impossibility that mechanical dynamics could yield mental experiences.

Isaac Newton ushered in a much weaker acceptation of mechanism that tolerated the antithetical, and as yet inexplicable, action at a distance of gravity. However, his work seemed to successfully predict the motion of both celestial and terrestrial bodies according to that principle, and the generation of philosophers who were inspired by Newton's example carried the mechanist banner nonetheless. Chief among them were French philosophers such as Julien Offray de La Mettrie and Denis Diderot.

Anthropic Mechanism

The debate over anthropic mechanism seems here to stay, at least for the time being. The thesis in anthropic mechanism is not that everything can be completely explained in mechanical terms (although some anthropic mechanists may *also* believe that), but rather that everything about human beings can be completely explained in mechanical terms, as surely as can everything about clockwork or gasoline engines.

One of the chief obstacles that all mechanistic theories have faced is providing a mechanistic explanation of the human mind; Descartes, for one, endorsed dualism in spite of endorsing a completely mechanistic conception of the material world because he argued that mechanism and the notion of a mind were logically incompatible. Hobbes, on the other hand, conceived of the mind and the will as purely mechanistic, completely explicable in terms of the effects of perception and the pursuit of desire, which in turn he held to be completely explicable in terms of the materialistic operations of the nervous system. Following Hobbes, other mechanists argued for a thoroughly mechanistic explanation of the mind, with one of the most influential and controversial expositions of the doctrine being offered by Julien Offray de La Mettrie in his *Man a Machine* (1748).

Today, as in the past, the main points of debate between anthropic mechanists and anti-mechanists are mainly occupied with two topics: the mind — and consciousness, in particular — and free will. Anti-mechanists argue that anthropic mechanism is incompatible with our commonsense intuitions: in philosophy of mind they argue that unconscious matter cannot completely explain the phenomenon of consciousness, and in metaphysics they argue that anthropic mechanism implies determinism about human action, which (they argue) is incompatible with our understanding of ourselves as creatures with free will. Contemporary philosophers who have argued for this position include Norman Malcolm and David Chalmers.

Anthropic mechanists typically respond in one of two ways. In the first, they agree with anti-mechanists that mechanism conflicts with some of our commonsense intuitions, but go on to argue that our commonsense intuitions are simply mistaken and need to be revised. Down this path lies eliminative materialism in philosophy of mind, and hard determinism on the question of free will. This option is popular with some scientists, but it is rejected by most philosophers, although not by its most well-known advocate, the eliminative materialist philosopher Paul Churchland. What is far from clear is how eliminative materialism is compatible with the freedom of will apparently required for anyone (including its adherents) to make truth claims. The second option, common amongst philosophers who adopt anthropic mechanism, is to argue that the arguments given for incompatibility are specious: whatever it is we mean by "consciousness" and "free will," they urge, it is fully compatible with a mechanistic understanding of the human mind and will. As a result they tend to argue for one or another non-eliminativist physicalist theories of mind, and for compatibilism on the question of free will. Contemporary philosophers who have argued for this sort of account include J. J. C. Smart and Daniel Dennett.

Gödelian Arguments

Some scholars have debated over what, if anything, Gödel's incompleteness theorems imply about anthropic mechanism. Much of the debate centres on whether the human mind is equivalent to a Turing machine, or by the Church-Turing thesis, any finite machine at all. If it is, and if the machine is consistent, then Gödel's incompleteness theorems would apply to it.

One of the earliest attempts to use incompleteness to reason about human intelligence was by Gödel himself in his 1951 Gibbs lecture entitled "Some basic theorems on the foundations of mathematics and their philosophical implications". In this lecture, Gödel uses the incompleteness theorem to arrive at the following disjunction: (a) the human mind is not a consistent finite machine, or (b) there exist Diophantine equations for which it cannot decide whether solutions exist. Gödel finds (b) implausible, and thus seems to have believed the human mind was not equivalent to a finite machine, i.e., its power exceeded that of any finite machine. He recognized that this was only a conjecture, since one could never disprove (b). Yet he considered the disjunctive conclusion to be a "certain fact".

In subsequent years, more direct anti-mechanist lines of reasoning were apparently floating around the intellectual atmosphere. In 1960, Hilary Putnam published a paper entitled "Minds and Machines," in which he points out the flaws of a typical anti-mechanist argument. Informally, this is the argument that the (alleged) difference between "what can be mechanically proven" and "what can be seen to be true by humans" shows that human intelligence is not mechanical in nature. Or, as Putnam puts it:

Let T be a Turing machine which "represents" me in the sense that T can prove just the mathematical statements I prove. Then using Gödel's technique I can discover a proposition that T cannot prove, and moreover I can prove this proposition. This refutes the assumption that T "represents" me, hence I am not a Turing machine.

Hilary Putnam objects that this argument ignores the issue of consistency. Gödel's technique can only be applied to consistent systems. It is conceivable, argues Putnam, that the human mind is inconsistent. If one is to use Gödel's technique to prove the proposition that T cannot prove, one must first prove (the mathematical statement representing) the consistency of T, a daunting and perhaps impossible task. Later Putnam suggested that while Gödel's theorems cannot be applied to humans, since they make mistakes and are therefore inconsistent, it may be applied to the human faculty of science or mathematics in general. If we are to believe that it is consistent, then either we cannot prove its consistency, or it cannot be represented by a Turing machine.

J. R. Lucas in Minds, Machines and Gödel (1963), and later in his book *The Freedom of the Will* (1970), lays out an anti-mechanist argument closely following the one described by Putnam, including reasons for why the human mind can be considered consistent. Lucas admits that, by Gödel's second theorem, a human mind cannot formally prove its own consistency, and even says (perhaps facetiously) that women and politicians are inconsistent. Nevertheless, he sets out arguments for why a male non-politician can be considered consistent. These arguments are philosophical in nature and are the subject of much debate; Lucas provides references to responses on his own website.

Another work was done by Judson Webb in his 1968 paper "Metamathematics and the Philosophy of Mind". Webb claims that previous attempts have glossed over whether one truly can see that the Gödelian statement *p* pertaining to oneself, is true. Using a different formulation of Gödel's theorems, namely, that of Raymond Smullyan and Emil Post, Webb shows one can derive convincing arguments for oneself of both the truth and falsity of *p*. He furthermore argues that all arguments about the philosophical implications of Gödel's theorems are really arguments about whether the Church-Turing thesis is true.

Later, Roger Penrose entered the fray, providing somewhat novel anti-mechanist arguments in his books, *The Emperor's New Mind* (1989) [ENM] and *Shadows of the Mind* (1994) [SM]. These books have proved highly controversial. Martin Davis responded to ENM in his paper "Is Mathematical Insight Algorithmic?" (ps), where he argues that Penrose ignores the issue of consistency. Solomon Feferman gives a critical examination of SM in his paper "Penrose's Gödelian argument" (pdf).

One of the most lucid statements of a Gödel based anti-mechanism argument can be found in Douglas Hofstadter's Pulitzer Prize winning book *Gödel, Escher, Bach: An Eternal Golden Braid.* This is particularly interesting, in that Hofstadter is widely viewed as one of the better known skeptics of such argument:

Looked at this way, Gödel's proof suggests – though by no means does it prove! – that there could be some high-level way of viewing the mind/brain, involving concepts which do not appear on lower levels, and that this level might have explanatory power that does not exist – not even in principle – on lower levels. It would mean that some facts could be explained on the high level quite easily, but not on lower levels at all. No matter how long and cumbersome a low-level statement were made, it would not explain the phenomena in question. It is analogous to the fact that, if you make derivation after derivation in Peano arithmetic, no matter how long and cumbersome you make them, you will never come up with one for G – despite the fact that on a higher level, you can see that the Gödel sentence is true.

What might such high-level concepts be? It has been proposed for eons, by various holistically or "soulistically" inclined scientists and humanists that consciousness is a phenomenon that escapes explanation in terms of brain components; so here is a candidate at least. There is also the ever-puzzling notion of free will. So perhaps these qualities could be "emergent" in the sense of requiring explanations which cannot be furnished by the physiology alone (*Gödel, Escher, Bach,* p. 708).

Explanation

Explanation, in philosophy, set of statements that makes intelligible the existence or occurrence of an object, event, or state of affairs. Among the most common forms of explanation are causal explanation (*see*causation); deductive-nomological explanation (*see*covering-law model), which involves subsuming the explanandum under a generalization from which it may be derived in a deductive argument (e.g., "All gases expand when heated; this gas was heated; therefore, this gas expanded"); and statistical explanation, which involves subsuming the explanandum under a generalization that gives it inductive support (e.g., "Most people who use tobacco contract cancer; this person used tobacco; therefore, this person contracted cancer"). Explanations of human behaviour typically appeal to the subject's beliefs and desires, as well as other facts about him, and proceed on the assumption that the behaviour in question is rational (at least to a minimum degree). Thus an explanation of why the subject removed his coat might cite the fact that the subject felt hot, that the subject desired to feel cooler, and that the subject believed that he would feel cooler if he took off his coat.

Theories of Explanation

Within the philosophy of science there have been competing ideas about what an explanation is. Historically, explanation has been associated with causation: to explain an event or phenomenon is to identify its cause. But with the growth and development of philosophy of science in the 20th century, the concept of explanation began to receive more rigorous and specific analysis. Of particular concern were theories that posited the existence of unobservable entities and processes (atoms, fields, genes, and so forth). These posed a dilemma: on the one hand, the staunch empiricist had to reject unobservable entities as a matter of principle; on the other, theories that appealed to unobservable entities were clearly producing revolutionary results. Thus philosophers of science sought some way to characterize the obvious value of these theories without abandoning the empiricist principles deemed central to scientific rationality.

A theory of explanation might treat explanations in either a realist or an epistemic (that is, anti-realist) sense. A realist interpretation of explanation holds that the entities or processes an explanation posits actually exist–the explanation is a literal description of external reality. An epistemic interpretation, on the contrary, holds that such entities or processes do not necessarily exist in any literal sense but are simply useful for organizing human experience and the results of scientific experiments–the point of an explanation is only to facilitate the construction of a consistent empirical model, not to furnish a literal description of reality. Thus Hempel's epistemic theory of explanation deals only in logical form, making no mention of any actual physical connection between the phenomenon to be explained and the facts purported to explain it, whereas Salmon's realist account emphasizes that real processes and entities are conceptually necessary for understanding exactly why an explanation works.

In contrast to these theoretical and primarily scientific approaches, some philosophers have favoured a theory of explanation grounded in the way people actually perform explanation. Ordinary Language Philosophy stresses the communicative or linguistic aspect of an explanation, its utility in answering questions and furthering understanding between two individuals, while an approach based in cognitive science maintains that explaining is a purely cognitive activity and that an explanation is a certain kind of mental representation that results from or aids in this activity. It is a matter of contention within cognitive science whether explanation is properly conceived as the process and results of belief revision or as the activation of patterns within a neural network.

This article focuses on the way thinking about explanation within the philosophy of science has changed since 1950. It begins by discussing the philosophical concerns that gave rise to the first theory of explanation, the deductive-nomological model. Discussions of this theory and standard criticisms of it are followed by an examination of attempts to amend, extend or replace this first model. There is particular emphasis on the most general aspects of explanation and on the extent to which later developments reflect the priorities and presuppositions of different philosophical traditions. There are many important aspects of explanation not covered, most notably the relation between the different types of explanation such as teleological, functional, reductive, psychological, and historical explanation — that are employed in various branches of human inquiry.

Most people, philosophers included, think of explanation in terms of causation. Very roughly, to explain an event or phenomenon is to identify its cause. The nature of causation is one of the perennial problems of philosophy, so on the basis of this connection one might reasonably attempt to trace thinking about the nature of explanation to antiquity. (Among the ancients, for example, Aristotle's theory of causation is plausibly regarded as a theory of explanation.) But the idea that the concept of explanation warrants independent analysis really did not begin to take hold until the 20th century. Generally, this change occurred as the result of the linguistic turn in philosophy. More specifically, it was the result of philosophers of science attempting to understand the nature of modern theoretical science.

Of particular concern were theories that posited the existence of unobservable entities and processes (for example, atoms, fields, genes, etc.). These posed a dilemma. On the one hand, the staunch empiricist had to reject unobservable entities as a matter of principle; on the other hand, theories that appealed to unobservables were clearly producing revolutionary results. A way was needed to characterize the obvious value of these theories without abandoning the empiricist principles deemed central to scientific rationality.

In this context it became common to distinguish between the literal truth of a theory and its power to explain observable phenomena. Although the distinction between truth and explanatory power is important, it is susceptible to multiple interpretations, and this remains a source of confusion even today. The problem is this: In philosophy the terms "truth" and "explanation" have both realist and epistemic interpretations. On a realist interpretation the truth and explanatory power of a theory are matters of the correspondence of language with an external reality. A theory that is both true and explanatory gives us insight into the causal structure of the world. On an epistemic interpretation, however, these terms express only the power of a theory to order our experience. A true and explanatory theory orders our experience to a greater degree than a false non-explanatory one. Hence, someone who denies that scientific theories are explanatory in the realist sense of the term may or may not be denying that they are explanatory in the epistemic sense. Conversely, someone who asserts that scientific theories are explanatory in the epistemic sense may or may not be claiming that they are explanatory in the realist sense. The failure to distinguish these senses of "explanation" can and does foster disagreements that are purely semantic in nature.

One common way of employing the distinction between truth and explanation is to say that theories that refer to unobservable entities may explain the phenomena, but they are not literally true. A second way is to say that these theories are true, but they do not really explain the phenomena. Although these statements are superficially contradictory, they can both be made in support of the same basic view of the nature of scientific theories. This, it is now easy to see, is because the terms 'truth' and 'explanation' are being used differently in each statement. In the first, 'explanation' is being used epistemically and 'truth' realistically; in the second, 'explanation' is being used realistically and 'truth' epistemically. But both statements are saying roughly the same thing, namely, that a scientific theory may be accepted as having a certain epistemic value without necessarily accepting that the unobservable entities it refers to actually exist. (This view is known as anti-realism.) One early 20th century philosopher scientist, Pierre Duhem, expressed himself according to the latter interpretation when he claimed:

A physical theory is not an explanation. It is a system of mathematical propositions, deduced from a small number of principles, which aim to represent as simply, as completely, and as exactly as possible a set of experimental laws. ([1906] 1962: p7)

Duhem Claimed that: To explain is to strip the reality of the appearances covering it like a veil, in order to see the bare reality itself. (op.cit.: p19)

Explanation was the task of metaphysics, not science. Science, according to Duhem, does not comprehend reality, but only gives order to appearance. However, the subsequent rise of analytic philosophy and, in particular, logical positivism made Duhem's acceptance of classical metaphysics unpopular. The conviction grew that, far from being explanatory, metaphysics was meaningless insofar as it issued claims that had no implications for experience. By the time Carl Hempel (who, as a logical positivist, was still fundamentally an anti-realist about unobservable entities) articulated the first real theory of explanation (1948) the explanatory power of science could be stipulated.

To explain the phenomena in the world of our experience, to answer the question "Why?" rather than only the question "What?", is one of the foremost objectives of all rational inquiry; and especially scientific research, in its various branches strives to go beyond a mere description of its subject matter by providing an explanation of the phenomena it investigates. (Hempel and Oppenheim 1948: p8)

For Hempel, answering the question "Why?" did not, as for Duhem, involve an appeal to a reality beyond all experience. Hempel employs the epistemic sense of explanation. For him the question "Why?" was an expression of the need to gain predictive control over our future experiences, and the value of a scientific theory was to be measured in terms of its capacity to produce this result.

Hempel's Theory of Explanation

According to Hempel, an Explanation is: ...an argument to the effect that the phenomenon to be explained ...was to be expected in virtue of certain explanatory facts. (1965 p. 336)

Hempel claimed that there are two types of explanation, what he called 'deductive-nomological' (DN) and 'inductive-statistical' (IS) respectively." Both IS and DN arguments have the same structure. Their premises each contain statements of two types: (1) initial conditions C, and (2) law-like generalizations L. In each, the conclusion is the event E to be explained:

C1, C2, C3,...Cn

L1, L2, L3,...Ln

E

The only difference between the two is that the laws in a DN explanation are universal generalizations, whereas the laws in IS explanations have the form of statistical generalizations. An example of a DN explanation containing one initial condition and one law-like generalization is:

C. The infant's cells have three copies of chromosome 21.

L. Any infant whose cells have three copies of chromosome 21 has Down's Syndrome.

E. The infant has Down's Syndrome.

An example of an IS explanation is:

C. The man's brain was deprived of oxygen for five continuous minutes.

L. Almost anyone whose brain is deprived of oxygen for five continuous minutes will sustain brain damage.

E. The man has brain damage.

For Hempel, DN explanations were always to be preferred to IS explanations. There were two reasons for this.

First, the deductive relationship between premises and conclusion maximized the predictive value of the explanation. Hempel accepted IS arguments as explanatory just to the extent that they approximated DN explanations by conferring a high probability on the event to be explained.

Second, Hempel understood the concept of explanation as something that should be understood fundamentally in terms of logical form. True premises are, of course, essential to something being a good DN explanation, but to qualify as a DN explanation (what he sometimes called a potential DN explanation) an argument need only exhibit the deductive-nomological structure. (This requirement placed Hempel squarely within the logical positivist tradition, which was committed to analyzing all of the epistemically significant concepts of science in logical terms.) There is, however, no corresponding concept of a potential IS explanation. Unlike DN explanations, the inductive character of IS explanations means that the relation between premises and conclusion can always be undermined by the addition of new information. (For example, the probability of brain damage, given that a man is deprived of oxygen for 7 minutes, is lowered somewhat by the information that the man spent this time at the bottom of a very cold lake.) Consequently, it is always possible that a proposed IS explanation, even if the premises are true, would fail to predict the fact in question, and thus have no explanatory significance for the case at hand.

Standard Criticisms of Hempel's Theory of Explanation

Hempel's dissatisfaction with statistical explanation was at odds with modern science, for which the explanatory use of statistics had become indispensable. Moreover, Hempel's requirement that IS explanations approximate the predictive power of DN explanations has the counterintuitive implication that for inherently low probability events no explanations are possible. For example, since smoking two packs of cigarettes a day for 40 years does not actually make it probable that a person will contract lung cancer, it follows from Hempel's theory that a statistical law about smoking will not be involved in an IS explanation of the occurrence of lung cancer. Hempel's view might be defended here by claiming that when our theories do not allow us to predict a phenomenon with a high degree of accuracy, it is because we have incomplete knowledge of the initial conditions. However, this seems to require us to base a theory of explanation on the now dubious metaphysical position that all events have determinate causes.

Another important criticism of Hempel's theory is that many DN arguments with true premises do not appear to be explanatory. Wesley Salmon raised the problem of relevance with the following example:

C1. Butch takes birth control pills.

C2: Butch is a man.

L: No man who takes birth control pills becomes pregnant.

E: Butch has not become pregnant.

Unfortunately, this reasoning qualifies as explanatory on Hempel's theory despite the fact that the premises seem to be explanatorily irrelevant to the conclusion.

Sylvain Bromberger raised the problem of asymmetry by pointing out that, while on Hempel's model one can explain the period of a pendulum in terms of the length of the pendulum together with the law of simple periodic motion, one can just as easily explain the length of a pendulum in terms of its period in accord with the same law. Our intuitions tell us that the first is explanatory, but the second is not. The same point is made by the following example:

C: The barometre is falling rapidly.

L: Whenever the barometre falls rapidly, a storm is approaching.

E: A storm is approaching.

While the falling barometre is a trustworthy indicator of an approaching storm, it is counterintuitive to say that the barometre explains the occurrence of the storm. Rather, it is the approaching storm that explains the falling barometre.

These two problems, relevance and asymmetry, expose the difficulty of developing a theory of explanation that makes no reference to causal relations. Reference to causal relations is not an option for Hempel, however, since causation heads the anti-realist's list of metaphysically suspect concepts. It would also undermine his view that explanation should be understood as an epistemic rather than a metaphysical relationship. Hempel's response to these problems was that they raise purely pragmatic issues. His model countenances many explanations that prove to be useless, but whether an explanation has any practical value is not, in Hempel's view, something that can be determined by philosophical analysis. This is a perfectly cogent reply, but it has not generally been regarded as an adequate one. Virtually all subsequent attempts to improve upon Hempel's theory accept the above criticisms as legitimate.

As noted above, Hempel's model requires that an explanation make use of at least one law-like generalization. This presents another sort of problem for the DN model. Hempel was careful to distinguish law-like generalizations from accidental generalizations. The latter are generalizations that may be true, but not in virtue of any law of nature. (for example, "All of my shirts are stained with coffee" may be true, but it is- I hope- just an accidental fact, not a law of nature.) Although the idea that explanation consists in subsuming events under natural laws has wide appeal in the philosophy of science, it is doubtful whether this requirement can be made consistent with Hempel's epistemic view of explanation. The reason is simply that no one has ever articulated an epistemically sound criterion for distinguishing between law-like generalizations and accidental generalizations. This is essentially just Hume's problem of induction, namely, that no finite number of observations can justify the claim that a regularity in nature is due to an natural necessity. In the absence of such a criterion, Hempel's model seems to violate the spirit of the epistemic view of explanation, as well as the idea that explanation can be understood in purely logical terms.

Contemporary Developments in the Theory of Explanation

Contemporary developments in the theory of explanation in many ways reflect the fragmented state of analytic philosophy since the decline of logical positivism. In this article we will look briefly at examples of how explanation has been conceived within the following five traditions: (1) Causal Realism, (2) Constructive Empiricism, (3) Ordinary Language Philosophy, (4) Cognitive Science and (5) Naturalism and Scientific Realism.

Explanation and Causal Realism

With the decline of logical positivism and the gathering success of modern theoretical science, philosophers began to regard continued skepticism about the reality of unobservable entities and processes as pointless. Different varieties of realism were articulated and against this background several different causal theories of explanation were developed. The idea behind them is the ordinary intuition noted at the beginning of this essay: to explain is to attribute a cause. Michael Scriven argued this point with notable force:

Let us take a case where we can be sure beyond any reasonable doubt that we have a correct explanation. As you reach for the dictionary, your knee catches the edge of the table and thus turns over the ink bottle, the contents of which proceed to run over the table's edge and ruin the carpet. If you are subsequently asked to explain how the carpet was damaged you have a complete explanation. You did it by knocking over the ink. The certainty of this explanation is primeval...This capacity for identifying causes is learnt, is better developed in some people than in others, can be tested, and is the basis for what we call judgments. (1959: p. 456)

Wesley Salmon's causal theory of explanation is perhaps the most influential developed within the realist tradition. Salmon had earlier developed a fundamentally epistemic view according to which an explanation is a list of statistically relevant factors. However he later rejected this, and any epistemic theory, as inadequate. His reason was that all epistemic theories are incapable of showing how explanations produce scientific understanding. This is because scientific understanding is not only a matter of having justified beliefs about the future. Salmon now insists that even a Laplacean Demon whose knowledge of the laws and initial conditions of the universe were so precise and complete as to issue in perfect predictive knowledge would lack scientific understanding. Specifically, he would lack the concepts of causal relevance and causal asymmetry and he could not distinguish between true causal processes and pseudo-processes. (As an example of the latter, consider the beam of a search light as it describes an arc through the sky. The movement of the beam is a pseudo-process since earlier stages of the beam do not cause later stages. By contrast, the electrical generation of the light itself, and the movement of the lamp housing are true causal processes.)

Salmon defends his causal realism by rejecting the Humean conception of causation as linked chains of events, and by attempting to articulate an epistemologically sound theory of continuous causal processes and causal interactions to replace it. The theory itself is detailed and does not lend itself to compression. It reads not so much as an analysis of the term 'explanation' as a set of instructions for producing an explanation of a particular phenomenon or event. One begins by compiling a list of statistically relevant factors and analyzing the list by a variety of methods. The procedure terminates in the creation of causal models of these statistical relationships and empirical testing to determine which of these models is best supported by the evidence.

Insofar as Salmon's theory insists that an adequate explanation has not been achieved until the fundamental causal mechanisms of a phenomenon have been articulated, it is deeply reductionistic. It is not clear, for example, how Salmon's model of explanation could ever generate meaningful explanations of mental events, which supervene on, but do not seem to be reducible to a unique set of causal relationships. Salmon's theory is also similar to Hempel's in at least one sense, and that is that both champion ideal forms of explanation, rather than anything that scientists or ordinary people are likely to achieve in the workaday world. This type of theorizing clearly has its place, but it has also been criticized by those who see explanation primarily as a form of communication between individuals. On this view, simplicity and ease of communication are not merely pragmatic, but essential to the creation of human understanding.

Explanation and Constructive Empiricism

In his book *The Scientific Image* (1980) Bas van Fraassen produced an influential defence of anti-realism. Terming his view "constructive empiricism" van Fraassen claimed that theoretical science was properly construed as a creative process of model construction rather than one of discovering truths about the unobservable world. While avoiding the fatal excesses of logical positivism he argued strongly against the realistic interpretation of theoretical terms, claiming that contemporary scientific realism is predicated on a dire misunderstanding of the nature of explanation. In support of his constructive empiricism van Fraassen produced an epistemic theory of explanation that draws on the logic of why-questions and draws on a Bayesian interpretation of probability.

Like Hempel, van Fraassen seeks to explicate explanation as a purely logical concept. However, the logical relation is not that of premises to conclusion, but one of question to answer. Following Bromberger, van Fraassen characterizes explanation as an answer to a why-question. Why-questions, for him, are essentially contrastive. That is, they always, implicitly or explicitly, ask: Why Pk, rather than some set of alternatives X= ? Why-questions also implicitly stipulate a relevance relation R, which is the explanatory relation (for example, causation) any answer must bear to the ordered pair .

Van Fraassen follows Hempel in addressing explanatory asymmetry and explanatory relevance as pragmatic issues. However, van Fraassen's question-answering model makes this view a bit more intuitive. The relevance relation is defined by the interests of the person posing the question. For example, an individual who asks for an explanation of an airline accident in terms of the human decisions that led to it can not be forced to accept an explanation solely in terms of the weather. van Fraassen deals with the problem of explanatory asymmetry by showing that this, too, is a function of context. For example, most people would say that bad weather explains plane crashes, but plane crashes don't explain bad weather. However, there are conditions (for example, unstable atmospheric conditions, an airplane carrying highly explosive cargo) that could combine to supply the latter explanation with an appropriate context.

Van Fraassen's model also avoids Hempel's problematic requirement of high probability for IS explanation. For van Fraassen, an answer will be potentially explanatory if it "favours" Pk over all the other members of the contrast class. This means roughly that the answer must confer greater probability on Pk than on any other Pi. It does not require that Pk actually be probable, or even that the probability of Pk be raised as a result of the answer, since favouring can actually result from an answer that lowers the probability of all other Pi relative to Pk. For van Fraassen, the essential tool for calculating the explanatory value of a theory is Bayes' Rule, which allows one to calculate the probability of a particular event relative to a set of background assumptions and some new information. From a Bayesian point of view, the rationality of a belief is relative to a set of background assumptions which are not themselves the subject of evaluation. Van Fraassen's theory of explanation is therefore deeply subjectivist: what counts as a good explanation for one person may not count as a good explanation for another, since their background assumptions may differ.

Van Fraassen's pragmatic account of explanation buttresses his anti-realist position, by showing that when properly analyzed there is nothing about the concept of explanation that demands a realistic interpretation of causal processes or unobservables. Van Fraassen does not make the positivist mistake of claiming that talk of such things is metaphysical nonsense. He claims only that a full appreciation of science does not depend on a realistic interpretation. His pragmatism also offers an alternative account of Salmon's Laplacean Demon. van Fraassen agrees with Salmon that an individual with perfect knowledge of the laws and initial conditions of the universe lacks something, but what he lacks is not objective knowledge of the difference between causal processes and pseudo processes. Rather, he simply lacks the human interests that make causation a useful concept.

Explanation and Ordinary Language Philosophy

Although van Fraassen's theory of explanation is based on the view that explanation is a process of communication, he still chooses to explicate the concept of explanation as a logical relationship between question and answer, rather than as a communicative relationship between two individuals. Ordinary Language Philosophy tends to emphasize this latter quality, rejecting traditional epistemology and metaphysics and focusing on the requirements of effective communication. For this school, philosophical problems do not arise because ordinary language is defective, but because we are in some way ignoring the communicative function of language. Consequently, the point of ordinary language analysis is not to improve upon ordinary usage by clarifying the meanings of terms for use in some ideal vocabulary, but rather to bring the full ordinary meanings of the terms to light.

Within this tradition Peter Achinstein (1983) developed an illocutionary theory of explanation. Like Salmon, Achinstein characterizes explanation as the pursuit of understanding. He defines the act of explanation as the attempt by one person to produce understanding in another by answering a certain kind of question in a certain kind of way. Achinstein rejects Salmon's narrow association of understanding with causation, as well as van Fraassen's analysis in terms of why-questions. For Achinstein there are many different kinds of questions that we ordinarily regard as attempts to gain understanding (for example, who-, what-, when-, and where-questions) and it follows that the act of answering any of these is properly regarded as an act of explanation.

According to Achinstein's theory S (a person) explains q (an interrogative expressing some question Q) by uttering u only if:

S utters u with the intention that his utterance of u render q understandable by producing the knowledge of the proposition expressed by u that it is a correct answer to Q. (1983: p.13)

Achinstein's approach is an interesting departure from the types of theory discussed above in that it draws freely both on the concept of intention as well as the irreducibly causal notion of "producing knowledge." This move clearly can not be countenanced by someone who sees explanation as a fundamentally logical concept. Even the causal realist who believes that explanations make essential reference to causes does not construe explanation itself in causal terms. Indeed, Achinstein's approach is so different from theories that we have discussed so far that it might be best construed as addressing a very different question. Whereas traditional theories have attempted to explicate the logic of explanation, Achinstein's theory may be best understood as an attempt to describe the process of explanation itself.

Like van Fraassen's theory, Achinstein's theory is deeply pragmatic. He stipulates that all explanations are given relative to a set of instructions (cf. van Fraassen's relevance relations) and indicates that these instructions are ultimately determined by the individual asking the question. So, for example, a person who ask for an explanation why the electrical power in the house has gone out implicitly instructs that the question be answered in a way that would be relevant to the goal of turning the electricity back on. An answer that explained the absence of an electrical current in scientific terms, say by reference to Maxwell's equations, would be inappropriate in this case.

Achinstein attempts to avoid van Fraassen's subjectivism, by identifying understanding with knowledge that a certain kind of proposition is true. These, he calls "content giving propositions" which are to be contrasted with propositions that have no real cognitive significance. For example, Achinstein would want to rule out as non-explanatory, answers to questions that are purely tautological, such as: Mr. Pheeper died because Mr. Pheeper ceased to live. Achinstein also counts as non explanatory the scientifically correct answer to a question like: What is the speed of light in a vacuum? For him 186,000 miles/ second is not explanatory because, as it stands, it is just an incomprehensibly large number offering no basis of comparison with velocities that are cognitively significant. This does not mean that speed of light in a vacuum can not be explained. For example, a more cognitively significant answer to the above question might be that light can travel 7 1/2 times around the earth in one second. (Thanks to Professor Norman Swartz for this example)

One of the main difficulties with Achinstein's theory is that the idea of a content-giving proposition remains too vague. His refusal to narrow the list of questions that qualify as requests for explanation makes it very difficult to identify any interesting property that an act of explanation must have in order to produce understanding. Moreover, Achinstein's theory suffers from epistemological problems of its own. His theory of explanation makes essential reference to the intention to produce a certain kind of knowledge-state, but it is unclear from what Achinstein says how a knowledge state can be the result of an illocutionary act simpliciter. Certainly, such acts can produce beliefs, but not all beliefs so produced will count as knowledge, and Achinstein's theory does not distinguish between the kinds of explanatory acts that are likely to result in such knowledge, and the kinds that will not.

Explanation and Cognitive Science

While explanation may be fruitfully regarded as an act of communication, still another departure from the standard relational analysis is to think of explaining as a purely cognitive activity, and an explanation as a certain kind of mental representation that results from or aids in this activity. Considered in this way, explaining (sometimes called 'abduction') is a universal phenomenon. It may be conscious, deliberative, and explicitly propositional in nature, but it may also be unconscious, instinctive, and involve no explicit propositional knowledge whatsoever. For example: a father, hearing a high-pitched wail coming from the next room, rushes to his daughter's aid. Whether he reacted instinctively, or on the basis of an explicit inference, we can say that the father's behaviour was the result of his having explained the wailing sound as the cry of his daughter.

From this perspective the term 'explanation' is neither a meta-logical nor a metaphysical relation. Rather, the term has been given a theoretical status and an explanatory function of its own; that is, we explain a person's behaviour by reference to the fact that he is in possession of an explanation. Put differently, 'explanation' has been subsumed into the theoretical vocabulary of science (with explanation itself being one of the problematic unobservables) an understanding of which was the very purpose of the theory of explanation in the first place.

Cognitive science is a diverse discipline and there are many different ways of approaching the concept of explanation within it. One major rift within the discipline concerns the question whether "folk psychology" with its reference to mental entities like intentions, beliefs and desires is fundamentally sound. Cognitive scientists in the artificial intelligence (AI) tradition argue that it is sound, and that the task of cognitive science is to develop a theory that preserves the basic integrity of belief-desire explanation. On this view, explaining is a process of belief revision, and explanatory understanding is understood by reference to the set of beliefs that result from that process. Cognitive scientists in the neuroscience tradition, in contrast, argue that folk psychology is not explanatory at all: in its completed state all reference to beliefs and desires will be eliminated from the vocabulary of cognitive science in favour of a vocabulary that allows us to explain behaviour by reference to models of neural activity. On this view explaining is a fundamentally neurological process, and explanatory understanding is understood by reference to activation patterns within a neural network.

One popular approach that incorporates aspects of both traditional AI and neuroscience makes use of the idea of a mental model (cf. Holland et al. [1986]) Mental models are internal representations that occur as a result of the activation of some part of a network of condition-action (or if-then) type rules. These rules are clustered in such a way that when a certain number of conditions becomes active, some action results. For example, here is a small cluster of rules that a simple cognitive system might use to distinguish different types of small furry mammals in a backyard environment.

(i) If [large, scurries, meows] then [cat].

(ii) If [small, scurries, squeaks] then [rat].

(iii) If [small, hops, chirps] then [squirrel].

(iv) If [squirrel or rat] then [flees].

(v) If [cat] then [approaches].

A mental model of a squirrel, then, can be described as an activation of rule (iii).

A key concept within the mental models framework is that of a default hierarchy. A set of rules such as those above, state a standard set of default conditions. When these are met, a set of expectations is generated. For example, the activation of rule (iii) generates expectations of type (iv). However, a viable representational system must be able to revise prior rule activations when expectations are contradicted by future experience. In the mental models framework, this is achieved by incorporating a hierarchy of rules below the default condition with more specific conditions at lower levels of the model whose actions will defeat default expectations. For example, default rule (iii) might be defeated by another rule as follows:

3. Level 1: If [small, hops, chirps] then [squirrel].

Level 2: If [flies] then [bird].

In other words, a system that identifies a small, hopping chirping animal as a squirrel generates a set of expectations about its future behaviour. If these expectations are contradicted by, for example, the putative squirrel flying, then the system will descend to a lower level of the hierarchy thereby allowing the system to reclassify the object as a bird.

Although this is just a cursory characterization of the mental models framework it is enough to show how explanation can be handled within it. In this context it is natural to think of explanation as a process that is triggered by a predictive failure. Essentially, when the expectations activated at Level 1 of the default hierarchy fail, the system searches lower levels of the hierarchy to find out why. If the above example were formulated in explicitly propositional terms, we would say that the failure of Level 1 expectations generated the question: Why did the animal, which I previously identified as a squirrel, fly? The answer supplied at level 2 is: Because the animal is not a squirrel, but a bird. Of course, Level 2 rules produce their own set of expectations, which must themselves be corroborated with future experience or defeated by future explanations. Clearly, the above example is a rudimentary form of explanation. Any viable system must incorporate learning algorithms which allow it to modify both the content and structure of the default hierarchy when its expectations are repeatedly undermined by experience. This will necessarily involve the ability to generalize over past experiences and activate entirely new rules at every level of the default hierarchy.

One can reasonably doubt whether philosophical questions about the nature of explanation are addressed by defining and ultimately engineering systems capable of explanatory cognition. To the extent that these questions are understood in purely normative terms, they obviously arise in regard to systems built by humans with at least as much force as they arise for humans themselves. In defence of the cognitive science approach, however, one might assert that the simple philosophical question "What is explanation?" is not well-formed. If we accept some form of epistemic relativity, the proper form of such a question is always "What is explanation in cognitive system S?" Hence, doubts about the significance of explanatory cognition in some system S are best expressed as doubts about whether system S-type explanation models human cognition accurately enough to have any real significance for human beings.

Explanation, Naturalism and Scientific Realism

Historically, naturalism is associated with the inclination to reject any kind of explanation of natural phenomena that makes essential reference to unnatural phenomena. Insofar as this view is understood simply as the rejection of *supernatural* phenomena (for example the actions of gods, irreducibly spiritual substances, etc.) it is uncontroversial within the philosophy of science. However, when it is understood to entail the rejection of irreducibly *non-natural* properties, (that is, the normative properties of 'rightness' and 'wrongness' that we appeal to in making evaluative judgments about human thought and behaviour), it is deeply problematic. The problem is just that the aim of the philosophy of science has always been to establish an *a priori* basis for making precisely these evaluative judgments about scientific inquiry itself. If they can not be made, then it follows that the goals of philosophical inquiry have been badly misconceived.

Most contemporary naturalists do not regard this as an insurmountable problem. Rather, they just reject the idea that philosophical inquiry can occur from a vantage point outside of science, and they deny that evaluative judgments we make about scientific reasoning and scientific concepts have any *a priori* status. Put differently, they think philosophical inquiry should be seen as a very abstract form of scientific inquiry, and they see the normative aspirations of philosophers as something that must be achieved by using the very tools and methods that philosophers have traditionally sought to justify.

The relevance of naturalism to the theory of explanation can be understood briefly as follows. Naturalism undermines the idea that knowledge is prior to understanding. If it is true that there will never be an inductive logic that can provide an *a priori* basis for calling an observed regularity a natural law, then there is, in fact, no independent way of establishing what is the case prior to understanding why it is the case. Because of this, some naturalists (for example, Sellars) have suggested a different way of thinking about the epistemic significance of explanation. The idea, basically, is that explanation is not something that occurs on the basis of pre-confirmed truths. Rather, successful explanation is actually part of the process of confirmation itself:

Our aim [is] to manipulate the three basic components of a world picture: (a) observed objects and events, (b) unobserved objects and events, (c) nomological connections, so as to achieve a maximum of "explanatory coherence." In this reshuffle no item is sacred. (Sellars, 1962: p356)

Many naturalists have since embraced this idea of "inference to the best explanation" (IBE) as a fundamental principle of scientific reasoning. Moreover, they have put this principle to work as an argument for realism. Briefly, the idea is that if we treat the claim that unobservable entities exist as a scientific hypothesis, then it can be seen as providing an explanation of the success of theories that employ them: namely, the theories are successful because they are (approximately) true. Anti-realism, by contrast, can provide no such explanation; on this view theories that make reference to unobservables are not literally true and so the success of scientific theories remains mysterious. It should be noted here that scientific realism has a very different flavour from the more foundational form of realism discussed above. Traditional realists do not think of realism as a scientific hypothesis, but as an independent metaphysical thesis.

Although IBE has won many converts in recent years it is deeply problematic precisely because of the way it employs the concept of explanation. While most people find IBE to be intuitively plausible, the fact remains that no theory of explanation discussed above can make sense of the idea that we accept a claim on the basis of its explanatory power. Rather, every such view stipulates as a condition of having explanatory power at all that a statement must be true or well-confirmed. Moreover, van Fraassen has argued that even if we can make sense of IBE, it remains a highly dubious principle of inductive inference.

The reason is that "inference to the best explanation" really can only mean "inference to the best explanation given to date." We are unable to compare proposed explanations to others that no one has yet thought of, and for this reason the property of being the best explanation can not be an objective measure of the likelihood that it is true.

One way of responding to these criticisms is to observe that Sellars' concept of explanatory coherence is based on a view about the nature of understanding that simply eludes the standard models of explanation. According to this view an explanation increases our understanding, not simply by being the correct answer to a particular question, but by increasing the coherence of our entire belief system. This view has been developed in the context of traditional epistemology (Harman, Lehrer) as well as the philosophy of science (Thagard, Kitcher). In the latter context, the terms "explanatory unification" and "consilience" have been introduced to promote the idea that good explanations necessarily tend to produce a more unified body of knowledge. Although traditionalists will insist that there is no *a priori* basis for thinking that a unified or coherent set of beliefs is more likely to be true, (counterexamples are, in fact, easy to produce) this misses the point that most naturalists reject the possibility of establishing IBE, or any other inductive principle, on purely *a priori* grounds.

The Current State of the Theory of Explanation

This brief summary may leave the reader with the impression that philosophers are hopelessly divided on the nature of explanation, but this is not really the case. Most philosophers of science would agree that our understanding of explanation is far better now than it was in 1948 when Hempel and Oppenheim published "Studies in the Logic of Explanation." While it serves expository purposes to represent the DN model and each of its successors as fatally flawed, this should not obscure the fact that these theories have brought real advances in understanding which succeeding models are required to preserve. At this point, fundamental disagreements on the nature of explanation fall into one of two categories. First, there are metaphysical disagreements. Realists and anti-realists continue to differ over what sort of ontological commitments one makes in accepting an explanation. Second, there are meta-philosophical disagreements. Naturalists and non-naturalists remain at odds concerning the relevance of scientific inquiry (namely, inquiry into the way scientists, ordinary people and computers actually think) to a philosophical theory of explanation. These disputes are unlikely to be resolved anytime soon. Fortunately, however, the significance of further research into the logical and cognitive structure of explanation does not depend on their outcome.

Sociological Explanation

There is a fundamental tension between so-called intuitive, or common sense, explanations of social events and basic sociological approaches to explanation. The former starts with individuals and their motives, while sociologists start with organizations and higher levels of abstraction. Common sense seems to tell us that people are the most fundamental unit of society, and so understanding an event requires understanding the motives of the particular people involved. That is wrong on three counts.

First, in modern, developed societies, not only have organizations have become numerous and complex, they are also the locus of power and they control income and social status. Government agencies, hospitals, corporations, unions, schools, universities, and countless other organizations dominate society and influence all social events. They are the most fundamental components of any society. It therefore seems self evident that explanations of social events must focus on organizations, not their individual members.

Second, we can never fully grasp all traits of unique people. We can only grasp a few attributes of any person at time. In fact, any subject matter can be represented only as a set of attributes. Analysis literally means to break something into its components, such as the person's age, gender, moodiness, or aggressiveness. This approach is no different than distilling a political organization into its components, i.e., size membership composition, location, and the like. Since there is no difference between analyzing individuals and analyzing organizations, one is no more important or fundamental than the other.

Third, if human beings are no more fundamental than, nor different from, any other set of attributes, they require no special theories or methods. There is no merit to the idea that an explanation is incomplete unless it accounts for human motives. So-called motivations add little to an explanation. We do not need to understand a fly's motives to predict that it will attempt to avoid the fly swatter. Any attempt to reduce social events to individual motivations only opens the door to an endless reduction cycle that can stop only at biochemical explanations. So-called motivations can be explained by a serious of causal hypotheses based on speculative assumptions. For example: a neighbour is observed gathering wood and taking into his house. One can only guess that the motive is to start a fire in the fireplace to keep warm. But many other guesses are possible, e.g., he is planning to burn down the house. The best explanation is determined by information about probabilities of each course of action and does not require any special methods. Even the person's assertions about his motives may turn out to be misleading. We know that social causation occurs independently of individual motivations. For example: overcrowding in cities does not intentionally cause disease. And, with the best of motives, a government program to hire the unemployed in Detroit attracted more job seekers and raised the unemployment rate. Also, many years ago a government program that increased benefits for the elderly raised their income to a level that disqualified many of them for free health insurance. Suppose we want to know why people panic in emergencies. The search for motives would focus on each individual's perceptions and predispositions. A simpler explanation would measure the ratio between the population's size and the number of available exits.

Therefore, the most fruitful an efficient to explanation of social events concentrates on (a) relationships between organizations and their membership and (b) relationships among organizations. This does not mean it is useless to examine mental constructs and other intervening processes. However, the fact remains that it is justifiable to ignore them. Otherwise, we would be committed to the impossible task of trying to account for endless chains of intervening variables. Incompleteness is inherent in the analytic process. It is not necessary to predict the feeling, motives, or behaviour of particular individuals. What matters is the outcome(s) of their actions and how the outcomes are distributed. For example, suppose that in a large school district, some high schools have recently hired more teachers with special math training. This changes the distribution of schools, with more of the specialized schools at the top to the distribution, and fewer at the bottom. One question is whether the distribution students in the district who able to demonstrate math skills being taught has also changed—whether there are more students in the top part of the test distribution.

The Human as the Biosocial

Contemporary science considers the human being on the basis of two different dimensions of his existence: the biological and the social. Human beings appeared on earth as a result of a long process of development. As biological creatures, they still retain a close genetic connection with the animal world. Man's organism has many features in common with the higher animals.

Man got ahead of the mammals thanks to the intensive development and differentiation of the cerebral cortex. The characteristic anatomical and physiological features of the human being are erect posture, free upper extremities, adapted for using and making tools, and advanced development of the means of communication. The need to maintain balance in the erect posture caused a certain curvature of the spinal column and a shift in the general centre of gravity.

Since the upper extremities were no longer used for body support and walking, the skeleton of the lower extremities became stronger and their muscles developed, the feet became arched to act as springs. All the systems of the internal organs have adapted to the erect posture, the means of delivering blood from the lower extremities to the heart and the brain have become more complex. The diaphragm has shifted from a vertical to a horizontal position, the muscles of the abdomen have come to perform a much greater role in the act of breathing. At a certain level of anthropogenesis, under the influence of labour activity and communication, biological development became what is, in effect, the historical development of social systems.

The human being is also a natural being and, as such, is endowed with natural vital forces, which take the form of inherited qualities. Birth gives man existence as a natural individual. Although he comes into the world with insufficiently formed anatomical and physiological systems, they are genetically programmed as uniquely human. The newborn child is not a "tabula rasa" (clean slate) on which the environment draws its fanciful spiritual patterns. Heredity equips the child not only with instincts. He is from the very beginning the possessor of a special ability, the ability to *imitate* adults, their actions, the noises they make. He has an inherent curiosity, an ability to enjoy bright objects. He is capable of being upset, disappointed, experiencing fear and joy. His smile is innate and it can be observed even in prematurely born babies. Smiling is the privilege of man. And these purely human innate potentials are developed in the course of his whole subsequent life in society. Many specific features even of the human being's physiological make-up (the round shape of the head, the sophisticated structure of the hands, the shape of the lips and the whole facial structure, the erect posture, etc.) are products of the social way of life, the result of interaction with other people.

To sum up, man is an integrated unity of the biological, the organismic and the personal, the natural and the social, the inherited and what he acquires during his life. Developing both historically and in the course of his individual development as a social being, man does not "opt out" of the multiform biotic flow. The physiological rhythm of the blood circulation, nutrition, breathing, sex life, the rhythmical vortices of the energy and information processes in the organism, birth, maturity and death, the phases of individual existence — childhood, adolescence, rebellious youth, young manhood, maturity, advanced life, old age, senility and complete decline—all this and much else is genetically programmed. Human beings are the towering peak of a great biological system, the latest to emerge in time, and the most complex.

Three forms of determination—the biotropic, the cosmotropic and sociotropic—operate in the human being. They embrace the whole history of humanity, regional and national traditions, the influence of a certain social group, of microconditions, the great power of biological heredity. The accuracy and purity of heredity is maintained by a specific material substratum, the apparatus of the genes, which for millions of years has carefully guarded man's racial essence as the highest biological species. If a chimpanzee were placed from birth in ideal conditions and surrounded by gifted teachers, it still would not change from an ape into a man. Heredity sets an impassable gulf between ape and man.

The genetically coded abilities of the child are the product of a long process of evolution, but even such apparently simple and seemingly innate abilities as the ability to distinguish ordinary sounds of speech and musical tones are formed only in the process of its living mastery of the historically shaped forms of language and music. The ability to think as a human being does not simply appear and mature in the process of the child's individual development; it is shaped by life in society. At the moment of birth a child is only a candidate human being, it cannot become a full member of the human race if isolated. It must learn to become human through communication, through being introduced to the world of people, of society, which regulates, guides and fills his behaviour with social meaning.

Every human being has amazingly obedient fingers; he can take up a brush and colours and begin to paint, but this does not make him into an artist. It is the same with consciousness, which is not our natural birthright. The conscious mental phenomena inherent in man are shaped during life by education, training, the active mastery of world culture, language, and a world-view. Thus, the social principle permeates the individual and determines the essentially human structure and mechanisms of his mentality, consciousness and mode of behaviour.

For various cognitive or practical purposes we may stress man's biological or social aspects, but we must always remember their essential unity.

In the past decade world science has devoted much attention to the problem of the relationship between the biological and the social in man. Paradoxically, it is the social conditions of life of modern man that have so urgently confronted us with the problem of his *natural* origin: the social has, as it were, "highlighted" the biological, sometimes to the point of vulgarisation, such as the assertion that nature has endowed man with "three brains", which despite their completely different structures have to function together and maintain contact. According to this view, the oldest of our brains is reptilian, the second was inherited from the lower mammals, and the third is the achievement of the higher mammals. This is the one that turned the living creature into man. So, figuratively speaking, when a doctor invites his patient to lie down on a couch, he is dealing simultaneously with a human being, a horse and a crocodile. Such views stem from the notion that man's biological essence is invariable. The conception of *socio-biologism* has also won some recognition in Western science, due probably to the striking successes of biological research in recent decades, particularly in the sphere of genetics, neurophysiology, ethology, etc.

To the question does man rely on "genes or society?" we often receive the answer that it is the genes that count most.

Some thinkers envisage man's biological destiny in an extremely optimistic and colourful light. They believe that the existing system of heredity fully reflects the results of his appearance as a unique biological species. Its significance is so great that it can virtually serve for an unlimited period, for the whole foreseeable future, and this precious hereditary basis of humanity must be preserved from any harmful external influences.

Others maintain that the human being as a biological species is already on the way to extinction. Thanks to the creation of his own environment and the successes of medicine, man has deviated from the stern discipline of natural selection and thus burdened himself with increased pressure from accumulated mutations.

A third school of thought works on the assumption that the human being, as a biologically young species, carries too many animal genes in his heredity. The social environment in which he lives is created not by the history of humanity but by the activity only of its elite.

The last two of these doctrines are based on the idea that man's genetic nature as a whole requires some adjustment or correction, that the near future threatens humanity with destruction through biological factors, and that in these conditions only genetics, by taking evolution into its own hands, can avert this grave menace.

On the crest of these ideas there emerges a somewhat elaborated form of eugenics, which imperatively declares that whether we want it or not, science must deliberately control the reproduction of the human race, and introduce some kind of partial selection for the "benefit" of humanity. Some Western scientists propose that the sperm of the "finest specimens of the human race" should be used for this purpose. It should be put into deep freeze for a long time to allow for objective assessment of the true value of the individuals concerned. Sperm thus preserved may then be used for mating purposes. The wife and the donor will be the biological parents while the husband (assumed to be inferior to the donor) remains only the "adopting parent". Exercises in "genetic engineering" even go as far as to assume an "adopting mother", in which case neither mother nor father is a truly biological parent. Even if one ignores the purely genetic implications of such selection, one is confronted by a host of moral and psychological questions. Who possesses the genotypes with the desirable features? Who should or could decide the question of what precisely is desirable? Who would dare, and by what right, to prevent the majority of men and women producing progeny, and limit this activity to an elite group? To whom can society entrust such a crucial decision? What are we to do about the incorrigible desire to perpetuate oneself in one's children? This hypertrophy of genetic factors and opportunities stems from the belittling of the social principle in man. Man is a natural being, but a *human natural* being. Nature gives the human being less than life in society requires of him. Life and the development of society may continue only through the biological form of human existence, and human biology can develop its genetic programme only in the context of the social reality. In its origin, biological law is socially conditioned. Only when swaddled in the "cotton wool" of social care can the child—the most helpless of all young animals—realise the species programme implanted in it by nature.

The animal is born with fur or feathers, it is clothed by nature. But the baby is born naked and has to be clothed by society. It must learn to be human. And this it does in constant communication with adults, in its lifetime acquisition of culture.

The influence of the social on the biological is demonstrated by the increase in longevity from approximately 18 years in the stone age to between 64 and 74 in modern times. The active period of life has also increased, particularly that of mental activity. The onset of old age has receded, the period of childhood has lengthened and sexual maturity has accelerated. The phenomenon of acceleration is regarded as an epochal shift, one of the most significant phenomena in contemporary biology, with serious medical, pedagogical and other social implications.

What regulates the relationship of the sexes? Why does one find the following stable ratio in human population: 103 boys to 100 girls? In post-war years, after the loss of so many males, the birth rate of boys increases.

Life shows that on the borderline between the biological and social the pressure of conflict sometimes reaches great intensity. Quite often it causes shifts and disruption. The number of diseases is ominously increasing, particularly those of the cardio-vascular, oncological and neuro-psychiatric types.

Physical time flows on smoothly but socio-biological time is constantly accelerating. Every hour and every minute of physical time is becoming more and more full of socio-psychological living content. The flow of contemporary life is like a violent mountain stream, it rushes us along at perilous speed. Man's psycho-physiological powers cannot always stand the pace. Everyone is trying to live faster, so as not to lag behind the general information front, to keep up with the accelerated development of culture. In the last 10 or 15 years the volume of scientific information, of discoveries and inventions, has outstripped everything previously achieved in human history. The sense organs and the human brain are fiercely and ceaselessly bombarded by all kinds of information.

When discussing biological factors, one should not reduce them to the genetic. More attention should be given to the physiological and ontogenetic aspects of development, and particularly to those that evoke a pathological effect, for it is these that modify the biology of the human being, who is also beginning to perceive even social factors in quite a different way. Dialectics does not simply put the social and the biological factors on an equal footing and attribute the human essence to the formula of biotropic-sociotropic determination favoured by some scientists. It stresses the dominant role of the social factors. Nor does dialectics accept the principles of vulgar sociologism, which ignores the significance of the biological principle in man.

As the highest intelligent being, man is the focal point of all forms of the motion of matter. They are represented in him hierarchically, and the highest ultimately guiding and regulative factor is the social, to which all other forms are subordinate. In other words a human being embodies and sums up, as it were, the whole development of the universe.

High though he stands in the universal hierarchy, a human being, when he becomes the target of scientific research, is dissected into small and even minute particles, each of which, the teeth, the stomach, the intestines, and so on, are investigated and treated separately. This is the result of the progressive differentiation of scientific knowledge, which enables us to penetrate deeper into the intricacies of human structural organisation. Without this it would be impossible to advance science. But in the course of such differentiation scientific thought tends to overlook the real and higher integrity of man, although he cannot be fully understood or treated without taking into account the whole. So there is a need for the opposite process of cognition, namely under standing of man as the highest unitary system.

The important thing is to overcome the obvious and blatant fascination with the analytical method and achieve a synthetic, complex approach, concentrating intellectual efforts in various fields on the problem of the human being as a whole. Such a "short-circuiting" of the sciences could produce a flash that would illuminate and help to identify new problems.

The independence of each separate science is an important fact, but it must be relative and should not develop into autonomy. The autonomy of the sciences that study man is a sign that they have lost the integrity of knowledge that is so essential to an understanding of the essence of the case, and to effective treatment or education. When discussing the disunity of man one must first of all realise that he is divided by the scientific scalpel into two: one half is studied by the natural sciences (biology, physiology, biochemistry, biophysics, etc.), while the other is the province of the social sciences, and also of medicine, which occupies an intermediary position and would appear to be all-embracing.

3

Quality, Quantity, Pseudo Quantity, and Measurement in Social Science

A quality (from Latin *qualitas*) is an attribute or a property. In contemporary philosophy the idea of qualities, and especially how to distinguish certain kinds of qualities from one another, remains controversial.

Background

Aristotle analyzed qualities in his logical work, the *Categories*. To him, qualities are hylomorphically–formal attributes, such as "white" or "grammatical". Categories of *state*, such as "shod" and "armed" are also non–essential qualities *(katà symbebekós)*. Aristotle observed: "one and the selfsame substance, while retaining its identity, is yet capable of admitting contrary qualities. The same individual person is at one time white, at another black, at one time warm, at another cold, at one time good, at another bad. This capacity is found nowhere else... it is the peculiar mark of substance that it should be capable of admitting contrary qualities; for it is by itself changing that it does so". Aristotle described four types of qualitative opposites: *correlatives, contraries, privatives* and *positives*.

John Locke presented a distinction between primary and secondary qualities in *An Essay Concerning Human Understanding*. For Locke, a quality is an idea of a sensation or a perception. Locke further asserts that qualities can be divided in two kinds: primary and secondary qualities. Primary qualities are intrinsic to an object—a thing or a person—whereas secondary qualities are dependent on the interpretation of the subjective mode and the context of appearance. For example, a shadow is a secondary quality.

It requires a certain lighting to be applied to an object. For another example, consider the mass of an object. Weight is a secondary quality since, as a measurement of gravitational force, it varies depending on the distance to, and mass of, very massive objects like the Earth, as described by Newton's law. It could be thought that mass is intrinsic to an object, and thus a primary quality. In the context of relativity, the idea of mass quantifying an amount of matter requires caution.

The relativistic mass varies for variously travelling observers; then there is the idea of rest mass or invariant mass (the magnitude of the energy-momentum 4-vector), basically a system's relativistic mass in its own rest frame of reference. (Note, however, that Aristotle drew a distinction between qualification and quantification; a thing's quality can vary in degree). Only an isolated system's invariant mass in relativity is the same as observed in variously travelling observers' rest frames, and conserved in reactions; moreover, a system's heat, including the energy of its massless particles such as photons, contributes to the system's invariant mass (indeed, otherwise even an isolated system's invariant mass would not be conserved in reactions); even a cloud of photons travelling in different directions has, as a whole, a rest frame and a rest energy equivalent to invariant mass. Thus, to treat rest mass (and by that stroke, rest energy) as an intrinsic quality distinctive of physical matter raises the question of what is to count as physical matter. Little of the invariant mass of a hadron (for example a proton or a neutron) consists in the invariant masses of its component quarks (in a proton, around 1%) apart from their gluonparticle fields; most of it consists in the quantum chromodynamics binding energy of the (massless) gluons.

Conceptions of Quality as Metaphysical and Ontological

Philosophy and common sense tend to see qualities as related either to subjective feelings or to objective facts. The qualities of something depends on the criteria being applied to and, from a neutral point of view, do not determine its value (the philosophical value as well as economic value). Subjectively, something might be good because it is useful, because it is beautiful, or simply because it exists. Determining or finding qualities therefore involves understanding what is useful, what is beautiful and what exists. Commonly, *quality* can mean degree of excellence, as in, "a quality product" or "work of average quality". It can also refer to a property of something such as "the addictive quality of nicotine". In his book, *Zen and the Art of Motorcycle Maintenance*, Robert M. Pirsig examines concepts of quality in classical and romantic, seeking a Metaphysics of Quality and a reconciliation of those views in terms of non-dualisticholism.

Quantity

Quantity is a property that can exist as a magnitude or multitude. Quantities can be compared in terms of "more", "less" or "equal", or by assigning a numerical value in terms of a unit of measurement. Quantity is among the basic classes of things along with quality, substance, change, and relation. Being a fundamental term, quantity is used to refer to any type of quantitative properties or attributes of things. Some quantities are such by their inner nature (as number), while others are functioning as states (properties, dimensions, attributes) of things such as heavy and light, long and short, broad and narrow, small and great, or much and little. A small quantity is sometimes referred to as a quantulum.

Two basic divisions of quantity, magnitude and multitude, imply the principal distinction between continuity (continuum) and discontinuity.

Under the names of multitude come what is discontinuous and discrete and divisible into indivisibles, all cases of collective nouns: *army, fleet, flock, government, company, party, people, chorus, crowd, mess, and number*. Under the names of magnitude come what is continuous and unified and divisible into divisibles, all cases of non-collective nouns: *the universe, matter, mass, energy, liquid, material, animal, plant, tree.*

Along with analyzing its nature and classification, the issues of quantity involve such closely related topics as the relation of magnitudes and multitudes, dimensionality, equality, proportion, the measurements of quantities, the units of measurements, number and numbering systems, the types of numbers and their relations to each other as numerical ratios.

Thus quantity is a property that exists in a range of magnitudes or multitudes. Mass, time, distance, heat, and angular separation are among the familiar examples of quantitative properties. Two magnitudes of a continuous quantity stand in relation to one another as a ratio, which is a real number.

Background

In Mathematics the concept of quantity is an ancient one extending back to the time of Aristotle and earlier. Aristotle regarded quantity as a fundamental ontological and scientific category. In Aristotle's ontology, quantity or quantum was classified into two different types, which he characterized as follows:

'Quantum' means that which is divisible into two or more constituent parts, of which each is by nature a 'one' and a 'this'. A quantum is a plurality if it is numerable, a magnitude if it is measurable. 'Plurality' means that which is divisible potentially into non-continuous parts, magnitude that which is divisible into continuous parts; of magnitude, that which is continuous in one dimension is length; in two breadth, in three depth. Of these, limited plurality is number, limited length is a line, breadth a surface, depth a solid. (Aristotle, book v, chapters 11-14, Metaphysics).

In his *Elements,* Euclid developed the theory of ratios of magnitudes without studying the nature of magnitudes, as Archimedes, but giving the following significant definitions:

A magnitude is a *part* of a magnitude, the less of the greater, when it measures the greater; A *ratio* is a sort of relation in respect of size between two magnitudes of the same kind.

For Aristotle and Euclid, relations were conceived as whole numbers (Michell, 1993). John Wallis later conceived of ratios of magnitudes as real numbers as reflected in the following:

When a comparison in terms of ratio is made, the resultant ratio often [namely with the exception of the 'numerical genus' itself] leaves the genus of quantities compared, and passes into the numerical genus, whatever the genus of quantities compared may have been. (John Wallis, *Mathesis Universalis*)

That is, the ratio of magnitudes of any quantity, whether volume, mass, heat and so on, is a number. Following this, Newton then defined number, and the relationship between quantity and number, in the following terms: "By *number* we understand not so much a multitude of unities, as the abstracted ratio of any quantity to another quantity of the same kind, which we take for unity" (Newton, 1728).

Quantitative Structure

Continuous quantities possess a particular structure that was first explicitly characterized by Hölder (1901) as a set of axioms that define such features as *identities* and *relations* between magnitudes. In science, quantitative structure is the subject of empirical investigation and cannot be assumed to exist *a priori* for any given property. The linear continuum represents the prototype of continuous quantitative structure as characterized by Hölder (1901) (translated in Michell & Ernst, 1996). A fundamental feature of any type of quantity is that the relationships of equality or inequality can in principle be stated in comparisons between particular magnitudes, unlike quality, which is marked by likeness, similarity and difference, diversity. Another fundamental feature is additivity. Additivity may involve concatenation, such as adding two lengths A and B to obtain a third A + B. Additivity is not, however, restricted to extensive quantities but may also entail relations between magnitudes that can be established through experiments that permit tests of hypothesized observable manifestations of the additive relations of magnitudes. Another feature is continuity, on which Michell (1999, p. 51) says of length, as a type of quantitative attribute, "what continuity means is that if any arbitrary length, a, is selected as a unit, then for every positive real number, *r*, there is a length b such that b = *r*a".

Quantity in Mathematics

Magnitude and multitude, the two principal types of quantities, are further divided as mathematical and physical. In formal terms, quantities—their ratios, proportions, order and formal relationships of equality and inequality—are studied by mathematics. The essential part of mathematical quantities consists of having a collection of variables, each assuming a set of values. These can be a set of a single quantity, referred to as a scalar when represented by real numbers, or have multiple quantities as do vectors and tensors, two kinds of geometric objects.

The mathematical usage of a quantity can then be varied and so is situationally dependent. Quantities can be used as being infinitesimal, arguments of a function, variables in an expression (independent or dependent), or probabilistic as in random and stochastic quantities. In mathematics, magnitudes and multitudes are also not only two distinct kinds of quantity but furthermore relatable to each other.

Number theory covers the topics of the discrete quantities as numbers: number systems with their kinds and relations. Geometry studies the issues of spatial magnitudes: straight lines, curved lines, surfaces and solids, all with their respective measurements and relationships.

Quantity in Physical Science

Establishing quantitative structure and relationships *between* different quantities is the cornerstone of modern physical sciences. Physics is fundamentally a quantitative science. Its progress is chiefly achieved due to rendering the abstract qualities of material entities into physical quantities, by postulating that all material bodies marked by quantitative properties or physical dimensions are subject to some measurements and observations. Setting the units of measurement, physics covers such fundamental quantities as space (length, breadth, and depth) and time, mass and force, temperature, energy, and quantum.

A distinction has also been made between intensive quantity and extensive quantity as two types of quantitative property, state or relation. The magnitude of an *intensive quantity* does not depend on the size, or extent, of the object or system of which the quantity is a property, whereas magnitudes of an *extensive quantity* are additive for parts of an entity or subsystems. Thus, magnitude does depend on the extent of the entity or system in the case of extensive quantity. Examples of intensive quantities are density and pressure, while examples of extensive quantities are energy, volume and mass.

Quantity in Logic and Semantics

In respect to quantity, propositions are grouped as universal and particular, applying to the whole subject or a part of the subject to be predicated. Accordingly, there are existential and universal quantifiers. In relation to the meaning of a construct, quantity involves two semantic dimensions: 1. extension or extent (determining the specific classes or individual instances indicated by the construct) 2. intension (content or comprehension or definition) measuring all the implications (relationships and associations involved in a construct, its intrinsic, inherent, internal, built-in, and constitutional implicit meanings and relations).

Quantity in Natural Language

In human languages, including English, number is a syntactic category, along with person and gender. The quantity is expressed by identifiers, definite and indefinite, and quantifiers, definite and indefinite, as well as by three types of nouns: 1. count unit nouns or countables; 2. mass nouns, uncountables, referring to the indefinite, unidentified amounts; 3. nouns of multitude (collective nouns). The word 'number' belongs to a noun of multitude standing either for a single entity or for the individuals making the whole. An amount in general is expressed by a special class of words called identifiers, indefinite and definite and quantifiers, definite and indefinite. The amount may be expressed by: singular form and plural from, ordinal numbers before a count noun singular (first, second, third...), the demonstratives; definite and indefinite numbers and measurements (hundred/hundreds, million/millions), or cardinal numbers before count nouns. The set of language quantifiers covers "a few, a great number, many, several (for count names); a bit of, a little, less, a great deal (amount) of, much (for mass names); all, plenty of, a lot of, enough, more, most, some, any, both, each, either, neither, every, no". For the complex case of unidentified amounts, the parts and examples of a mass are indicated with respect to the following: a measure of a mass (two kilos of rice and twenty bottles of milk or ten pieces of paper); a piece or part of a mass (part, element, atom, item, article, drop); or a shape of a container (a basket, box, case, cup, bottle, vessel, jar).

Further Examples

Some further examples of quantities are:

- 1.76 litres (liters) of milk, a continuous quantity
- 2ðr metres, where *r* is the length of a radius of a circle expressed in metres (or metres), also a continuous quantity
- one apple, two apples, three apples, where the number is an integer representing the count of a denumerable collection of objects (apples)
- 500 people (also a count)
- a *couple* conventionally refers to two objects
- *a few* usually refers to an indefinite, but usually small, number greater than two.
- *several* refers to an indefinite, but usually small, number - usually indefinitely greater than "a few".

Scale (Social Sciences)

In the social sciences, scaling is the process of measuring or ordering entities with respect to quantitative attributes or traits. For example, a scaling technique might involve estimating individuals' levels of extraversion, or the perceived quality of products. Certain methods of scaling permit estimation of magnitudes on a continuum, while other methods provide only for relative ordering of the entities.

The level of measurement is the type of data that is measured.

Comparative and Non Comparative Scaling

With comparative scaling, the items are directly compared with each other (example: Do you prefer Pepsi or Coke?). In noncomparative scaling each item is scaled independently of the others (example: How do you feel about Coke?).

Composite Measures

Composite measures of variables are created by combining two or more separate empirical indicators into a single measure. Composite measures measure complex concepts more adequately than single indicators, extend the range of scores available and are more efficient at handling multiple items.

In addition to scales, there are two other types of composite measures. Indexes are similar to scales except multiple indicators of a variable are combined into a single measure.

The index of consumer confidence, for example, is a combination of several measures of consumer attitudes. A *typology* is similar to an index except the variable is measured at the nominal level.

Indexes are constructed by accumulating scores assigned to individual attributes, while scales are constructed through the assignment of scores to patterns of attributes.

While indexes and scales provide measures of a single dimension, typologies are often employed to examine the intersection of two or more dimensions. Typologies are very useful analytical tools and can be easily used as independent variables, although since they are not unidimensional it is difficult to use them as a dependent variable.

Data Types

The type of information collected can influence scale construction. Different types of information are measured in different ways.

1. Some data are measured at the nominal level. That is, any numbers used are mere labels; they express no mathematical properties. Examples are SKU inventory codes and UPC bar codes.
2. Some data are measured at the ordinal level. Numbers indicate the relative position of items, but not the magnitude of difference. An example is a preference ranking.
3. Some data are measured at the interval level. Numbers indicate the magnitude of difference between items, but there is no absolute zero point. Examples are attitude scales and opinion scales.
4. Some data are measured at the ratio level. Numbers indicate magnitude of difference and there is a fixed zero point. Ratios can be calculated. Examples include: age, income, price, costs, sales revenue, sales volume, and market share.

Scale Construction Decisions

- What level of data is involved (nominal, ordinal, interval, or ratio)?
- What will the results be used for?
- Should you use a scale, index, or typology?
- What types of statistical analysis would be useful?
- Should you use a comparative scale or a noncomparative scale?
- How many scale divisions or categories should be used (1 to 10; 1 to 7; “3 to +3)?
- Should there be an odd or even number of divisions? (Odd gives neutral centre value; even forces respondents to take a non-neutral position.)
- What should the nature and descriptiveness of the scale labels be?
- What should the physical form or layout of the scale be? (graphic, simple linear, vertical, horizontal)
- Should a response be forced or be left optional?

Comparative Scaling Techniques

- Pairwise comparison scale – a respondent is presented with two items at a time and asked to select one (example : Do you prefer Pepsi or Coke?). This is an ordinal level technique when a measurement model is not applied. Krus and Kennedy (1977) elaborated the paired comparison scaling within their domain-referenced model. The Bradley–Terry–Luce (BTL) model (Bradley and Terry, 1952; Luce, 1959) can be applied in order to derive measurements provided the data derived from paired comparisons possess an appropriate structure. Thurstone’s Law of comparative judgement can also be applied in such contexts.
- Rasch model scaling – respondents interact with items and comparisons are inferred between items from the responses to obtain scale values. Respondents are subsequently also scaled based on their responses to items given the item scale values. The Rasch model has a close relation to the BTL model.
- Rank-ordering – a respondent is presented with several items simultaneously and asked to rank them (example : Rate the following advertisements from 1 to 10.). This is an ordinal level technique.
- Bogardus social distance scale – measures the degree to which a person is willing to associate with a class or type of people. It asks how willing the respondent is to make various

associations. The results are reduced to a single score on a scale. There are also non-comparative versions of this scale.

- Q-Sort – Up to 140 items are sorted into groups based on rank-order procedure.
- Guttman scale – This is a procedure to determine whether a set of items can be rank-ordered on a unidimensional scale. It utilizes the intensity structure among several indicators of a given variable. Statements are listed in order of importance. The rating is scaled by summing all responses until the first negative response in the list. The Guttman scale is related to Rasch measurement; specifically, Rasch models bring the Guttman approach within a probabilistic framework.
- Constant sum scale – a respondent is given a constant sum of money, script, credits, or points and asked to allocate these to various items (example : If you had 100 Yen to spend on food products, how much would you spend on product A, on product B, on product C, etc.). This is an ordinal level technique.
- Magnitude estimation scale – In a psychophysics procedure invented by S. S. Stevens people simply assign numbers to the dimension of judgment. The geometric mean of those numbers usually produces a power law with a characteristic exponent. In cross-modality matching instead of assigning numbers, people manipulate another dimension, such as loudness or brightness to match the items. Typically the exponent of the psychometric function can be predicted from the magnitude estimation exponents of each dimension.

Non-Comparative Scaling Techniques

- Continuous rating scale (also called the graphic rating scale) – respondents rate items by placing a mark on a line. The line is usually labelled at each end. There are sometimes a series of numbers, called scale points, (say, from zero to 100) under the line. Scoring and codification is difficult.
- Likert scale – Respondents are asked to indicate the amount of agreement or disagreement (from strongly agree to strongly disagree) on a five- to nine-point scale. The same format is used for multiple questions. This categorical scaling procedure can easily be extended to a magnitude estimation procedure that uses the full scale of numbers rather than verbal categories.
- Phrase completion scales – Respondents are asked to complete a phrase on an 11-point response scale in which 0 represents

the absence of the theoretical construct and 10 represents the theorized maximum amount of the construct being measured. The same basic format is used for multiple questions.

- Semantic differential scale – Respondents are asked to rate on a 7 point scale an item on various attributes. Each attribute requires a scale with bipolar terminal labels.
- Stapel scale – This is a unipolar ten-point rating scale. It ranges from +5 to 5 and has no neutral zero point.
- Thurstone scale – This is a scaling technique that incorporates the intensity structure among indicators.
- Mathematically derived scale – Researchers infer respondents' evaluations mathematically. Two examples are multi dimensional scaling and conjoint analysis.

Scale Evaluation

Scales should be tested for reliability, generalizability, and validity. Generalizability is the ability to make inferences from a sample to the population, given the scale you have selected. Reliability is the extent to which a scale will produce consistent results. Test-retest reliability checks how similar the results are if the research is repeated under similar circumstances. Alternative forms reliability checks how similar the results are if the research is repeated using different forms of the scale. Internal consistency reliability checks how well the individual measures included in the scale are converted into a composite measure.

Scales and indexes have to be validated. Internal validation checks the relation between the individual measures included in the scale, and the composite scale itself. External validation checks the relation between the composite scale and other indicators of the variable, indicators not included in the scale. Content validation (also called face validity) checks how well the scale measures what is supposed to measured. Criterion validation checks how meaningful the scale criteria are relative to other possible criteria. Construct validation checks what underlying construct is being measured. There are three variants of construct validity. They are convergent validity, discriminant validity, and nomological validity (Campbell and Fiske, 1959; Krus and Ney, 1978). The coefficient of reproducibility indicates how well the data from the individual measures included in the scale can be reconstructed from the composite scale.

4

The Lure and Disappointment of Rational Choice Theory

Rational Choice Theory

Rational choice theory, also known as choice theory or rational action theory, is a framework for understanding and often formally modelling social and economic behaviour. Rationality, interpreted as "wanting more rather than less of a good", is widely used as an assumption of the behaviour of individuals in microeconomic models and analysis and appears in almost all economics textbook treatments of human decision-making.

It is also central to some of modern political science, sociology, and philosophy. It attaches "wanting more" to instrumental rationality, which involves seeking the most cost-effective means to achieve a specific goal without reflecting on the worthiness of that goal. Gary Becker was an early proponent of applying rational actor models more widely. He won the 1992 Nobel Memorial Prize in Economic Sciences for his studies of discrimination, crime, and human capital.

Definition and Scope

The "rationality" described by rational choice theory is different from the colloquial and most philosophical use of the word. Typically, "rationality" means "sane" or "in a thoughtful clear-headed manner,." Rational choice theory uses a specific and narrower definition of "rationality" simply to mean that an individual acts *as if* balancing costs against benefits to arrive at action that maximizes personal advantage. In rational choice theory, all decisions, crazy or sane, are postulated as mimicking such a "rational" process. Thus rationality is seen as a property of patterns of choices, rather than of individual choices: there is nothing irrational in preferring fish to meat the first time, but there is something irrational in preferring fish to meat *and* preferring meat to fish, regularly.

Early neoclassical economists writing about rational choice, e.g. William Stanley Jevons, did assume that agents make consumption choices as to maximize their happiness. Twentieth century refinements of rational choice theory have eliminated such presumptions. In essence, the rationality assumed under modern rational choice theory is considerably narrower than its name might suggest—it mandates just a consistent ranking of choice alternatives. Contemporary work done under the rational choice theory paradigm typically does not investigate the origins, nature, or validity of the vast array of human motivations of human desire.

Although models used in rational choice theory are diverse, everyone assumes that individuals choose the best action according to personal identificative functions, and constraint facing them. Most idealistic models have additional assumptions. The proponents of rational choice models associated with the Chicago school of economics do not claim that a model's assumptions are a full description of reality, only that good or bad models can aid reasoning and provide help in formulating falsifiable hypothesis, whether intuitive or not. In this view, the only way to judge the success of a hypothesis is empirical tests. To use an example from Milton Friedman, if a theory that says that the behaviour of the leaves of a tree is explained by their rationality passes the empirical test, it is seen as successful. Personal rationality is not seen as an egotistical good, but rather a utilitarianistic one under certain circumstances.

However, it may not be possible to empirically test or falsify the rationality assumption, so that the theory leans heavily toward being a tautology (true by definition) since there is no effort to explain individual goals. Nonetheless, empirical tests can be conducted on some of the results derived from the models. In recent years the theoretical vision of rational choice theory has been subject to more and more doubt by the experimental results of behavioural economics. This criticism has encouraged many social scientists to utilize concepts of bounded rationality to replace the "absolute" rationality of rational choice theory: this points to the difficulties of data-processing and decision-making associated with many choices in economics, political science, and sociology. More economists these days are learning from other fields, such as psychology, in order to get a more accurate view of human decision-making than offered by rational choice theory. For example, the behavioural economist and experimental psychologist Daniel Kahneman won the Nobel Memorial Prize in Economic Sciences in 2002 for his work in this field.

Because of the relative success of economics at understanding markets, rational choice theory has also become increasingly employed in social sciences other than economics, such as sociology and political science in recent decades. It has had far-reaching impacts on the study of political science, especially in fields like the study of interest groups, elections, behaviour in legislatures, coalitions, and bureaucracy. Models that rely on rational choice theory often adopt methodological individualism, the assumption that social situations or collective behaviours are the result of individual actions alone, with no role for larger institutions. The poor fit between this and a sociological conception of social situations partially explains the theory's limited use in sociology. Among other things, sociology's emphasis on the determination of individual tastes and perspectives by social institutions often conflicts with rational choice theory's methodological assumption that tastes and perspectives are given and static.

Actions, Assumptions, and Individual Preferences

The basic idea of rational choice theory is that patterns of behaviour in societies reflect the choices made by individuals as they try to maximize their benefits and minimize their costs. In other words, people make decisions about how they should act by comparing the costs and benefits of different courses of action. As a result, patterns of behaviour will develop within the society that result from those choices.

The idea of rational choice, where people compare the costs and benefits of certain actions, is easy to see in economic theory. Since people want to get the most useful products at the lowest price, they will judge the benefits of a certain object (for example, how useful is it or how attractive is it) compared to similar objects. Then they will compare prices (or costs). In general, people will choose the object that provides the greatest reward at the lowest cost.

Rational decision making entails choosing a "rational" action given one's preferences, the actions one could take, and expectations about the outcomes of those actions. Actions are often expressed as a set, for example a set of j exhaustive and exclusive actions:

$$A = \{a_1, \ldots, a_i, \ldots, a_j\}$$

For example, if a person is to vote for either Roger or Sara or to abstain, their set of possible voting actions is:

$$A = \{Roger, Sara, abstain\}$$

Individuals can also have similar sets of possible outcomes.

Rational choice theory makes three assumptions about individuals' preferences for actions:

- Completeness – all actions can be ranked in an order of preference (indifference between two or more is possible).
- Transitivity – if action a_1 is preferred to a_2, and action a_2 is preferred to a_3, then a_1 is preferred to a_3. In other words, all actions can be compared with other actions.
- Independence of irrelevant alternatives - If A is preferred to B out of the choice set {A,B}, then introducing a third alternative X, thus expanding the choice set to {A,B,X}, must not make B preferable to A.

Together these assumptions form the result that given a set of exhaustive and exclusive actions to choose from, an individual can rank them in terms of his preferences, and that his preferences are consistent.

An individual's preferences can also take forms:

- Strict preference occurs when an individual prefers a_1 to a_2, but not a_2 to a_1.
- In some models, a weak preference can be held in which an individual has a preference for *at least* a_j, similar to the mathematical operator $\leq$.
- Indifference occurs when an individual does not prefer a_1 to a_2, or a_2 to a_1.

In more complex models, other assumptions are often incorporated, such as the assumption of independence axiom. Also, with dynamic models that include decision-making over time, time inconsistency may affect an individual's preferences.

Research that took off in the 1980s sought to develop models which drop these assumptions and argue that such behaviour could still be rational, Anand (1993).

This work, often conducted by economic theorists and analytical philosophers, suggests ultimately that the assumptions or axioms above are not completely general and might at best be regarded as approximations.

Other Assumptions

At the same time, is often claimed from behavioural or social disciplines that rational choice theory makes some descriptively unrealistic assumptions in order to generate tractable and testable predictions. These can include:

- An individual has full or perfect information about exactly what will occur due to any choice made. More complex models rely on probability to describe outcomes.
- An individual has the cognitive ability and time to weigh every choice against every other choice. Studies about the limitations of this assumption are included in theories of bounded rationality.

Even more realistic theories of human action include such components as Amos Tversky and Daniel Kahneman's prospect theory, which reflects the empirical finding as that, contrary to rational choice theory, individuals attach extra value to items that they already own compared to similar items owned by others. To rational choice theory, the amount that an individual is willing to pay for an item (such as a drinking mug) should equal the amount he or she is willing to be paid in order to part with it. In experiments, the latter price is typically significantly higher than the former. Behavioural economics includes a large number of other amendments to its picture of human behaviour that go against pure economic rationality.

Utility Maximization

Often preferences are described by their utility function or *payoff function*. This is an ordinal number an individual assigns over the available actions, such as:

$$u(a_i) > u(a_j)$$

The individual's preferences are then expressed as the relation between these ordinal assignments. For example, if an individual prefers the candidate Sara over Roger over abstaining, their preferences would have the relation:

$$u(Sara) > u(Roger) > u(abstain)$$

Criticism

Both the assumptions and the behavioural predictions of rational choice theory have sparked criticism from various camps. As mentioned above, some economists have developed models of bounded rationality, which hope to be more psychologically plausible without completely abandoning the idea that reason underlies decision-making processes.

Other economists have developed more theories of human decision-making that allow for the roles of uncertainty, institutions, and determination of individual tastes by their socioeconomic environment (cf. Fernandez-Huerga, 2008).

Martin Hollis and Edward J. Nell's 1975 book offers both a philosophical critique of neo-classical economics and an innovation in the field of economic methodology. Further they outlined an alternative vision to neo-classicism based on a rationalist theory of knowledge. Within neo-classicism, the authors addressed consumer behaviour (in the form of indifference curves and simple versions of revealed preference theory) and marginalist producer behaviour in both product and factor markets. Both are based on rational optimizing behaviour. They consider imperfect as well as perfect markets since neo-classical thinking embraces many market varieties and disposes of a whole system for their classification.

However, the authors believe that the issues arising from basic maximizing models have extensive implications for econometric methodology (Hollis and Nell, 1975, p. 2). In particular it is this class of models – rational behaviour as maximizing behaviour – which provide support for specification and identification. And this, they argue, is where the flaw is to be found. Hollis and Nell (1975) argued that positivism (broadly conceived) has provided neo-classicism with important support, which they then show to be unfounded. They base their critique of neo-classicism not only on their critique of positivism but also on the alternative they propose, rationalism. Indeed, they argue that rationality is central to neo-classical economics – as rational choice – and that this conception of rationality is misused. Demands are made of it that it cannot fulfill.

In their 1994 work, *Pathologies of Rational Choice Theory*, Donald P. Green and Ian Shapiro argue that the empirical outputs of rational choice theory have been limited. They contend that much of the applicable literature, at least in political science, was done with weak statistical methods and that when corrected many of the empirical outcomes no longer hold. When taken in this perspective, rational choice theory has provided very little to the overall understanding of political interaction - and is an amount certainly disproportionately weak relative to its appearance in the literature. Yet, they concede that cutting edge research, by scholars well-versed in the general scholarship of their fields (such as work on the U.S. Congress by Keith Krehbiel, Gary Cox, and Mat McCubbins) has generated valuable scientific progress.

Duncan K. Foley (2003, p. 1) has also provided an important criticism of the concept of *rationality* and its role in economics. He argued that

"Rationality" has played a central role in shaping and establishing the hegemony of contemporary mainstream economics. As the specific claims of robust neoclassicism fade into the history of economic thought, an orientation toward situating explanations of economic phenomena in relation to rationality has increasingly become the touchstone by which mainstream economists identify themselves and recognize each other. This is not so much a question of adherence to any particular conception of rationality, but of taking rationality of individual behaviour as the unquestioned starting point of economic analysis.

Foley (2003, p. 9) went on to argue that

The concept of rationality, to use Hegelian language, represents the relations of modern capitalist society one-sidedly. The burden of rational-actor theory is the assertion that 'naturally' constituted individuals facing existential conflicts over scarce resources would rationally impose on themselves the institutional structures of modern capitalist society, or something approximating them. But this way of looking at matters systematically neglects the ways in which modern capitalist society and its social relations in fact constitute the 'rational', calculating individual. The well-known limitations of rational-actor theory, its static quality, its logical antinomies, its vulnerability to arguments of infinite regress, its failure to develop a progressive concrete research program, can all be traced to this starting-point.

Schram and Caterino (2006) contains a fundamental methodological criticism of rational choice theory for promoting the view that the natural science model is the only appropriate methodology in social science and that political science should follow this model, with its emphasis on quantification and mathematization. Schram and Caterino argue instead for methodological pluralism. The same argument is made by William E. Connolly, who in his work Neuropolitics shows that advances in neuroscience further illuminate some of the problematic practices of rational choice theory.

More recently Edward J. Nell and Karim Errouaki (2011, Ch. 1) argued that:

The DNA of neoclassical economics is defective. Neither the induction problem nor the problems of methodological individualism can be solved within the framework of neoclassical assumptions. The neoclassical approach is to call on rational economic man to solve both.

Economic relationships that reflect rational choice should be 'projectible'. But that attributes a deductive power to 'rational' that it cannot have consistently with positivist (or even pragmatist) assumptions (which require deductions to be simply analytic). To make rational calculations projectible, the agents may be assumed to have idealized abilities, especially foresight; but then the induction problem is out of reach because the agents of the world do not resemble those of the model.

The agents of the model can be abstract, but they cannot be endowed with powers actual agents could not have. This also undermines methodological individualism; if behaviour cannot be reliably predicted on the basis of the 'rational choices of agents', a social order cannot reliably follow from the choices of agents.

Furthermore, Pierre Bourdieu fiercely opposed rational choice theory as grounded in a misunderstanding of how social agents operate. Bourdieu argued that social agents do not continuously calculate according to explicit rational and economic criteria. According to Bourdieu, social agents operate according to an implicit practical logic—a practical sense—and bodily dispositions. Social agents act according to their "feel for the game" (the "feel" being, roughly, habitus, and the "game" being the field).

An evolutionary psychology perspective is that many of the seeming contradictions and biases regarding rational choice can be explained as being rational in the context of maximizing biological fitness in the ancestral environment but not necessarily in the current one. Thus, when living at subsistence level where a reduction of resources may have meant death it may have been rational to place a greater value on losses than on gains. It may also explain differences between groups such as males being less risk-averse than females since males have more variable reproductive success than females. While unsuccessful risk-seeking may limit reproductive success for both sexes, males may potentially increase their reproductive success much more than females from successful risk-seeking.

Benefits

Describing the decisions made by individuals as rational and utility maximizing may seem to be a tautological explanation of their behaviour that provides very little new information. While there may be many reasons for a rational choice theory approach, two are important for the social sciences. First, assuming humans make decisions in a rational rather than a stochastic manner implies that their behaviour can be modelled and thus predictions can be made about future actions. Second, the mathematical formality of rational choice theory allows social scientists to derive results from their models that may have otherwise not been seen, and to submit these theoretical results for empirical verification. Despite these benefits, there is nothing about rational choice theory that tells scholars that they should reject other methods of investigating questions about the economy and society, such as the sociological determination of individual tastes.

Choice-Supportive Bias

In cognitive science, choice-supportive bias is the tendency to retroactively ascribe positive attributes to an option one has selected. It is a cognitive bias. For example, if a person buys a computer from Apple instead of a computer (PC) running Windows, he is likely to ignore or downplay the faults of Apple computers while amplifying those of Windows computers. Conversely, he is also likely to notice and amplify advantages of Apple computers and not notice or de-emphasize those of Windows computers.

What is remembered about a decision can be as important as the decision itself, especially in determining how much regret or satisfaction one experiences. Research indicates that the process of making and remembering choices yields memories that tend to be distorted in predictable ways. In cognitive science, one predictable way that memories of choice options are distorted is that positive aspects tend to be remembered as part of the chosen option, whether or not they originally were part of that option, and negative aspects tend to be remembered as part of rejected options. Once an action has been taken, the ways in which we evaluate the effectiveness of what we did may be biased. It is believed this may influence our future decision-making.

These biases may be stored as memories, which are attributions that we make about our mental experiences based on their subjective qualities, our prior knowledge and beliefs, our motives and goals, and the social context. True and false memories arise by the same mechanism because when the brain processes and stores information, it cannot tell the difference from where they came from.

General Definition

The tendency to remember one's choices as better than they actually were, where people tend to over attribute positive features to options they chose and negative features to options not chosen.

Theory

Experiments in cognitive science and social psychology have revealed a wide variety of biases in areas such as statistical reasoning, social attribution, and memory.

Choice-supportive memory distortion is thought to occur during the time of memory retrieval and was the result of the belief that, "I chose this option, therefore it must have been the better option." It is also possible that choice-supportive memories arise because an individual is only paying attention to certain pieces of information when making a decision or to post-choice cognitive dissonance. In addition, biases can also arise because they are closely related to the high level cognitive operations and complex social interactions.

Memory distortions may sometimes serve a purpose because it may be in our interest to not remember some details of an event or to forget others altogether.

Making a Selection

The objective of a choice is generally to pick the best option. Thus, after making a choice, a person is likely to maintain the belief that the chosen option was better than the options rejected. Every choice has an upside and a downside. The process of making a decision mostly relies upon previous experiences. Therefore, a person will remember not only the decision made but also the reasoning behind making that decision.

Motivation

Motivation may also play a role in this process because when a person remembers the option that they chose as being the best option, it should help reduce regret about their choice. This may represent a positive illusion that promotes well-being.

Cases When Individual is not in Control

There are cases where an individual is not always in control of which options are received. People often end up with options that were not chosen but, instead were assigned by others, such as job assignments made by bosses, course instructors assigned by a registrar, or vacation spots selected by other family members. However, being assigned (random or not) to an option leads to a different set of cognitions and memory attributions that tend to favour the alternative (non-received) option and may emphasize regret and disappointment.

- Assigned Options: Making a choice or having a choice made for you by other people in your best interest can prompt memory attributions that support that choice. Current experiments show no choice-supportive memory bias for assigned options. However, choices which are made on a person's behalf in their best interest do show a tendency for choice-supportive memory bias.

- Random Selection: People do not show choice-supportive biases when choices are made randomly for them. This is because choice-supportive memory bias tends to arise during the act of making the decision.

How Choice-Supportive Bias Relates to Self

People's conception of who they are is shaped by the memories of the choices they make; the college favoured over the one renounced, the job chosen over the one rejected, the candidate elected instead of another one not selected. Memories of chosen as well as forgone alternatives can affect one's sense of well-being. Regret for options not taken can cast a shadow, whereas satisfaction at having made the right choice can make a good outcome seem even better.

Positive Illusions

Choice-supportive bias often results in memories that depict the self in an overly favourable light. In general, cognitive biases loosen our grasp on reality because the line between reality and fantasy can become fuzzy if one's brain has failed to remember a particular event. Positive illusions are generally mild and are important contributors to our sense of well being. However, we all need to be aware that they do exist as part of human nature.

Memory Storage

Human beings are blessed with having an intelligent and complex mind, which allows us to remember our past, be able to optimize the present, and plan for the future. Remembering involves a complex interaction between the current environment, what one expects to remember, and what is retained from the past.

The mechanisms of the brain that allow memory storage and retrieval serve us well most of the time, but occasionally get us into trouble.

Memories Change over Time

There is now abundant evidence that memory content can undergo systematic changes. After some period of time and if the memory is not used often, it may become forgotten.

- Memory Retention: It is recognized that retention is best for experiences that are pleasant, intermediate for experiences that are unpleasant, and worst for experiences that are neutral. Generic memories provide the basis for inferences that can bring about distortions. These distortions in memory do not appear to displace an individual's specific memories, but rather they supplement and fill in the gaps when the memories are lost. It has been shown that a wide variety of strategic and systematic processes are used to activate different areas of the brain in order to retrieve information.
- Credibility of a Memory: People have a way to self-check memories, in which a person may consider the plausibility of the retrieved memory by asking themselves is this event even possible. For example, if a person remembers seeing a pig fly, they must conclude that it was from a dream because pigs cannot fly in the real world. Memory does not provide people with perfect reproductions of what happened, it only consists of constructions and reconstructions of what happened.

Brain Areas of Interest

There is extensive evidence that the amygdala is involved in effectively influencing memory. Emotional arousal, usually fear based, activates the amygdala and results in the modulation of memory storage occurring in other brain regions. The forebrain is one of the targets of the amygdala. The forebrain receives input from amygdala and calculates the emotional significance of the stimulus, generates an emotional response, and transmits it to cerebral cortex. This can alter the way neurons respond to future input, and therefore cognitive biases, such as choice-supportive bias can influence future decisions.

Stress Hormones Affect Memory

Effects of stress-related hormones, such as epinephrine and glucocorticoids are mediated by influences involving the amygdala. It has been shown in experiments with rats that when they are given systemic injections of epinephrine while being trained to perform a task, they show an enhanced memory of performing the task. In effect the stronger the emotion that is tied to the memory, the more likely the individual is to remember. Therefore, if the memory is stored and retrieved properly it is less likely to be distorted.

Brain Mapping

A PET scan or fMRI can be used to identify different regions of the brain that are activated during specific memory retrieval.

fMRI Study

- True versus False Memories: One study asked subjects to remember a series of events while being monitored by an fMRI to see which areas "light up." When an individual remembered a greater number of true memories than false memories, it showed a cluster spanning the right superior temporal gyrus and lateral occipital cortex.

  However, when the reverse occurred (when an individual remembered a greater number of false memories than true) the brain area that showed activation was the left insula. These findings may provide some insight as to which areas of the brain are involved with storing memories and later retrieving them.

Choice-Supportive Bias Increases with Age

Studies now show that as people age, their process of memory retrieval changes. Although general memory problems are common to everyone because no memory is perfectly accurate, older adults are more likely than younger adults to show choice-supportive biases.

Aging of the Brain

Normal aging may be accompanied by neuropathy in the frontal brain regions. Frontal regions help people encode or use specific memorial attributes to make source judgments, controls personality and the ability to plan for events. These areas can attribute to memory distortions and regulating emotion.

Regulation of Emotion

In general, older adults are more likely to remember emotional aspects of situations than are younger adults. For example, on a memory characteristic questionnaire, older adults rated remembered events as having more associated thoughts and feelings than did younger adults. As a person ages, regulating personal emotion becomes a higher priority, whereas knowledge acquisition becomes less of a powerful motive.

Therefore choice-supportive bias would arise because their focus was on how they felt about the choice rather than on the factual details of the options. Studies have shown that when younger adults are encouraged to remember the emotional aspect of a choice, they are more likely to show choice-supportive bias. This may be related to older adults' greater tendency to show a positivity effect in memory.

Rely on Familiarity

Older adults rely more than younger adults on categorical or general knowledge about an event to recognize particular elements from the event. Older adults are also less likely to correctly remember contextual features of events, such as their colour or location. This may be because older adults remember (or rely on) fewer source identifying characteristics than the young. Consequently, older adults must more often guess or base a response on less specific information, such as familiarity. As a result, if they can't remember something, they are more likely to fill in the missing gaps with things that are familiar to them.

Getting the 'Gist'

Older adults are more reliant on gist-based retrieval. A number of studies suggest that using stereotypes or general knowledge to help remember an event is less cognitively demanding than relying on other types of memorial information and thus might require less reflective activity. This shift towards gist-based processes might occur as a compensation for age decrements in verbatim memory.

Inhibition

The episodic memory and inhibition accounts of age-related increases in false memories. Inhibition of a memory may be related to an individual's hearing capacity and attention span. If the person cannot hear what is going on around them or is not paying much attention, the memory cannot be properly stored and therefore cannot be accurately retrieved.

Examples of Choice-Supportive Bias

Deciding between Two Used Cars: Henkel and Mather tested the role of beliefs at the time of retrieval about which option was chosen by giving participants several hypothetical choices like deciding between two used cars. After making several choices, participants left and were asked to return a week later. At that point, Henkel and Mather reminded them which option they had chosen for each choice and gave them a list of the features of the two options; some new positive and negative features were mixed in with the old features. Next, participants were asked to indicate whether each option was new, had been associated with the option they chose, or had been associated with the option they rejected. Participants favoured whichever option Henkel and Mather had told them they had chosen in their memories. These findings show that beliefs at the time of retrieval about which option was chosen shape both which features are attributed to the options and how vividly they are remembered.

Remembering High School Grades

One study looked at the accuracy and distortion in memory for high school grades. The relation between accuracy and distortion of autobiographical memory content was examined by verifying 3,220 high school grades recalled by 99 freshman college students. It was shown that most errors inflated the actual high school grade, meaning that these distortions are attributed to memory reconstructions in a positive and emotionally gratifying direction. In addition, their findings indicate that the process of distortion does not cause the actual unpleasant memory loss of getting the bad grade. This is because there was no correlation found between the percentage of accuracy recall and the degree of asymmetry, or distortion. This shows that the distortion in memories of high school grades arises after the content has been forgotten by another mechanism.

A 50 Year Study of College Grades

Many similar studies have been performed, such as a fifty-year study of remembering high school grades. In this study one to 54 years after graduating, 276 alumni correctly recalled 3,025 of 3,967 college grades. The number of omission errors increased with the retention interval and better students made fewer errors. The accuracy of recall increased with confidence in recall. Eighty-one percent of errors of commission inflated the actual grade. This data suggested that distortions occur soon after graduation, remain constant during the retention interval, and are greater for better students and for courses students enjoyed most. Therefore, sometime in between when the memory is stored and when it is retrieved some time later, the distortion may arise.

Methods for Testing Choice-Supportive Bias

Written Scenario Memory Tests: Researchers have used written scenarios in which participants are asked to make a choice between two options. Later, on a memory test, participants are given a list of positive and negative features, some of which were in the scenario and some of which are new. A choice-supportive bias is seen when both correct and incorrect attributions tend to favour the chosen option, with positive features more likely to be attributed to the chosen option and negative features to the rejected option.

- Deception: Henkel and Mather (2007) found that giving people false reminders about which option they chose in a previous experiment session led people to remember the option they were told they had chosen as being better than the other option. This reveals that choice-supportive biases arise in large part when remembering past choices, rather than being the result of biased processing at the time of the choice.

Deese/Roediger–McDermott Paradigm

The Deese–Roediger–McDermott paradigm (DRM) consists of a participant listening to an experimenter read lists of thematically related words (e.g. table, couch, lamp, desk); then after some period of time the experimenter will ask if a word was presented in the list. Participants often report that related but non-presented words (e.g. chair) were included in the encoding series, essentially suggesting that they 'heard' the experimenter say these non-presented words (or critical lures). Incorrect 'yes' responses to critical lures, often referred to as false memories, are remarkably high under standard DRM conditions.

Relation to Cognitive Dissonance

The theory of cognitive dissonance proposes that people have a motivational drive to reduce dissonance. Choice-supportive bias is potentially related to the aspect of cognitive dissonance explored by Jack Brehm (1956) as postdecisional dissonance. Within the context of cognitive dissonance, choice-supportive bias would be seen as reducing the conflict between "I prefer X" and "I have committed to Y".

Individualism

Individualism is the moral stance, political philosophy, ideology, or social outlook that emphasizes the moral worth of the individual. Individualists promote the exercise of one's goals and desires and so value independence and self-reliance and advocate that interests of the individual should achieve precedence over the state or a social group, while opposing external interference upon one's own interests by society or institutions such as the government.

Individualism makes the individual its focus and so starts "with the fundamental premise that the human individual is of primary importance in the struggle for liberation." Liberalism, existentialism and anarchism are examples of movements that take the human individual as a central unit of analysis. Individualism thus involves "the right of the individual to freedom and self-realization".

It has also been used as a term denoting "The quality of being an individual; individuality" related to possessing "An individual characteristic; a quirk." Individualism is thus also associated with artistic and bohemian interests and lifestyles where there is a tendency towards self-creation and experimentation as opposed to tradition or popular mass opinions and behaviours as so also with humanist philosophical positions and ethics.

Etymology

In the English language, the word "individualism" was first introduced, as a pejorative, by the Owenites in the late 1830s, although it is unclear if they were influenced by Saint-Simonianism or came up with it independently. A more positive use of the term in Britain came to be used with the writings of James Elishama Smith, who was a millenarian and a Christian Israelite. Although an early Owenite socialist, he eventually rejected its collective idea of property, and found in individualism a "universalism" that allowed for the development of the "original genius." Without individualism, Smith argued, individuals cannot amass property to increase one's happiness. William Maccall, another Unitarian preacher, and probably an acquaintance of Smith, came somewhat later, although influenced by John Stuart Mill, Thomas Carlyle, and German Romanticism, to the same positive conclusions, in his 1847 work "Elements of Individualism".

The Individual

An individual is a person or any specific object in a collection. In the 15th century and earlier, and also today within the fields of statistics and metaphysics, individual means "indivisible", typically describing any numerically singular thing, but sometimes meaning "a person." (q.v. "The problem of proper names"). From the 17th century on, individual indicates separateness, as in individualism. Individuality is the state or quality of being an individual; a person separate from other persons and possessing his or her own needs, goals, and desires.

Individualism and Society

Individualism holds that a person taking part in society attempts to further his or her own interests, or at least demands the *right* to serve his or her own interests, without taking the interests of society into consideration (an individualist need not be an egoist). The individualist does not favour any philosophy that requires the sacrifice of the self-interest of the individual for higher social causes. Jean-Jacques Rousseau, however, claims that his concept of "general will" in the "social contract" is not the simple collection of individual wills and that it furthers the interests of the individual (the constraint of law itself would be beneficial for the individual, as the lack of respect for the law necessarily entails, in Rousseau's eyes, a form of ignorance and submission to one's passions instead of the preferred autonomy of reason).

Societies and groups can differ in the extent to which they are based upon predominantly "self-regarding" (individualistic, and arguably self-interested) rather than "other-regarding" (group-oriented, and group, or society-minded) behaviour. Ruth Benedict made a distinction, relevant in this context, between "guilt" societies (e.g., medieval Europe) with an "internal reference standard", and "shame" societies (e.g., Japan, "bringing shame upon one's ancestors") with an "external reference standard", where people look to their peers for feedback on whether an action is "acceptable" or not (also known as "group-think").

Individualism is often contrasted either with totalitarianism or with collectivism, but in fact there is a spectrum of behaviours at the societal level ranging from highly individualistic societies through mixed societies to collectivist.

Individuation Theories

The principle of individuation , or *principium individuationis*, describes the manner in which a thing is identified as distinguished from other things. For Carl Jung individuation is a process of transformation whereby the personal and collective unconscious is brought into consciousness (by means of dreams, active imagination or free association to take some examples) to be assimilated into the whole personality. It is a completely natural process necessary for the integration of the psyche to take place. Jung considered individuation to be the central process of human development. In *L'individuation psychique et collective*, Gilbert Simondon developed a theory of individual and collective individuation in which the individual subject is considered as an effect of individuation rather than a cause.

Thus, the individual atom is replaced by a never-ending ontological process of individuation. Individuation is an always incomplete process, always leaving a "pre-individual" left-over, itself making possible future individuations. The philosophy of Bernard Stiegler draws upon and modifies the work of Gilbert Simondon on individuation and also upon similar ideas in Friedrich Nietzsche and Sigmund Freud. For Stiegler "the *I*, as a psychic individual, can only be thought in relationship to *we*, which is a collective individual. The *I* is constituted in adopting a collective tradition, which it inherits and in which a plurality of *I*'s acknowledge each other's existence."

Emotional Self-Interest

Emotional self-interest is defined by Nayef Al-Rodhan as "self-interest driven by neurochemically-mediated emotions". As he suggests in his general theory of human nature, "emotional amoral egoism", human behaviour is primarily governed by self-interest. Humans first seek to ensure survival, and then they seek to dominate. These facets of human nature are a product of genetically coded survival instincts modified by the totality of our environment and expressed as neurochemically-mediated emotions and actions. Accordingly, once humans' basic needs have been filled, they may employ measured self-interest. In some instances this may result in positive consequences like greater cooperation between individuals and societies. However, Al-Rodhan cautions that excessive general self-interest risks leading to deception, criminality, and conflict.

Based on his understanding of human nature, Al-Rodhan suggests introducing mechanisms that will check unregulated general self-interest. Good governance should include adequate checks on government powers and effective law enforcement, as well as the defence of human rights and their extension to include basic physiological and emotional needs.

Methodological Individualism

Methodological individualism is the view that social phenomena can only be understood by examining how they result from the motivations and actions of individual agents. In economics, people's behaviour is explained in terms of rational choices, as constrained by prices and incomes. The economist accepts individuals' preferences as givens. Becker and Stigler provide a forceful statement of this view:

On the traditional view, an explanation of economic phenomena that reaches a difference in tastes between people or times is the terminus of the argument: the problem is abandoned at this point to whoever studies and explains tastes (psychologists? anthropologists? phrenologists? sociobiologists?). On our preferred interpretation, one never reaches this impasse: the economist continues to search for differences in prices or incomes to explain any differences or changes in behaviour.

Political Individualism

With the abolition of private property, then, we shall have true, beautiful, healthy Individualism. Nobody will waste his life in accumulating things, and the symbols for things. One will live. To live is the rarest thing in the world. Most people exist, that is all.

Oscar Wilde, *The Soul of Man under Socialism*, 1891

Individualists are chiefly concerned with protecting individual autonomy against obligations imposed by social institutions (such as the state or religious morality). For L. Susan Brown "Liberalism and anarchism are two political philosophies that are fundamentally concerned with individual freedom yet differ from one another in very distinct ways. Anarchism shares with liberalism a radical commitment to individual freedom while rejecting liberalism's competitive property relations."

Civil libertarianism is a strain of political thought that supports civil liberties, or which emphasizes the supremacy of individual rights and personal freedoms over and against any kind of authority (such as a state, a corporation, social norms imposed through peer pressure, etc.). Civil libertarianism is not a complete ideology; rather, it is a collection of views on the specific issues of civil liberties and civil rights. Because of this, a civil libertarian outlook is compatible with many other political philosophies, and civil libertarianism is found on both the right and left in modern politics. For scholar Ellen Meiksins Wood "there are doctrines of individualism that are opposed to Lockean individualism(...)and non-lockean individualism may encompass socialism".

Liberalism

Liberalism (from the Latin *liberalis*, "of freedom; worthy of a free man, gentlemanlike, courteous, generous") is the belief in the importance of individual freedom. This belief is widely accepted in the United States, Europe, Australia and other Western nations, and was recognized as an important value by many Western philosophers throughout history, in particular since the Enlightenment. It is often rejected by collectivist, Islamic, or confucian societies in Asia or the Middle East (though Taoists were and are known to be individualists). The Roman Emperor Marcus Aurelius wrote praising "the idea of a polity administered with regard to equal rights and equal freedom of speech, and the idea of a kingly government which respects most of all the freedom of the governed".

Modern liberalism has its roots in the Age of Enlightenment and rejects many foundational assumptions that dominated most earlier theories of government, such as the Divine Right of Kings, hereditary status, and established religion. John Locke is often credited with the philosophical foundations of classical liberalism. He wrote "no one ought to harm another in his life, health, liberty, or possessions."

In the 17th century, liberal ideas began to influence governments in Europe, in nations such as The Netherlands, Switzerland, England and Poland, but they were strongly opposed, often by armed might, by those who favoured absolute monarchy and established religion. In the 18th century, in America, the first modern liberal state was founded, without a monarch or a hereditary aristocracy. The American *Declaration of Independence* includes the words (which echo Locke) "all men are created equal; that they are endowed by their Creator with certain unalienable rights; that among these are life, liberty, and the pursuit of happiness; that to insure these rights, governments are instituted among men, deriving their just powers from the consent of the governed."

Liberalism comes in many forms. According to John N. Gray, the essence of liberalism is toleration of different beliefs and of different ideas as to what constitutes a good life.

Anarchism

Anarchism is generally defined as the political philosophy which holds the state to be undesirable, unnecessary, and harmful, or alternatively as opposing authority and hierarchical organization in the conduct of human relations. Proponents of anarchism, known as "anarchists", advocate stateless societies based on non-hierarchical voluntary associations.

For influential Italian anarchist Errico Malatesta "All anarchists, whatever tendency they belong to, are individualists in some way or other. But the opposite is not true; not by any means. The individualists are thus divided into two distinct categories: one which claims the right to full development for all human individuality, their own and that of others; the other which only thinks about its own individuality and has absolutely no hesitation in sacrificing the individuality of others. The Tsar of all the Russias belongs to the latter category of individualists. We belong to the former."

Individualist Anarchism

Individualist anarchism refers to several traditions of thought within the anarchist movement that emphasize the individual and their will over any kinds of external determinants such as groups, society, traditions, and ideological systems. Individualist anarchism is not a single philosophy but refers to a group of individualistic philosophies that sometimes are in conflict.

In 1793, William Godwin, who has often been cited as the first anarchist, wrote *Political Justice*, which some consider to be the first expression of anarchism. Godwin, a philosophical anarchist, from a rationalist and utilitarian basis opposed revolutionary action and saw a minimal state as a present "necessary evil" that would become increasingly irrelevant and powerless by the gradual spread of knowledge. Godwin advocated individualism, proposing that all cooperation in labour be eliminated on the premise that this would be most conducive with the general good.

An influential form of individualist anarchism, called "egoism," or egoist anarchism, was expounded by one of the earliest and best-known proponents of individualist anarchism, the German Max Stirner. Stirner's *The Ego and Its Own*, published in 1844, is a founding text of the philosophy. According to Stirner, the only limitation on the rights of the individual is their power to obtain what they desire, without regard for God, state, or morality. To Stirner, rights were *spooks* in the mind, and he held that society does not exist but "the individuals are its reality". Stirner advocated self-assertion and foresaw unions of egoists, non-systematic associations continually renewed by all parties' support through an act of will, which Stirner proposed as a form of organization in place of the state. Egoist anarchists claim that egoism will foster genuine and spontaneous union between individuals. "Egoism" has inspired many interpretations of Stirner's philosophy. It was re-discovered and promoted by German philosophical anarchist and LGBT activist John Henry Mackay.

Josiah Warren is widely regarded as the first American anarchist, and the four-page weekly paper he edited during 1833, *The Peaceful Revolutionist*, was the first anarchist periodical published. For American anarchist historian Eunice Minette Schuster "It is apparent...that Proudhonian Anarchism was to be found in the United States at least as early as 1848 and that it was not conscious of its affinity to the Individualist Anarchism of Josiah Warren and Stephen Pearl Andrews...William B. Greene presented this Proudhonian Mutualism in its purest and most systematic form." Henry David Thoreau (1817–1862) was an important early influence in individualist anarchist thought in the United States and Europe. Thoreau was an American author, poet, naturalist, tax resister, development critic, surveyor, historian, philosopher, and leading transcendentalist. He is best known for his books *Walden*, a reflection upon simple living in natural surroundings, and his essay, *Civil Disobedience*, an argument for individual resistance to civil government in moral opposition to an unjust state. Later Benjamin Tucker fused Stirner's egoism with the economics of Warren and Proudhon in his eclectic influential publication *Liberty*.

From these early influences individualist anarchism in different countries attracted a small but diverse following of bohemian artists and intellectuals,free love and birth control advocates, individualist naturistsnudists, freethought and anti-clerical activists as well as young anarchist outlaws in what came to be known as illegalism and individual reclamation. These authors and activists included Oscar Wilde, Emile Armand, Han Ryner, Henri Zisly, Renzo Novatore, Miguel Gimenez Igualada, Adolf Brand and Lev Chernyi among others.

Philosophical Individualism

Ethical Egoism: Ethical egoism (also called simply egoism) is the normative ethical position that moral agents ought to do what is in their own self-interest. It differs from psychological egoism, which claims that people *do* only act in their self-interest. Ethical egoism also differs from rational egoism, which holds merely that it is rational to act in one's self-interest. These doctrines may, though, be combined with ethical egoism.

Ethical egoism contrasts with ethical altruism, which holds that moral agents have an obligation to help and serve others. Egoism and altruism both contrast with ethical utilitarianism, which holds that a moral agent should treat one's self (also known as the subject) with no higher regard than one has for others (as egoism does, by elevating self-interests and "the self" to a status not granted to others), but that one also should not (as altruism does) sacrifice one's own interests to help others' interests, so long as one's own interests (i.e. one's own desires or well-being) are substantially-equivalent to the others' interests and well-being. Egoism, utilitarianism, and altruism are all forms of consequentialism, but egoism and altruism contrast with utilitarianism, in that egoism and altruism are both agent-focused forms of consequentialism (i.e. subject-focused or subjective), but utilitarianism is called agent-neutral (i.e. objective and impartial) as it does not treat the subject's (i.e. the self's, i.e. the moral "agent's") own interests as being more or less important than if the same interests, desires, or well-being were anyone else's.

Ethical egoism does not, however, require moral agents to harm the interests and well-being of others when making moral deliberation; e.g. what is in an agent's self-interest may be incidentally detrimental, beneficial, or neutral in its effect on others. Individualism allows for others' interest and well-being to be disregarded or not, as long as what is chosen is efficacious in satisfying the self-interest of the agent. Nor does ethical egoism necessarily entail that, in pursuing self-interest, one ought always to do what one wants to do; e.g. in the long term, the fulfilment of short-term desires may prove detrimental to the self. Fleeting pleasance, then, takes a back seat to protracted eudaemonia. In the words of James Rachels, "Ethical egoism [...] endorses selfishness, but it doesn't endorse foolishness."

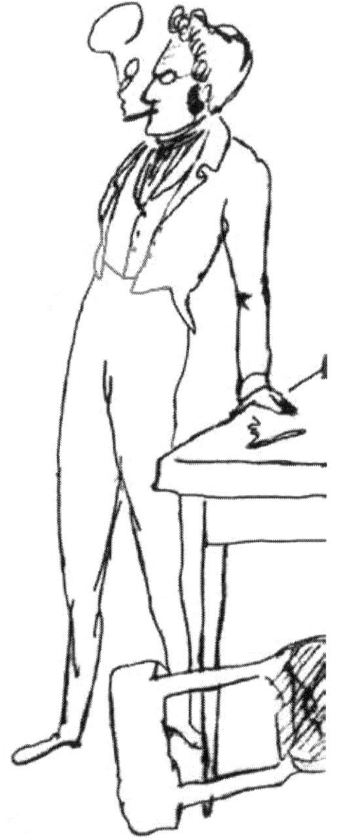

Figure: *Caricature of Max Stirner taken from a sketch by Friedrich Engels. Egoist philosopher Max Stirner has been called a proto-existentialist philosopher while at the same time is a central theorist of individualist anarchism*

Ethical egoism is sometimes the philosophical basis for support of libertarianism or individualist anarchism as in Max Stirner, although these can also be based on altruistic motivations. These are political positions based partly on a belief that individuals should not coercively prevent others from exercising freedom of action.

Existentialism

Existentialism is a term applied to the work of a number of 19th- and 20th-century philosophers who, despite profound doctrinal differences, generally held that the focus of philosophical thought should be to deal with the conditions of existence of the individual person and his or her emotions, actions, responsibilities, and thoughts. The early 19th century philosopher Søren Kierkegaard, posthumously regarded as the father of existentialism, maintained that the individual solely has the responsibilities of giving one's own life meaning and living that life passionately and sincerely, in spite of many existential obstacles and distractions including despair, angst, absurdity, alienation, and boredom.

Subsequent existential philosophers retain the emphasis on the individual, but differ, in varying degrees, on how one achieves and what constitutes a fulfilling life, what obstacles must be overcome, and what external and internal factors are involved, including the potential consequences of the existence or non-existence of God. Many existentialists have also regarded traditional systematic or academic philosophy, in both style and content, as too abstract and remote from concrete human experience. Existentialism became fashionable in the post-World War years as a way to reassert the importance of human individuality and freedom.

Freethought

Freethought holds that individuals should not accept ideas proposed as truth without recourse to knowledge and reason. Thus, freethinkers strive to build their opinions on the basis of facts, scientific inquiry, and logical principles, independent of any logical fallacies or intellectually limiting effects of authority, confirmation bias, cognitive bias, conventional wisdom, popular culture, prejudice, sectarianism, tradition, urban legend, and all other dogmas. Regarding religion, freethinkers hold that there is insufficient evidence to scientifically validate the existence of supernatural phenomena.

Humanism

Humanism is a perspective common to a wide range of ethical stances that attaches importance to human dignity, concerns, and capabilities, particularly rationality. Although the word has many senses, its meaning comes into focus when contrasted to the supernatural or to appeals to authority. Since the 19th century, humanism has been associated with an anti-clericalism inherited from the 18th-century Enlightenment *philosophes*. 21st century

Humanism tends to strongly endorse human rights, including reproductive rights, gender equality, social justice, and the separation of church and state. The term covers organized non-theistic religions, secular humanism, and a humanistic life stance.

Hedonism

Philosophical hedonism is a meta-ethical theory of value which argues that pleasure is the only intrinsic good and pain is the only intrinsic bad. The basic idea behind hedonistic thought is that pleasure (an umbrella term for all inherently likable emotions) is the only thing that is good in and of itself or by its very nature. The normative implications of this are evaluating character or behaviour as morally good to the extent that one is concerned with pleasure/pain qua pleasure/pain or an action leads to a greater balance of pleasure over pain than any other would.

Libertinism

A libertine is one devoid of most moral restraints, which are seen as unnecessary or undesirable, especially one who ignores or even spurns accepted morals and forms of behaviour sanctioned by the larger society. Libertines, also known as rakes, placed value on physical pleasures, meaning those experienced through the five senses. As a philosophy, libertinism gained new-found adherents in the 17th, 18th, and 19th centuries, particularly in France and Britain. Notable among these were John Wilmot, 2nd Earl of Rochester, and the Marquis de Sade. "Libertine" is defined today as "a dissolute person; usually a person who is morally unrestrained".

Objectivism

Objectivism is a system of philosophy created by philosopher and novelist Ayn Rand (1905–1982) that holds: reality exists independent of consciousness; human beings gain knowledge rationally from perception through the process of concept formation and inductive and deductive logic; the moral purpose of one's life is the pursuit of one's own happiness or rational self-interest. Rand thinks the only social system consistent with this morality is full respect for individual rights, embodied in pure *laissez faire* capitalism; and the role of art in human life is to transform man's widest metaphysical ideas, by selective reproduction of reality, into a physical form—a work of art—that he can comprehend and to which he can respond emotionally. Objectivism celebrates man as his own hero, "with his own happiness as the moral purpose of his life, with productive achievement as his noblest activity, and reason as his only absolute."

Philosophical Anarchism

Philosophical anarchism is an anarchist school of thought which contends that the State lacks moral legitimacy and - in contrast to revolutionary anarchism - does not advocate violent revolution to eliminate it but advocate peaceful evolution to superate it. Though philosophical anarchism does not necessarily imply any action or desire for the elimination of the State, philosophical anarchists do not believe that they have an obligation or duty to obey the State, or conversely, that the State has a right to command. Philosophical anarchism is a component especially of individualist anarchism. Philosophical anarchists of historical note include Mohandas Gandhi, William Godwin, Pierre-Joseph Proudhon, Max Stirner, Benjamin Tucker, and Henry David Thoreau. Contemporary philosophical anarchists include A. John Simmons and Robert Paul Wolff.

Subjectivism

Subjectivism is a philosophical tenet that accords primacy to subjective experience as fundamental of all measure and law. In extreme forms like Solipsism, it may hold that the nature and existence of every object depends solely on someone's subjective awareness of it. For example, Wittgenstein wrote in Tractatus Logico-Philosophicus: "The subject doesn't belong to the world, but it is a limit of the world" (proposition 5.632). Metaphysical subjectivism is the theory that reality is what we perceive to be real, and that there is no underlying true reality that exists independently of perception. One can also hold that it is consciousness rather than perception that is reality (subjective idealism). In probability, a subjectivism stands for the belief that probabilities are simply degrees-of-belief by rational agents in a certain proposition, and which have no objective reality in and of themselves.

Ethical subjectivism stands in opposition to moral realism, which claims that moral propositions refer to objective facts, independent of human opinion; to error theory, which denies that any moral propositions are true in any sense; and to non-cognitivism, which denies that moral sentences express propositions at all.

The most common forms of ethical subjectivism are also forms of moral relativism, with moral standards held to be relative to each culture or society (c.f. cultural relativism), or even to every individual. The latter view, as put forward by Protagoras, holds that there are as many distinct scales of good and evil as there are subjects in the world. Moral subjectivism is that species of moral relativism that relativizes moral value to the individual subject.

Horst Matthai Quelle was a Spanish languageGerman anarchist philosopher influenced by Max Stirner. He argued that since the individual gives form to the world, he is those objects, the others and the whole universe. One of his main views was a "theory of infinite worlds" which for him was developed by pre-socratic philosophers.

Solipsism

Solipsism is the philosophical idea that only one's own mind is sure to exist. The term comes from Latin*solus* (alone) and *ipse* (self). Solipsism as an epistemological position holds that knowledge of anything outside one's own mind is unsure.

The external world and other minds cannot be known, and might not exist outside the mind. As a metaphysical position, solipsism goes further to the conclusion that the world and other minds do not exist. As such it is the only epistemological position that, by its own postulate, is both irrefutable and yet indefencible in the same manner.

Although the number of individuals sincerely espousing solipsism has been small, it is not uncommon for one philosopher to accuse another's arguments of entailing solipsism as an unwanted consequence, in a kind of reductio ad absurdum. In the history of philosophy, solipsism has served as a skeptical hypothesis.

Economic Individualism

The doctrine of economic individualism holds that each individual should be allowed autonomy in making his or her own economic decisions as opposed to those decisions being made by the state, the community, the corporation etc. for him or her.

Classical Liberalism

Classical liberalism is a political ideology that developed in the 19th century in England, Western Europe, and the Americas. It followed earlier forms of liberalism in its commitment to personal freedom and popular government, but differed from earlier forms of liberalism in its commitment to free markets and classical economics.

Notable classical liberals in the 19th century include Jean-Baptiste Say, Thomas Malthus, and David Ricardo. Classical liberalism was revived in the 20th century by Ludwig von Mises and Friedrich Hayek, and further developed by Milton Friedman, Robert Nozick, Loren Lomasky, and Jan Narveson. The phrase *classical liberalism* is also sometimes used to refer to all forms of liberalism before the 20th century.

Individualist Anarchism and Economics

In regards to economic questions within individualist anarchism there are adherents to mutualism (Pierre Joseph Proudhon, Emile Armand, early Benjamin Tucker); natural rights positions (early Benjamin Tucker, Lysander Spooner, Josiah Warren); and egoistic disrespect for "ghosts" such as private property and markets (Max Stirner, John Henry Mackay, Lev Chernyi, later Benjamin Tucker, Renzo Novatore, illegalism).

Mutualism

Mutualism is an anarchist school of thought which can be traced to the writings of Pierre-Joseph Proudhon, who envisioned a society where each person might possess a means of production, either individually or collectively, with trade representing equivalent amounts of labour in the free market. Integral to the scheme was the establishment of a mutual-credit bank which would lend to producers at a minimal interest rate only high enough to cover the costs of administration. Mutualism is based on a labour theory of value which holds that when labour or its product is sold, in exchange, it ought to receive goods or services embodying "the amount of labour necessary to produce an article of exactly similar and equal utility". Receiving anything less would be considered exploitation, theft of labour, or usury.

Libertarian Socialism

Libertarian socialism (sometimes called social anarchism, and sometimes left libertarianism) is a group of political philosophies that promote a non-hierarchical, non-bureaucratic, stateless society without private property in the means of production. Libertarian socialism is opposed to all coercive forms of social organization, and promotes free association in place of government and opposes what it sees as the coercive social relations of capitalism, such as wage labour. The term libertarian socialism is used by some socialists to differentiate their philosophy from state socialism or by some as a synonym for left anarchism.

Adherents of libertarian socialism assert that a society based on freedom and equality can be achieved through abolishing authoritarian institutions that control certain means of production and subordinate the majority to an owning class or political and economic elite. Libertarian socialism also constitutes a tendency of thought that promotes the identification, criticism and practical dismantling of illegitimate authority in all aspects of life.

Accordingly, libertarian socialists believe that "the exercise of power in any institutionalized form—whether economic, political, religious, or sexual—brutalizes both the wielder of power and the one over whom it is exercised". Libertarian socialists generally place their hopes in decentralized means of direct democracy such as libertarian municipalism, citizens' assemblies, trade unions and workers' councils.

Political philosophies commonly described as libertarian socialist include most varieties of anarchism (especially anarchist communism, anarchist collectivism, anarcho-syndicalism, mutualism) as well as autonomism, communalism, participism, some versions of "utopian socialism and individualist anarchism, and also libertarian Marxist philosophies such as council communism and Luxemburgism.

Left-Libertarianism

Left-libertarianism (sometimes synonymous with left-wing libertarianism and libertarian socialism) is a term that has been used to describe several different libertarian political movements and theorists.

Left-libertarianism, as defended by contemporary theorists such as Peter Vallentyne, Hillel Steiner, and Michael Otsuka, is a doctrine that has a strong commitment to personal liberty *and* has an egalitarian view concerning natural resources, believing that it is illegitimate for anyone to claim private ownership of resources to the detriment of others. Some left-libertarians of this type support some form of income redistribution on the grounds of a claim by each individual to be entitled to an equal share of natural resources. Social anarchists, including Murray Bookchin, anarcho-communists such as Peter Kropotkin and anarcho-collectivists such as Mikhail Bakunin, are sometimes called left-libertarian. Noam Chomsky also refers to himself as a left libertarian.

The term is sometimes used synonymously with libertarian socialism or used in self-description by geoists who support individuals paying rent to the community for the use of land. Left libertarian parties, such as Green, share with "traditional socialism a distrust of the market, of private investment, and of the achievement ethic, and a commitment to expansion of the welfare state."

Right-Libertarianism

Right-libertarianism or right libertarianism is a phrase used by some to describe either non-collectivist forms of libertarianism or a variety of different libertarian views some label "right" of mainstream libertarianism including "libertarian conservatism".

Stanford Encyclopedia of Philosophy calls it "right libertarianism" but states: "Libertarianism is often thought of as 'right-wing' doctrine. This, however, is mistaken for at least two reasons. First, on social—rather than economic—issues, libertarianism tends to be 'left-wing'. It opposes laws that restrict consensual and private sexual relationships between adults (e.g., gay sex, non-marital sex, and deviant sex), laws that restrict drug use, laws that impose religious views or practices on individuals, and compulsory military service. Second, in addition to the better-known version of libertarianism—right-libertarianism—there is also a version known as 'left-libertarianism'. Both endorse full self-ownership, but they differ with respect to the powers agents have to appropriate unappropriated natural resources (land, air, water, etc.)."

Individualism as Creative Independent Lifestyle

The anarchist writer and bohemian Oscar Wilde wrote in his famous essay *The Soul of Man under Socialism* that "Art is individualism, and individualism is a disturbing and disintegrating force. There lies its immense value. For what it seeks is to disturb monotony of type, slavery of custom, tyranny of habit, and the reduction of man to the level of a machine." For anarchist historian George Woodcock "Wilde's aim in *The Soul of Man under Socialism* is to seek the society most favourable to the artist...for Wilde art is the supreme end, containing within itself enlightenment and regeneration, to which all else in society must be subordinated...Wilde represents the anarchist as aesthete." The word individualism in this way has been used to denote a personality with a strong tendency towards self-creation and experimentation as opposed to tradition or popular mass opinions and behaviours.

Anarchist writer Murray Bookchin describes a lot of individualist anarchism as people who "expressed their opposition in uniquely personal forms, especially in fiery tracts, outrageous behaviour, and aberrant lifestyles in the cultural ghettos of fin de sicle New York, Paris, and London. As a credo, individualist anarchism remained largely a bohemian lifestyle, most conspicuous in its demands for sexual freedom ('free love') and enamored of innovations in art, behaviour, and clothing."

In relation to this view of individuality, French Individualist anarchist Emile Armand advocates egoistical denial of social conventions and dogmas to live in accord to one's own ways and desires in daily life since he emphasized anarchism as a way of life and practice. In this way he manifests "So the anarchist individualist tends to reproduce himself, to perpetuate his spirit in other individuals who will share his views and who will make it possible for a state of affairs to be established from which authoritarianism has been banished. It is this desire, this will, not only to live, but also to reproduce oneself, which we shall call "activity".

In the book *Imperfect garden : the legacy of humanism*, humanist philosopher Tzvetan Todorov identifies individualism as an important current of socio-political thought within modernity and as examples of it he mentions Michel de Montaigne, François de La Rochefoucauld, Marquis de Sade, and Charles Baudelaire In La Rochefoucauld, he identifies a tendency similar to stoicism in which "the honest person works his being in the manner of an sculptor who searches the liberation of the forms which are inside a block of marble, to extract the truth of that matter." In Baudelaire he finds the dandy trait in which one searches to cultivate "the idea of beauty within oneself, of satisfying one´s passions of feeling and thinking."

The Russian-American poet Joseph Brodsky once manifested that "The surest defence against Evil is extreme individualism, originality of thinking, whimsicality, even—if you will—eccentricity. That is, something that can't be feigned, faked, imitated; something even a seasoned imposter couldn't be happy with." Ralph Waldo Emerson famously declared", "Whoso would be a man must be a nonconformist"—a point of view developed at length in both the life and work of (Henry David) Thoreau. Equally memorable and influential on Walt Whitman is Emerson's idea that "a foolish consistency is the hobgoblin of small minds, adored by little statesmen and philosophers and divines."...Emerson opposes on principle the reliance on social structures (civil, religious) precisely because through them the individual approaches the divine second hand, mediated by the once original experience of a genius from another age: "An institution," as he explains, "is the lengthened shadow of one man." To achieve this original relation one must "Insist on one's self; never imitate" for if the relationship is secondary the connection is lost."

Subjective Probability?

Subjective probability is a measurement of a likely outcome determined by an individual's personal viewpoint. Unlike most forms of probability, which are based on mathematics, subjective probability has little to no actual mathematical data involved in its outcome. The most important factor in this form of probability is the viewpoint of the individual making the decision. This is often a first or final step in determining an unpredictable outcome and is a common means of assessing group mentality or making decisions without data. In most cases, probability is the study of situations to determine their absolute outcome. The likelihood an area will receive rain, that a person will turn left at an intersection or any number of other choices is broken down into a series of mathematical equations. These numbers are manipulated to find underlying causal factors, which will show the likelihood of certain actions taking place.

The term subjective means 'relative to a subject,' which is precisely the meaning of this kind of probability. A person makes an assessment as to a likely outcome based on his own personal beliefs and experiences. This form of decision making has a huge amount of inaccuracy and bias when attempting to replicate real-world situations, so it is often used for other purposes.

An example of the difference between the two forms of probability is in pre-calling the outcome of a sporting event. In standard probability, previous encounters between the participants are broken down into mathematical information. The potential interactions between key individuals are determined, and the process finds the likelihood of one group winning over another. With subjective probability, a person calculates the winner based on her personal experience with the participants and what she has seen in the past. Both methods are common and both have a similar accuracy rate, when performed by professionals.

When subjective probability is used to determine the mentality of a group, it is often accomplished through polling. A large group is asked its opinions on a certain subject, and the numbers show the mindset. At the end of the study, most of the group may believe in the inevitability of a certain outcome. This does not mean the outcome is more likely—it simply means the members believe it to be more likely. While this data is subjective, it reflects the thoughts of a group, which may lead organizations to act a certain way.

It is also common to use subjective probability to determine outcomes where there isn't enough data for a normal decision. When faced with a series of options and no additional information, a person will subconsciously calculate the various outcomes of different actions. She will then make a decision based on a 'gut-feeling' or hunch; in essence, she makes a decision based on subjective probability.

Subjective Expected Utility

Subjective expected utility is a method in decision theory in the presence of risk, promoted by L. J. Savage in 1954 following previous work by Ramsey and von Neumann. The theory of subjective expected utility combines two subjective concepts: first, a personal utility function, and second a personal probability distribution (based on Bayesian probability theory).

Savage proved that, if you adhere to axioms of rationality, if you believe an uncertain event has possible outcomes $\{x_i\}$ each with a utility to you of $u(x_i)$ then your choices can be explained as arising from a function in which you believe that there is a subjective probability of each outcome is $P(x_i)$, and your subjective expected utility is the expected value of the utility,

$$\sum_i u(x_i)\, P(x_i).$$

You may be able to make a decision which changes the possible outcomes to $\{y_j\}$ in which case your subjective expected utility will become

$$\sum_j u(y_j)\, P(y_j).$$

Which decision you prefer depends on which subjective expected utility is higher. Different people may make different decisions because they may have different utility functions or different beliefs about the probabilities of different outcomes.

Savage assumed that it is possible to take convex combinations of decisions and that preferences would be preserved. So if you prefer $x(=\{x_i\})$ to y and s to t then you will prefer $\lambda x + (1-\lambda)s$ to $\lambda y + (1-\lambda)t$, for $0 < \lambda < 1$.

Experiments have shown that many individuals do not behave in a manner consistent with subjective expected utility, e.g. most prominently Allais (1953) and Ellsberg (1961).

Empirical Evidence

Empirical evidence (also empirical data, sense experience, empirical knowledge, or the a posteriori) is a source of knowledge acquired by means of observation or experimentation. Empirical evidence is information that justifies a belief in the truth or falsity of an empirical claim. In the empiricist view, one can only claim to have knowledge when one has a true belief based on empirical evidence. This stands in contrast to the rationalist view under which reason or reflection alone is considered to be evidence for the truth or falsity of some propositions. The senses are the primary source of empirical evidence. Although other sources of evidence, such as memory, and the testimony of others ultimately trace back to some sensory experience, they are considered to be secondary, or indirect.

In another sense, empirical evidence may be synonymous with the outcome of an experiment. In this sense, an empirical result is a unified confirmation. In this context, the term *semi-empirical* is used for qualifying theoretical methods which use in part basic axioms or postulated scientific laws and experimental results. Such methods are opposed to theoretical *ab initio* methods which are purely deductive and based on first principles.

In science, empirical evidence is required for a hypothesis to gain acceptance in the scientific community. Normally, this validation is achieved by the scientific method of hypothesis commitment, experimental design, peer review, adversarial review, reproduction of results, conference presentation and journal publication. This requires rigorous communication of hypothesis (usually expressed in mathematics), experimental constraints and controls (expressed necessarily in terms of standard experimental apparatus), and a common understanding of measurement.

Statements and arguments depending on empirical evidence are often referred to as a posteriori ("from the later") as distinguished from *a priori* ("from the earlier"). *A priori* knowledge or justification is independent of experience (for example "All bachelors are unmarried"); whereas *a posteriori* knowledge or justification is dependent on experience or empirical evidence (for example "Some bachelors are very happy"). The notion of the distinction between A priori and a posteriori as tantamount to the distinction between empirical and non-empirical knowledge comes from Kant's Critique of Pure Reason.

The standard positivist view of empirically acquired information has been that observation, experience, and experiment serve as neutral arbiters between competing theories. However, since the 1960s, a persistent critique most associated with Thomas Kuhn, has argued that these methods are influenced by prior beliefs and experiences. Consequently it cannot be expected that two scientists when observing, experiencing, or experimenting on the same event will make the same theory-neutral observations. The role of observation as a theory-neutral arbiter may not be possible. Theory-dependence of observation means that, even if there were agreed methods of inference and interpretation, scientists may still disagree on the nature of empirical data.

Empirical Research

Empirical research is a way of gaining knowledge by means of direct and indirect observation or experience. Empirical evidence (the record of one's direct observations or experiences) can be analyzed quantitatively or qualitatively. Through quantifying the evidence or making sense of it in qualitative form, a researcher can answer empirical questions, which should be clearly defined and answerable with the evidence collected (usually called data). Research design varies by field and by the question being investigated. Many researchers combine qualitative and quantitative forms of analysis to better answer questions which cannot be studied in laboratory settings, particularly in the social sciences and in education.

In some fields, quantitative research may begin with a research question (e.g., "Does listening to vocal music during the learning of a word list have an effect on later memory for these words?") which is tested through experimentation in a lab. Usually, a researcher has a certain theory regarding the topic under investigation. Based on this theory some statements, or hypotheses, will be proposed (e.g., "Listening to vocal music has a negative effect on learning a word list."). From these hypotheses predictions about specific events are derived (e.g., "People who study a word list while listening to vocal music will remember fewer words on a later memory test than people who study a word list in silence."). These predictions can then be tested with a suitable experiment. Depending on the outcomes of the experiment, the theory on which the hypotheses and predictions were based will be supported or not.

Terminology

The term empirical was originally used to refer to certain ancient Greek practitioners of medicine who rejected adherence to the dogmatic doctrines of the day, preferring instead to rely on the observation of phenomena as perceived in experience. Later empiricism referred to a theory of knowledge in philosophy which adheres to the principle that knowledge arises from experience and evidence gathered specifically using the senses.

In scientific use the term empirical refers to the gathering of data using only evidence that is observable by the senses or in some cases using calibrated scientific instruments. What early philosophers described as empiricist and empirical research have in common is the dependence on observable data to formulate and test theories and come to conclusions.

Usage

The researcher attempts to describe accurately the interaction between the instrument (or the human senses) and the entity being observed. If instrumentation is involved, the researcher is expected to calibrate his/her instrument by applying it to known standard objects and documenting the results before applying it to unknown objects. In other words, it describes the research that has not taken place before and their results.

In practice, the accumulation of evidence for or against any particular theory involves planned research designs for the collection of empirical data, and academic rigor plays a large part of judging the merits of research design. Several typographies for such designs have been suggested, one of the most popular of which comes from Campbell and Stanley (1963). They are responsible for popularizing the widely cited distinction among pre-experimental, experimental, and quasi-experimental designs and are staunch advocates of the central role of randomized experiments in educational research.

Scientific Research

Accurate analysis of data using standardized statistical methods in scientific studies is critical to determining the validity of empirical research. Statistical formulas such as regression, uncertainty coefficient, t-test, chi square, and various types of ANOVA (analyses of variance) are fundamental to forming logical, valid conclusions. If empirical data reach significance under the appropriate statistical formula, the research hypothesis is supported. If not, the null hypothesis is supported (or, more correctly, not rejected), meaning no effect of the independent variable(s) was observed on the dependent variable(s).

It is important to understand that the outcome of empirical research using statistical hypothesis testing is never proof. It can only *support* a hypothesis, *reject* it, or do neither. These methods yield only probabilities.

Among scientific researchers, empirical *evidence* (as distinct from empirical *research*) refers to objective evidence that appears the same regardless of the observer. For example, a thermometre will not display different temperatures for each individual who observes it. Temperature, as measured by an accurate, well calibrated thermometre, is empirical evidence. By contrast, non-empirical evidence is subjective, depending on the observer. Following the previous example, observer A might truthfully report that a room is warm, while observer B might truthfully report that the same room is cool, though both observe the same reading on the thermometre. The use of empirical evidence negates this effect of personal (i.e., subjective) experience or time.

Empirical Cycle

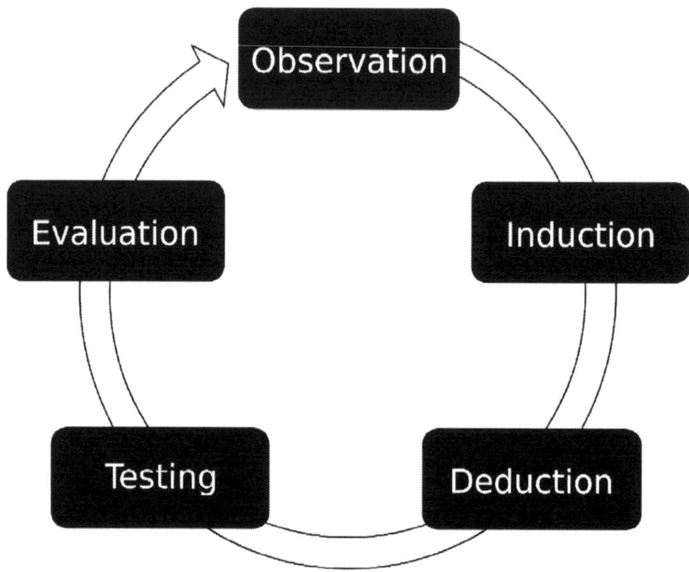

Figure: *Empirical cycle according to A.D. de Groot*

A.D. de Groot's empirical cycle:

1. *Observation:* The collecting and organisation of empirical facts; Forming hypothesis.
2. *Induction:* Formulating hypothesis.
3. *Deduction:* Deducting consequences of hypothesis as testable predictions.
4. *Testing:* Testing the hypothesis with new empirical material.
5. *Evaluation:* Evaluating the outcome of testing

5

Popper's Social Philosophy

Karl Popper: Critical Rationalism

"Critical Rationalism" is the name Karl Popper (1902-1994) gave to a modest and self-critical rationalism. He contrasted this view with "uncritical or comprehensive rationalism," the received justificationist view that only what can be proved by reason and/or experience should be accepted. Popper argued that comprehensive rationalism cannot explain how proof is possible and that it leads to inconsistencies. Critical rationalism today is the project of extending Popper's approach to all areas of thought and action. In each field the central task of critical rationalism is to replace allegedly justificatory methods with critical ones.

Section 2 explains how critical rationalism arose out of the breakdown of Popper's first justificationist attempt to account for scientific progress. Section 2 also presents Popper's first application of his non-justificationist perspective to new fields in his *The Open Society and Its Enemies*. Section 3 first explains Joseph Agassi's view of the critical appraisal of metaphysical theories in scientific contexts as well as his view of piecemeal rationality, and secondly portrays William Bartley's more comprehensive view of non-justificationism. Section 4 discusses Imré Lakatos's extension of critical rationalism to mathematics. Section 5 portrays Hans Albert's systematic version of critical rationalism. His perspective incorporated results of Popper, Agassi and Bartley and extended them to social and political theory. Section 6 suggests that Mario Bunge's fallibilism % which he developed independently of critical rationalists % is sufficiently close to their views to count here: he develops critical tools for achieving progress without justification in virtually all areas of thought. Section 7 discusses attempts to develop critical rationalism in new and simpler ways. These views seek to do without frameworks and methodological rules; their originators are Jagdish Hattiangadi, Gunnar Andersson, and David Miller. These theories deprive rational thought of needed steering mechanisms. Section 8 presents the reintroduction of forms of justification designed to be compatible with Popper's criticism of induction. These have been developed by Alan Musgrave, Volker Gadenne and John Watkins. Section 9 explains how Popper's emphasis on the importance of methodological rules in science has led to a critical rationalist sociology of science.

The main task of this sociology of science is to examine existing rules and methods as furthering or hindering research. Section 10 calls attention to the alternative philosophical anthropology which Agassi has proposed as a framework for critical rationalism. Whereas Popper saw rationality as contrary to human nature's craving for security, Agassi sees rationality as natural, but partial and improvable. Section 11 describes how Popper's original political manifesto in *The Open Society and Its Enemies* has led to attempts to use his arguments to defend both right-leaning and left-leaning political theories. Section 12 returns to Popper's early researches in educational theory. His philosophy led to concerted efforts to develop a new pedagogy which emphasizes active problem solving as the best learning method. This pedagogy should promote autonomy and critical thinking. Section 13 concludes with the suggestion that the success or the failure of the project of substituting critical for allegedly justificatory methods has still to be judged.

Critical rationalism emerged from research by the Würzburg school of psychology. This school sought to develop a deductivist philosophy of science to complement their deductivist psychology. While working on this program, Karl Popper stumbled onto a non-justificationist theory of scientific knowledge: he explained the growth of knowledge without proof. Non-justificationism, that is, the theory that no theory can be proven, is at least as old as Socrates, but Popper's version of it is the first that also purports to explain the growth of knowledge. Popper and other critical rationalists took on the project of explaining the growth of knowledge without justification. This project has produced various competing theories of rationality and has been extended to many fields. This article will concentrate on the internal logic and problems involved in the development of critical methods capable of producing the growth of knowledge.

Of the numerous justificationist predecessors let only this be said. The overwhelming majority of those who comment on critical rationalism claim that critical rationalism is somehow incoherent and that inductivism is better. A major exception was Bertrand Russell. He appreciated the logical strength of critical rationalism and knew the logical weakness of induction. Nevertheless he clung to induction. He thought that critical rationalism was a philosophy of despair. Whether his judgment of critical rationalism was correct depends on whether its development can bring progress. To show this progress, new critical rationalist ideas are described and presented below. This should provide an answer to Russell that he amply deserves.

Popper and Non-Justificationism

Inductive inferences have observations as premises and theories as conclusions. They are notoriously invalid but often are deemed unavoidable. Critical rationalism views them as unnecessary. This point of view grew gradually out of Karl Popper's attempt to describe science without their use in *Die beiden Grundprobleme der Erkenntnistheorie* (1932-33), where he still operated within the framework of justificationism, that is, while viewing the aim of scientific method as the proper (justified) assessment of the truth value of certain sentences. He hoped to build a theory of the proper assessment of sentences, that is, of the possibility of proving the truth or falsity of some sentences. He began with the fact that a theory is false if it contradicts a singular sentence describing some observation reports. Popper then said that such singular sentences were veridical, that is, truthful as opposed to illusory, so they may be used to produce final proofs of the falsity of some universal sentences. For example, the singular sentence, "That swan is black," if it is a true report of some observation, can be used to produce a final proof of the falsity of the universal sentence, "All swans are white." But, he argued, proof of universal sentences or the demonstration that they are probable requires inductive inferences. As a consequence no such putative proof can be valid.

Popper himself found the theory he presented in *Die beiden Grundprobleme der Erkenntnistheorie* without chapter 5 inadequate for three reasons. The first reason is that singular statements are not veridical. He began work on this problem in chapter 5 of *Die beiden Grundprobleme.* This chapter contains a theory of science which differs on important points from the theory found in the rest of that volume. The second reason that Popper's first attempt broke down is that one can circumvent refutations by *ad hoc* stratagems, as Hans Reichenbach quickly pointed out in a note which responded to Popper's first publication of his view in *Erkenntnis*. The third reason was Popper's inability to handle the problem of the demarcation of science from non-science with his idea that we show how science properly assigns truth values to sentences with no inductive inference. On a justificationist theory of the task of the philosophy of science such as Reichenbach's, which was identical to Popper's theory as he wrote *Die beiden Grundprobleme* without chapter 5, science should be demarcated by the proper assignment of truth values: science is the set of sentences with justifiably assigned truth values. The task of the philosophy of science is to explain how these assignments are properly made. (Reichenbach said the calculus of probabilities serves that purpose.) Popper argued that it is not possible to properly assign either the truth value True or some degree of probability to universal sentences. He called such sentences "fictions", which is a term he had earlier taken over from Hans Vaihinger. On the theory presented in *Die beiden Grundprobleme* without chapter 5, after science had done its job, there were still, on the one hand, some fictions which ought to be deemed scientific such as the theories of the Würzburg school in psychology and, perhaps, as he said later, Einstein's physics, and, on the other hand, other fictions which should be deemed unscientific, such as the psychologies of Freud and Adler. He could not distinguish between these two sets of theories within his justificationist framework, since, on this view, only proofs or refutations of these theories could do that. He asserted, however, that no proof was possible and refutations could establish only the falsity of universal propositions.

As a consequence of these three difficulties Popper developed an entirely different theory of science in chapter 5, then in *Logik der Forschung*. In order to overcome the problems his first view faced, he adopted two central strategies. First, he reformulated the task of the philosophy of science. Rather than presenting scientific method as a tool for properly assigning truth values to sentences, he presented rules of scientific method as conducive to the growth of knowledge. Apparently he still held that only proven or refuted sentences could take truth values. But this view is incompatible with his new philosophy of science as it appears in his *Logik der Forschung*: there he had to presume that some non-refuted theories took truth values, that is, that they are true or false as the case may be, even though they have been neither proved nor refuted. It is the job of scientists to discover their falsity when they can. So, he worked around the difficulty posed by the fact that, on the one hand, he had to assume that theories were refutable and thus had truth values, whereas, on the other hand, he thought that only proven or refuted theories had truth values at all. He argued that his view could be interpreted as realist or as antirealist. He hedged his bets as best he could and appealed to Mach, who had stipulated that one should avoid participation in any metaphysical dispute.

In *Logik der Forschung* Popper solved his three initial difficulties in the following ways. First, instead of claiming that singular sentences were veridical, he said that basic statements are only provisionally accepted, provided that they were repeatable and so testable. He thereby introduced the following rule: consider only repeatable basic statements. He claimed that the provisional acceptance of basic statements does not disqualify them as refutations of theories—no longer simply universal sentences—because for the most part we can agree on which basic sentences we provisionally assume to be true. Second, he proposed the rule that one should always replace some theory which is contradicted by a basic statement by whichever new alternative has the highest degree of falsifiability. This rule should guarantee that refutations lead to progress. Reichenbach had declared that there was no logic of scientific method, that is, no proof or refutation. The basis for his claim that there could be no refutation was that any theory could be protected from a putative refutation with some ad hoc maneuver. Popper responded to Reichenbach with his *Logik der Forschung* (Logic of Research) and by introducing methodology into his deliberations. The methodological rule enabled him to avoid ad hoc protection of theories and thus enabled him to show how theories could be refuted. Third, he introduced the rule: only refutable theories—the term "fiction" no longer appears in his work—are scientific and may be deemed scientific.

This view was no longer justificationist, that is, it no longer claimed properly to assign truth values to sentences. All "assignments" are conjectural. But Popper had at that point no non-justificationist theory of rationality in general; his theory applied to science alone. He did not at that point notice problems which his theory raised for the broader framework of rationality which all philosophers of science had used since antiquity, the framework that identified the rational with the proven.

The conflict between Popper's new theory of science and his older theory that only proven or refuted sentences can take truth values was removed by Tarski. Tarski's definition of truth, as Tarski explained to Popper, allows for non-proven but still true sentences. Tarski thereby did away with the theory of truth that had given Popper so much trouble. Tarski did not necessarily offer Popper an adequate theory of truth for his philosophy of science. But Tarski did free him from a false theory which was a great impediment to the construction of a truly fallibilist, realist theory of science. Popper never clearly explained the importance that Tarski had for him at the time.

This failure to explain how the logic of his problem changed as a result of Tarski's theory was part of his repression of the fact that he had held a justificationist theory of truth for a long time, even after he began writing a fallibilist book. After his meeting with Tarski, he was free to develop his fallibilist theory of science in new ways, because he could claim that theories could be true even though there was no proof of them. During his earlier years in London, during 1946-1965 or so, he returned to the possibilities this fact opened up.

In *Logik der Forschung* Popper developed a theory of the growth of scientific knowledge without justification. But he had no general theory of rationality without justification. Indeed, he still limited rationality to science and methodology. However, at least three problems arose for this limited view of rationality.

Popper maintained at that point that scientists gain knowledge not by proofs but by refutations of good conjectures and by replacing them with new and better ones. These new conjectures avoid earlier mistakes, explain more, and invite new tests. He originally thought of this theory as *eo ipso* a theory of rationality: outside of science and methodology he made no allowance for rationality. He identified research, science and methodology, as the title of his book indicates.

Difficulties piled up fast. First, if rationality is limited to science, how is methodology rational? Methodology can only be rational if methodology is the empirical study of science—as Whewell said—or if non-empirical research can be rational. Popper could not view methodology as a science of science because he held that it is not merely descriptive but also prescriptive. Yet it should be rational.

The second problem arose as Popper tried to apply his methodology of the physical sciences to the social sciences. *The Poverty of Historicism* and *The Open Society and Its Enemies* defend the open society on the grounds that only open societies preserve reason, that is, criticism, and as a consequence only open societies can be civilized. But why is a choice for the open society rational? He had no answer. He merely said that the acceptance of reason was a consequence of sympathy for others. Nothing can be said to convince those to change their minds who accept the barbaric consequences of fascism or communism.

The third problem concerns metaphysics. Before he had ever developed his own philosophy of science, he had defended in his doctoral dissertation the view that metaphysical hypotheses can serve as working hypotheses in the construction of scientific theories. His discussion there merely concerned the use of physicalist metaphysics as a guide for psychological research. He said that this was fine, but one should not decide *a priori* that a view of psychological processes as physical is needed or even possible. Scientific research—he was not clear then what that meant—should decide this. He was later pressed, however, to decide between competing metaphysical theories with which to interpret science, even in the absence of a scientific answer. Was the world determined or not? Questions such as this raised the question as to whether one metaphysical theory can be better or worse than another and whether one could find out which one is better. He gave up his earlier view of rationality as limited to scientific research and methodology, but he still insisted that for science some metaphysical theories are merely heuristic, and no more than that.

To extend his theory that rationality consisted of scientific research and methodology alone, Popper loosened his standard of rationality. Rejecting the older standard of rationality — proof – - as too high, he began to view the standard for science, refutability, as too high for the rationality that obtains outside science. Whereas earlier he had replaced justification with refutation, he now replaced refutation with criticism. Popper thereby created a new philosophical perspective by generalizing his theory of scientific research. The name he gave to this extension is "critical rationalism." Popper introduced it in the introduction to his *Conjectures and Refutations*, where he characterized it briefly as the critical attitude. He used it also to describe views he developed earlier, in *The Open Society and Its Enemies*.

Could his critical rationalism apply to other fields? Could various fields also not only do without (epistemological) justification but also raise their levels of rationality with the use of critical methods? Critical rationalism became a project to employ critical methods as a substitute for epistemological justification in all areas of life.

Joseph Agassi and William Bartley

Outside of Popper's own efforts to develop this project, the first two most significant endeavours were undertaken by Joseph Agassi and William Bartley. Although Agassi's efforts began somewhat earlier than Bartley's, their development overlaps considerably; the two were in conversation with each other for much of the time that they were working out their ideas as Popper's students. I begin with Agassi, who developed Popper's philosophy piecemeal and then turn to Bartley who attempted to give critical rationalism a comprehensive statement, that is, a version of it which would explain how a critical rationalist could adopt a critical stance toward any idea whatsoever, including its own claims.

Agassi began with his dissertation, in which he posed the question, How can metaphysics be used to guide scientific research without making science subordinate to it? Duhem had warned that, were science to concern itself with metaphysics, it would be subordinate to it. Encouraging scientists to engage in metaphysical debates would cause dissent and lead them away from science's main task of constructing empirical theories.

Agassi's project was to show how metaphysical research could facilitate empirical progress without tyrannizing science. He did this by extending Popper's theory of the methods of scientific practice to include the critical, and thereby progressive, use of metaphysical theories to guide scientific research. On his view metaphysics need not be a mere heuristic, that is, a source of ideas, but rather a systematic guide to scientific research and a provisional standard for desirable theories. Metaphysics can be useful in advancing science by giving guidelines for the search for empirical explanations and by deepening the understanding of the world offered by science. But, he also said, it can help achieve these aims only when used critically. A critical stance toward metaphysics is possible when two or more metaphysical research programs compete with each other to construct empirically refutable theories. This, he argued, is just what happened when Faraday used his metaphysical field theory as the framework within which he constructed physical (field) theories. His competitors tried to explain the same phenomena under the Newtonian assumption that all forces act at a distance. Faraday's theory of electro-magnetic events eventually had an enormous impact, because his metaphysics enabled him to construct better physical theories than his competitors.

Bartley developed a comprehensive version of critical rationalism. He argued that there were two problems that showed Popper's original version was too limited. Popper encountered the first of these as he wrote *The Open Society and Its Enemies* where he discussed the problem: Why should one be rational? He conceded that rationality is limited, as its choice is pre-rational, a decision based on feelings. Bartley viewed Popper's problem of the limits of the ability to argue rationally in favour of rationality as parallel to a problem he (Bartley) had earlier encountered in religious philosophy: defenders of religion claim that commitment to some religion is just as rational as commitment to rationality: each individual has to choose some starting point, and each starting point must be arbitrary. Each starting point then is just as pre-rational as the other, since each choice is beyond the limits of reason.

Bartley viewed the inability to defend rationality rationally as amounting to the inability to show the superiority of rational methods to solve problems over any other method. Bartley saw this limitation as an important defect. But in Popper's approach to rationality as critical rather than justificatory, he found a way to overcome it. For, he argued, on the one hand, the theory of rationality as proof should itself be proven, but in fact it is not provable, whereas, on the other hand, the theory of rationality as readiness to appraise theories critically should itself be open to criticism, and this is quite possible. It is then no longer the case that the adoption of a rational approach to problems is no more rational than commitments to belief systems, such as those of some religion: the theory that rational practice means holding all theories open to criticism, may itself be held open to criticism. This also means that the use of rational methods to solve problems may be rationally defended, that is, we may use rationality to answer objections to the use of rationality.

Could this theory allow one to hold religious beliefs rationally by holding them open to criticism? Bartley never answered this question explicitly. He hinted that he did believe this was the case, and some have understood him as adopting this position. Some critical rationalists are believers and some are not. Standards here remain vague. The winner of the Popper essay prize argued that Christians were also critical rationalists, because they discussed, for example, the theological significance of their religious experiences and have developed their views at Church councils. (Elliot 2004) Agassi has pointed out that the Talmudic tradition is highly critical within certain bounds, yet cannot be said to have a high degree of rationality. If all critical discussions, even those within sects, qualify their practitioners as critical rationalists, then critical rationalism itself dissolves. To take seriously the replacement of justification with criticism, Agassi suggests, requires demarcation between effective and ineffective critical methods.

Bartley called his view "comprehensively critical rationalism" to distinguish it from Popper's critical rationalism. It should not merely explain how one can conduct rational inquires in specific fields, but it should apply to the theory of rationality itself. Bartley added a list of critical standards one may use to evaluate ideas in any area whatsoever: a proposed idea should be a solution to an important problem, internally consistent, not refuted, and consistent with science. The first three are incorporated into virtually all critical rationalist theories. The fourth has been treated with more caution: science might also be mistaken, especially when it contains competing theories. A new metaphysical alternative may be inconsistent with established physical theory, as Faraday's was, yet be quite important for progress.

John Watkins considered Bartley's theory a reinforced dogmatism with a "Heads I win, tails you lose" strategy: If comprehensive critical rationalism faces no effective criticism it wins, but if it does, it thereby shows that it can meet its own standards and then again it wins. This criticism overlooks the fact that, if it faces effective criticism, it is shown to be wrong. Bartley's standard is a necessary condition of rationality, but meeting it is no reason for clinging to an effectively criticized theory.

Bartley's ideal of holding all ideas open to criticism has been an important part of critical rationalism. But it soon became apparent that the problems of how to develop critical rationalism were more important than demonstrating just how comprehensive it could be or of maintaining this comprehensive position. In order to see how and why this realization came about it is useful to return to Agassi.

Agassi deems the focus of Bartley's of approach to be misplaced: it unduly emphasizes the defence of rationality as rationally defencible. Rationality does not need defence; it needs improvement, Agassi says. And we may try to improve it piecemeal. We are all rational to some degree and are all interested from time to time in using reason more effectively than we now do. We cannot help but be rational, since thinking is, like seeing, innate to some extent. No one is always rational or perfectly rational any time. Our best hope, then, is to use rationality to improve the partial and limited rationality which we all use to one degree or another. We use a bootstrap process in that we use the rational methods we now have at hand to develop better methods, whereby the methods we use may very well be corrected or even discarded.

Agassi also applied Popper's non-justificationism to the historiography of science. Like many, Popper wanted the theory of science to describe science, but he hardly tried to apply his view to the history of science. Agassi developed a far wider picture of the history of science from Popper's viewpoint, contrasting the traditional inductivist and conventionalist historiographies with a non-justificationist one. Inductivism distorts the history of science as it is the view of innovations as either completely right or quite useless; conventionalism distorts the history of science because it explains away radical changes. John Wettersten extended this application to the historiography of psychology, explaining how a non-justificationist approach was needed to remove peculiar distortions there.

Critical Rationalism in Mathematics

In *Proofs and Refutations* Imré Lakatos extended the range of critical rationalism into mathematics. This area is just where one would expect that it would be the most difficult to develop a theory of the growth of knowledge by criticism rather than by proof, or, as Lakatos put it, by proofs and refutations. Putative counter-examples, he illustrated historically, often refute "proofs" and thus require improvements.

Lakatos did not provide for the use of frameworks to formulate problems in mathematics, nor did he discuss the rules which mathematicians should follow in formulating and criticizing proofs. He forcefully argued against premature formalization, but he did not allow for the modern method of introducing a field axiomatically from the start. His theory of response to criticism only shows that varying ways of responding to problematical cases are available.

As a beginning this is fine. But caring for the central task of critical rationalism, that is, for the development of critical methods (in mathematics) as an alternative to the quest for justifications, requires the replacement of justificationist methods with critical ones. Is this at all possible? Answers to this question might enlighten us about the rationality of mathematical research. They might supplement and/or improve Lakatos's portrayal of mathematical research by accounts of the ways it proceeds, and explain how decisions about the direction of research are made rationally.

Several thinkers have taken up this question; but with only one exception, they have sought to use Lakatos's justificationist methodology of scientific research programs. The exception is Peggy Marchi who broke off her research before she had constructed any developed view. Three thinkers, however, have made attempts to take Lakatos' methodology of research programs in a critical spirit and then apply it to the history of mathematics.

D.D. Spalt (Spalt 1981) argues that Lakatos' methodology of research programs is inapplicable to the history of mathematics as mathematicians are more open skeptical and critical than Lakatos' methodology describes. This confirms Lakatos's turn away from a critical approach, but does not help us further since it does not go on to ask if a genuinely critical approach, say, to the use of research programs such as Agassi's would help us. But Spalt also finds no mathematicians who follow any clear research program at all. He defends a view of mathematics which has great similarity to Feyerabend's view of science: there is no methodology which can describe all mathematical research.

G. Giorello (Giorello 1981) argues that Lakatos' theory of scientific research programs is better applicable to mathematical research than Popper's or Kuhn's. Teun Koetsier in turn found Giorello's argument inadequate (Koetsier 1991 pp. 145ff.). This is not surprising, since Lakatos' methodology of research programs is sketchy.

Koetsier was not satisfied with Giorello's vague results nor with Spalt's negative ones. He proposed a revision of Lakatos' theory which would enable him to describe how mathematical research proceeds. His revised version is closer to Agassi's theory of research programs, which, Agassi suggested, might be used to explain how mathematical problems were chosen and how mathematical research was coordinated.

Lakatos's historical reconstructions of mathematical developments are Popperian in that they portray not only mathematical theorems and their proofs, but also their refutations, and their replacement by new ones. Koetsier criticizes this portrayal. He finds instead that the aim of mathematical research has been directed at refining mathematical theorems. The refined theorems are then by and large accepted and entered into the body of mathematical knowledge, where they then stay, subject only to further refinements. Koetsier agrees, however, that Lakatos's theory does show how mathematicians work when solving problems within some narrowly defined areas of research. This research is fallible, he agrees, and this allows it to progress by the discovery of difficulties with previous theories which are overcome by succeeding ones.

Koetsier discusses clusters of mathematical theories that are part of identifiable research traditions. These traditions pose their own problems and are identifiable by their offerings of clusters of mathematical theorems. Each tradition, however, is not replaced by some competing one as in the case of science, where one explanation is superseded by another leading to the rejection of the former. In this respect the theories of science of Popper and/or Lakatos cannot be applied to the history of mathematics. Rather, each theory progresses in its domain and the results it produces are largely cumulative.

In order to explain how progress is made in such research traditions, Koetsier employs the suggestion made by Marchi that theorems should be taken as analogous to facts. (Marchi 1976) Whereas scientists seek to explain facts, mathematicians seek to prove theorems. Theorems are, just as facts, accepted provisionally. Instead of seeking to explain them as in science, mathematicians seek to prove them. Mathematics grows as new theorems are discovered and proved.

This theory leads back to the problem posed by Agassi and Marchi: How is research coordinated? Koetsier finds that Lakatos's theory of mathematics describes "local" mathematical research rather well. It describes how they solve problems within some cluster of theories and/or methods. He finds various research traditions, which have been used to set problems. But, he does not explain how such traditions arise nor why they are chosen. Mathematical research is, then, coordinated by interests in particular kinds of mathematical objects and/or particular methods. But, how are these chosen? Why do they change?

Koetsier also Faces the Question: Which theorems should mathematicians prove and why? He notes that some are central and others that seem simply too ad hoc to bother with. But, how does one decide? He offers a list of measures by which to judge the importance of theorems. His list of methods for appraising the ad hoc nature of theorems is interesting but still rather ad hoc. (Koetsier p. 170-171)

Agassi's theory of metaphysical research programs might have helped him here. Unlike Lakatos' inferior and subsequent theory, Agassi's was designed to solve the problems of "How is scientific research coordinated?" or "How do scientists choose their problems?" and "How can we explain simultaneous discoveries?" His answer is that problems in science are often chosen for their relevance to metaphysical problems. He developed at some length and in some depth the conflict between Faraday's field theory and Newton's atomic theory to show how problems were chosen which bore on this controversy and how the two metaphysical research programs could compete against each other.

How much of the choice of problems in the history of mathematics can be explained by Agassi's conjecture that they are regularly chosen due to their relevance to metaphysical problems? This is still an open question. But some problems clearly were. Among them are problems concerning irrational numbers, whether numbers exist in a Platonic world, problems concerning the nature of infinitesimals or irrational numbers or the square root of minus one or the nature of transfinite numbers as well as questions concerning the possibilities of non-Euclidean geometries. A history of mathematics written from this point of view might be enlightening, if it could portray underlying metaphysical concerns as focusing mathematical research on certain kinds of problems and the development of methods to deal with them.

It should be noted that J. O. Wisdom had portrayed the development of the calculus as a response to the criticisms of Berkeley before Lakatos began his research (Wisdom 1939; 1941). His view is less radical than Lakatos's however, since Lakatos, but not Wisdom, said that the growth of mathematical knowledge by proofs and refutations continues even after the introduction of new formal methods of logic. The formal proofs in the logical language are indeed, Lakatos says, immune from refutations, but the translations from the mathematical into the logical language are always open to question.

Hans Albert

In the 1960s, Hans Albert began to apply critical rationalism to social and political theory. His writings have become the standard statement of critical rationalism in the German-speaking world, if not elsewhere. He argues that any attempt at justification faces a three-pronged difficulty that is traceable to Agrippa: One alternative leads to an infinite regress as one seeks to prove one assumption but then needs to assume some new one; a second alternative lands in a circular argument as one assumes what one seeks to prove; a third alternative takes some arbitrary starting point and holds to it dogmatically. Outside of these three unacceptable moves, justificationism offers no other alternative. Since none of these three alternatives provide any justification at all, we should abandon the quest for justification. Instead we should hold all theories open to criticism, as Popper and Bartley have proposed. He takes over Agassi's theory of research programs, but, due to his emphasis on the comprehensive nature of critical rationalism, tends to side with Bartley more than Agassi on questions of rationality. He has never, however, had any open dispute with Popper, Bartley or Agassi even though the three thinkers disagree on various significant points. He builds what he can from their points of view into his own version and avoids controversial issues among critical rationalists, while developing polemics against its detractors.

His major project is to explain how the theory of rationality proposed by Popper, Bartley and Agassi is, or can be made to be, applicable to virtually all areas of human endeavour—ethics, politics, social science, science, and so forth. He has from time to time presented this as an alternative to the so-called Frankfurt School that was especially influential in Germany in the late 60s and 70s. Its members thought themselves capable of deep analyses of society to show what went wrong in German history—why, for example, Germany was authoritarian. Members of this school berated alternatives such as Albert's as "positivist," by which they seemed to have meant that it did not take into account the human dimensions of imperfect institutions. Because it looked at them too narrowly from an empirical, technical perspective it passed over too quickly the unhappy consequences they have. Albert countered that the failure to separate descriptive and prescriptive questions leads to the failure of the Frankfurt School to draw a realistic picture of society and such a picture is the necessary foundation for any adequate theory of social reform, which critical rationalism by no means opposes. It attempts rather to make it realistic. The political ideas of critical rationalism as presented by Popper and by Albert were the most popular in Germany next to those of the Frankfurt School. Albert also presented critical rationalism as superior to the hermeneutic theories of Hans-Otto Apel and Hans Georg Gadamer.

Albert has dealt extensively with methodology in economics, criticizing neo-classical economics for its unrealistic assumptions about the rationality of human actions, and its presumptions that there can be a measure of the social welfare of society. But he views the tradition of neoclassical economics as the best that the social sciences have to offer. He hopes to reform it by making its psychological assumptions more realistic. Here he decidedly parts company with Popper, who is far more skeptical about the use of theories of human nature, especially psychological ones. Albert rejects what he consider to be the exaggerated assumptions of rational-choice economics, and he suggests Popper's methodological individualism is not the same as the one that economists often use. But he has not constructed any systematic alternative.

Mario Bunge and Fallibilism

The researches mentioned so far grew directly out of Popper's non-justificationist theory of science. Mario Bunge developed a non-justificationist theory of science, especially of physics, before he had ever heard of Popper, and he does not view his work a part of the project known as critical rationalism. It nevertheless can count as a version of critical rationalism: it is a non-justificationist effort to improve standards of criticism. Bunge describes the crucial event in the later development of his philosophy as the realization that frameworks—he calls them systems–were crucial for the growth of knowledge. Bunge's "systems" differ from the "frameworks," whose usefulness is emphasized by some critical rationalists, if they differ at all, in taking as the best critical methods and most progressive research the formal, precise wording of theories. Bunge apparently feels more affinity with those thinkers who emphasize the use of formal methods and who futilely seek justification, than with those who deny the possibility of justification and deem the use of formal methods more limited than he does.

This is understandable, since he holds that the attainment of precision is crucial for rationality and, on his view precision is best obtained with formal methods, and sometimes can be obtained only in this way. As a corollary of this attitude, he proposes to respond to difficulties first with small changes that preserve systems, and move to larger ones when these prove inadequate. This is the exact opposite of what Popper said, as he advocated that one should always prefer that theory which has the highest degree of falsifiability. These thinkers, however, do not disagree about the aim of the philosophy of science, which is to improve critical standards so that the best possible theories are created and honed, but rather about the best means for doing that. In the wake of Einstein, Agassi resolves this conflict by proposing that both approaches can be used simultaneously.

Critical Rationalism without Frameworks of Methodological Rules

In contrast to critical rationalists who emphasize the need for both theoretical frameworks and methodological rules, there are also critical rationalists who dispense with both. Jagdish Hattiangadi, Gunnar Andersson and David Miller are examples. Hattiangadi says that all problems are contradictions encountered in attempts to master everyday problems of survival. Theoretical frameworks play no role in the formulation of problems, though traditions apparently do. It is hard to see the difference. One of the difficulties that his view encounters is that it makes it impossible to define problems well. For, the problem posed by the assumptions {p, ~p, a, b, c} turns out to be the same as the problem posed by the assumptions {p, ~p, x, y, z}. Another difficulty the theory faces is that it should, but does not, present a contradiction to earlier versions of critical rationalism that it allegedly improves upon. Moreover, some problems are due to gaps in our knowledge that are not contradictions. Formulations of good problems thus require frameworks that include some selection rules.

Posing problems of knowledge in terms of the identification of methodological rules for gaining knowledge was the crucial breakthrough that enabled Popper to move beyond his early *Die beiden Grundprobleme*. When one dispenses with them, one has an ad hoc approach to critical methods. They grow of themselves, Hattiangadi suggests, as attempts to solve practical problems. No other special critical activity is needed or useful. He explains the growth of critical methods as part of the struggle for survival: those who use the best methods to solve practical problems survive and reproduce themselves best. This view runs the danger of relapsing into Hegelianism, since it judges as best any intellectual development which is successful. Should fundamentalist Hinduism or Islam or Christianity (or all of them together) win the day, will they then be the best expression of rationality?

Gunnar Andersson views Popper's introduction of methodological rules as quite unnecessary: all contradictions between theories and observations pose problems and all responses to them should be prima facie acceptable. He takes off the table the most crucial aspect of the project of critical rationalism: how can we best improve our critical methods and our capacity to learn from mistakes? Even without any appeal to an evolutionary process such as that used by Hattiangadi, Andersson assumes that science will do just fine without critical studies of its methods. He does not discuss his optimism or the fears of those who do not share it. He says virtually nothing about non-scientific inquiry and rational action.

David Miller's critical rationalism is the third example of attempts to characterize rationality without explaining how the use of theoretical frameworks or methodological rules furthers it or hinders it. He concentrates on improving criticism of the logic of justification; he ignores Popper's crucial move from the mere portrayal of the logic of research to the formulation of methodological rules. He agrees that science is better off because it handles theories critically, but does not bother with the details. He ignores the question: How is the use that science makes of criticism distinct, if at all, from other uses of it? However, he apparently sides with Bartley's comprehensively critical rationalism. He has effectively bolstered Popper's arguments against attempts to use induction to establish any degree of probability of any theory and effectively criticized Popper's theory of verisimilitude. Having concluded that there is no evidence which can increase the probability that a theory is true, he concludes that there can be no good reasons whatsoever for any theory or any course of action. All we can ask, he suggests, is: Why not? We only have reasons for the rejection of theories, never for their endorsement.

But it does not follow from his correct observation that we can have no evidence which increases the probability that a theory is true, that there are no good reasons to consider any theory true. Miller suggests that in the interest of truth we should not make fanciful claims. But he says nothing about reasons for preferring, say, highly explanatory theories over less explanatory ones, or ones that solve problems better than others, or that we can improve our methods of elimination of theories beyond the mere random quest for contradictions. On a commonsense understanding of good reasons, all these possibilities may constitute good reasons for preferring some theories over others, even if they do not increase the probability that any theory is true.

On Miller's view it seems a person can declare true any unrefuted theory, say a minimal astrological theory, or Descartes' theory that souls have no extension, without violating any rationalist precept. He does not offer any selection procedure. He relies entirely on the interest in the truth, which, he claims, prevents arbitrariness. This is hardly enough: arbitrariness is not obvious. He rejects the possibility of taking advantage of our ability to assign truth values as we fancy, as it is frivolous; he does not tell us how to spot the frivolous. Talmudists and scholastics certainly have an interest in truth, are hardly frivolous, and use arguments extensively, yet they are hardly rational in any way comparable to the rationality of scientists. Popper's mature philosophy began as he specified rules that should prevent frivolity. He saw the need for methodological rules to make criticism effective.

Some critics say Miller's version of critical rationalism seems to have lost its way. By limiting himself so severely to logical analysis and neglecting the methodological aspects of rationality, Miller gives his philosophy a characteristic typical of positivism; by limiting his considerations to logic, he suggests that almost anything goes.

Theoretical frameworks are needed to direct rational thought and conduct, and methodological rules are needed to improve criticism and to maintain critical standards. Popper took over from the psychology of Otto Selz the idea that rational thought is directed because it is problem-oriented: without problems to direct thought it becomes a random process. And without frameworks we cannot formulate and choose problems well.

Miller can defend his view by explaining that he, too, recommends procedures to select theories to consider true. This takes us back to the problems of social standards of rationality, of problem-solving, of desiderata and of methods of critique which other critical rationalists are engaged in solving. About all this he remains silent. Yet his view that there are no good reasons for considering some statements true seems to render these redundant. If they are redundant, he should explain how we can do without them; if not, he is saying what most critical rationalists agree about.

Critical Rationalism, Truth and Best Theories

Alan Musgrave, Volker Gadenne and John Watkins all came out of Popper's circle. But Musgrave and Gadenne nevertheless focus on the search for some assurance that the theories they trust really are trustworthy; Watkins wants some empirical standard to determine which theory is now the best. Their peculiarity is that they seek methods of selecting credible theories or the best theories, while recognizing the validity of the criticisms of methods of justification launched by critical rationalists.

Musgrave endorses Popper's arguments that show the impossibility of sensible assignments to theories of some measure of probability. But he finds wanting Popper's way of avoiding skepticism, because Popper fails to offer reasons for beliefs. Only if it does that can Popper respond to the charge that his view is too skeptical. Musgrave regards his effort, then, as a vital defence of critical rationalism. In order to provide the needed defence, he seeks a standard for reasonable belief. He says that Popper has such a solution: we should believe that theory which has best withstood criticism is true. He adds that Popper should have said so more clearly.

Skepticism is the theory that no theory is any better than any other. Critical rationalism offers tentative rules for the choice of theories to examine, not to believe in. Musgrave endorses Popper's criticism of all attempts to specify the probability of any theory being true. He considers his position fallibilist and critical rationalist, because he accepts evidence to justify belief in a theory only if the evidence results from attempts to refute it. And, he claims, no evidence justifies claims that a theory is true, but only belief in a theory. Belief in a theory that has withstood criticism is justified, then, but not the claim that it is true. It is not clear why Musgrave suggests that the task of justifying beliefs is less insoluble and less superfluous than that of justifying theories.

Volker Gadenne resembles Musgrave somewhat. He agrees with Popper that theoretical science may very well do without evidence for belief, but he disagrees with him about actions: these require decisions as to which hypothesis is best. He suggests, then, that confirmed theories are preferable as a pragmatic ground for belief. Unlike Musgrave, he realizes that Popper's theory of corroboration cannot serve this purpose, as it allots the least probable theories, the ones that take the most risks, the highest degree of corroboration. But acting on them is still most risky. He therefore has a different theory of corroboration. He separates content from degree of corroboration in order to justify choosing the most highly corroborated theories to guide actions.

Admittedly we do need standards to limit the risk of the application of theories, as Agassi has pointed out. As a matter of principle, Agassi notes, we may demand that theories be tested in severe ways in order to reduce risk. But this procedure is not designed to increase belief or confidence in hypotheses or likelihood of theories. (It is not clear what Gadenne claims for corroboration.) For example, two theories might be equally applicable to some practical situation, one of which may by more risky, because it has more consequences than its competitor. We may still prefer it as a basis for action, even though we have, according to Gadenne's theory, more reason to believe the weaker theory. The stronger theory may enable us to do more. We have, for example, introduced nuclear energy even though we have far less reason, on Gadenne's standards for belief, to believe that using nuclear power is less risky than using coal. We use gene-technology for various purposes, even though Gadenne's theory of belief offers reasons to refrain from using it. We thus have standards for application of theories in technology and other areas of life which are quite independent of belief, thus apparently refuting Gadenne's theory.

Gadenne might respond by contending that the belief in question is not belief in a theory but belief in the success of its application. So, before applying it, we try to increase our belief that the application will succeed. But this is also not the case. We seek to anticipate problems and to test, as well as we can, whether some given application will lead to success or not. We try to apply risky theories because they promise more. When we know we are taking considerable risks, we anticipate them as best we can, and prepare to change course quickly. When we do not anticipate risks, but hope for great success, we simply act to test our hopes. The realization that these always may be frustrated may lead to total paralysis on the basis of Gadenne's theory of the need for corroboration as a means of choice of theories that enable us to act. Planning to solve our problems and realize our hopes employs theories with explanatory power. It also takes into account criticism of possible courses of action, and requires decisions. Belief or reassurance or corroboration are not required. Gadenne's theory, just like Musgrave's, leads us back to numerous insoluble and superfluous problems in the search for justification: How much corroboration must we seek before we act?

Judges must justify the sentences they impose on criminals. Proposals to take risks with the environment or to defend it should be justified too%on a case by case basis. Social standards have to be sufficiently agreed upon to allow for a consensus. On the core doctrine of critical rationalism, such standards cannot have epistemological justification; they are based on conjectures as to how we can avoid mistakes, and when there are different candidates, they are all subject to criticism. More cannot be done, and so all decisions are unjustified and so they all incur risks.

John Watkins intended his theory to go beyond Popper's suggestion that we should choose the theory that has the highest degree of explanatory power. He wished to explain why the theory corroborated to the highest degree is the best now available. But it is hard to see why one theory has to be identified as the best. It is often the case that one theory will be better in one respect and another in some other respect. Such a situation poses problems for both theories. It is reasonable to attempt to solve problems facing each theory quite independently of which theory is now the best on available evidence—if indeed, such a judgment can be made in any sensible way. The attempt to reduce all the good qualities to one quality which is fundamental or the most important is quixotic, as Popper's failed attempt to reduce all good qualities of theory to high degree of testability illustrates. (In the development of his theory of metaphysical research programs Agassi first pointed out that explanatory power can vary independently from testability.) The refined theory of corroboration which Watkins offers is quite irrelevant to practice, where what counts is adequacy for the task at hand and not some abstract measure of current success. Also, in practice we do not want to know which theory is the best, but how various serious alternatives may be improved. Furthermore, there is no point in trying to say which theory is the best at any given time with such a difficult procedure as Watkins has offered: before we have determined which of two alternatives is the best, both alternatives will very likely have been modified and we will have to start all over again.

Theories should have good qualities before we set about criticizing them, if we are not to waste our time in a random search. These good qualities are methodological: What does the theory explain? What problems does it solve? How can it be criticized? They are not epistemological: What evidence do we have for its truth? How can we be reassured we are on the right track? How do we know it corresponds to what the truth is like? Watkins views himself as a critical rationalist even though he stresses corroboration, because he does not relate corroboration to appraisals of the truth or probability of theories, but rather to other good qualities of theories. But he changes the project of critical rationalism from substituting methods of criticism for methods of justification to the quixotic project of determining which theory is best at any given time on the basis of its corroboration.

Critical Rationalist Sociology of Science

A crucial feature of critical rationalism is the theory that social norms determine the degree of rationality which individuals are able to exercise. This is a direct outgrowth of Popper's use of methodological rules to explain the growth of science. Because science is a social activity, Popper argued, Robinson Crusoe could not do science. One individual, he suggested, cannot both put forth and criticize theories adequately. Rationality comes from cooperation. To be effective in bringing about the growth of knowledge, criticism should follow social rules.

This feature of critical rationalism has led to a critical rationalist sociology of science and technology. The task of this sociology is the appraisal of the rules of science and technology. Do they encourage or hinder the formulation and circulation of bold conjectures and their effective critical appraisal? This effort began with Agassi's criticisms of Popper's rule to always prefer the theory with the highest degree of testability: Sometimes a testable theory has a higher explanatory power than some competitor, he argued, but also has a lower degree of testability than this competitor. We may, then, prefer it. The same holds for Popper's rule that all basic statements used in science should be repeatable: an independently testable explanation of a basic statement is sufficient. From these studies he moved on to inquiries into science as an open society. Even in the face of the traditional association of science with openness of debate and discussion, a variety of modern thinkers such as Michael Polanyi and Thomas Kuhn have opposed this view.

John Wettersten has continued critical rationalist studies in the sociology of science with examinations of how adventurous and conservative styles of research complement and compete with each other, how stylistic standards can hinder research, how a problem-oriented approach may improve standards in science and technology, and how critical rationalism may be used to guide sociological research. Wettersten has developed critical studies of alternative approaches to the sociology of science: a critical rationalist approach aims at minimizing the idealization of science, but without explaining scientific knowledge away.

I.C. Jarvie has recently studied how and when Popper added a theory of the institutions of science to his theory of the logic of science (Jarvie 2001) . In *The Open Society and Its Enemies* Popper explicitly added a social dimension to his view of science which was only implicit in *Logik der Forschung.* Popper did not, however, move on to sociological studies of science. He was so concerned not to explain away scientific knowledge as a mere social phenomena that he did not engage in the social studies of science even though his view called for such studies. He did not see that the effort to minimize idealized versions of science by describing how science encourages and hinders research poses no temptation to explain away scientific knowledge.

Philosophical Anthropology and Critical Rationality

As rationality is never perfect, and as idealization is to be minimized, Jarvie and Agassi tried to solve a number of central issues in the social sciences under the assumption that rationality is a matter of degree. This invites a new philosophical anthropology. In order to understand human nature it is desirable to desist from seeking all-or-nothing theories of humanity as, for example, a mere machine or of rationality as perfect. Human rationality cannot be understood apart from its mechanical or biological or social or rational aspects; human mechanism and biology and society cannot be understood apart from their rational aspects.

Critical Rationalism and Political Society

In addition to being a study of the methodology of the social sciences Popper's *The Open Society and Its Enemies* is a political manifesto. It sets minimal conditions for democratic politics: it must avoid utopian social engineering. The exclusive use of piecemeal social engineering requires that societies be open and that critical appraisal of government policies be carried out. Governments must set abstract conditions for how a society functions, but they should leave individuals free to act as they choose. This freedom includes the right of individuals to build their own social groups.

John Watkins and Bryan Magee have added significant observations about Popper's contribution. Watkins pointed out that

Popper's theory offered a basis for a pluralistic society which traditional theories of rationality cannot: justificationist theories allow only one view to be justified given the evidence at any time, whereas critical rationalism allows for a range of defencible theories which may democratically compete in the political arena. Magee (1995) has argued that Popper's philosophy offered a good antidote for those who would reject existing society as no good on the basis of utopian standards and demand radical reform. It explained why all societies have grave defects, that they could be corrected to some degree piecemeal, but that no radical change of society had any hope of making the situation any better.

Popper's abstract demarcation of closed and open societies does not touch most political controversies today, which concern disagreements among defenders of the open society. As a consequence, critical rationalists such as Jeremy Shearmur and Gerard Radnitzky have attempted to pull Popper's theory toward Hayek and laissez-faire economics, whereas others, such Malachi Hacohen, Agassi and Helmut Schmidt have found in his theory a framework for theories of active social reform. Popper said very little about competing democratic forms of government and what he has said is not necessarily connected to his philosophical deliberations in any obvious way.

Popper's observation that reform has unintended and unknown consequences which may then require further adjustments or backtracking has been read as a support for Hayek's demand that all government should be severely limited. Popper's observation that no society is perfect and his demand that social reform should eliminate some of its worst aspects have been read as support of a moderate socialism.

Popper and Education Theory

Popper began his research as a student of the Pedagogical Institute of the University of Vienna. Members of the Würzburg School such as Karl Bühler and Otto Selz were closely associated with the school reform movement led by Eduard Burger. Selz explained how learning could be improved when it centred on active problem solving. Popper adopted his view and argued that the memorization of important material by repetition would be replaced with a Selzian, problem-orientated approach. Wettersten has explained this as a beginning of integrated psychology and pedagogy that Popper has further developed by adding to it his methodological insights. Other critical rationalists followed this lead stressing the import of active problem solving, and adding the formation of conjectures and exercises in criticism and improvement of them. Also, emphasizing Popper's insight that science only makes advances in social settings, they have added the demand not to ignore the fact that learning involves social interaction, whereby autonomy, as the needed prerequisite for critical thinking, is also deemed a prime goal of any good pedagogy.

Conclusion

The salient points of critical rationalism open new possibilities in ethics, which until now has been merely couched in terms of the need to be critical and open. A problem-oriented ethics may replace traditional rule and consequence oriented ones. The use of critical standards of debate to appraise the history of philosophy opens up new perspectives as illustrated in the work of Curtis on Darwin's reception (Curtis 1987) and Wettersten's study of the reception to Whewell. It offers new paths for the study of related fields such as economics, where Kurt Klappholz and Lawrence Boland have led the way, for the study of methods and historiography of psychology as mentioned, and the possibility of a new theory of institutions as structures which individuals use to solve problems and appraise alternatives.

Various efforts such as these are still too fresh to be appraised and various defenders of critical rationalism differ on crucial issues. Just what, if any, its long-term impact will be is still quite open; debates among its exponents and between them and opponents are still on-going. The crucial issue is whether and to what degree methods of criticism can be substituted for epistemological methods of justification in all areas of life. This is the way we can face the stimulating criticism of Russell, who viewed critical rationalism as defeatist. Only the exhibition of bold, fruitful thinking may answer it. There is ongoing research to develop a critical theory of the history of philosophy, of the sociology of science, of political philosophy, of ethical theory, and of social and political institutions. If critical rationalism is merely a theory of weak justification as Musgrave, Gadenne and Watkins would have it, or if it ignores problems of the direction of research and intellectual standards as perhaps Hattiangadi, Andersson and Miller do, then it may deservedly be forgotten.

Karl Popper: Political Philosophy

Among philosophers, Karl Popper (1902-1994) is best known for his contributions to the philosophy of science and epistemology. Most of his published work addressed philosophical problems in the natural sciences, especially physics; and Popper himself acknowledged that his primary interest was nature and not politics. However, his political thought has arguably had as great an impact as has his philosophy of science. This is certainly the case outside of the academy. Among the educated general public, Popper is best known for his critique of totalitarianism and his defence of freedom, individualism, democracy and an "open society." His political thought resides squarely within the camp of Enlightenment rationalism and humanism. He was a dogged opponent of totalitarianism, nationalism, fascism, romanticism, collectivism, and other kinds of (in Popper's view) reactionary and irrational ideas.

Popper's rejection of these ideas was anchored in a critique of the philosophical beliefs that, he argued, underpinned them, especially a flawed understanding of the scientific method. This approach is what gives Popper's political thought its particular philosophical interest and originality—and its controversy, given that he locates the roots of totalitarianism in the ideas of some of the West's most esteemed philosophers, ancient as well as modern. His defence of a freed and democratic society stems in large measure from his views on the scientific method and how it should be applied to politics, history and social science. Indeed, his most important political texts—*The Poverty of Historicism* (1944) and *The Open Society and Its Enemies* (1945)—offer a kind of unified vision of science and politics. As explained below, the people and institutions of the open society that Popper envisioned would be imbued with the same critical spirit that marks natural science, an attitude which Popper called critical rationalism. This openness to analysis and questioning was expected to foster social and political progress as well as to provide a political context that would allow the sciences to flourish.

The Critique of the Closed Society

A central aim of *The Open Society and Its Enemies* as well as *The Poverty of Historicism* was to explain the origin and nature of totalitarianism. In particular, the rise of fascism, including in Popper's native Austria, and the ensuing Second World War prompted Popper to begin writing these two essays in the late 1930s and early 1940s, while he was teaching in New Zealand. He described these works as his "war effort" (*Unended Quest,* 115).

The arguments in the two essays overlap a great deal. (In fact, *The Open Society* began as a chapter for *Poverty.*) Yet there is a difference in emphasis. *The Poverty of Historicism* is concerned principally with the methodology of the social sciences, and, in particular, how a flawed idea, which Popper dubbed "historicism," had led historians and social scientists astray methodologically and which also served as a handmaiden to tyranny. *The Open Society*, a much longer and, according to Popper, a more important work, included in-depth discussion of historicism and the methods of the social sciences. But it also featured an inquiry into the psychological and historical origins of totalitarianism, which he located in the nexus of a set of appealing but, he argued, false ideas. These included not only historicism but also what he labelled "holism" and "essentialism." Together they formed the philosophical substrate of what Popper called the "closed society." The "closed society" is what leads to totalitarianism.

Open versus Closed Societies

According to Popper, totalitarianism was not unique to the 20th century. Rather, it "belongs to a tradition which is just as old or just as young as our civilization itself" (*Open Society, Vol. I*, 1). In *The Open Society*, Popper's search for the roots of totalitarianism took him back to ancient Greece. There he detected the emergence of what he called the first "open society" in democratic Athens of the 5th century B.C.E., Athenians, he argued, were the first to subject their own values, beliefs, institutions and traditions to critical scrutiny and Socrates and the city's democratic politics exemplified this new attitude. But reactionary forces were unnerved by the instability and rapid social change that an open society had unleashed. (Socrates was indicted on charges of corrupting the youth and introducing new gods.) They sought to turn back the clock and return Athens to a society marked by rigid class hierarchy, conformity to the customs of the tribe, and uncritical deference to authority and tradition—a "closed society." This move back to tribalism was motivated by a widely and deeply felt uneasiness that Popper called the "strain of civilization." The structured and organic character of closed societies helps to satisfy a deep human need for regularity and a shared common life, Popper said. In contrast, the individualism, freedom and personal responsibility that open societies *necessarily* engender leave many feeling isolated and anxious, but this anxiety, Popper said, must be born if we are to enjoy the greater benefits of living in an open society: freedom, social progress, growing knowledge, and enhanced cooperation. "It is the price we have to pay for being human" (*Open Society Vol. 1*, 176).

Popper charged that Plato emerged as the philosophical champion of the closed society and in the process laid the groundwork for totalitarianism. Betraying the open and critical temper of his mentor Socrates, in his *Republic* Plato devised an elaborate system that would arrest all political and social change and turn philosophy into an enforcer, rather than a challenger, of authority. It would also reverse the tide of individualism and egalitarianism that had emerged in democratic Athens, establishing a hierarchical system in which the freedom and rights of the individual would be sacrificed to the collective needs of society.

Popper noted that Plato's utopian vision in the *Republic* was in part inspired by Sparta, Athen's enemy in the Peloponnesian War and, for Popper, an exemplar of the closed society. Spartan society focused almost exclusively on two goals: internal stability and military prowess. Toward these ends, the Spartan constitution sought to create a hive-like, martial society that always favoured the needs of the collective over the individual and required a near total control over its citizenry. This included a primitive eugenics, in which newborn infants deemed insufficiently vigorous were tossed into a pit of water. Spartan males judged healthy enough to merit life were separated from their families at a young age and provided an education consisting mainly of military training.

The training produced fearsome warriors who were indifferent to suffering, submissive to authority, and unwaveringly loyal to the city. Fighting for the city was an honour granted solely to the male citizenry, while the degrading toil of cultivating the land was the lot reserved to an enslaved tribe of fellow Greeks, the helots. Rigid censorship was imposed on the citizenry, as well as laws that strictly limited contact with foreigners. Under this system, Sparta became a dominant military power in ancient Greece, but, unsurprisingly, made no significant contributions to the arts and sciences. Popper described Sparta as an "arrested tribalism" that sought to stymie "equalitarian, democratic and individualistic ideologies," such as found in Athens (*Open Society Vol. 1*, 182). It was no coincidence, he said, that the Nazis and other modern-day totalitarians were also inspired by the Spartans.

Holism, Essentialism and Historicism

Popper charged that three deep philosophical predispositions underpinned Plato's defence of the closed society and, indeed, subsequent defences of the closed society during the next two-and-a-half millennia. These ideas were *holism*, *essentialism*, and *historicism*.

Holism may be defined as the view that adequate understanding of certain kinds of entities requires understanding them as a whole.

This is often held to be true for biological and social systems, for example, an organism, an ecosystem, an economy, or a culture. A corollary that is typically held to follow from this view is that such entities have properties that cannot be reduced to the entities' constituent parts. For instance, some philosophers argue that human consciousness is an emergent phenomenon whose properties cannot be explained solely by the properties of the physical components (nerve cells, neurotransmitters, and so forth) that comprise the human brain. Similarly, those who advocate a holistic approach to social inquiry argue that social entities cannot be reduced to the properties of the individuals that comprise them. That is, they reject *methodological individualism* and support *methodological holism*, as Popper called it.

Plato's holism, Popper argued, was reflected in his view that the city—the Greek *polis*—was prior to and, in a sense, more real than the individuals who resided in it. For Plato "[o]nly a stable whole, the permanent collective, has reality, not the passing individuals" (*Open Society Vol. 1*, 80). This view in turn implied that the city has real needs that supersede those of individuals and was thus the source of Plato's ethical collectivism. According to Popper, Plato believed that a just society required individuals to sacrifice their needs to the interests of the state. "Justice for [Plato]," he wrote, "is nothing but health, unity and stability of the collective body" (OSE I, 106). Popper saw this as profoundly dangerous. In fact, he said, the view that some collective social entity—be it, for example, a city, a state, society, a nation, or a race—has needs that are prior and superior to the needs of actual living persons is a central ethical tenet of all totalitarian systems, whether ancient or modern. Nazis, for instance, emphasized the needs of the Aryan race to justify their brutal policies, whereas communists in the Soviet Union spoke of class aims and interests as the motor of history to which the individual must bend. The needs of the race or class superseded the needs of individuals. In contrast, Popper held, members of an open society see the state and other social institutions as human designed, subject to rational scrutiny, and always serving the interests of individuals—and never the other way around. True justice entails equal treatment of individuals rather than Plato's organistic view, in which justice is identified as a well functioning state.

Also abetting Plato's support for a closed society was a doctrine that Popper named "methodological essentialism". Adherents of this view claim "that it is the task of pure knowledge or 'science' to discover and to describe the true nature of things, i.e., their hidden reality or essence" (*Open Society Vol. 1*, 31). Plato's theory of the Forms exemplified this approach. According to Plato, understanding of any kind of thing—for example, a bed, a triangle, a human being, or a city—requires understanding what Plato called its Form. The Forms are timeless, unchanging and perfect exemplars of sensible things found in our world. Coming to understand a Form, Plato believed, requires rational examination of its essence. Such understanding is governed by a kind of intuition rather than empirical inquiry. For instance, mathematical intuition provides the route to understanding the essential nature of triangles—that is, their Form—as opposed to attempting to understand the nature of triangles by measuring and comparing actual sensible triangles found in our world.

Although Forms are eternal and unchanging, Plato held that the imperfect copies of them that we encounter in the sensible world invariably undergo decay. Extending this theory presented a political problem for Plato. In fact, according to Popper, the disposition to decay was the core political problem that Plato's philosophy sought to remedy. The very nature of the world is such that human beings and the institutions that they create tend to degrade over time. For Plato, this included cities, which he believed were imperfect copies of the Form of the city. This view of the city, informed by Plato's methodological essentialism, produced a peculiar political science, Popper argued. It required, first, understanding the true and best nature of the city, that is, its Form. Second, in order to determine how to arrest (or at least slow) the city's decay from its ideal nature, the study of politics must seek to uncover the laws or principles that govern the city's natural tendency towards decay and thereby to halt the degradation. Thus Plato's essentialism led him to seek a theory of historical change—a theory that brings order and intelligibility to the constant flux of our world. That is, Plato's essentialism led to what Popper labelled "historicism."

Historicism is the view that history is governed by historical laws or principles and, further, that history has a necessary direction and end-point. This being so, historicists believe that the aim of philosophy—and, later, history and social science—must be to predict the future course of society by uncovering the laws or principles that govern history. Historicism is a very old view, Popper said, predating Athens of the 5th century B.C.E. Early Greek versions of historicism held that the development of cities naturally and necessarily moves in cycles: a golden age followed by inevitable decay and collapse, which in some versions paves the way for rebirth and a new golden age. In Plato's version of this "law of decay," the ideal city by turns degenerates from timarchy (rule by a military class) to oligarchy to democracy and then, finally, dictatorship. But Plato did not merely describe the gradual degeneration of the city; he offered a philosophical explanation of it, which relied upon his theory of the Forms and thus methodological essentialism. Going further, Plato sought to provide a way to arrest this natural tendency toward decay. This, Popper argued, was the deep aim of the utopian society developed in the *Republic*—a newly fabricated closed society as the solution to natural tendency toward moral and political decline. It required creation of a rigid and hierarchical class society governed by philosopher kings, whose knowledge of the Forms would stave off decay as well as ensure the rulers' incorruptibility. Tumultuous democratic Athens would be replaced with a stable and unchanging society. Plato saw this as justice, but Popper argued that it had all the hallmarks of totalitarianism, including rigid hierarchy, censorship, collectivism, central planning—all of which would be reinforced through propaganda and deception, or, as Plato called them, "noble lies."

Plato's deep mistrust of democracy was no doubt in part a product of experience. As a young man he saw the citizens of Athens, under the influence of demagogues, back ill-advised military campaigns that ultimately led to the Spartan victory over the city in 404 B.C.E. After democracy was re-established following the Spartan occupiers' departure in 403 B.C.E., he witnessed the Athenian people's vote to execute its wisest citizen, Socrates. Popper as a young man had also witnessed the collapse of democracy, in his native Austria and throughout Europe. But he drew very different lessons from that experience. For him, democracy remained a bulwark against tyranny, not its handmaiden. For reasons explained in the next section, Popper held that by rejecting democracy Plato's system destroyed not only individual freedom but also the conditions for social, political, scientific and moral progress.

Popper's criticism of Plato sparked a lively and contentious debate. Prior to publication of *The Open Society*, Plato was widely regarded as the wellspring of enlightened humanism in the Western tradition. Popper's recasting of Plato as a proto-fascist was scandalous. Classists rose to Plato's defence and accused Popper of reading Plato ahistorically, using dubious or tendentious translations of his words, and failing to appreciate the ironic and literary elements in Plato's dialogues. These criticisms exposed errors in Popper's scholarship. But Popper was nonetheless successful in drawing attention to potential totalitarian dangers of Plato's utopianism. Subsequent scholarship could not avoid addressing his arguments.

Although Plato was the principle target of Popper's criticisms in the *Open Society*, he also detected dangerous tendencies in other ancient Greek philosophers' ideas, most notably Aristotle's. Plato's greatest student, Popper argued, had inherited his teacher's essentialism but had given it a teleological twist. Like Plato, Aristotle believed that knowledge of an entity required grasping its essence. However, Plato and Aristotle differed in their understanding of the relationship between an entity's essence and how that essence was manifested in the sensible world. Plato held that the entities found in the sensible world were imperfect, decaying representation of the Forms. Thus his understanding of history, Popper argued, was ultimately pessimistic: the world degrades over time. Plato's politics was an attempt to arrest or at least slow this degradation. In contrast, Aristotle understood an entity's essence as a bundle of potentialities that become manifest as the entity develops through time. An entity's essence acts as a kind of internal motor that impels the entity toward its fullest development, or what Aristotle called its *final cause*. The oak tree, for example, is the final cause of an acorn, the end towards which it strives.

Herein Popper detected an implicit historicism in Aristotle's epistemology. Though Aristotle himself produced no theory of history, his essentialism wedded to his teleology naturally lent itself to the notion that a person's or a state's true nature can only be understood as it is revealed through time. "Only if a person or a state develops, and only by way of its history, can we get to *know* anything about its 'hidden undeveloped essence'" (*Open Society Vol. II*, 7). Further, Popper argued that Aristotle's essentialism naturally aligned with the notion of historical destiny: a state's or a nation's development is predetermined by its "hidden undeveloped essence."

Popper believed that he had revealed deep links between ancient Greek philosophy and hostility toward the open society. In Plato's essentialism, collectivism, holism and historicism, Popper detected the philosophical underpinning for Plato's ancient totalitarian project. As we shall see in the next section, Popper argued that these very same ideas were at the heart of modern totalitarianism, too. Though for Popper Plato was the most important ancient enemy of the open society, in Aristotle's teleological essentialism Popper found a key link connecting ancient and modern historicism. In fact, the idea of historical destiny that Aristotle's thought generated was at the core of the thought of two 19th century philosophers, G.W.F. Hegel and Karl Marx, whom Popper charged with facilitating the emergence of modern closed societies.

The "far-reaching historicist consequences" of Aristotle's essentialism "were slumbering for more than twenty centuries, 'hidden and undeveloped'," until the advent of Hegel's philosophical system (*Open Society Vol. 1*, 8).

Hegel, Marx and Modern Historicism

History was central to both Hegel's and Marx's philosophy, and for Popper their ideas exemplified historicist thinking and the political dangers that it entailed. Hegel's historicism was reflected in his view that the dialectal interaction of ideas was the motor of history. The evolution and gradual improvement of philosophical, ethical, political and religious ideas determines the march of history, Hegel argued. History, which Hegel sometimes described as the gradual unfolding of "Reason," comes to an end when all the internal contradictions in human ideas are finally resolved.

Marx's historical materialism famously inverted Hegel's philosophy. For Marx, history was a succession of economic and political systems, or "modes of production" in Marx's language. As technological innovations and new ways of organizing production led to improvements in a society's capacity to meet human material needs, new modes of production would emerge. In each new mode of production, the political and legal system, as well as the dominant moral and religious values and practices, would reflect the interests of those who controlled the new productive system. Marx believed that the capitalist mode of production was the penultimate stage of human history.

The productive power unleashed by new technologies and factory production under capitalism was ultimately incompatible with capitalism as an economic and political system, which was marked by inefficiency, instability and injustice. Marx predicted that these flaws would inevitably lead to revolution followed by establishment of communist society. This final stage of human development would be one of material abundance and true freedom and equality for all.

According to Popper, though they disagreed on the mechanism that directed human social evolution, both Hegel and Marx, like Plato, were historicists because they believed that trans-historical laws governed human history. This was the key point for Popper, as well as the key error and danger.

The deep methodological flaw of historicism, according to Popper, is that historicists wrongly see the goal of social science as *historical forecast*—to predict the general course of history. But such prediction is not possible, Popper said. He provided two arguments that he said demonstrated its impossibility. The first was a succinct logical argument: Human knowledge grows and changes overtime, and knowledge in turn affects social events. (That knowledge might be, for example, a scientific theory, a social theory, or an ethical or religious idea.) We cannot predict what we will know in the future (otherwise we would already know it), therefore we cannot predict the future. As long as it is granted that knowledge affects social behaviour and that knowledge changes overtime—two premises that Popper considered incontestable—then the view that we can predict the future cannot be true and historicism must be rejected. This argument, it should be noted, also reflected Popper's judgment that the universe is nondeterministic: that is, he believed that prior conditions and the laws of nature do not completely causally determine the future, including human ideas and actions. Our universe is an "open" universe, he said.

Popper's second argument against the possibility of historical forecasting focused on the role of laws in social explanations. According to Popper, historicists wrongly believe that genuine social science must be a kind of "theoretical history" in which the aim is to uncover laws of historical development that explain and predict the course of history (*Poverty of Historicism*, 39). But Popper contended that this represents a fundamental misunderstanding of scientific laws. In fact, Popper argued, *there isno such thing as a law of historical development*. That is, there are no trans-historical laws that determine the transition from one historical period to the next. Failure to understand why this is so represented a deep philosophical error. There may be sociological laws that govern human behaviour within particular social systems or institutions, Popper said. For instance, the laws of supply and demand are kinds of social laws governing market economies. But the future course of history cannot be predicted and, in particular, laws that govern the general trajectory of history do not exist. Popper does not deny that there can be historical *trends*—a tendency towards greater freedom and equality, more wealth or better technology, for instance, but unlike genuine laws, trends are always dependent upon conditions. Change the conditions and the trends may alter or disappear. A trend towards greater freedom or knowledge could be disrupted by, say, the outbreak of a pandemic disease or the emergence of a new technology that facilitates authoritarian regimes. Popper acknowledges that in certain cases natural scientists can predict the future—even the distance future—with some confidence, as is the case with astronomy, for instance. But this type of successful long-range forecasting can occur only in physical systems that are "well-isolated, stationary and recurrent," such as the solar system (*Conjectures and Refutations*, 339). Social systems can never be isolated and stationary, however.

Utopian Social Engineering

So historicism as social science is deeply defective, according to Popper. But he also argued that it was politically dangerous and that this danger stemmed from historicism's natural and close allegiance with what Popper called "utopian social engineering." Such social planning "aims at remodelling the 'whole of society' in accordance with a definite plan or blueprint," as opposed to social planning that aims at gradual and limited adjustments. Popper admitted that the alliance between historicism and utopian engineering was "somewhat strange" (*Poverty of Historicism*, 73). Because historicists believe that laws determine the course of history, from their vantage it is ultimately pointless to try to engineer social change. Just as a meteorologist can forecast the weather, but not alter it, the same holds for social scientists, historicists believe. They can predict future social developments, but not cause or alter them. Thus "out-and-out historicism" is against utopian planning—or even against social planning altogether (*Open Society Vol. 1*, 157). For this reason Marx rejected attempts to design a socialist system; in fact he derided such projects as "utopian." Nonetheless, the connection between historicism and utopian planning remains strong, Popper insisted. Why?

First, historicism and utopian engineering share a connection to utopianism. Utopians seek to establish an ideal state of some kind, one in which all conflicts in social life are resolved and ultimate human ends—for example, freedom, equality, true happiness—are somehow reconciled and fully realized. Attaining this final goal requires radical overhaul of the existing social world and thus naturally suggests the need for utopian social engineering. Many versions of historicism are thus inclined towards utopianism. As noted above, both Marx's and Hegel's theory of history, for instance, predict an end to history in which all social contradictions will be permanently resolved. Second, historicism and utopian social engineering both tend to embrace holism. Popper said that historicists, like utopian engineers, typically believe that "society as a whole" is the proper object of scientific inquiry. For the historicist, society must be understood in terms of social wholes, and to understand the deep forces that move the social wholes, you must understand the laws of history. Thus the historicists' anticipation of the coming utopia, and their knowledge of the historical tendencies that will bring it about, may tempt them to try to intervene in the historical process and therefore, as Marx said, "lessen the birth pangs" associated with the arrival of the new social order. So while a philosophically consistent historicism might seem to lead to political quiescence, the fact is that historicists often cannot resist political engagement. In addition, Popper noted that even less radical versions of historicism, such as Plato's, permit human intervention.

Popper argued that utopian engineering, though superficially attractive, is fatally flawed: it invariably leads to multitudinous unintended and usually unwelcome consequences. The social world is so complex, and our understanding of it so incomplete, that the full impact of any imposed change to it, especially grand scale change, can never be foreseen. But, because of their unwarranted faith in their historical prophesies, the utopian engineers will be methodologically ill equipped to deal with this reality. The unintended consequences will be unanticipated, and he or she will be forced to respond to them in a haphazard and ill-informed manner: "[T]he greater the holistic changes attempted, the greater are their unintended and largely unexpected repercussions, forcing on the holistic engineer the expedient of piecemeal *improvisation*" or the "notorious phenomenon of *unplanned planning*"(*Poverty of Historicism*, 68-69). One particularly important cause of unintended consequences that utopian engineers are generally blind to is what Popper called the "human factor" in all institutional design. Institutions can never wholly govern individuals' behaviour, he said, as human choice and human idiosyncrasies will ensure this. Thus no matter how thoroughly and carefully an institution is designed, the fact that institutions are filled with human beings results in a certain degree of unpredictability in their operation. But the historicists' holism leads them to believe that individuals are merely pawns in the social system, dragged along by larger social forces outside their control. The effect of the human factor is that utopian social engineers inevitably are forced, despite themselves, to try to alter human nature itself in their bid to transform society. Their social plan "substitutes for [the social engineers'] demand that we build a new society, fit for men and women to live in, the demand that we 'mould' these men and women to fit into this new society" (*Poverty of Historicism*, 70).

Achieving such molding requires awesome and total power and thus in this way utopian engineering naturally tends toward the most severe authoritarian dictatorship. But this is not the only reason that utopian engineering and tyranny are allied. The central planning that it requires invariably concentrates power in the hands of the few, or even the one. This is why even utopian projects that officially embrace democracy tend towards authoritarianism. Authoritarian societies are in turn hostile to any public criticism, which deprives the planners of needed feedback about the impact of their policies, which further undermines the effectiveness of utopian engineering. In addition, Popper argued that the utopian planners' historicism makes them indifferent to the misery that their plans cause. Having uncovered what they believe is inevitable en route to utopia, they all too easily countenance any suffering as a necessary part of that process, and, moreover, they will be inclined to see such suffering as outweighed by the benefits that will flow to all once utopia is reached.

Popper's discussion of utopian engineering and its link to historicism is highly abstract. His criticisms are generally aimed at "typical" historicists and utopian planners, rather than actual historical or contemporary figures. This reluctance to name names is somewhat surprising, given that Popper himself later stated that the political disasters of the 1930s and 40s were the impetus for his foray into political philosophy. Exactly whom did Popper think was guilty of social science malpractice? A contemporary reader with a passing familiarity with 20th-century history is bound to suppose that Popper had in mind the horrors of the Soviet Union when he discussed utopian planning. Indeed, the attempts to transform the Soviet Union into a modern society—the "five year plans," rapid industrialization, collectivization of agriculture, and so forth—would seem to feature all the elements of utopian engineering.

They were fuelled by Marxist historicism and utopianism, centrally planned, aimed at wholesale remodelling of Russian society, and even sought to create a new type of person—"New Soviet Man"—through indoctrination and propaganda. Moreover, the utopian planning had precisely the pernicious effects that Popper predicted. The Soviet Union soon morphed into a brutal dictatorship under Stalin, criticism of the leadership and their programs was ruthlessly suppressed, and the various ambitious social projects were bedeviled by massive unintended consequences. The collectivization of agriculture, for instance, led to a precipitous drop in agricultural production and some 10 million deaths, partly from the unintended consequence of mass starvation and partly from the Soviet leaders' piecemeal improvisation of murdering incorrigible peasants. However, when writing *Poverty* and *The Open Society*, Popper regarded the Soviet experiments, at least the early ones, as examples of piecemeal social planning rather than the utopian kind. His optimistic assessment is no doubt explained partly by his belief at the time that the Russian revolution was a progressive event, and he was thus reluctant to criticize the Soviet Union (Hacohen, 396-397). In any event, the full horrors of the Soviet social experiments were not yet known to the wider world. In addition, the Soviets during the Second World War were part of the alliance against fascism, which Popper saw as a much greater threat to humanity. In fact, initially Popper viewed totalitarianism as an exclusively right-wing phenomenon. However, he later became a unambiguous opponent of Soviet-style communism, and he dedicated the 1957 publication in book form of *The Poverty of Historicism* to the "memory of the countless men, women and children of all creeds or nations or races who fell victims to the fascist and communist belief in Inexorable Laws of Historical Destiny."

Freedom, Democracy and the Open Society

Having uncovered what he believed were the underlying psychological forces abetting totalitarianism (the strain of civilization) as well as the flawed philosophical ideas (historicism, holism and essentialism), Popper provided his own account of the values and institutions needed to sustain an open society in the contemporary world. He viewed modern Western liberal democracies as open societies and defended them as "the best of all political worlds of whose existence we have any historical knowledge" (*All Life Is Problem Solving*, 90). For Popper, their value resided principally in the individual freedom that they permitted and their ability to self-correct peacefully over time.

That they were democratic and generated great prosperity was merely an added benefit. What gives the concept of an open society its interest is not so much the originality of the political system that Popper advocated, but rather the novel grounds on which he developed and defended this political vision. Popper's argument for a free and democratic society is anchored in a particular epistemology and understanding of the scientific method.

He held that all knowledge, including knowledge of the social world, was conjectural and that freedom and social progress ultimately depended upon the scientific method, which is merely a refined and institutionalized process of trial and error. Liberal democracies in a sense both embodied and fostered this understanding of knowledge and science.

Minimalist Democracy

Popper's view of democracy was simple, though not simplistic, and minimalist. Rejecting the question *Who should rule?* as the fundamental question of political theory, Popper proposed a new question: *"How can we so organize political institutions that bad or incompetent rulers can be prevented from doing too much damage?"* (*Open Society Vol. 1*, 121). This is fundamentally a question of institutional design, Popper said. Democracy happens to be the best type of political system because it goes a long way toward solving this problem by providing a nonviolent, institutionalized and regular way to get rid of bad rulers—namely by voting them out of office. For Popper, the value of democracy did not reside in the fact that the people are sovereign. (And, in any event, he said, "the people do not rule anywhere, it is always governments that rule" [*All Life Is Problem Solving*, 93]). Rather, Popper defended democracy principally on pragmatic or empirical grounds, not on the "essentialist" view that democracy by *definition* is rule by the people or on the view that there is something intrinsically valuable about democratic participation. With this move, Popper is able to sidestep altogether a host of traditional questions of democratic theory, e.g.. On what grounds are the people sovereign? Who, exactly, shall count as "the people"? How shall they be represented? The role of the people is simply to provide a regular and nonviolent way to get rid of incompetent, corrupt or abusive leaders.

Popper devoted relatively little thought toward the design of the democratic institutions that permit people to remove their leaders or otherwise prevent them from doing too much harm. But he did emphasize the importance of instituting checks and balances into the political system. Democracies must seek "institutional control of the rulers by balancing their power against other powers" (Ibid.) This idea, which was a key component of the "new science" of politics in the 18th century, was expressed most famously by James Madison in Federalist Paper #51. "A dependence on the people is, no doubt, the primary control on the government," Madison wrote, "but experience has taught mankind the necessity of auxiliary precautions." That is, government must be designed such that "ambition must be made to counteract ambition." Popper also argued that two-party systems, such as found in the United States and Great Britain, are superior to proportional representation systems; he reasoned that in a two-party system voters are more easily able to assign failure or credit to a particular political party, that is, the one in power at the time of an election. This in turn fosters self-criticism in the defeated party: "Under such a system ... parties are from time to time forced to learn from their mistakes" (*All Life Is Problem Solving*, 97). For these reasons, government in a two-party system better mirrors the trial-and-error process found in science, leading to better public policy. In contrast, Popper argued that proportional representation systems typically produce multiple parties and coalitional governments in which no single party has control of the government. This makes it difficult for voters to assign responsibility for public policy and thus elections are less meaningful and government less responsive. (It should be noted that Popper ignored that divided government is a typical outcome in the U.S. system. It is relevantly infrequent for one party to control the presidency along with both chambers of the U.S. congress, thus making it difficult for voters to determine responsibility for public policy successes and failures.)

Importantly, Popper's theory of democracy did not rely upon a well-informed and judicious public. It did not even require that the public, though ill-informed, nonetheless exercises a kind of collective wisdom. In fact, Popper explicitly rejected *vox populi vox dei* as a "classical myth". "We are democrats," Popper wrote, "not because the majority is always right, but because democratic traditions are the least evil ones of which we know" (*Conjectures and Refutations*, 351). Better than any other system, democracies permit the change of government without bloodshed. Nonetheless Popper expressed the hope that public opinion and the institutions that influence it (universities, the press, political parties, cinema, television, and so forth) could become more rational overtime by embracing the scientific tradition of critical discussion—that is, the willingness to submit one's ideas to public criticism and habit of listening to another person's point of view.

Piecemeal Social Engineering

So the chief role of the citizen in Popper's democracy is the small but important one of removing bad leaders. How then is public policy to be forged and implemented? Who forges it? What are its goals? Here Popper introduced the concept of "*piecemeal social engineering*," which he offered as a superior approach to the utopian engineering described above. Unlike utopian engineering, piecemeal social engineering must be "small scale," Popper said, meaning that social reform should focus on changing one institution at a time. Also, whereas utopian engineering aims for lofty and abstract goals (for example, perfect justice, true equality, a higher kind of happiness), piecemeal social engineering seeks to address concrete social problems (for example, poverty, violence, unemployment, environmental degradation, income inequality). It does so through the creation of new social institutions or the redesign of existing ones. These new or reconfigured institutions are then tested through implementation and altered accordingly and continually in light of their effects. Institutions thus may undergo gradual improvement overtime and social ills gradually reduced. Popper compared piecemeal social engineering to physical engineering. Just as physical engineers refine machines through a series of small adjustments to existing models, social engineers gradually improve social institutions through "piecemeal tinkering." In this way, "[t]he piecemeal method permits repeated experiments and continuous readjustments" (*Open Society Vol 1.*, 163). Only such social experiments, Popper said, can yield reliable feedback for social planners. In contrast, as discussed above, social reform that is wide ranging, highly complex and involves multiple institutions will produce social experiments in which it is too difficult to untangle causes and effects. The utopian planners suffer from a kind of hubris, falsely and tragically believing that they possess reliable experimental knowledge about how the social world operates. But the "piecemeal engineer knows, like Socrates, how little he knows. He knows that we can learn only from our mistakes" (*Poverty of Historicism*, 67).

Thus, as with his defence of elections in a democracy, Popper's argument for piecemeal social engineering rests principally on its compatibility with the trial-and-error method of the natural sciences: a theory is proposed and tested, errors in the theory are detected and eliminated, and a new, improved theory emerges, starting the cycle over. Via piecemeal engineering, the process of social progress thus parallels scientific progress. Indeed, Popper says that piecemeal social engineering is the only approach to public policy that can be genuinely scientific: "This—and no Utopian planning or historical prophecy—would mean the introduction of scientific method into politics, since the whole secret of scientific method is a readiness to learn from mistakes" (*Open Society Vol 1.*, 163).

Negative Utilitarianism

If piecemeal social engineers should target specific social problems, what criteria should they use to determine which problems are most urgent? Here Popper introduced a concept that he dubbed "negative utilitarianism," which holds that the principal aim of politics should be to reduce suffering rather than to increase happiness. "[I]t is my thesis," he wrote, "that human misery is the most urgent problem of a rational public policy" (*Conjectures and Refutations*, 361). He made several arguments in favour of this view.

First, he claimed that there is no moral symmetry between suffering and happiness: "In my opinion ... human suffering makes a direct moral appeal, namely, an appeal for help, while there is no similar call to increase the happiness of a man who is doing well anyway" (*Open Society Vol. 1*, 284). He added:

A further criticism of the Utilitarian formula 'Maximize pleasure' is that it assumes, in principle, a continuous pleasure-pain scale which allows us to treat degrees of pain as negative degrees of pleasure. But, from a moral point of view, pain cannot be outweighed by pleasure, and especially not one man's pain by another man's pleasure (Ibid.).

In arguing against what we might call "positive utilitarianism," Popper stressed the dangers of utopianism. Attempts to increase happiness, especially when guided by some ideal of complete or perfect happiness, are bound to lead to perilous utopian political projects. "It leads invariably to the attempt to impose our scale of 'higher' values upon others, in order to make them realize what seems to us of greatest importance for their happiness; in order, as it were to save their souls. It leads to Utopianism and Romanticism" (*Open Society Vol 11.*, 237). In addition, such projects are dangerous because they tend to justify extreme measures, including severe human suffering in the present, as necessary measures to secure a much greater human happiness in the future. "[W]e must not argue that the misery of one generation may be considered as a mere means to the end of securing the lasting happiness of some later generation or generations" (*Conjectures and Refutations*, 362). Moreover, such projects are doomed to fail anyway, owing to the unintended consequences of social planning and the irreconcilability of the ultimate humans ends of freedom, equality, and happiness. Thus Popper's rejection of positive utilitarianism becomes part of his broader critique of utopian social engineering, while his advocacy of negative utilitarianism is tied to his support for piecemeal social engineering. It is piecemeal engineering that provides the proper approach to tackling the identifiable, concrete sources of suffering in our world.

Finally, Popper offered the pragmatic argument that negative utilitarianism approach "adds to clarify the field of ethics" by requiring that "we formulate our demands negatively" (*Open Society Vol. 1*, 285.). Properly understood, Popper says, the aim of science is "the elimination of false theories ... rather than the attainment of established truths" (Ibid.). Similarly, ethical public policy may benefit by aiming at "the elimination of suffering rather than the promotion of happiness" (Ibid.). Popper thought that reducing suffering provides a clearer target for public policy than chasing after the will-o'-the-wisp, never-ending goal of increasing happiness. In addition, he argued, it easier to reach political agreement to combat suffering than to increase happiness, thus making effective public policy more likely. "For new ways of happiness are theoretical, unreal things, about which it may be difficult to form an opinion. But misery is with us, here and now, and it will be with us for a long time to come. We all know it from experience" (*Conjectures and Refutations*, 346). Popper thus calls for a public policy that aims at reducing and, hopefully, eliminating such readily identifiable and universally agreed upon sources of suffering as "poverty, unemployment, national oppression, war, and disease" (*Conjectures and Refutations,* 361).

Libertarian, Conservative or Social Democrat?

Popper's political thought would seem to fit most comfortably within the liberal camp, broadly understood. Reason, toleration, nonviolence and individual freedom formed the core of his political values, and, as we have seen, he identified modern liberal democracies as the best-to-date embodiment of an open society. But where, precisely, did he reside within liberalism? Here Popper's thought is difficult to categorize, as it includes elements of libertarianism, conservatism, and socialism—and, indeed, representatives from each of these schools have claimed him for their side.

The case for Popper's libertarianism rests mainly on his emphasis on freedom and his hostility to large-scale central planning. He insisted that freedom—understood as individual freedom—is the most important political value and that efforts to impose equality can lead to tyranny. "Freedom is more important than equality," he wrote, and "the attempt to realize equality endangers freedom" (*Unended Quest,* 36.) Popper also had great admiration for Friedrich Hayek, the libertarian economist from the so-called Austrian school, and he drew heavily upon his ideas in his critique of central planning. However, Popper also espoused many views that would be anathema to libertarians. Although he acknowledged "the tremendous benefit to be derived from the mechanism of free markets," he seemed to regard economic freedom as important mainly for its instrumental role in producing wealth rather than as an important end in itself (*Open Society Vol 11.*, 124). Further, he warned of the dangers of unbridled capitalism, even declaring that "the injustice and inhumanity of the unrestrained 'capitalist system' described by Marx cannot be questioned" (Ibid.). The state therefore must serve as a counteracting force against the predations of concentrated economic power: "We must construct social institutions, enforced by the power of the state, for the protection of the economically weak from the economically strong" (*Open Society Vol 11.*, 125). This meant that the "principle of non-intervention, of an unrestrained economic system, has to be given up" and replaced by "economic interventionism" (Ibid.) Such interventionism, which he also called "protectionism," would be implemented via the piecemeal social engineering described above. This top-down and technocratic vision of politics is hard to reconcile with libertarianism, whose adherents, following Hayek, tend to believe that such social engineering is generally counterproductive, enlarges the power and thus the danger of the state, and violates individual freedom.

It is in this interventionist role for the state where the socialistic elements of Popper's political theory are most evident. In his intellectual autobiography *Unended Quest*, Popper says that he was briefly a Marxist in his youth, but soon rejected the doctrine for what he saw as its adherents' dogmatism and embrace of violence. Socialism nonetheless remained appealing to him, and he remained a socialist for "several years" after abandoning Marxism (*Unended Quest*, 36). "For nothing could be better," he wrote, "than living a modest, simple, and free life in an egalitarian society" (Ibid.). However, eventually he concluded that socialism was "no more than a beautiful dream," and the dream is undone by the conflict between freedom and equality (Ibid.).

But though Popper saw utopian efforts to create true social and economic equality as dangerous and doomed to fail anyway, he continued to support efforts by the state to reduce and even eliminate the worst effects of capitalism. As we saw above, he advocated the use of piecemeal social engineering to tackle the problems of poverty, unemployment, disease and "rigid class differences." And it is clear that for Popper the solutions to these problems need not be market-oriented solutions. For instance, he voiced support for establishing a minimum income for all citizens as a means to eliminate poverty. It seems then that his politics put into practice would produce a society more closely resembling the so-called social democracies of northern Europe, with their more generous social welfare programs and greater regulation of industry, than the United States, with its more laissez-faire capitalism and comparatively paltry social welfare programs. That said, it should be noted that in later editions of *The Open Society*,

Popper grew somewhat more leery of direct state intervention to tackle social problems, preferring tinkering with the state's legal framework, if possible, to address them. He reasoned that direct intervention by the state always empowers the state, which endangers freedom.

Evidence of Popper's conservatism can be found in his opposition to radical change. His critique of utopian engineering at times seems to echo Edmund Burke's critique of the French Revolution. Burke depicted the bloodletting of the Terror as an object lesson in the dangers of sweeping aside all institutions and traditions overnight and replacing them with an abstract and untested social blueprint. Also like Burke and other traditional conservatives, Popper emphasized the importance of tradition for ensuring order, stability and well-functioning institutions. People have an inherent need for regularity and thus predictability in their social environment, Popper argued, which tradition is crucial for providing. However, there are important differences between Popper's and Burke's understanding of tradition. Popper included Burke, as well as the influential 20th-century conservative Michael Oakeshott, in the camp of the "anti-rationalists." This is because "their attitude is to accept tradition as something just given"; that is, they "accept tradition *uncritically*" (*Conjectures and Refutations*, 120, 122, Popper's emphasis). Such an attitude treats the values, beliefs and practices of a particular tradition as "taboo." Popper, in contrast, advocated a "*critical* attitude" toward tradition (Ibid., Popper's emphasis). "We free ourselves from the taboo if we think about it, and if we ask ourselves whether we should accept it or reject" (Ibid.). Popper emphasized that a critical attitude does not require stepping outside of all traditions, something Popper denied was possible. Just as criticism in the sciences always targets particular theories and also always takes place from the standpoint of some theory, so to for social criticism with respect to tradition. Social criticism necessarily focuses on particular traditions and does so from the standpoint of a tradition. In fact, the critical attitude toward tradition is itself a tradition — namely the *scientific* tradition — that dates back to the ancient Greeks of the 5th and 6th century B.C.E.

Popper's theory of democracy also arguably contained conservative elements insofar as it required only a limited role for the average citizen in governing. As we saw above, the primary role of the public in Popper's democracy is to render a verdict on the success or failure of a government's policies. For Popper public policy is not to be created through the kind of inclusive public deliberation envisioned by advocates of radical or participatory democracy. Much less is it to be implemented by ordinary citizens. Popper summed up his view by quoting Pericles, the celebrated statesman of Athenian democracy in 5th-century B.C.E.: "'Even if only a few of us are capable of devising a policy or putting it into practice, all of us are capable of judging it'." Popper added, "Please note that [this view] discounts the notion of rule by the people, and even of popular initiative. Both are replaced with the very different idea of *judgement by the people*" (*Lessons of This Century*, 72, Popper's emphasis). This view in some ways mirrors traditional conservatives' support for rule by "natural aristocrats," as Burke called them, in a democratic society. Ideally, elected officials would be drawn from the class of educated gentlemen, who would be best fit to hold positions of leadership owing to their superior character, judgment and experience. However, in Popper's system, good public policy in a democracy would result not so much from the superior wisdom or character of its leadership but rather from their commitment to the scientific method. As discussed above, this entailed implementing policy changes in a piecemeal fashion and testing them through the process of trial and error. Popper's open society is technocratic rather than aristocratic.

Antinomianism

In Christianity, an antinomian is "one who holds that under the gospel dispensation of grace the moral law is of no use or obligation because faith alone is necessary to salvation". Many antinomians, however, believe that Christians will obey the moral law despite their freedom from it. The distinction between antinomian and other Christian views on the moral law is that antinomians believe that obedience to the law is motivated by an internal principle flowing from belief rather than any external compulsion.

The term *antinomianism* emerged soon after the Protestant Reformation (c.1517) and has historically been used as a pejorative against Christian thinkers or sects who carried their belief in justification by faith further than was customary. Antinomianism in modern times is commonly seen as the theological opposite to Legalism or Works righteousness, the notion that obedience to religious law earns salvation. This makes antinomianism an exaggeration of justification by faith alone.

Examples are Martin Luther's critique of antinomianism and the Antinomian Controversy of the 17th century Massachusetts Bay Colony. Although the term originated in the 16th century, the topic has its roots in Christian views on the old covenant extending back to the 1st century. It can also be extended to any individual who rejects a socially established morality. Few groups, other than Christian anarchists or Jewish anarchists, explicitly call themselves antinomian.

Christianity

Antinomianism has been a point of doctrinal contention in the history of Christianity, especially in Protestantism. Given the Protestant belief in justification through faith alone, versus on the basis of merit or good works or works of mercy, most Protestants consider themselves saved without having to keep the commandments of the Mosaic Law as a whole. However, consistent with the Reformed formula, "We are justified by faith alone but not by a faith that is alone", salvific faith has overall been seen as one that effected obedience, in contrast to rejecting moral constraint.

The term "antinomianism" was coined by Martin Luther during the Reformation, to criticize extreme interpretations of the new Lutheran soteriology. The contemporary Evangelical theologian J. I. Packer states that Antinomianism "which means being anti-law, is a name for several views."

A general consensus has been historically reached as to which laws of the Old Testament Christians are still enjoined to keep. These moral laws, as opposed to civil or ceremonial laws, are derivative of what St. Paul refers to as the natural law (Rom. 2.14-15). Mosaic law has authority only insofar as it reflects the commands of Christ and the natural law. Christian sects and theologians who believe that they are freed from more moral constraint than is customary are often called "antinomian" by their critics. Thus the classic Methodist commentator Adam Clarke held, "The Gospel proclaims liberty from the ceremonial law: but binds you still faster under the moral law. To be freed from the ceremonial law is the Gospel liberty; to pretend freedom from the moral law is Antinomianism."

Gnosticism

Although the term designating this error came into use only in the sixteenth century, the doctrine itself can be traced in the teaching of the earlier heresies. Early Gnostic sects were accused of failure to follow the Mosaic Law in terms that suggest the modern term "antinomian". Some Gnostic sects did not accept parts of the Old Testament moral law. For example, the Manichaeans held that their spiritual being was unaffected by the action of matter and regarded carnal sins as being, at worst, forms of bodily disease. Marcionism, though technically not gnostic, rejected the Hebrew Bible in its entirety. Such deviations from the moral law were criticized by proto-orthodox rivals of the Gnostics, who ascribed various aberrant and licentious acts to them. A biblical example of such criticism can be found in Revelation 2:6–15, which criticizes the Nicolaitanes, an early Gnostic sect.

Lutheranism

The term "antinomianism" was coined by Martin Luther during the Reformation, to criticize extreme interpretations of the new Lutheran soteriology. The Lutheran Church benefited from early antinomian controversies by becoming more precise in distinguishing between Law and Gospel and justification and sanctification. Martin Luther developed 258 theses during his six antinomian disputations, which continue to provide doctrinal guidance to Lutherans today.

Upon hearing that he was being charged with rejection of the Old Testament moral law, Luther responded: "And truly, I wonder exceedingly, how it came to be imputed to me, that I should reject the Law or ten Commandments, there being extant so many of my own expositions (and those of several sorts) upon the Commandments, which also are daily expounded, and used in our Churches, to say nothing of the Confession and Apology, and other books of ours." In his "Introduction to Romans," Luther stated that saving faith is, "a living, creative, active and powerful thing, this faith. Faith cannot help doing good works constantly. It doesn't stop to ask if good works ought to be done, but before anyone asks, it already has done them and continues to do them without ceasing. Anyone who does not do good works in this manner is an unbeliever...Thus, it is just as impossible to separate faith and works as it is to separate heat and light from fire!"

First Antinomian Controversy

As early as 1525, Johannes Agricola, in his commentary on Luke, advanced his idea that the law was a futile attempt of God to work the restoration of mankind. He maintained that while non-Christians were still held to the Mosaic law, Christians were entirely free from it, being under the Gospel alone. He viewed sin as a malady or impurity rather than an offence rendering the sinner guilty and damnable before God. The sinner was the subject of God's pity rather than of his wrath. To Agricola, the purpose of repentance was to abstain from evil rather than the contrition of a guilty conscience. The law had no role in repentance, which came about after one came to faith and was caused by the knowledge of the love of God alone. In contrast, Philipp Melanchthon urged that repentance must precede faith, and that knowledge of the moral law is needed to produce repentance. He later wrote in the Augsburg Confession, that repentance had two parts. "One is contrition, that is, terrors smiting the conscience through the knowledge of sin; the other is faith, which is born of the Gospel, or of absolution, and believes that for Christ's sake, sins are forgiven, comforts the conscience, and delivers it from terrors."

Shortly after Melanchthon drew up the *1527 Articles of Visitation* in June, Agricola began to be verbally aggressive toward him, but Martin Luther succeeded in smoothing out the difficulty at Torgau in December 1527. However, Agricola did not change his ideas, and later depicted Luther as disagreeing with him. After Agricola moved to Wittenberg, he still maintained that while the law must be used in the courthouse, it must not be used in the church. He said that repentance comes from hearing the good news only and does not precede but rather follows faith. He continued to disseminate this doctrine in books, despite receiving various warnings from Luther.

Luther, with reluctance, at last believed he had to make public comment against antinomianism and its promoters in 1538 and 1539. Agricola apparently yielded, and Luther's book *Against the Antinomians* (1539) was to serve as Agricola's recantation. This was the first use of the term Antinomian. But the conflict flared up again, and Agricola sued Luther. He said that Luther had slandered him in his disputations, *Against the Antinomians*, and in his *On the Councils and Churches* (1539). But before the case could be brought to trial, Agricola, though he had bound himself to remain at Wittenberg, left the city and moved to Berlin, where he had been offered a position as preacher to the court. After his arrival there, he made peace with the Saxons, acknowledged his "error", and gradually conformed his doctrine to that which he had before opposed and assailed. He still used such terms as gospel and repentance in a different manner than Luther.

Second Antinomian Controversy

The antinomian doctrine, however, was not eliminated from Lutheranism. Melanchthon and those who agreed with him, called Philippists, were checked by the Gnesio-Lutherans in the Second Antinomian Controversy during the Augsburg Interim. The Philippists ascribed to the Gospel alone the ability to work repentance, to the exclusion of the law. They blurred the distinction between Law and Gospel by considering the Gospel itself to be a moral law. They did not identify Christ's fulfillment of the law with the commandments which humans are expected to follow. As a result, the Book of Concord rejects antinomianism in the last confession of faith. The Formula of Concord rejects antinominism in the fifth article, *On the Law and the Gospel* and in the sixth article, *On the Third Use of the Law.*

Calvinism

A number of seventeenth-century English writers in the Reformed tradition held antinomian beliefs. None of these individuals argued that Christians would not obey the law. Instead, they believed that believers would spontaneously obey the law without external motivation. Antinomianism during this period is likely a reaction against Arminianism, as it emphasized free grace in salvation to the detriment of any participation on the part of the believer. John Eaton is often identified as the father of English antinomianism.

From the latter part of the 18th century, critics of Calvinists accused them of antinomianism. Such charges were frequently raised by Arminian Methodists, who subscribed to a synergistic soteriology that contrastedwith Calvinism's monergistic doctrine of justification.

The controversy between Arminian and Calvinistic Methodists produced the notable Arminian critique of Calvinism: Fletcher's *Five Checks to Antinomianism* (1771–75).

The Westminster Confession of Faith states: "Faith, thus receiving and resting on Christ and His righteousness, is the alone instrument of justification; yet it is not alone in the person justified, but is ever accompanied with all other saving graces, and is no dead faith, but works by love."

Quakers

Quakers were charged with antinomianism due to their rejection of a graduate clergy and a clerical administrative structure, as well as their reliance on the Spirit (as revealed by the Inner Light of God within each person) rather than the Scriptures.

They also rejected civil legal authorities and their laws (such as the paying of tithes to the State church and the swearing of oaths) when they were seen as inconsistent with the promptings of the Inner Light of God.

Jesuits

Blaise Pascal accused the Jesuits of antinomianism in his *Lettres provinciales*, charging that Jesuit casuistry undermined moral principles.

Charges against Other Groups

Other Protestant groups that have been accused of antinomianism include the Anabaptists and Mennonites. In the history of American Puritanism, Roger Williams and Anne Hutchinson were accused of antinomian teachings by the Puritan leadership of Massachusetts, see Antinomian Controversy.

The Ranters of 17th century England were one of the most outright antinomian sects in the history of Christianity. New Covenant Theology has been accused of antinomianism for their belief that the Ten Commandments have been abrogated, but they point out that nine of these ten are renewed under the New Covenant's Law of Christ.

Biblical Law in Christianity

The question of the obligation to follow the Mosaic Law was a point of contention in the Early Christian Church. Many early converts were Greek and thus had less interest in adherence to the Law of Moses than did the earliest Christians, who were primarily Jewish and already accustomed to the Law. Thus, as Christianity spread into new cultures, the early church was pressured to decide which laws were still required of Christians, and which were no longer required under the New Covenant. The New Testament, (especially the book of Acts) is interpreted by some as recording the church slowly abandoning the "ritual laws" of Judaism, such as circumcision, Sabbath and kosher law, while remaining in full agreement on adherence to the "divine law", or Jewish laws on morality, such as the Ten Commandments. Thus, the early Christian church incorporated ideas sometimes seen as *partially antinomian* or parallel to Dual-covenant theology, while still upholding the traditional laws of moral behaviour.

The first major dispute over Christian antinomianism was a dispute over whether circumcision was required of Christians. This happened at the Council of Jerusalem, which is dated to about 50 AD and recorded in the book of Acts 15:5.

But some believers who belonged to the sect of the Pharisees stood up and said, 'It is necessary for them to be circumcised and ordered to keep the law of Moses.'

—NRSV

The apostles and elders met at Jerusalem, and after a spirited discussion, their conclusion, later called the *Apostolic Decree*, possibly a major act of differentiation of the Church from its Jewish roots (the first being the Rejection of Jesus), was recorded in Acts 15:19-21:

Acts 15:(19) Wherefore my [James] sentence is, that we trouble not them, which from among the Gentiles are turned to God: (20) But that we write unto them, that they abstain from pollutions of idols, and from fornication, and from things strangled, and from blood. (21) For Moses of old time hath in every city them that preach him, being read in the synagogues every sabbath day.

—KJV

Beginning with Augustine of Hippo, many have seen a connection to Noahide Law, while some modern scholars reject the connection to *Noahide Law*.

James sets out a preliminary list of commands which Gentiles should obey. Gentiles were not required to be circumcised, but were required to obey the four beginning requirements to be part of the larger congregation. This passage shows that the remainder of the commandments would follow as they studied "Moses" in the Synagogues. If Gentiles did not follow this reduced requirement, they risked being put out of the Synagogue and missing out on a Torah education (in Leviticus 17 and 20). James's list still includes some dietary commands, but many of those also passed out of some Christian traditions quite early. Acts 10:9-16 describes the following vision, which was used to excuse early gentile Christians from the Mosaic dietary laws. (9) ...Peter went up upon the housetop to pray about the sixth hour: (10) And he became very hungry, and would have eaten: but while they made ready, he fell into a trance, (11) And saw heaven opened, and a certain vessel descending unto him, as it had been a great sheet knit at the four corners, and let down to the earth: (12) Wherein were all manner of fourfooted beasts of the earth, and wild beasts, and creeping things, and fowls of the air. (13) And there came a voice to him, Rise, Peter; kill, and eat. (14) But Peter said, Not so, Lord; for I have never eaten any thing that is common or unclean. (15) And the voice spake unto him again the second time, What God hath cleansed, that call not thou common. (16) This was done thrice: and the vessel was received up again into heaven.

—KJV

Peter was perplexed about the vision in Acts 10. His subsequent explanation of the vision in Acts 11 gives no credence to antinomianism as it relates to the inapplicability of the Mosaic dietary laws.

Though the *Apostolic Decree* is no longer observed by many Christian denominations today, it is still observed in full by the Greek Orthodox.

In the Letter to the Hebrews (Hebrews 7:11-28), it is written that under the Old Testament Law, priests had to be from the tribe of Levi, Aaron and his sons:

Bring his sons and dress them in tunics and put headbands on them. Then tie sashes on Aaron and his sons. The priesthood is theirs by a lasting ordinance. In this way you shall ordain Aaron and his sons.

—Exodus 29:8-9

It is pointed out that Jesus was from the tribe of Judah, and thus Jesus could not be a priest under the Old Testament Law, as Jesus is not a descendant of Aaron. It states that the Law had to change for Jesus to be the High Priest: "For when there is a change of the priesthood, there must also be a change of the law." (Hebrews 7:12)

Supporting Pauline Passages

The Apostle Paul, in his Letters, says that believers are saved by the unearned grace of God, not by good works, "lest anyone should boast", and placed a priority on orthodoxy (right belief) before orthopraxy (right practice). The soteriology of Paul's statements in this matter has long been a matter of dispute. The ancient gnostics interpreted Paul, for example in 2 Peter 3:16, to be referring to the manner in which embarking on a path to enlightenment ultimately leads to enlightenment, which was their idea of what constituted salvation. In what has become the modern Protestant orthodoxy, however, this passage is interpreted as a reference to justification by trusting Christ.

Paul used the term *freedom in Christ*, for example, Galatians 2:4. Some understood this to mean "lawlessness" (i.e. not obeying Mosaic Law). For example, in Acts 18:12-16, Paul is accused of "persuading .. people to worship God in ways contrary to the law."

In Acts 21:21James the Just explained his situation to Paul:

And they are informed of thee, that thou teachest all the Jews which are among the Gentiles to forsake Moses, saying that they ought not to circumcise their children, neither to walk after the customs.

—KJV

Colossians 2:13-14 is sometimes presented as proof of Paul's antinomistic views. For example, the NIV translates these verses: "...he forgave us all our sins, having canceled the written code, with its regulations, that was against us and that stood opposed to us; he took it away, nailing it to the cross." But, the NRSV translates this same verse as: "...he forgave us all our trespasses, erasing the record that stood against us with its legal demands. He set this aside, nailing it to the cross." This latter translation makes it sound as though it is a *record of trespasses*, rather than *the Law itself*, that was "nailed to the cross." The interpretation partly depends on the original Greek word ÷åéñüãñáöïí which, according to Strong's G5498, literally means "something written by hand;" it is variously translated as "written code" or "record", as in a record of debt.

2 Corinthians 3:6-17 says,

"Who also hath made us able ministers of the new testament; not of the letter, but of the spirit: for the letter killeth, but the spirit giveth life. But if the ministration of death, written and engraven in stones, was glorious, so that the children of Israel could not stedfastly behold the face of Moses for the glory of his countenance; which glory was to be done away: How shall not the ministration of the spirit be rather glorious? For if the ministration of condemnation be glory, much more doth the ministration of righteousness exceed in glory. For even that which was made glorious had no glory in this respect, by reason of the glory that excelleth. For if that which is done away was glorious, much more that which remaineth is glorious. Seeing then that we have such hope, we use great plainness of speech: And not as Moses, which put a veil over his face, that the children of Israel could not stedfastly look to the end of that which is abolished: But their minds were blinded: for until this day remaineth the same vail untaken away in the reading of the old testament; which vail is done away in Christ. But even unto this day, when Moses is read, the vail is upon their heart. Nevertheless when it shall turn to the Lord, the vail shall be taken away. Now the Lord is that Spirit: and where the Spirit of the Lord is, there is liberty." (KJV)

Some cite Acts 13:39 (for what purpose?): "And by him all that believe are justified from all things, from which ye could not be justified by the law of Moses." But this is more about Justification (theology) than *antinomianism*.

Romans 6 states twice that believers are not under the law: Romans 6:14 "For sin shall not have dominion over you: for ye are not under the law, but under grace" and Romans 6:15 "What then? shall we sin, because we are not under the law, but under grace? God forbid.". KJV

Galatians 3:1-5 describes the Galatians as "foolish" for relying on being observant to the Law: "(1) O foolish Galatians, who hath bewitched you, that ye should not obey the truth, before whose eyes Jesus Christ hath been evidently set forth, crucified among you? (2) This only would I learn of you, Received ye the Spirit by the works of the law, or by the hearing of faith? (3) Are ye so foolish? having begun in the Spirit, are ye now made perfect by the flesh? (4) Have ye suffered so many things in vain? if it be yet in vain. (5) He therefore that ministereth to you the Spirit, and worketh miracles among you, doeth he it by the works of the law, or by the hearing of faith?" KJV

Galatians 3:23-25 says that the purpose of the Law was to lead people to Christ, once people believe in Christ, they are no longer under the Law:

"(23) But before faith came, we were kept under the law, shut up unto the faith which should afterwards be revealed. (24) Wherefore the law was our schoolmaster to bring us unto Christ, that we might be justified by faith.(25) But after that faith is come, we are no longer under a schoolmaster." KJV

In Galatians 4:21-31, Paul compares the Old Covenant with the New Covenant through Supersessionism. In this comparison, he equates each covenant with a woman, using the wives of Abraham as examples. The old covenant is equated with the slave woman, Hagar, and the new covenant is equated with the free woman Sarah.(Galatians 4:22-26). He concludes this example by saying that we are not children of the slave woman, but children of the free woman. In other words, we are not under the old covenant, we are under the new covenant.

"(22) For it is written, that Abraham had two sons, the one by a bondmaid, the other by a freewoman. (23) But he who was of the bondwoman was born after the flesh; but he of the freewoman was by promise. (24) Which things are an allegory: for these are the two covenants; the one from the mount Sinai, which gendereth to bondage, which is Agar. (25) For this Agar is mount Sinai in Arabia, and answereth to Jerusalem which now is, and is in bondage with her children. (26) But Jerusalem which is above is free, which is the mother of us all." KJV(Galatians 4:30-31)

Romans 10:4 is sometimes translated: "For Christ is the end of the law for righteousness to every one that believeth." (KJV) The key word here is *telos* (Strong's G5056). Robert Badenas argues that *telos* is correctly translated as goal, not end, so that Christ is the *goal* of the Law. Andy Gaus' version of the New Testament translates this verse as: "Christ is what the law aims at: for every believer to be on the right side of [God's] justice."

Also cited (where? by whom?) is Ephesians 2:15: "Having abolished in his flesh the enmity, even the law of commandments contained in ordinances; for to make in himself of twain one new man, so making peace" KJV. Another passage cited is Romans 7:1-7, especially Romans 7:4 "Wherefore, my brethren, ye also are become dead to the law by the body of Christ; that ye should be married to another, even to him who is raised from the dead, that we should bring forth fruit unto God" and Romans 7:6 "But now we are delivered from the law, that being dead wherein we were held; that we should serve in newness of spirit, and not in the oldness of the letter." KJV

The first covenant (made with Israel, as recorded in the Old Testament) is compared with the new covenant in Hebrews 8-9. In Hebrews 8:6-7: "But the ministry Jesus has received is as superior to theirs as the covenant of which he is mediator is superior to the old one, and it is founded on better promises. For if there had been nothing wrong with that first covenant, no place would have been sought for another."

It goes on to say that the problem with the first covenant was with the people who were supposed to keep it, and that in the new covenant: "I will put my laws into their minds, and write them on their hearts, and I will be their God, and they shall be my people." Hebrews 8:10

The first covenant was said to be obsolete, and would soon disappear: "By calling this covenant "new," he has made the first one obsolete; and what is obsolete and aging will soon disappear." Hebrews 8:13. It identifies the first covenant which is disappearing in Hebrews 9:1-5. Particularly the "stone tables of the covenant" in Hebrews 9:4 referred directly to the Ten Commandments.

"Now the first covenant had regulations for worship and also an earthly sanctuary. A tabernacle was set up. In its first room were the lampstand, the table and the consecrated bread; this was called the Holy Place. Behind the second curtain was a room called the Most Holy Place, which had the golden altar of incense and the gold-covered ark of the covenant. This ark contained the gold jar of manna, Aaron's staff that had budded, and the stone tablets of the covenant. Above the ark were the cherubim of the Glory, overshadowing the atonement cover." (Hebrews 9:1-5)

Some scholars consider Jesus' Sermon on the Mount (particularly the Antitheses) to be an antitype of the proclamation of the Ten Commandments or Mosaic Covenant by Moses from the Biblical Mount Sinai.

Opposing Pauline Passages

Those who oppose antinomianism invoke Paul as upholding obedience to the law, in living out a saving faith:

- "For as many as have sinned without law shall also perish without law: and as many as have sinned in the law shall be judged by the law; (For not the hearers of the law are just before God, but the doers of the law shall be justified." Romans 2:12–13 KJV
- "Do we then make void the law through faith? God forbid: yea, we establish the law." Romans 3:31 KJV
- "Because the carnal mind is enmity against God: for it is not subject to the law of God, neither indeed can be. So then they that are in the flesh cannot please God." Romans 8:7–8 KJV
- "While he answered for himself, Neither against the law of the Jews, neither against the temple, nor yet against Cæsar, have I offended any thing at all." Acts 25:8 KJV
- "Say I these things as a man? or saith not the law the same also? For it is written in the law of Moses, Thou shalt not muzzle the mouth of the ox that treadeth out the corn. Doth God take care for oxen? " 1 Corinthians 9:8-9 KJV
- "Let your women keep silence in the churches: for it is not permitted unto them to speak; but they are commanded to be under obedience, as also saith the law." 1 Corinthians 14:34 KJV (Need cite for these selections -)
- "But now I have written unto you not to keep company, if any man that is called a brother be a fornicator, or covetous, or an idolater, or a railer, or a drunkard, or an extortioner; with such an one no not to eat." 1 Corinthians 5:11 KJV
- "Know ye not that the unrighteous shall not inherit the kingdom of God? Be not deceived: neither fornicators, nor idolaters, nor adulterers, nor effeminate, nor abusers of themselves with mankind, Nor thieves, nor covetous, nor drunkards, nor revilers, nor extortioners, shall inherit the kingdom of God." 1 Corinthians 6:9-10:26 KJV
- "Neither be ye idolaters, as were some of them; as it is written, The people sat down to eat and drink, and rose up to play." 1 Corinthians 10:7 KJV
- "The wife is bound by the law as long as her husband liveth; but if her husband be dead, she is at liberty to be married to whom she will; only in the Lord." 1 Corinthians 7:39 KJV

- "Wherefore, my dearly beloved, flee from idolatry." 1 Corinthians 10:14 KJV
- "Now the works of the flesh are manifest, which are these; Adultery, fornication, uncleanness, lasciviousness, Idolatry, witchcraft, hatred, variance, emulations, wrath, strife, seditions, heresies, Envyings, murders, drunkenness, revellings, and such like: of the which I tell you before, as I have also told you in time past, that they which do such things shall not inherit the kingdom of God." Galatians 5:19–21 KJV
- "For this ye know, that no whoremonger, nor unclean person, nor covetous man, who is an idolater, hath any inheritance in the kingdom of Christ and of God. Let no man deceive you with vain words: for because of these things cometh the wrath of God upon the children of disobedience. " Ephesians 5:5-6 KJV
- "Mortify therefore your members which are upon the earth; fornication, uncleanness, inordinate affection, evil concupiscence, and covetousness, which is idolatry." Colossians 3:5 KJV
- "But if any provide not for his own, and specially for those of his own house, he hath denied the faith, and is worse than an infidel." 1 Timothy 5:8 KJV
- "Children, obey your parents in the Lord: for this is right. Honour thy father and mother; (which is the first commandment with promise." Ephesians 6:1-2 KJV (Need cite for these selections -)

Theology

The *Catholic Encyclopedia* article on "Judaizers" notes: "Paul, on the other hand, not only did not object to the observance of the Mosaic Law, as long as it did not interfere with the liberty of the Gentiles, but he conformed to its prescriptions when occasion required (1 Corinthians 9:20). Thus he shortly after the Council of Jerusalem circumcised Timothy (Acts 16:1-3), and he was in the very act of observing the Mosaic ritual when he was arrested at Jerusalem (21:26 sqq.)."

The *Jewish Encyclopedia* article on "Gentile: Gentiles May Not Be Taught the Torah" notes the following reconciliation: "R. Emden, in a remarkable apology for Christianity contained in his appendix to "Seder 'Olam," gives it as his opinion that the original intention of Jesus, and especially of Paul, was to convert only the Gentiles to the seven moral laws of Noah and to let the Jews follow the Mosaic law—this explains the apparent contradictions in the New Testament regarding the laws of Moses and the Sabbath."

The Tübingen school of historians founded by F. C. Baur holds that in Early Christianity, there was conflict between Pauline Christianity and the Jerusalem Church led by James the Just, Simon Peter, and John the Apostle, the so-called "Jewish Christians" or "Pillars of the Church." In many places Paul writes that he was an observant Jew, and that Christians should "uphold the Law" (Romans 3:31). In Galatians 2:14, part of the Incident at Antioch, Paul publicly accused Peter of judaizing. Even so, he says sins remain sins, and upholds by several examples the kind of behaviour that the church should not tolerate (e.g., Galatians 5:19-21, 1 Cor 6:9-10). In 1 Corinthians 7:10-16 he cites Jesus' teaching on divorce ("not I but the Lord") and does not reject it, but goes on to proclaim his own teaching ("I, not the Lord"), an extended counsel regarding a specific situation which some interpret as conforming to what the Lord said. But, this may mean he received direct knowledge of what the Lord wanted him to teach through the Holy Ghost (Galatians 2:6-10).

Paul versus James

The Epistle of James, in contrast, states that our good works justify before men, our faith after salvation, and we are to obey the Law of God, that "a person is justified by works and not by faith alone", that "faith without works is dead" (James 2:14–26). Historically, this statement has been difficult for Protestants to reconcile with their belief in justification by faith alone. Martin Luther, believing that his doctrines were refuted by this passage, suggested that the Epistle might be a forgery, and relegated it to an appendix in his Bible (although he later came to accept it as part of the canon). Though this may be interpreted through the word "justified." It speaks that faith in Jesus Christ is the first step and that faith is justified through good works, he goes on to say that without spreading your love and faith, it is dead. Literature which discusses this includes the article on *James 2:20* in *Law and Gospel. Romans* 2:6, Ephesians 2:8-10, and Joint Declaration on the Doctrine of Justification.

James also wrote: "For whoever keeps the whole law and yet stumbles at just one point is guilty of breaking all of it. For he who said, 'Do not commit adultery,' also said, 'Do not murder.' If you do not commit adultery but do commit murder, you have become a lawbreaker." James 2:10-11. One interpretation is that people who want to keep the Old Testament Law must perfectly keep all of the Law—"an impossible task." James appeals to his readers to follow the

"Royal Law of Love" instead in the preceding verses (James 2:8-9). But the scholar Alister McGrath says that James was the leader of a Judaizing party that taught that Gentiles must obey the entire Mosaic Law.

Paul made a statement that appears to agree with James, saying that "both" faith produced as a result of repentance (the initial requirement for justification) "and" works (the evidence or proof of true faith) must exist together:

"So then, King Agrippa, I was not disobedient to the vision from heaven. First to those in Damascus, then to those in Jerusalem and in all Judea, and to the Gentiles also, I preached that they should repent and turn to God and *prove their repentance by their deeds.*" Acts 26:19-20 (NIV)

Jesus

The Torah prescribes the death penalty for desecrating the Sabbath by working (Exodus 31:14-17). To avoid any possibility of breaking the Torah commands, the Pharisees formulated strict interpretations and numerous traditions which they treated as laws. According to the Christians, Jesus criticized the Pharisees for this (Mark 7:7-9). The *Jewish Encyclopedia* article on Jesus notes:

"Jesus, however, does not appear to have taken into account the fact that the Halakah was at this period just becoming crystallized, and that much variation existed as to its definite form; the disputes of Bet Hillel and Bet Shammai were occurring about the time of his maturity."

In the Gospel of Mark, Jesus' disciples were picking grain for food on the Sabbath (Mark 2:23-28). When the Pharisees challenged Jesus over this, he pointed to Biblical precedent and declared that "the Sabbath was made for man, not man for the Sabbath". Some claim Jesus rejected complete adherence to the Torah. Most scholars hold that Jesus did not reject the law, but directed that it should be obeyed in context. E. P. Sanders notes, "No substantial conflict existed between Jesus and the Pharisees with regard to Sabbath, food, and purity laws .... The church took some while to come to the position that the Sabbath need not be kept, and it is hard to think that Jesus explicitly said so." There may be passages where the words of Jesus have been misinterpreted and were not really in contradiction with the Jewish law.

In the Gospel of Matthew, Jesus is sometimes said to refer to people he sees as "wicked" with the term *ergazomenoi tçn anomian* (ñãáæüìåîïé ôtí íìì0áí) - e.g. Matthew 7:21-23, Matthew 13:40-43. Due to this negative context, the term has almost always been translated as "evildoers", although it literally means "workers of lawlessness". In Hebrew, lawlessness would imply "Torahlessness". Matthew appears to present Jesus as equating wickedness with encouraging antinomianism. Scholars view Matthew as having been written by or for a Jewish audience, the so-called Jewish Christians. Several scholars argue that Matthew artificially lessened a claimed rejection of Jewish law so as not to alienate his intended audience. But, Jesus called for full adherence to the commandments (Matthew 5:19-21) He declared: "Do not think that I have come to abolish the Law or the Prophets; I have not come to abolish them but to fulfill them." (Matthew 5:17). A parallel verse to Matthew 7:21 is James 1:22.

1 *John 3:4 states:* "Everyone who commits sin is guilty of lawlessness; sin is lawlessness."

Buddhism

Among some Buddhist groups there are types of 'antinomianism' which may act as a gloss for 'left-handed attainment' (Sanskrit: Vamachara): naturalist/spontaneous antinomianism, ritualist/ philosophical antinomianism, and empirical antinomianism. There may also be those who subscribe to all or some combination of these three types. Not all Buddhist schools accept antinomian thought as skillful.

Naturalist antinomians believe that enlightened beings may spontaneously break monastic codes of conduct while living out a natural state of enlightened mind. Another view is that an enlightened mind responds to circumstances based on Buddhist morality, rather than the legalism of the monastic codes, and that the "break" is not therefore spontaneous. There are tales of Buddhists who perform acts that appear to be bizarre or immoral, sometimes referred to as 'crazy wisdom' (Tibetan: yeshe chölwa). The movement of the Nyönpa in Seventeenth Century Tibet has strong associations with antinomian behaviour as well.

Ritualist antinomians, such as some Tantric Buddhists, may practice which seemingly may appear to be breaking the codes of conduct in specific religious rituals designed to teach non-duality or other philosophical concept. (refer Panchamakara; Ganachakra).

Empirical antinomians may break or disregard traditional ethical or moral rules that they believe are unconducive to the individual's contemplative life. They view such codification as having arisen in specific historical-cultural contexts and, as such, not always supportive of Buddhist training. Thus the individual and the community must test and verify which rules promote or hinder enlightenment.

Hinduism

Islam: In Islam, the law—which applies not only to religion, but also to areas such as politics, banking, and sexuality—is called *sharîah*, and it is traditionally organized around four primary sources:

1. the Qurân, which is Islam's central religious text;
2. the sunnah, which refers to actions practised during the time of the prophet Muhammad, and is often thought to include the *hadith*, or recorded words and deeds of Muhammad;
3. *ijma*, which is the consensus of the *'ulama*, or class of Islamic scholars, on points of practice;
4. *qiyas*, which—in Sunni Islam—is a kind of analogical reasoning conducted by the 'ulama' upon specific laws that have arisen through appeal to the first three sources; in Shiah Islam, *'aql* ("reason") is used in place of *qiyas*

Actions, behaviour, or beliefs that are considered to violate any or all of these four sources—primarily in matters of religion—can be termed "antinomian". Depending on the action, behaviour, or belief in question, a number of different terms can be used to convey the sense of "antinomian": *shirk* ("association of another being with God"); *bidah* ("innovation"); *kufr* ("disbelief"); *haram* ("forbidden"); etc.

As an example, the 10th-century Sufimystic Mansur Al-Hallaj was executed for *shirk* for, among other things, his statement *ana al-$aqq*, meaning "I am the Truth". As *al-$aqq* ("the Truth") is one of the 99 names of God in Islamic tradition, this would imply he was saying: "I am God." Expressions like these are known as *Shathiyat*. Another individual who has often been termed antinomian is Ibn al-¿Arabi, a 12th–13th century scholar and mystic whose doctrine of *wa%dat al-wujûd* ("unity of being") has sometimes been interpreted as being pantheistic, and thus *shirk*.

Apart from individuals, entire groups of Muslims have also been called antinomian. One of these groups is the Ismailism Shîîs, who have always had strong millenarian tendencies arising partly from persecution directed at them by Sunnîs. Influenced to a certain extent by Gnosticism, the Ismailis developed a number of beliefs and practices—such as their belief in the *imamah* and an esoteric exegesis of the Quran—that were different enough from Sunnî orthodoxy for them to be condemned as *shirk* and, hence, to be seen as antinomian. Certain other groups that evolved out of Shiah belief, such as the Alawites and the Bektashis, have also been considered antinomian. The Bektashis, particularly, have many practices that are especially antinomian in the context of Islam, such as the consumption of alcohol, the non-wearing of the *hijab* ("veil") by women, and gathering in the *cemevi* in preference to the mosque.

Left-Hand Path

In contemporary studies of esotericism, antinomianism is regarded as "a central ingredient in Left-Hand Path spiritualities," and understood as "nonconformity through the concept of transgression". This extends the modern usage of the term, from simply implying that "moral laws are relative in meaning and application", to include the avowed irreligion manifest in modern Satanism.

Nonreligious Usage

In his study of late-20th-century western society the historian Eric Hobsbawm stated that there was a new fusion of demotic and antinomian characteristics that made the period distinct, and appeared to be likely to extend into the future. For him there is now a readiness by the mass of people to have little sense of obligation to obey any set of rules that they consider arbitrary, or even just constraining, whatever its source. This may be facilitated by one or more of several changes. These include the tendency to live outside settled communities, the growth of enough wealth for most people to have a wide choice of styles of living and a popularised assumption that individual freedom is an unqualified good.

George Orwell was a frequent user of antinomian in a secular (and always approving) sense. In his 1940 essay on Henry Miller, "Inside the Whale", the word appears several times, including one in which he calls A. E. Housman a writer in "a blasphemous, antinomian, 'cynical' strain", meaning defiant of arbitrary societal rules.

Negative Utilitarianism

The basic idea of utilitarianism is to do the greatest good for the greatest number. A related idea, negative utilitarianism, requires us to prevent the greatest amount of suffering for the greatest number. According to its proponents, the greatest harms are more consequential than the greatest goods.

Would you rather avoid being tortured for a day, or engage in your favourite activity for a day? For many, the answer is obvious:

avoid torture. This synchs well with humanity's empirically demonstrated aversion to risk. It also makes sense evolutionarily, as avoiding pain was probably more adaptive than merely seeking pleasure.

Negative utilitarianism seems like a reasonable enough philosophy, at least at first. What could possibly be wrong with minimizing harm? Well, it turns out that the optimal implementation of negative utilitarianism would be to kill off all of humanity in the quickest and most painless way possible. That way, the probability of Earth-originating sentients experiencing harm in the future is reduced to zero. From the perspective of negative utilitarianism, this is the best possible outcome.

Hah! Now I'll bet you think negative utilitarianism sounds like a horrible idea, don't you? The problem is that it may be a philosophically appealing viewpoint to a subset of humanity. One challenge of futuristic technologies is that they may make possible the existence of groups that are unaccountable in practice. I'm not saying I *want* such groups to exist, or that such groups existing is a *good idea*, just that it could *actually happen* and we might be hard pressed to do anything about it. A prototype of such a scenario is given in the novel *Aristoi*, where aristocrats uses nanotechnology and brain-computer interfaces to ensure absolute dominance over the rest of humanity.

If an *Aristoi* class decides that negative utilitarianism makes sense, then from their perspective, it could be quite appealing to destroy all of humanity. Do we have any *intelligent strategies* for averting such a possibility?

Social Engineering (Political Science)

Social engineering is a discipline in social science that refers to efforts to influence popular attitudes and social behaviours on a large scale, whether by governments or private groups.

A social engineer is one who tries to influence popular attitudes, social behaviours, and resource management on a large scale. Social engineering is the application of the scientific method for social concern. Social engineers use the methods of science to analyze and understand social systems, so as to arrive at appropriate decisions as scientists, and not as politicians. In the political arena, the counterpart of social engineering is political engineering.

Decision-making can affect the safety and survival of literally billions of people. As expressed by German sociologist Ferdinand

Tönnies in his study *The Present Problems of Social Structure*, society can no longer operate successfully using outmoded methods of social management. To achieve the best outcomes, all conclusions and decisions must use the most advanced techniques and include reliable statistical data, which can be applied to a social system. In other words, social engineering is a data-based scientific system used to develop a sustainable design so as to achieve the intelligent management of Earth's resources with the highest levels of freedom, prosperity, and happiness within a population.

For various reasons, the term has been imbued with negative connotations. However, virtually all law and governance has the effect of seeking to change behaviour and could be considered "social engineering" to some extent. Prohibitions on murder, rape, suicide and littering are all policies aimed at discouraging undesirable behaviours. In British and Canadian jurisprudence, changing public attitudes about a behaviour is accepted as one of the key functions of laws prohibiting it. Governments also influence behaviour more subtly through incentives and disincentives built into economic policy and tax policy, for instance, and have done so for centuries.

History

The term *sociale ingenieurs* was introduced in an essay by the Dutch industrialist J.C. Van Marken in 1894. The idea was that modern employers needed the assistance of specialists—"social engineers"—in handling the *human* problems of the planet, just as they needed technical expertise (ordinary engineers) to deal with the problems of dead matter (materials, machines, processes). The term was brought to America in 1899, when the notion of "social engineering" was also launched as the name of the task of the social engineer in this sense. "Social engineering" was the title of a small journal in 1899 (from 1900 named "Social Service"), and in 1909 the title of a book by its former editor, William H. Tolman (translated in French in 1910), marking the end of the usage of the terminology in the sense of Van Marken. With the Social Gospel sociologist Edwin L. Earp's *The Social Engineer*, published during the "efficiency craze" of 1911 in the U.S., the usage of the term was launched that has since then been standard: the one building on a metaphor of social relations as "machineries", to be dealt with in the manner of the technical engineer.

Before one can engage in social engineering, one must have reliable information about the society that is to be engineered and effective tools to carry out the engineering. Both of these became available only relatively recently: roughly within the past one hundred years. The development of social science made it possible to gather and analyze information about social attitudes and trends, which is necessary in order to judge the initial state of society before an engineering attempt and the success or failure of that attempt after it has been implemented. At the same time, the development of modern communications technology and the media provided the tools through which social engineering could be carried out.

While social engineering can be carried out by any organization. Whether large or small, public or private, the most comprehensive (and often the most effective) campaigns of social engineering are those initiated by powerful central governments.

Extremely intensive social engineering campaigns occurred in countries with authoritarian governments. In the 1920s, the government of the Soviet Union embarked on a campaign to fundamentally alter the behaviour and ideals of Soviet citizens, to replace the old social frameworks of Tsarist Russia with a new Soviet culture, to create the New Soviet man. The Soviets used newspapers, books, film, mass relocations, and even architectural design tactics to serve as "social condenser" and change personal values and private relationships. Similar examples are the Chinese "Great Leap Forward" and "Cultural Revolution" program and the Khmer Rouge's plan of deurbanization of Cambodia. In Singapore, the government's housing policies attempt to promote a mix of all races within each subsidized housing district in order to foster social cohesion and national loyalty while providing citizens with affordable housing. In Tanzania in the 1970s, the government pursued a policy of enforced villagisation under Operation Vijiji in order to promote collective farming.

Non-authoritarian regimes tend to rely on more sustained social engineering campaigns that create more gradual, but ultimately far-reaching, change. Examples include the "War on Drugs" in the United States, the increasing reach of intellectual property rights and copyright, and the promotion of elections as a political tool. The campaign for promoting elections, which is by far the most successful of the three examples, has been in place for over two centuries. Social theorists of the Frankfurt School in Weimar Germany like Theodor Adorno had also observed the new phenomenon of mass culture and commented on its new manipulative power, when the rise of the Nazis drove them out of the country around 1930 (many of them became connected with the Institute for Social Research in the United States). The Nazis themselves were no strangers to the idea of influencing political attitudes and redefining personal relationships. The Nazi propaganda machine under Joseph Goebbels was a synchronized, sophisticated and effective tool for creating public opinion.

In a similar vein the Greek military junta of 1967–1974 attempted to steer Greek public opinion not only by propaganda but also by inventing new words and slogans such as *palaiokommatismos* (old-partyism), *Ellas Ellinon Christianon* (Greece of Christian Greeks), and *Ethnosotirios Epanastasis* (nation-saving revolution, meaning *coup d'état*).

Social engineering can be used as a means to achieve a wide variety of different results, as illustrated by the different governments and other organizations that have employed it. The discussion of the possibilities for such manipulation became especially active following World War II, with the advent of television, and continuing discussion of techniques of social engineering, particularly in advertising, is still quite pertinent in the western model of consumer capitalism.

Karl Popper

In his classic political science book, *The Open Society and Its Enemies*, volume I, *The Spell of Plato*, Karl Popper examined the application of the critical and rational methods of science to the problems of the open society. In this respect, he made a crucial distinction between the principles of *democratic* social engineering (what he called "piecemeal social engineering") and *Utopian* social engineering.

Popper Wrote: the piecemeal engineer will adopt the method of searching for, and fighting against, the greatest and most urgent evil of society, rather than searching for, and fighting for, its greatest ultimate good.

According to Popper, the difference between "piecemeal social engineering" and "Utopian social engineering" is:

the difference between a reasonable only method of improving matters which has so far been really successful, at any time, and in any place, and a method which, wherever it has been tried, has led only to the use of violence in place of reason, and if not to its own abandonment, at any rate to that of its original blueprint.

Piecemeal Social Engineering and the Politics of the Critical Rationalist Attack on Holism

If one wants a brief political introduction to the confused mind of this conservative thinker, then look no further than his essay on piecemeal and holistic social engineering. This essay, written in 1944 is tragically bad, it shows the depths of his technocratic understanding of politics (as engineers building and modifying institutions), the peculiar conservative motivations behind his confidence in the fundamental similarity of the natural and social sciences and the principles of experimentation, test and falsification therein and the lengths he will go to misrepresent the ultimate target of his scientific scepticism, namely Marxism, or any utopian or holistics (much of the same thing in Popper's book) and their pretensions towards total critique and total transformation of the prevailing order.

There are fundamental incongruities in Popper's argument. Many stem from the idea that social processes can be observed like natural laws as there are certain features of social organisation that act in a law like limiting way upon what can arise. Popper constantly conflates what is proper to the domain of scientific inquiry with conclusions about the possibilities of change in social and political life. In his mind-set piecemeal social reform is the only form of 'social engineering' that is in actually practiced.

This involves adaption of institutions and the creation of new ones (examples given include the decision of a monopoly to reduce prices). In Poppers view holistic social transformations only really ever effect piecemeal change, yet they do so in a manner that negates the benefits of such change, as the prejudice of total critique circumscribes a proper estimation of the effects of such practices. In fact, for Popper, the peculiar human problem of social engineering lies in that it can never fully predict its effects on social behaviour, given such factors as the variability of outcomes and reactions. Because Holistic transformations can not be tested (as a total transformation is necessary for the experiment to have effectivity) this precludes the possibility of there being a proper scientific basis to such meta-adjustment. In fact, Popper draws this conclusion: 'The holistics approach is incompatible with a truly scientific attitude'.

Yet we are lead immediately to question in what sense piecemeal social engineering (that is to say minor reforms) are compatible with a truly scientific attitude. They are unfortunately, at least in the manner that Popper construes the question, wholely inadequate. What Popper provides as evidence of the possibility of minor social reform lies in the practical experience of the individuals involved. He confesses this is not properly scientific (as in the example of someone who knows when to queue for a cinema ticket in order to ensure a reservation), but pre-scientific - nevertheless, the practical experience forms the basis on which social engineers can make measured calculations as to technologically based social intervention. Yet because of his peculiar technocratic construction of politics, he only judges the more holistic total transformation on the basis of such a conception of politics. All of a sudden experience is lost from the equation, Popper simply does not see how a holistic change could be based in mass collective experience and shared interests - he sees the aritculation of these as being utopian excesses of his type of constructed political agency.

He needs to posit an especially scientific character to his enemy inorder to discredit it, he can only view social experimentation and knowledge production in his own narrow way, within his own blinkered bourgeois mentality of isolated individuals. Hence projects that claim the necessity of a total transformation, for popper do not derive this from the more quotidian pre-scientific experiences, but from a pre-established schema that is beyond question: hence a political project is reduced to a validity claim in science, and they never meet Poppers standards. Yet it has long been an argument within Marxism that the possibility of a different society lies very much within the existing configuration of society, that the social forms characteristic of the contemporary world and the experiene of the social agents within it, allow for the passibility of their overcoming, and in some cases are posited as a necessary overcoming.

Popper conflates very different conceptions of holistic social change implicitly judging them by his own, unstated totalisations. Whole states and whole histories of determinative, creative social agency are ignored here.

Social Order

In social sciences, social order is a set of linked social structures, social institutions and social practices which conserve, maintain and enforce ways of relating and behaving.

A "social order" is a relatively persistent system of institutions, patterns of interactions and customs, capable of continually reproducing at least those conditions essential for its own existence. The concept refers to all those facts of society which remain relatively constant over time. These conditions could include both property, exchange and power relations, but also cultural forms, communication relations and ideological systems of values.

Social order as discussed in this article primarily refers to these structures and not to "order in society" with which it should not be confused. In this way, a society might be chaotic and dysfunctional but there is still a social order in a sheer sociological sense.

Sociology

The issue of social order, how and why it is that social orders exists at all, is historically central to sociology. Thomas Hobbes is recognized as the first to clearly formulate the problem, to answer which he conceived the notion of a social contract. Social theorists (such as Karl Marx, Émile Durkheim, Talcott Parsons, and Jürgen Habermas) have proposed different explanations for what a social order consists of, and what its real basis is. For Marx, it is the relations of production or economic structure which is the basis of a social order. For Durkheim, it is a set of shared social norms. For Parsons, it is a set of social institutions regulating pattern of action-orientations, which again are based on a frame of cultural values. For Habermas, it is all of these, as well as communicative action.

Principle of Extensiveness

Another key factor concerning social order is the principle of extensiveness. This states the more norms and the more important the norms are to a society, the better these norms tie and hold together the group as a whole.

A good example of this is smaller religions based around the U.S., such as the Amish. Many Amish live together in communities and because they share the same religion and values, it is easier for them to succeed in upholding their religion and views because their way of life is the norm for their community.

Groups and Networks

In every society people belong to groups, such as businesses, families, churches, athletic groups, or neighbourhoods. The structure inside of these groups mirrors that of the whole society. There are networks and ties between groups as well as inside of each of the groups that create social order.

Some people belong to more than one group, which sometimes causes conflict. The individual may encounter a situation in which he or she has to choose one group over another. Many who have studied these groups believe that it is necessary to have ties between groups to strengthen the society as a whole and to promote pride within each group. Others believe that it is best to have stronger ties within a group so that social norms and values are reinforced.

Status Groups

"Status groups" can be based on a person's characteristics such as race, ethnicity, sexual orientation, religion, caste, region, occupation, physical attractiveness, gender, education, age, etc. They are defined as "a subculture having a rather specific rank (or status) within the stratification system. That is, societies tend to include a hierarchy of status groups, some enjoying high ranking and some low." One example of this hierarchy is the prestige of a school teacher compared to that of a garbage man.

A certain lifestyle usually distinguishes the members of different status groups. For example, around the holidays a Jewish family may celebrate Hanukkah while a Christian family may celebrate Christmas. Other cultural differences such as language and cultural rituals identify members of different status groups.

Inside of a status group there are more, smaller groups. For instance, one can belong to a status group based on one's race and a social class based on financial ranking. This may cause strife for the individual in this situation when he or she feels they must choose to side with either their status group or their social class. For example, a wealthy African American man who feels he has to take a side on an issue on which the opinions of poor African Americans and wealthy white Americans are divided, and finds his class and status group opposed.

Values and Norms

Values can be defined as "internal criteria for evaluation". Values are also split into two categories, there are individual values, which pertains to something that we think has worth and then there are social values. Social values are our desires modified according to ethical principles or according to the group we associate with: friends, family, or co-workers. Norms tell us what people ought to do in a given situation. Unlike values, norms are enforced externally – or outside of oneself. A society as a whole determines norms, and they can be passed down from generation to generation.

6

The Enlightenment and its Enemies

Enlightenment

The Enlightenment is the period in the history of western thought and culture, stretching roughly from the mid-decades of the seventeenth century through the eighteenth century, characterized by dramatic revolutions in science, philosophy, society and politics; these revolutions swept away the medieval world-view and ushered in our modern western world. Enlightenment thought *culminates* historically in the political upheaval of the French Revolution, in which the traditional hierarchical political and social orders (the French monarchy, the privileges of the French nobility, the political power and authority of the Catholic Church) were violently destroyed and replaced by a political and social order informed by the Enlightenment ideals of freedom and equality for all, founded, ostensibly, upon principles of human reason. The Enlightenment *begins* with the scientific revolution of the sixteenth and seventeenth centuries.

The rise of the new science progressively undermines not only the ancient geocentric conception of the cosmos, but, with it, the entire set of presuppositions that had served to constrain and guide philosophical inquiry. The dramatic success of the new science in explaining the natural world, in accounting for a wide variety of phenomena by appeal to a relatively small number of elegant mathematical formulae, promotes philosophy (in the broad sense of the time, which includes natural science) from a handmaiden of theology, constrained by its purposes and methods, to an independent force with the power and authority to challenge the old and construct the new, in the realms both of theory and practice, on the basis of its own principles. D'Alembert, a leading figure of the French Enlightenment, characterizes his eighteenth century, in the midst of it, as "the century of philosophy *par excellence*", because of the tremendous intellectual progress of the age, the advance of the sciences, and the enthusiasm for that progress, but also because of the characteristic expectation of the age that philosophy (in this broad sense) would dramatically improve human life.

The task of characterizing philosophy in (or of) the Enlightenment confronts the obstacle of the wide diversity of Enlightenment thought. The Enlightenment is associated with the French thinkers of the mid-decades of the eighteenth century, the so-called "*philosophes*", (Voltaire, Diderot, D'Alembert, Montesquieu, et cetera). The *philosophes* constitute an informal society of men of letters who collaborate on a loosely defined project of Enlightenment centred around the project of the Encyclopedia. But the Enlightenment has broader boundaries, both geographical and temporal, than this suggests. In addition to the French, there was a very significant Scottish Enlightenment (key figures were Francis Hutcheson, David Hume, Adam Smith, and Thomas Reid) and a very significant German Enlightenment (*die Aufklärung*, key figures of which include Christian Wolff, Moses Mendelssohn, G.E. Lessing and Immanuel Kant). But all these Enlightenments were but particular nodes or centres in a far-flung and varied intellectual development. Given the variety, Enlightenment philosophy is characterized here in terms of general tendencies of thought, not in terms of specific doctrines or theories.

Only late in the development of the German Enlightenment, when the Enlightenment was near its end, does the movement become self-reflective; the question of "What is Enlightenment?" is debated in pamphlets and journals. In his famous definition of "enlightenment" in his essay "An Answer to the Question: What is Enlightenment?" (1784), which is his contribution to this debate, Immanuel Kant expresses many of the tendencies shared among Enlightenment philosophies of divergent doctrines. Kant defines "enlightenment" as humankind's release from its self-incurred immaturity; "immaturity is the inability to use one's own understanding without the guidance of another." Enlightenment is the process of undertaking to think for oneself, to employ and rely on one's own intellectual capacities in determining what to believe and how to act. Enlightenment philosophers from across the geographical and temporal spectrum tend to have a great deal of confidence in humanity's intellectual powers, both to achieve systematic knowledge of nature and to serve as an authoritative guide in practical life. This confidence is generally paired with suspicion or hostility toward other forms or carriers of authority (such as tradition, superstition, prejudice, myth and miracles), insofar as these are seen to compete with the authority of reason. Enlightenment philosophy tends to stand in tension with established religion, insofar as the release from self-incurred immaturity in this age, daring to think for oneself, awakening one's intellectual powers, generally requires opposing the role of established religion in directing thought and action.

The faith of the Enlightenment – if one may call it that – is that the process of enlightenment, of becoming progressively self-directed in thought and action through the awakening of one's intellectual powers, leads ultimately to a better, more fulfilled human existence.

This entry describes the main tendencies of Enlightenment thought in the following main sections: (1) The True: Science, Epistemology, and Metaphysics in the Enlightenment; (2) The Good: Political Theory, Ethical Theory and Religion in the Enlightenment; (3) The Beautiful: Aesthetics in the Enlightenment.

The True: Science, Epistemology and Metaphysics in the Enlightenment

In this era dedicated to human progress, the advancement of the natural sciences is regarded as the main exemplification of, and fuel for, such progress. Isaac Newton's epochal accomplishment in his *Principia Mathematica* (1687), which, very briefly described, consists in the comprehension of a diversity of physical phenomena – in particular the motions of heavenly bodies, together with the motions of sublunary bodies – in few relatively simple, universally applicable, mathematical laws, was a great stimulus to the intellectual activity of the eighteenth century and served as a model and inspiration for the researches of a number of Enlightenment thinkers. Newton's system strongly encourages the Enlightenment conception of nature as an orderly domain governed by strict mathematical-dynamical laws and the conception *of ourselves* as capable of knowing those laws and thus plumbing the secrets of nature through the exercise of our unaided faculties. – The conception of nature, and of how we know it, changes significantly with the rise of modern science.

It belongs centrally to the agenda of Enlightenment philosophy to contribute to the new knowledge of nature, and to provide a metaphysical framework within which to place and interpret this new knowledge.

Rationalism and the Enlightenment

René Descartes' rationalist system of philosophy is foundational for the Enlightenment in this regard. Descartes (1596–1650) undertakes to establish the sciences upon a secure metaphysical foundation. The famous method of doubt Descartes employs for this purpose exemplifies (in part through exaggerating) an attitude characteristic of the Enlightenment. According to Descartes, the investigator in foundational philosophical research ought to doubt all propositions that can be doubted. The investigator determines whether a proposition is dubitable by attempting to construct a possible scenario under which it is false. In the domain of fundamental scientific (philosophical) research, no other authority but one's own conviction is to be trusted, and not one's own conviction either, until it is subjected to rigorous skeptical questioning. With his method, Descartes casts doubt upon the senses as authoritative source of knowledge. He finds that God and the immaterial soul are both better known, on the basis of innate ideas, than objects of the senses. Through his famous doctrine of the dualism of mind and body, that mind and body are two distinct substances, each with its own essence, the material world (allegedly) known through the senses becomes denominated as an "external" world, insofar as it is external to the ideas with which one immediately communes in one's consciousness. Descartes' investigation thus establishes one of the central epistemological problems, not only of the Enlightenment, but also of modernity: the problem of objectivity in our empirical knowledge. If our evidence for the truth of propositions about extra-mental material reality is always restricted to mental content, content immediately before the mind, how can we ever be certain that the extra-mental reality is not other than we represent it as being? The solution Descartes puts forward to this problem depends on our having prior and certain knowledge of God. In fact, Descartes argues that *all* human knowledge (not only knowledge of the material world through the senses) depends on metaphysical knowledge of God.

However dubious Descartes' grounding of all scientific knowledge in metaphysical knowledge of God, his system contributes significantly to the advance of natural science in the period. He attacks the long-standing assumptions of the scholastic-aristotelians whose intellectual dominance stood in the way of the development of the new science; he developed a conception of matter that enabled mechanical explanation of physical phenomena; and he developed some of the fundamental mathematical resources – in particular, a way to employ algebraic equations to solve geometrical problems – that enabled the physical domain to be explained with precise, simple mathematical formulae. Furthermore, his grounding of physics, and all knowledge, in a relatively simple and elegant rationalist metaphysics provides a model of a rigorous and complete secular system of knowledge. Though it is typical of the Enlightenment thinkers of the eighteenth century (for example Voltaire in his *Letters on the English Nation*, 1734) to embrace Newton's physical system in preference to Descartes', Newton's system itself depends on Descartes' earlier work, a dependence of which Newton himself was aware.

Cartesian philosophy is also foundational for the Enlightenment through igniting various controversies in the latter decades of the seventeenth century that provide the context of intellectual tumult out of which the Enlightenment springs. Among these controversies are the following: Are mind and body two distinct sorts of substances, as Descartes argues, and if so, what is the nature of each, and how are they related to each other, both in the human being (which presumably "has" both a mind and a body) and in a unified world system? If matter is inert (as Descartes claims), what can be the source of motion and the nature of causality in the physical world? And of course the various epistemological problems: the problem of objectivity, the role of God in securing our knowledge, the doctrine of innate ideas, et cetera.

Baruch Spinoza's systematic rationalist metaphysics, which he develops in his *Ethics* (1677) in part in response to problems in the Cartesian system, is also an important basis for Enlightenment thought. Spinoza develops, in contrast to Cartesian dualism, an ontological monism according to which there is not only one *kind* of substance, but one substance, God or nature, with two attributes, corresponding to mind and body. Spinoza's denial, on the basis of strict philosophical reasoning, of the existence of a transcendent supreme being, his identification of God with nature, gives strong impetus to the strands of atheism and naturalism that thread through Enlightenment philosophy. Spinoza's rationalist principles also lead him to assert a strict determinism and to deny any role to final causes or teleology in explanation.

The rationalist metaphysics of Leibniz (1646–1716) is also foundational for the Enlightenment, particularly the German Enlightenment (*die Aufklärung*), which is founded to a great extent on the Leibnizean rationalist system of Christian Wolff (1679–1754). Leibniz articulates, and places at the head of metaphysics, the great rationalist principle, the principle of sufficient reason, which states that everything that exists has a sufficient reason for its existence. This principle exemplifies the faith, so important for the Enlightenment, that the universe is fully intelligible to us through the exercise of our natural powers of reason. The problem arises, in the face of skeptical questioning, of how this principle itself can be known or grounded. Wolff attempts to derive it from the logical principle of non-contradiction (in his *First Philosophy or Ontology*, 1730). Criticism of this alleged derivation gives rise to the general question of how formal principles of logic can possibly serve to ground substantive knowledge of reality. Whereas Leibniz exerts his influence through scattered writings on various topics, some of which elaborate plans for a systematic metaphysics which are never executed by Leibniz himself, Wolff exerts his influence on the German Enlightenment through his development of a rationalist system of knowledge in which he attempts to demonstrate all the propositions of science from first principles, known a priori.

Wolff's rationalist metaphysics is characteristic of the Enlightenment by virtue of the *pretensions* of human reason within it, not by reason's success in establishing its claims. Much the same could be said of the great rationalist philosophers of the seventeenth century. Through their articulation of the *ideal* of scientia, of a complete science of reality, composed of propositions derived demonstratively from a priori first principles, these philosophers exert great influence on the Enlightenment. But they fail, rather spectacularly, to realize this ideal. To the contrary, what they bequeath to the eighteenth century is metaphysics, in the words of Kant, as "a battlefield of endless controversies." However, the controversies themselves – regarding the nature of God, mind, matter, substance, cause, et cetera, and the relations of each of these to the others – provide tremendous fuel to Enlightenment thought.

Empiricism and the Enlightenment

Despite the confidence in and enthusiasm for human reason in the Enlightenment – it is sometimes called "the Age of Reason" – the rise of empiricism, both in the practice of science and in the theory of knowledge, is characteristic of the period. The enthusiasm for reason in the Enlightenment is not for the faculty of reason as an independent source of knowledge (at least not primarily), which is actually put on the defencive in the period, but rather for the human cognitive faculties generally; the Age of Reason contrasts with an age of religious faith, not with an age of sense experience. Of course, as outlined above, the great seventeenth century rationalist metaphysical systems of Descartes, Spinoza and Leibniz exert significant influence on philosophy in the Enlightenment; moreover, the eighteenth-century Enlightenment has a rationalist strain, perhaps best exemplified by the system of Christian Wolff. Still, that the *Encyclopedia* of Diderot and D'Alembert is dedicated to three empiricists, Francis Bacon, John Locke and Isaac Newton, indicates the general ascendency of empiricism in the period.

If the founder of the rationalist strain of the Enlightenment is Descartes, then the founder of the empiricist strain is Francis Bacon (1561–1626). Though Bacon's work belongs to the Renaissance, the revolution he undertook to effect in the sciences inspires and influences Enlightenment thinkers. The Enlightenment, as the age in which experimental natural science matures and comes into its own, admires Bacon as "the father of experimental philosophy." Bacon's revolution (enacted in, among other works, *The New Organon*, 1620) involves conceiving the new science as (1) founded on empirical observation and experimentation; (2) arrived at through the method of induction; and (3) as ultimately aiming at, and as confirmed by, enhanced practical capacities (hence the Baconian motto, "knowledge is power").

Though each of these elements of Bacon's revolution is significant for natural science in the Enlightenment, the point about method deserves special emphasis. Granted that Newton's work stands as the great exemplar of the accomplishments of natural science for the eighteenth century, the most salient contrast between Newton's work and that of the great rationalist systems lies in their methods. Whereas the great rationalist philosophers of the seventeenth century conceive of scientific knowledge of nature as consisting in a system in which statements expressing the observable phenomena of nature are *deduced* from first principles, known a priori, Newton's method begins with the observed phenomena of nature and reduces its multiplicity to unity by induction, that is, by finding mathematical laws or principles from which the observed phenomena can be derived or explained. The contrast between the great success of Newton's "bottom-up" procedure and the seemingly endless and fruitless conflicts among philosophers regarding the meaning and validity of first principles of reason naturally favours the rise of the Newtonian (or Baconian) method of acquiring knowledge of nature in the eighteenth century.

The tendency of natural science toward progressive independence from metaphysics in the eighteenth century is correlated with this point about method. The rise of modern science in the sixteenth and seventeenth centuries proceeds through its separation from the presuppositions, doctrines and methodology of theology; natural science in the eighteenth century proceeds to separate itself from metaphysics as well. Newton proves the capacity of natural science to succeed independently of a priori, clear and certain first principles. The characteristic Enlightenment suspicion of all allegedly authoritative claims the validity of which is obscure, which is directed first of all against religious dogmas, extends to the claims of metaphysics as well. While there are significant Enlightenment thinkers who are metaphysicians – again, one thinks of Christian Wolff – the general thrust of Enlightenment thought is anti-metaphysical.

John Locke's *Essay Concerning Human Understanding* (1690) exerts tremendous influence on the age, in good part through the epistemological rigor that it displays, which is at least implicitly anti-metaphysical. Locke undertakes in this work to examine the human understanding in order to determine the limits of human knowledge; he thereby institutes a prominent pattern of Enlightenment epistemology. Locke finds the source of all our ideas, the ideas out of which human knowledge is constructed, in the senses and argues influentially against the rationalists' doctrine of innate ideas. Locke's sensationalism exerts great influence in the French Enlightenment, primarily through being taken up and radicalized by the *philosophe*, Abbé de Condillac. In his *Treatise on Sensations* (1754), Condillac attempts to explain how all human knowledge arises out of sense experience. Locke's epistemology, as developed by Condillac and others, contributes greatly to the emerging science of psychology in the period.

Locke and Descartes both pursue a method in epistemology that brings with it the epistemological problem of objectivity. Both examine our knowledge by way of examining the ideas we encounter directly in our consciousness. This method comes to be called "the way of ideas". Though neither for Locke nor for Descartes do *all* of our ideas represent their objects by way of *resembling* them (e.g., our idea of God does not represent God by virtue of resembling God), our alleged knowledge of our environment through the senses does depend largely on ideas that allegedly resemble external material objects. The way of ideas implies the epistemological problem of how we can know that these ideas do in fact resemble their objects. How can we be sure that these objects do not appear one way before the mind and exist in another way (or not at all) in reality outside the mind? George Berkeley, an empiricist philosopher influenced by John Locke, avoids the problem by asserting the metaphysics of idealism: the (apparently material) objects of perception are nothing but ideas before the mind. However, Berkeley's idealism is less influential in, and characteristic of, the Enlightenment, than the opposing positions of materialism and Cartesian dualism. Thomas Reid, a prominent member of the Scottish Enlightenment, responds to this epistemological problem in a way more characteristic of the Enlightenment in general. He attacks the way of ideas and argues that the immediate objects of our (sense) perception are the common (material) objects in our environment, not ideas in our mind. Reid mounts his defence of naïve realism as a defence of common sense over against the doctrines of the philosophers. The defence of common sense, and the related idea that the results of philosophy ought to be of use to common people, are characteristic ideas of the Enlightenment, particularly pronounced in the Scottish Enlightenment.

Skepticism in the Enlightenment

Skepticism enjoys a remarkably strong place in Enlightenment philosophy, given that confidence in our intellectual capacities to achieve systematic knowledge of nature is a leading characteristic of the age. This oddity is at least softened by the point that much skepticism in the Enlightenment is merely methodological, a tool meant to serve science, rather than a philosophical position embraced on its own account. The instrumental role for skepticism is exemplified prominently in Descartes' *Meditations on First Philosophy* (1641), in which Descartes employs radical skeptical doubt to attack prejudices derived from learning and from sense experience and to search out principles known with certainty which may serve as a secure foundation for a new system of knowledge. Given the negative, critical, suspicious attitude of the Enlightenment towards doctrines traditionally regarded as well founded, it is not surprising that Enlightenment thinkers employ skeptical tropes (drawn from the ancient skeptical tradition) to attack traditional dogmas in science, metaphysics and religion.

However, skepticism is not merely a methodological tool in the hands of Enlightenment thinkers. The skeptical cast of mind is one prominent manifestation of the Enlightenment spirit. The influence of Pierre Bayle, another founding figure of the Enlightenment, testifies to this. Bayle was a French Protestant, who, like many European philosophers of his time, was forced to live and work in politically liberal and tolerant Holland in order to avoid censorship and prison. Bayle's *Historical and Critical Dictionary* (1697), a strange and wonderful book, exerts great influence on the age. The form of the book is intimidating: a biographical dictionary, with long scholarly entries on obscure figures in the history of culture, interrupted by long scholarly footnotes, which are in turn interrupted by further footnotes. Rarely has a work with such intimidating scholarly pretentions exerted such radical and liberating influence in the culture. It exerts this influence through its skeptical questioning of religious, metaphysical, and scientific dogmas. Bayle's eclecticism and his tendency to follow arguments without pre-arranging their conclusions make it difficult to categorize his thought. But it is the attitude of inquiry that Bayle displays, rather than any doctrine he espouses, that mark his as distinctively Enlightenment thought. He is fearless and presumptuous in questioning all manner of dogma. His attitude of inquiry resembles both that of Descartes' meditator and that of the person undergoing enlightenment as Kant defines it, the attitude of coming to think for oneself, of daring to know. This epistemological attitude, as manifest in distrust of authority and reliance on one's own capacity to judge, expresses the Enlightenment valuing of individualism and self-determination.

This skeptical/critical attitude underlies a significant tension in the age. While it is common to conceive of the Enlightenment as supplanting the authority of tradition and religious dogma with the authority of reason, in fact the Enlightenment is characterized by a crisis of authority regarding any belief. This is perhaps best illustrated with reference to David Hume's skepticism, as developed in Book One of *A Treatise of Human Nature* (1739–40) and in his later *Enquiries Concerning Human Understanding* (1748). While one might take Hume's skepticism to imply that he is an outlier with respect to the Enlightenment, it is more convincing to see Hume's skepticism as a flowering of a crisis regarding authority in belief that is internal to the Enlightenment. Hume articulates a variety of skepticisms. His "skepticism with regard to the senses" is structured by the epistemological problem bound up with the way of ideas, described above. Hume also articulates skepticism with regard to reason in an argument that is anticipated by Bayle. Hume begins this argument by noting that, though rules or principles in demonstrative sciences are certain or infallible, given the fallibility of our faculties, our applications of such rules or principles in demonstrative inferences yield conclusions that cannot be regarded as certain or infallible. On reflection, our conviction in the conclusions of demonstrative reasoning must be qualified by an assessment of the likelihood that we made a mistake in our reasoning. Thus, Hume writes, "all knowledge degenerates into probability" (*Treatise*, I.iv.i). Hume argues further that, given this degeneration, for any judgment, our assessment of the likelihood that we made a mistake, and the corresponding diminution of certainty in the conclusion, is another judgment about which we ought make a further assessment, which leads to a further diminution of certainty in our original conclusion, leading "at last [to] a total extinction of belief and evidence". Hume also famously questions the justification of inductive reasoning and causal reasoning. According to Hume's argument, since in causal reasoning we take our past observations to serve as evidence for judgments regarding what will happen in relevantly similar circumstances in the future, causal reasoning depends on the assumption that the future course of nature will resemble the past; and there is no non-circular justification of this essential assumption. Hume concludes that we have no rational justification for our causal or inductive judgments. Hume's skeptical arguments regarding causal reasoning are more radical than his skeptical questioning of reason as such, insofar as they call into question even *experience itself* as a ground for knowledge and implicitly challenge the credentials of Newtonian science itself, the very pride of the Enlightenment. The question implicitly raised by Hume's powerful skeptical arguments is whether *any* epistemological authority at all can withstand critical scrutiny. The Enlightenment begins by unleashing skepticism in attacking limited, circumscribed targets, but once the skeptical genie is out of the bottle, it becomes difficult to maintain conviction in any authority. Thus, the despairing attitude that Hume famously expresses in the conclusion to Book One of the *Treatise*, as the consequence of his epistemological inquiry, while it clashes with the self-confident and optimistic attitude we associate with the Enlightenment, in fact reflects an essential possibility in a distinctive Enlightenment problematic regarding authority in belief.

Science of Man and Subjectivism in the Enlightenment

Though Hume finds himself struggling with skepticism in the conclusion of Book One of the *Treatise*, the project of the work as he outlines it is not to advance a skeptical viewpoint, but to establish a science of the mind. Hume is one of many Enlightenment thinkers who aspire to be the "Newton of the mind"; he aspires to establish the basic laws that govern the elements of the human mind in its operations. Alexander Pope's famous couplet in *An Essay on Man* (1733) ("Know then thyself, presume not God to scan/ The proper study of mankind is man") expresses well the intense interest humanity gains in itself within the context of the Enlightenment, as a partial substitute for its traditional interest in God and the transcendent domain. Just as the sun replaces the earth as the centre of our cosmos in Copernicus' cosmological system, so humanity itself replaces God at the centre of humanity's consciousness in the Enlightenment. Given the Enlightenment's passion for science, the self-directed attention naturally takes the form of the rise of the scientific study of humanity in the period.

The enthusiasm for the scientific study of humanity in the period incorporates a tension or paradox concerning the place of humanity in the cosmos, as the cosmos is re-conceived in the context of Enlightenment philosophy and science. Newton's success early in the Enlightenment of subsuming the phenomena of nature under universal laws of motion, expressed in simple mathematical formulae, encourages the conception of nature as a very complicated machine, whose parts are material and whose motions and properties are fully accounted for by deterministic causal laws.

But if our conception of nature is of an exclusively material domain governed by deterministic, mechanical laws, and if we at the same time deny the place of the supernatural in the cosmos, then how does humanity itself fit into the cosmos? On the one hand, the achievements of the natural sciences in general are the great pride of the Enlightenment, manifesting the excellence of distinctively human capacities.

The pride and self-assertiveness of humanity in the Enlightenment expresses itself, among other ways, in humanity's making the study of itself its central concern. On the other hand, the study of humanity in the Enlightenment typically yields a portrait of us that is the opposite of flattering or elevating. Instead of being represented as occupying a privileged place in nature, as made in the image of God, humanity is represented typically in the Enlightenment as a fully natural creature, devoid of free will, of an immortal soul, and of a non-natural faculty of intelligence or reason.

The very title of J.O. de La Mettrie's *Man a Machine* (1748), for example, seems designed to deflate humanity's self-conception, and in this respect it is characteristic of the Enlightenment "science of man". It is true of a number of works of the Enlightenment, perhaps especially works in the more radical French Enlightenment – notable here are Helvétius's *Of the Spirit* (1758) and Baron d'Holbach's *System of Nature* (1770) – that they at once express the remarkable self-assertiveness of humanity characteristic of the Enlightenment in their scientific aspirations while at the same time painting a portrait of humanity that dramatically deflates its traditional self-image as occupying a privileged position in nature.

The methodology of epistemology in the period reflects a similar tension. Given the epistemological role of Descartes' famous "*cogito, ergo sum*" in his system of knowledge, one might see Descartes' epistemology as already marking the transition from an epistemology privileging knowledge of God to one that privileges self-knowledge instead. However, in Descartes' epistemology, it remains true that knowledge of God serves as the necessary foundation for all human knowledge. Hume's *Treatise* displays such a re-orientation less ambiguously. As noted, Hume means his work to comprise a science of the mind or of man. In the Introduction, Hume describes the science of man as effectively a foundation for all the sciences since all sciences "lie under the cognizance of men, and are judged of by their powers and faculties." In other words, since all science is human knowledge, scientific knowledge *of humanity* is the foundation of the sciences. Hume's placing the science of man at the foundation of all the sciences both exemplifies the privilege afforded to "mankind's study of man" within the Enlightenment and provides an interpretation of it. But Hume's methodological privileging of humanity in the system of sciences contrasts sharply with what he says in the body of his science about humanity. In Hume's science of man, reason as a faculty of knowledge is skeptically attacked and marginalized; reason is attributed to other animals as well; belief is shown to be grounded in custom and habit; and free will is denied. So, even as knowledge of humanity supplants knowledge of God as the keystone of the system of knowledge, the scientific perspective on humanity starkly challenges humankind's self-conception as occupying a privileged position in the order of nature.

Immanuel Kant explicitly enacts a revolution in epistemology modelled on the Copernican in astronomy. As characteristic of Enlightenment epistemology, Kant, in his *Critique of Pure Reason* (1781, second edition 1787) undertakes both to determine the limits of our knowledge, and at the same time to provide a foundation of scientific knowledge of nature, and he attempts to do this by examining our human faculties of knowledge critically. Even as he draws strict limits to rational knowledge, he attempts to defend reason as a faculty of knowledge, as playing a necessary role in natural science, in the face of skeptical challenges that reason faces in the period. According to Kant, scientific knowledge of nature is not merely knowledge of what *in fact* happens in nature, but knowledge of the causal laws of nature according to which what in fact happens *must* happen. But how is knowledge of necessary causal connection in nature possible? Hume's investigation of the idea of cause had made clear that we cannot know causal necessity through experience; experience teaches us at most what in fact happens, not what *must* happen. In addition, Kant's own earlier critique of principles of rationalism had convinced him that the principles of ("general") logic also cannot justify knowledge of *real* necessary connections (in nature); the formal principle of non-contradiction can ground at best the deduction of one *proposition* from another, but not the claim that one *property* or *event* must follow from another in the course of nature. The generalized epistemological problem Kant addresses in the *Critique of Pure Reason* is: how is science possible (including natural science, mathematics, metaphysics), given that all such knowledge must be (or include) knowledge of real, substantive (not merely logical or formal) necessities. Put in the terms Kant defines, the problem is: how is synthetic, a priori knowledge possible?

According to the Copernican Revolution in epistemology which Kant presents as the solution to this problem, objects must conform themselves to human knowledge rather than knowledge to objects. According to Kant's arguments, certain cognitive forms lie ready in the human mind – prominent examples are the pure concepts of substance and cause and the forms of intuition, space and time; given sensible representations must conform themselves to these forms in order for human experience (as empirical knowledge of nature) to be possible at all. According to Kant's epistemological revolution, we can acquire scientific knowledge of nature because we constitute it a priori according to certain cognitive forms; for example, we can know nature as a causally ordered domain because we originally synthesize a priori the given manifold of sensibility according to the category of causality, which has its source in the human mind.

Kant saves rational knowledge of nature by limiting rational knowledge to nature. According to Kant's argument, we can have rational knowledge only of the domain of possible experience, not of supersensible objects such as God and the soul. Moreover Kant's solution brings with it a kind of idealism: given the mind's role in constituting objects of experience, we know objects only as *appearances*, only as they are for us, not as they are in themselves. This is the subjectivism of Kant's epistemology. Kant's epistemology exemplifies Enlightenment thought by replacing the theocentric conception of knowledge of the rationalist tradition with an anthropocentric conception.

However, Kant means his system to make room for humanity's practical and religious aspirations toward the transcendent as well.

According to Kant's idealism, the realm of nature is limited to a realm of appearances, and we can intelligibly think supersensible objects such as God, freedom and the soul, though we cannot have knowledge of them. Through the postulation of a realm of unknowable noumena (things in themselves) over against the realm of nature as a realm of appearances, Kant manages to make place for practical concepts that are central to our understanding of ourselves even while grounding our scientific knowledge of nature as a domain governed by deterministic causal laws. Though Kant's idealism is highly controversial from the outset, it represents the Enlightenment's most serious attempt to understand the cosmos in such a way that the Enlightenment's conception of nature and the Enlightenment's conception of ourselves (as morally free, as having dignity, as perfectible, et cetera) fit together in a single system.

Emerging Sciences and the *Encyclopedia*

The commitment to careful observation and description of phenomena as the starting point of science, and then the success at explaining and accounting for observed phenomena through the method of induction, naturally leads to the development of new sciences for new domains in the Enlightenment. Many of the human and social sciences have their origins in the eighteenth century, in the context of the Enlightenment (e.g., history, anthropology, aesthetics, psychology, economics, even sociology), though most are only formally established as autonomous disciplines in universities later. The emergence of new sciences is aided by the development of new scientific tools, such as models for probabilistic reasoning, a kind of reasoning that gains new respect and application in the period. Despite the multiplication of sciences in the period, the ideal remains to comprehend the diversity of our scientific knowledge as a unified system of science; however, this ideal of unity is generally taken as regulative, as an ideal to emerge in the ever-receding end-state of science, rather than as enforced from the beginning by regimenting science under a priori principles.

As exemplifying these and other tendencies of the Enlightenment, one work deserves special mention: the *Encyclopedia*, edited by Denis Diderot and Jean La Rond d'Alembert. The *Encyclopedia* (subtitled: "*systematic dictionary of the sciences, arts and crafts*") was published in 28 volumes (17 of text, 11 of plates) over 21 years (1751–1772), and consists of over 70,000 articles, contributed by over 140 contributors, among them many of the luminaries of the French Enlightenment. The work aims to provide a compendium of existing human knowledge, a compendium to be transmitted to subsequent generations, a transmission intended to contribute to the progress and dissemination of human knowledge and to a positive transformation of human society. The orientation of the *Encyclopedia* is decidedly secular and implicitly anti-authoritarian. Accordingly, the French state of the *ancien régime* subjects the project to censorship, and it is completed only through the persistence of Diderot. The collaborative nature of the project, especially in the context of state opposition, contributes significantly to the formation of a shared sense of purpose among the wide variety of intellectuals who belong to the French Enlightenment. The knowledge contained in the *Encyclopedia* is self-consciously social both in its production – insofar as it is immediately the product of what the title page calls "a society of men of letters" – and in its address – insofar as it is primarily meant as an instrument for the education and improvement of society. It is a striking feature of the *Encyclopedia*, and one by virtue of which it exemplifies the Baconian conception of science characteristic of the period, that its entries cover the whole range and scope of knowledge, from the most abstract theoretical to the most practical, mechanical and technical.

The Good: Political Theory, Ethical Theory and Religion in the Enlightenment

Political Theory: The Enlightenment is most identified with its political accomplishments. The era is marked by three political revolutions, which together lay the basis for modern, republican, constitutional democracies: The English Revolution (1688), the American Revolution (1775–83), and the French Revolution (1789–99). The success at explaining and understanding the natural world encourages the Enlightenment project of re-making the social/political world, in accord with the true models we allegedly find in our reason. Enlightenment philosophers find that the existing social and political orders do not withstand critical scrutiny; they find that existing political and social authority is shrouded in religious myth and mystery and founded on obscure traditions. The negative work of criticizing existing institutions is supplemented with the positive work of constructing in theory the model of institutions as they ought to be. We owe to this period the basic model of government founded upon the consent of the governed; the articulation of the political ideals of freedom and equality and the theory of their institutional realization; the articulation of a list of basic individual human rights to be respected and realized by any legitimate political system; the articulation and promotion of toleration of religious diversity as a virtue to be respected in a well ordered society; the conception of the basic political powers as organized in a system of checks and balances; and other now-familiar features of western democracies. However, for all the enduring accomplishments of Enlightenment political philosophy, it is not clear that human reason proves powerful enough to put a concrete, positive authoritative ideal in place of the ideals negated by rational criticism. As in the epistemological domain, reason shows its power more convincingly in criticizing authorities than in establishing them. Here too the question of the limits of reason is one of the main philosophical legacies of the period.

These limits are arguably vividly illustrated by the course of the French Revolution. The explicit ideals of the French Revolution are the Enlightenment ideals of individual freedom and equality; but, as the revolutionaries attempt to devise rational, secular institutions to put in place of those they have violently overthrown, eventually they have recourse to violence and terror in order to control and govern the people. The devolution of the French Revolution into the Reign of Terror is perceived by many as proving the emptiness and hypocrisy of Enlightenment reason, and is one of the main factors which account for the end of the Enlightenment as an historical period.

The political revolutions of the Enlightenment, especially the French and the American, were informed and guided to a significant extent by prior political philosophy in the period. Though Thomas Hobbes, in his *Leviathan* (1651), defends the absolute power of the political sovereign, and is to that extent opposed to the revolutionaries and reformers in England, this work is a founding work of Enlightenment political theory. Hobbes' work originates the modern social contract theory, which incorporates Enlightenment conceptions of the relation of the individual to the state. According to the general social contract model, political authority is grounded in an agreement (often understood as ideal, rather than real) among individuals, each of whom aims in this agreement to advance his rational self-interest by establishing a common political authority over all.

Thus, according to the general contract model (though this is more clear in later contract theorists such as Locke and Rousseau than in Hobbes himself), political authority is grounded not in conquest, natural or divinely instituted hierarchy, or in obscure myths and traditions, but rather in the rational consent of the governed. In initiating this model, Hobbes takes a naturalistic, scientific approach to the question of how political society ought to be organized (against the background of a clear-eyed, unsentimental conception of human nature), and thus decisively influences the Enlightenment process of secularization and rationalization in political and social philosophy.

Baruch Spinoza also greatly contributes to the development of Enlightenment political philosophy in its early years. Spinoza's *Tractatus Theologico-Politicus* (1677) is his main work dedicated to political philosophy, but the metaphysical doctrines of the *Ethics* lay the groundwork for his influence on the age. Spinoza's arguments against Cartesian dualism and in favour of substance monism, the claim in particular that there can only be one substance, God or nature, was taken to have radical implications in the domains of politics, ethics and religion throughout the period. Spinoza's employment of philosophical reason leads to the radical conclusion of denying the existence of a transcendent, creator, providential, law-giving God; this establishes the opposition between the teachings of philosophy, on the one hand, and the traditional orienting practical beliefs (moral, religious, political) of the people, on the other hand, an opposition that is one important aspect of the culture of the Enlightenment. In his political writings, Spinoza, building on his rationalist naturalism, opposes superstition, argues for toleration and the subordination of religion to the state, and pronounces in favour of qualified democracy. Liberalism is perhaps the most characteristic political philosophy of the Enlightenment, and Spinoza is one of its originators.

However, John Locke's *Second Treatise of Government* (1690) is the classical source of modern liberal political theory. In his *First Treatise of Government*, Locke attacks Robert Filmer's *Patriarcha* (1680), which epitomizes the sort of political theory the Enlightenment opposes. Filmer defends the right of kings to exercise absolute authority over their subjects on the basis of the claim that they inherit the authority God vested in Adam at creation. Though Locke's assertion of the natural freedom and equality of human beings in the *Second Treatise* is starkly and explicitly opposed to such a view, it is striking that the cosmology underlying Locke's assertions is closer to Filmer's than to Spinoza's. According to Locke, in order to understand the nature and source of legitimate political authority, we have to understand our relations in the state of nature. Drawing upon the natural law tradition, Locke argues that it is evident to our natural reason that we are all absolutely subject to our Lord and Creator, but that, in relation to each other, we exist naturally in a state of equality "wherein all the power and jurisdiction is reciprocal, no one having more than another" (*Second Treatise*, §4). We also exist naturally in a condition of freedom, insofar as we may do with ourselves and our possessions as we please, within the constraints of the fundamental law of nature. The law of nature "teaches all mankind ... that, being all equal and independent, no one ought to harm another in his life, health, liberty, or possessions" (§6). That we are governed in our natural condition by such a substantive moral law, legislated by God and known to us through our natural reason, implies that the state of nature is not the war of all against all that Hobbes claims it is. However, since there is lacking any human authority over all to judge of disputes and enforce the law, it is a condition marred by "inconveniencies", in which possession of natural freedom, equality and possessions is insecure. According to Locke, we rationally quit this natural condition by contracting together to set over ourselves a political authority, charged with promulgating and enforcing a single, clear set of laws, for the sake of guaranteeing our natural rights, liberties and possessions.

The civil, political law, founded ultimately upon the consent of the governed, does not cancel the natural law, according to Locke, but merely serves to draw that law closer. "[T]he law of nature stands as an eternal rule to all men" (§135). Consequently, when established political power violates that law, the people are justified in overthrowing it. Locke's support for the right to revolt against a government that opposes the purposes for which legitimate government is founded is significant both within the context of the political revolution in the context of which he writes (the English revolution) and through the influence of his writings on the revolutionaries in the American colonies almost a hundred years later.

Though Locke's liberalism has been tremendously influential, his political theory is founded on doctrines of natural law and religion that are not nearly as evident as Locke assumes. Locke's reliance on the natural law tradition is typical of Enlightenment political and moral theory. According to the natural law tradition, as the Enlightenment makes use of it, we can know through the use of our unaided reason that we all – all human beings, universally – stand in particular moral relations to each other. The claim that we can apprehend through our unaided reason a *universal* moral order exactly because moral qualities and relations (in particular human freedom and equality) belong to the nature of things, is attractive in the Enlightenment for obvious reasons. However, as noted above, the scientific apprehension of nature in the period does not support, and in fact opposes, the claim that the alleged moral qualities and relations (or, indeed, that *any* moral qualities and relations) are *natural*. According to a common Enlightenment assumption, as humankind clarifies the laws of nature through the advance of natural science and philosophy, the true moral and political order will be revealed with it.

This view is expressed explicitly by the *philosophe* Marquis de Condorcet, in his *Sketch for a Historical Picture of the Progress of the Human Mind* (published posthumously in 1795 and which, perhaps better than any other work, lays out the paradigmatically Enlightenment view of history of the human race as a continual progress to perfection). But, in fact, advance in knowledge of the laws of nature in the science of the period does not help with discernment of a natural political or moral order. This asserted relationship between natural scientific knowledge and the political and moral order is under great stress already in the Enlightenment. With respect to Lockean liberalism, though his assertion of the moral and political claims (natural freedom, equality, et cetera) continues to have considerable force for us, the grounding of these claims in a religious cosmology does not. The question of how to ground our claims to natural freedom and equality is one of the main philosophical legacies of the Enlightenment.

The rise and development of liberalism in Enlightenment political thought has many relations with the rise of the mercantile class (the bourgeoisie) and the development of what comes to be called "civil society", the society characterized by work and trade in pursuit of private property. Locke's *Second Treatise* contributes greatly to the project of articulating a political philosophy to serve the interests and values of this ascending class. Locke claims that the end or purpose of political society is the preservation and protection of property (though he defines property broadly to include not only external property but life and liberties as well). According to Locke's famous account, persons acquire rightful ownership in external things that are originally given to us all by God as a common inheritance, independently of the state and prior to its involvement, insofar as we "mix our labour with them".

The civil freedom that Locke defines, as something protected by the force of political laws, comes increasingly to be interpreted as the freedom to trade, to exchange without the interference of governmental regulation. Within the context of the Enlightenment, economic freedom is a salient interpretation of the individual freedom highly valued in the period. Adam Smith, a prominent member of the Scottish

Enlightenment, describes in his *An Inquiry into the Nature and Causes of the Wealth of Nations* (1776) some of the laws of civil society, as a sphere distinct from political society as such, and thus contributes significantly to the founding of political economy (later called merely "economics"). His is one of many voices in the Enlightenment advocating for free trade and for minimal government regulation of markets. The trading house floor, in which people of various nationalities, languages, cultures, religions come together and trade, each in pursuit of his own self-interest, but, through this pursuit, supplying the wants of their respective nations and increasing its wealth, represents for some Enlightenment thinkers the benign, peaceful, universal rational order that they wish to see replace the violent, confessional strife that characterized the then-recent past of Europe.

However, the liberal conception of the government as properly protecting economic freedom of citizens and private property comes into conflict in the Enlightenment with the valuing of democracy. James Madison confronts this tension in the context of arguing for the adoption of the U.S. Constitution (in his Federalist #10). Madison argues that popular government (pure democracy) is subject to the evil of factions; in a pure democracy, a majority bound together by a private interest, relative to the whole, has the capacity to impose its particular will on the whole. The example most on Madison's mind is that those without property (the many) may seek to bring about governmental re-distribution of the property of the propertied class (the few), perhaps in the name of that other Enlightenment ideal, equality. If, as in Locke's theory, the government's protection of an individual's freedom is encompassed within the general end of protecting a person's property, then, as Madison argues, the proper form of the government cannot be pure democracy, and the will of the people must be officially determined in some other way than by directly polling the people.

Jean-Jacques Rousseau's political theory, as presented in his *On the Social Contract* (1762), presents a contrast to the Lockean liberal model. Though commitment to the political ideals of freedom and equality constitutes a common ground for Enlightenment political philosophy, it is not clear not only how these values have a home in nature as Enlightenment science re-conceives it, but also how concretely to interpret each of these ideals and how properly to balance them against each other. Contrary to Madison, Rousseau argues that direct (pure) democracy is the only form of government in which human freedom can be realized. Human freedom, according to Rousseau's interpretation, is possible only through governance according to what he calls "the general will," which is the will of the body politic, formed through the original contract, concretely determined in an assembly in which all citizens participate. Rousseau's account intends to avert the evils of factions by structural elements of the original contract. The contract consists in the self-alienation by each associate of all rights and possessions to the body politic. Because each alienates all, each is an equal member of the body politic, and the terms and conditions are the same for all.

The emergence of factions is avoided insofar as the good of each citizen is, and is understood to be, equally (because wholly) dependent on the general will. Legislation supports this identification with the general will by preserving the original equality established in the contract, prominently through maintaining a measure of economic equality. The (ideal) relation of the individual citizen to the state is quite different on Rousseau's account than on Locke's; in Rousseau's account, the individual must be actively engaged in political life in order to maintain the identification of his supremely authoritative will with the general will, whereas in Locke the emphasis is on the limits of governmental authority with respect to the expressions of the individual will. Though Locke's liberal model is more representative of the Enlightenment in general, Rousseau's political theory, which in some respects presents a revived classical model modified within the context of Enlightenment values, in effect poses many of the enduring questions regarding the meaning and interpretation of political freedom and equality within the modern state.

Both Madison and Rousseau, like most political thinkers of the period, are influenced by Baron de Montesquieu's *The Spirit of the Laws* (1748), which is one of the founding texts of modern political theory. Though Montesquieu's treatise belongs to the tradition of liberalism in political theory, given his scientific approach to social, legal and political systems, his influence extends beyond this tradition. Montesquieu argues that the system of legislation for a people varies appropriately with the particular circumstances of the people. He provides specific analysis of how climate, fertility of the soil, population size, et cetera, affect legislation. He famously distinguishes three main forms of governments: republics (which can either be democratic or aristocratic), monarchies and despotisms. He describes leading characteristics of each. His argument that functional democracies require the population to possess civic virtue in high measure, a virtue that consists in valuing public good above private interest, influences later Enlightenment theorists, including both Rousseau and Madison. He describes the threat of factions to which Madison and Rousseau respond in different (indeed opposite) ways. He provides the basic structure and justification for the balance of political powers that Madison later incorporates into the U.S. Constitution.

Ethical Theory

Many of the leading issues and positions of contemporary philosophical ethics take shape within the Enlightenment. Prior to the Enlightenment in the West, ethical reflection begins from and orients itself around religious doctrines concerning God and the afterlife. The highest good of humanity, and, accordingly, the content and grounding of moral duties, are conceived in immediately religious terms. During the Enlightenment, this changes, certainly within philosophy, but to some significant degree, within the population of western society at large. As the processes of industrialization, urbanization, and dissemination of education advance in this period, happiness in this life, rather than union with God in the next, becomes the highest end for more and more people. Also, the violent religious wars that bloody Europe in the early modern period motivate the development of secular, this-worldly ethics, insofar as they indicate the failure of religious doctrines concerning God and the afterlife to establish a stable foundation for ethics. In the Enlightenment, philosophical thinkers confront the problem of developing ethical systems on a secular, broadly naturalistic basis for the first time since the rise of Christianity eclipsed the great classical ethical systems. However, the changes in our understanding of nature and cosmology, effected by modern natural science, make recourse to the systems of Plato and Aristotle problematic. The Platonic identification of the good with the real and the Aristotelian teleological understanding of natural things are both difficult to square with the Enlightenment conception of nature. The general philosophical problem emerges in the Enlightenment of how to understand the source and grounding of ethical duties, and how to conceive the highest good for human beings, within a secular, broadly naturalistic context, and within the context of a transformed understanding of the natural world.

In ethical thought, as in political theory, Hobbes' thought is an important provocation in the Enlightenment. Hobbes understands what is good, as the end of human action, to be "whatsoever is the object of any man's appetite or desire," and evil to be "the object of his hate, and aversion," "there being nothing simply and absolutely so; nor any common rule of good and evil, to be taken from the nature of the objects themselves" (*Leviathan*, chapter 6). Hobbes' conception of human beings as fundamentally motivated by their perception of what is in their own best interest implies the challenge, important for Enlightenment moral philosophy, to construct moral duties of justice and benevolence out of such limited materials.

The basis of human action that Hobbes posits is immediately intelligible and even shared with other animals to some extent; a set of moral duties constructed out of such a basis would be likewise intelligible, de-mystified, and fit within the larger scheme of nature. Bernard Mandeville is sometimes grouped with Hobbes in the Enlightenment, especially by critics of them both, because he too, in his popular *Fable of the Bees; or, Private Vices, Public Benefits* (1714), sees people as fundamentally motivated by their perceived self-interest, and then undertakes to tell a story about how moral virtue, which involves conquering one's own appetite and serving the interests of others, can be understood to arise out of this basis.

Samuel Clarke, an influential rationalist British thinker early in the Enlightenment, undertakes to show in his *Discourse concerning the Unchangeable Obligations of Natural Religion* (1706), against Hobbes explicitly, that the absolute difference between moral good and moral evil lies in the immediately discernible nature of things, independently of any compacts or positive legislation by God or human beings. Clarke writes that "in men's dealing ... one with another, it is undeniably more fit, absolutely and in the nature of the thing itself, that all men should endeavour to promote the universal good and welfare of all; than that all men should be continually contriving the ruin and destruction of all". Likewise for the rest of what morality enjoins upon us. According to Clarke, that some actions (those we call morally good or required) are "fit to be done" and others not fit is grounded upon the immediately evident relations in which things stand to each other in nature, just as "the proportions of lines or numbers" are evident to the rational perception of a reasonable being. Like Clarke's, Christian Wolff's rationalist practical philosophy also grounds moral duties in an objective rational order.

However, the objective quality on which moral requirements are grounded for Wolff is not the "fitness" of things to be done but rather their perfection. Wolff counts as a founder of the German *Aufklärung* in part because of his attempted derivation of ethical duties from an order of perfection in things, discernable through reason, independently of divine commands. Rationalist ethics so conceived faces the following obstacles in the Enlightenment. First, as implied above, it becomes increasingly implausible that the objective, mind-independent order is really as rationalist ethicists claim it to be. Second, even if the objective realm were ordered as the rationalist claims, it remains unclear how this order gives rise (on its own, as it were) to obligations binding on our wills. David Hume famously exposes the fallacy of deriving a prescriptive statement (that one ought to perform some action) from a description of how things stand in relation to each other in nature. Prima facie, there is a gap between the rationalist's objective order and a set of prescriptions binding on our wills; if a supreme legislator must be re-introduced in order to make the conformity of our actions to that objective order binding on our wills, then the alleged existence of the objective moral order does not do the work the account asks of it in the first place.

Alongside the rationalist strand of ethical philosophy in the Enlightenment, there is also a very significant empiricist strand. Empirical accounts of moral virtue in the period are distinguished, both by grounding moral virtue on an empirical study of human nature, and by grounding cognition of moral duties and moral motivation in human sensibility, rather than in reason. The Third Earl of Shaftesbury, author of the influential work *Characteristics of Men, Manners, Opinions, Times* (1711), is a founding figure of the empiricist strand. Shaftesbury, like Clarke, is provoked by Hobbes' egoism to provide a non-egoistic account of moral virtue. Shaftesbury conceives the core notion of the goodness of things teleologically: something is good if it contributes to the well-being or furtherance of the system of which it is a part. Individual animals are members of species, and therefore they are good as such insofar as they contribute to the well-being of the species of which they are a part. Thus, the good of things, including human beings, for Shaftesbury as for Clarke, is an objective quality that is knowable through reason.

However, though we can know what is good through reason, Shaftesbury maintains that reason alone is not sufficient to motivate human action. Shaftesbury articulates the structure of a distinctively human moral sensibility. Moral sensibility depends on the faculty of reflection. When we reflect on first-order passions such as gratitude, kindness and pity, we find ourselves approving or liking them and disapproving or disliking their opposites. By virtue of our receptivity to such feelings, we are capable of virtue and have a sense of right and wrong. In this way, Shaftesbury defines the moral sense that plays a significant role in the theories of subsequent Enlightenment thinkers such as Francis Hutcheson and David Hume.

In the rationalist tradition, the conflict within the breast of the person between the requirements of morality and self-interest is canonically a conflict between the person's reason and her passions. Shaftesbury's identification of a moral sentiment in the nature of humanity renders this a conflict within sensibility itself, a conflict between different sentiments, between a self-interested sentiment and an unegoistic sentiment. Though both Shaftesbury and Hutcheson, no less than Clarke, oppose Hobbes's egoism, it is nonetheless true that the doctrine of moral sensibility softens moral demands, so to speak. Doing what is morally right or morally good is intrinsically bound up with a distinctive kind of pleasure on their accounts. It is significant that both Shaftesbury and Hutcheson, the two founders of modern moral sense theory, articulate their ethical theory in conjunction with an aesthetic theory. Arguably the pleasure we feel in the apprehension of something beautiful is *disinterested pleasure*. Our susceptibility to aesthetic pleasure can be taken to reveal that we apprehend and respond to objective (or, anyway, universal) values, not only or necessarily on the basis of reason, but through our natural sensibility instead. Thus, aesthetics, as Shaftesbury and Hutcheson independently develop an account of it, gives encouragement to their doctrines of moral sensibility. But an account of moral virtue, unlike aesthetics, requires an account of moral *motivation*. As noted above, both Shaftesbury and Hutcheson want to do justice to the idea that proper moral motivation is not the pursuit of pleasure, even disinterested pleasure, but rather an immediate response to the perception of moral value. The problem of giving a satisfying account of moral motivation is a difficult one for empiricist moral philosophers in the Enlightenment.

While for Shaftesbury, at the beginning of the moral sense tradition, moral sense tracks a mind-independent order of value, David Hume, motivated in part by a more radical empiricism, is happy to let the objective order go. We have no access through reason to an independent order of value which moral sense would track. For Hume, morality is founded completely on our sentiments. Hume is often regarded as the main originator of so-called "ethical subjectivism", according to which moral judgments or evaluations (regarding actions or character) do not make claims about independent facts but merely express the subject's feelings or attitudes with respect to actions or character. Such subjectivism is relieved of the difficult task of explaining how the objective order of values belongs to the natural world as it is being reconceived by natural science in the period; however, it faces the challenge of explaining how error and disagreement in moral judgments and evaluations are possible. Hume's account of the standards of moral judgment follows that of Hutchenson in relying centrally on the "natural" responses of an ideal observer or spectator.

Hume's ethics is exemplary of philosophical ethics in the Enlightenment by virtue of its belonging to the attempt to provide a new, empirically grounded science of human nature, free of theological presuppositions. As noted above, the attempts by the members of the French Enlightenment to present a new understanding of human nature are strongly influenced by Locke's "sensationalism", which, radicalized by Condillac, amounts to the attempt to base all contents and faculties of the human mind on the senses. Typically, the French *philosophes* draw more radical or iconoclastic implications from the new "science of man" than English or Scottish Enlightenment figures. Claude-Adrien Helvétius (1715–1771) is typical here. In *De l'ésprit* (1758), Helvétius follows the Lockean sensationalism of Condillac and pairs it with the claim that human beings are motivated in their actions only by the natural desire to maximize their own pleasure and minimize their pain. *De l'ésprit*, though widely read, gives rise to strong negative reactions in the time, both by political and religious authorities (the Sorbonne, the Pope and the Parliament of Paris all condemn the book) and by prominent fellow *philosophes*, in great part because Helvétius's psychology seems to critics to render moral imperatives and values without basis, despite his best attempts to derive them. Helvétius attempts to ground the moral equality of all human beings by portraying all human beings, whatever their standing in the social hierarchy, whatever their special talents and gifts, as equally products of the nature we share plus the variable influences of education and social environment. But, to critics, Helvétius's account portrays all human beings as equal only by virtue of portraying all as equally worthless (insofar as the claim to equality is grounded on all being equally determined by external factors). However, Helvétius's ideas, in *De l'ésprit* as well as in its posthumously published sequel *De l'homme* (1772), exert a great deal of influence, especially his case for the role of pleasure and pain in human motivation and the role of education and social incentives in shaping individuals into contributors to the social good. Helvétius is sometimes regarded as the father of modern utilitarianism through his articulation of the greatest happiness principle and through his influence on Bentham.

Helvétius is typical in the respect that he is radical in the revisions he proposes, not in common moral judgments or customs of the time, but rather regarding the philosophical grounding of those judgments and customs. But there are some philosophers in the Enlightenment who are radical in the revisions they propose regarding the content of ethical judgments themselves. The Marquis de Sade is merely the most notorious example, among a set of Enlightenment figures (including also the Marquis de Argens and Diderot himself in some of his writings) who, within the context of the new naturalism and its emphasis on the pursuit of pleasure, celebrate the avid pursuit of sexual pleasure and explicitly challenge the sexual mores, as well as the wider morality, of their time. The more or less fictionalized, philosophically self-conscious "libertine" is one significant expression of Enlightenment ethical thought.

If the French Enlightenment tends to advance this-worldly happiness as the highest good for human beings more insistently than the Enlightenment elsewhere, then Rousseau's voice is, in this as in other respects, a discordant voice in that context. Rousseau advances the cultivation and realization of *human freedom* as the highest end for human beings and thereby gives expression to another side of Enlightenment ethics. As Rousseau describes it, the capacity for individual self-determination puts us in a problematic relation to our natural desires and inclinations and to the realm of nature generally, insofar as that realm is constituted by mechanistic causation. Though Rousseau places a great deal of emphasis on human freedom, and makes significant contributions to our understanding of ourselves as free, he does not address very seriously the problem of the place of human freedom in the cosmos as it is conceived within the context of Enlightenment naturalism.

However, Rousseau's writings help Kant to the articulation of a practical philosophy that addresses many of the tensions in the Enlightenment. Kant follows Rousseau, and disagrees with empiricism in ethics in the period, in emphasizing human freedom, rather than human happiness, as the central orienting concept of practical philosophy. Though Kant presents the moral principle as a principle of practical reason, his ethics also disagrees significantly with rationalist ethics in the period. According to Kant, rationalists such as Wolff, insofar as they take moral prescriptions to follow from an end (in Wolff's case, the end of perfection) that is given to the will externally, do not understand us as autonomous in our moral activity. Through interpreting the faculty of the will itself as practical reason, Kant understands the moral principle as internally legislated, thus as not only compatible with freedom, but as equivalent to the principle of a free will, as a principle of autonomy. As noted above, rationalists in ethics in the period are challenged to explain how the objective moral order which reason in us allegedly discerns gives rise to valid prescriptions binding on our wills (the gap between *is* and *ought*). For Kant, the moral order is not independent of our will, but rather represents the formal constraints of willing as such. Kant's account thus both avoids the is-ought gap and interprets moral willing as expressive of our freedom.

Moreover, by virtue of his interpretation of the moral principle as the principle of pure practical reason, Kant is able to redeem the ordinary sense of moral requirements as over-riding, as potentially opposed to the claims of one's happiness, and thus as different in kind from the deliverances of prudential reasoning. This ordinary sense of moral requirements is not easily accommodated within the context of Enlightenment empiricism and naturalism. Kant's stark dichotomy between a person's practical reason and her sensible nature is strongly criticized, both by the subsequent Romantic generation and in the contemporary context; but this dichotomy is bound up with an important benefit of Kant's view – much promoted by Kant himself – within the context of the Enlightenment. Elaborated in the context of Kant's idealism as a contrast between the "realm of freedom" and the "realm of nature", the dichotomy enables Kant's proposed solution to the conflict between freedom and nature that besets Enlightenment thought. As noted above, Kant argues that the application of the causal principle is restricted to the realm of nature, thus making room for freedom, compatibly with the causal determination of natural events required by scientific knowledge. Additionally, Kant attempts to show that morality "leads ineluctably to" religious belief (in the supersensible objects of God and of the immortal soul) while being essentially not founded on religious belief, thus again vindicating the ordinary understanding of morality while still furthering Enlightenment values and commitments.

Religion and the Enlightenment

Though the Enlightenment is sometimes represented as the enemy of religion, it is more accurate to see it as critically directed against various (arguably contingent) features of religion, such as superstition, enthusiasm, fanaticism and supernaturalism. Indeed the effort to discern and advocate for a religion purified of such features – a "rational" or "natural" religion – is more typical of the Enlightenment than opposition to religion as such. Even Voltaire, who is perhaps the most persistent, powerful, vocal Enlightenment critic of religion, directs his polemic mostly against the Catholic Church in France – "*l'infâme*" in his famous sign-off in his letters, "*Écrasez l'infâme*" ("Crush the infamous") refers to the Church, not to religion as such. However, controversy regarding the truth-value or reasonableness of religious belief in general, Christian belief in particular, and controversy regarding the proper place of religion in society, occupies a particularly central place in the Enlightenment. It's as if the terrible, violent confessional strife in the early modern period in Europe, the bloody drawn-out wars between the Christian sects, was removed to the intellectual arena in the Enlightenment and became a set of more general philosophical controversies.

Alongside the rise of the new science, the rise of Protestantism in western Christianity also plays an important role in generating the Enlightenment. The original Protestants assert a sort of individual liberty with respect to questions of faith against the paternalistic authority of the Church. The "liberty of conscience", so important to Enlightenment thinkers in general, and asserted against all manner of paternalistic authorities (including Protestant), descends from this Protestant assertion. The original Protestant assertion initiates a crisis of authority regarding religious belief, a crisis of authority that, expanded and generalized and even, to some extent, secularized, becomes a central characteristic of the Enlightenment spirit. The original Protestant assertion against the Catholic Church bases itself upon the authority of scripture. However, in the Enlightenment, the authority of scripture is strongly challenged, especially when taken literally. Developing natural science renders acceptance of a literal version of the Bible increasingly untenable. But authors such as Spinoza (in his *Tractatus Theologico-Politicus*) present ways of interpreting scripture according to its spirit, rather than its letter, in order to preserve its authority and truth, thus contributing to the Enlightenment controversy of whether some rationally purified version of the religion handed down in the culture belongs to the true philosophical representation of the world or not; and, if so, what its content is.

It is convenient to discuss religion in the Enlightenment by presenting four characteristic forms of Enlightenment religion in turn: deism, religion of the heart, fideism and atheism.

Deism. Deism is the form of religion most associated with the Enlightenment. According to deism, we can know by the natural light of reason that the universe is created and governed by a supreme intelligence; however, although this supreme being has a plan for creation from the beginning, the being does not interfere with creation;

the deist typically rejects miracles and reliance on special revelation as a source of religious doctrine and belief, in favour of the natural light of reason.

Thus, a deist typically rejects the divinity of Christ, as repugnant to reason; the deist typically demotes the figure of Jesus from agent of miraculous redemption to extraordinary moral teacher. Deism is the form of religion fitted to the new discoveries in natural science, according to which the cosmos displays an intricate machine-like order; the deists suppose that the supposition of God is necessary as the source or author of this order. Though not a deist himself, Isaac Newton inadvertently encourages deism in his *Opticks* (1704) by arguing that we must infer from the order and beauty in the world to the existence of an intelligent supreme being as the cause of this order and beauty. Samuel Clarke, perhaps the most important proponent and popularizer of Newtonian philosophy in the early eighteenth century, supplies some of the more developed arguments for the position that the correct exercise of unaided human reason leads inevitably to the well-grounded belief in God. He argues that the Newtonian physical system implies the existence of a transcendent cause, the creator God. In his first set of Boyle lectures, *A Demonstration of the Being and Attributes of God* (1705), Clarke presents the metaphysical or "argument *a priori*" for God's existence.

This argument concludes from the rationalist principle that whatever exists must have a sufficient reason or cause of its existence to the existence of a transcendent, necessary being who stands as the cause of the chain of natural causes and effects. Clarke also supports the empirical argument from design, the argument that concludes from the evidence of order in nature to the existence of an intelligent author of that order. In his second set of Boyle lectures, *A Discourse Concerning the Unchangeable Obligations of Natural Religion* (1706), Clarke argues as well that the moral order revealed to us by our natural reason requires the existence of a divine legislator and an afterlife, in which the supreme being rewards virtue and punishes vice. In his Boyle lectures, Clarke argues directly against the deist philosophy and maintains that what he regards as the one true religion, Christianity, is known as such on the basis of miracles and special revelation; still, Clarke's arguments on the topic of natural religion are some of the best and most widely-known arguments in the period for the general deist position that natural philosophy in a broad sense grounds central doctrines of a universal religion. Enlightenment deism first arises in England. In *On the Reasonableness of Christianity* (1695), Locke aims to establish the compatibility of reason and the teachings of Christianity. Though Locke himself is (like Newton, like Clarke) not a deist, the major English deists who follow (John Toland, *Christianity Not Mysterious* [1696]); Anthony Collins, *A Discourse of Freethinking* [1713]; Matthew Tindal, *Christianity as Old as Creation* [1730]) are influenced by Locke's work. Voltaire carries deism across the channel to France and advocates for it there over his long literary career. Toward the end-stage, the farcical stage, of the French revolution, Robespierre institutes a form of deism, the so-called "Cult of the Supreme Being", as the official religion of the French state. Deism plays a role in the founding of the American republic as well. Many of the founding fathers (Jefferson, Franklin, Madison, Paine) author statements or tracts that are sympathetic to deism; and their deistic sympathies influence the place given (or not given) to religion in the new American state that they found.

Religion of the Heart. Opposition to deism derives sometimes from the perception of it as coldly rationalistic. The God of the deists, arrived at through a priori or empirical argument and referred to as the Prime Mover or Original Architect, is often perceived as distant and unconcerned with the daily struggles of human existence, and thus as not answering the human needs from which religion springs in the first place. Some important thinkers of the Enlightenment – notably Shaftesbury and Rousseau – present religion as founded on natural human sentiments, rather than on the operations of the intellect. Rousseau has his Savoyard Vicar declare, in his Profession of Faith in *Emile* (1762), that the idea of worshiping a beneficent deity arose in him initially as he reflected on his own situation in nature and his "heart began to glow with a sense of gratitude towards the author of our being". The Savoyard Vicar continues: "I adore the supreme power, and melt into tenderness at his goodness. I have no need to be taught artificial forms of worship; the dictates of nature are sufficient. Is it not a natural consequence of self-love to honour those who protect us, and to love such as do us good?" This "natural" religion – opposed to the "artificial" religions enforced in the institutions – is often classed as a form of deism. But it deserves separate mention, because of its grounding in natural human sentiments, rather than in metaphysical or natural scientific problems of cosmology.

Fideism. Deism or natural religion of various sorts tends to rely on the claim that reason or human experience supports the hypothesis that there is a supreme being who created or authored the world. In one of the most important philosophical texts on natural religion to appear during the Enlightenment, David Hume's *Dialogues Concerning Natural Religion* (published posthumously in 1779), this supposition is criticized relentlessly, incisively and in detail. Naturally, the critical, questioning attitude characteristic of the Enlightenment in general is directed against the arguments on which natural religion is based. In Part Nine of the *Dialogues,* Samuel Clarke's "argument a priori" (as defended by the character Demea) is dispatched fairly quickly, but with a battery of arguments. But Hume is mainly concerned in the *Dialogues* with the other major pillar of natural religion in the Enlightenment, the "empirical" argument, the teleological argument or the argument from design. Cleanthes, the character who advances the design argument in the dialogue, proceeds from the rule for empirical reasoning that like effects prove like causes. He reasons that, given the resemblance between nature, which displays in many respects a "curious adaptation of means to ends", and a man-made machine, we must infer the cause of nature to be an intelligence like ours, though greater in proportion as nature surpasses in perfection the products of human intelligence. Philo, the skeptical voice in the *Dialogues*, presses Cleanthes' argument on many fronts. He points out that the argument is only as strong as the similarity between nature or parts of nature and man-made machines, and further, that a close scrutiny reveals that analogy to be weak. Moreover, according to the logic of the argument, the stronger the evidence for an author (or authors) of nature, the *more like us* that author (or authors) should be taken to be. Consequently, according to Philo, the argument does not support the conclusion that *God* exists, taking God to be unitary, infinite, perfect, et cetera. Also, although the existence of evil and disorder in nature may serve actually to strengthen the case for the argument, given the disorder in human creations as well, the notion that God authors evil and disorder is disturbing. If one denies that there is disorder and evil in nature, however implausibly, the effect is to emphasize again the dissimilarity between nature and human products and thus weaken the central basis of the argument. With these and other considerations, Philo puts the proponent of the empirical argument in a difficult dialectical position. But Cleanthes is not moved. He holds the inference from the phenomenon of the curious adaptation of means to ends in nature to the existence of an intelligent and beneficent author to be so natural as to be impervious to the philosophical cavils raised by Philo. And, in the ambiguous conclusion of the work, Philo seems to agree. Though Hume himself seems to have been an atheist, one natural way to take the upshot of his *Dialogues* is that religious belief is so "natural" to us that rational criticism cannot unseat it. The ambiguous upshot of the work can be taken to be the impotence of rational criticism in the face of religious belief, rather than the illegitimacy of religious belief in the face of rational criticism. This tends toward fideism, the view according to which religious faith maintains its truth over against philosophical reasoning, which opposes but cannot defeat it. Fideism is most often associated with thinkers whose beliefs run contrary to the trends of the Enlightenment (Blaise Pascal, Johann-Georg Hamann, Søren Kierkegaard), but the skeptical strain in the Enlightenment, from Pierre Bayle through David Hume, expresses itself not only in atheism, but also in fideism.

Atheism. Atheism is more present in the French Enlightenment than elsewhere. In the writings of Denis Diderot, atheism is partly supported by an expansive, dynamic conception of nature. According to the viewpoint developed by Diderot, we ought to search for the principles of natural order within natural processes themselves, not in a supernatural being. Even if we don't yet know the internal principles for the ordering and development of natural forms, the appeal to a transcendent author of such things is reminiscent, to Diderot's ear, of the appeal to Aristotelian "substantial forms" that was expressly rejected at the beginning of modern science as explaining nothing. The appeal to a transcendent author does not extend our understanding, but merely marks and fixes the limits of it. Atheism (combined with materialism) in the French Enlightenment is perhaps most identified with the Baron d'Holbach, whose *System of Nature* (1770) generated a great deal of controversy at the time for urging the case for atheism explicitly and emphatically. D'Holbach's system of nature is strongly influenced by Diderot's writings, though it displays less subtlety and dialectical sophistication. Though most Enlightenment thinkers hold that morality requires religion, in the sense that morality requires belief in a transcendent law-giver and in an after-life, d'Holbach (influenced in this respect by Spinoza, among others) makes the case for an ethical naturalism, an ethics that is free of any reference to a supernatural grounding or aspiration. Like Helvétius before him, d'Holbach presents an ethics in which virtue consists in enlightened self-interest. The metaphysical background of the ethics he presents is deterministic materialism. The Prussian enlightened despot, Frederick the Great, famously criticizes d'Holbach's book for exemplifying the incoherence that troubles the Enlightenment generally: while d'Holbach provides passionate moral critiques of existing religious and social and political institutions and practices, his own materialist, determinist conception of nature allows no place for moral "oughts" and prescriptions and values.

The Beautiful: Aesthetics in the Enlightenment

Modern systematic philosophical aesthetics not only first emerges in the context of the Enlightenment, but also flowers brilliantly there. As Ernst Cassirer notes, the eighteenth century not only thinks of itself as the "century of philosophy", but also as "the age of criticism," where criticism is centrally (though not only) art and literary criticism (Cassirer 1932, 255). Philosophical aesthetics flourishes in the period because of its strong affinities with the tendencies of the age. Alexander Baumgarten, the German philosopher in the school of Christian Wolff, founds systematic aesthetics in the period, in part through giving it its name. "Aesthetics" is derived from the Greek word for "senses", because for Baumgarten a science of the beautiful would be a science of the sensible, a science of sensible cognition. The Enlightenment in general re-discovers the value of the senses, not only in cognition, but in human lives in general, and so, given the intimate connection between beauty and human sensibility, the Enlightenment is naturally particularly interested in aesthetics. Also, the Enlightenment includes a general recovery and affirmation of the value of pleasure in human lives, against the past of Christian asceticism, and the flourishing of the arts, of the criticism of the arts and of the philosophical theorizing about beauty, promotes and is promoted by this recovery and affirmation. The Enlightenment also enthusiastically embraces the discovery and disclosure of rational order in nature, as manifest most clearly in the development of the new science. It seems to many theorists in the Enlightenment that the faculty of taste, the faculty by which we discern beauty, reveals to us some part of this order, a distinctive harmony, unities amidst variety. Thus, in the phenomenon of aesthetic pleasure, human sensibility discloses to us rational order, thus binding together two enthusiasms of the Enlightenment.

French Classicism and German Rationalism

In the early Enlightenment, especially in France, the emphasis is upon the discernment of an objective rational order, rather than upon the subject's sensual aesthetic pleasure. Though Descartes' philosophical system does not include a theory of taste or of beauty, his mathematical model of the physical universe inspires the aesthetics of French classicism. French classicism begins from the classical maxim that the beautiful is the true. Nicolas Boileau writes in his influential didactic poem, *The Art of Poetry* (1674), in which he lays down rules for good versification within different genres, that "Nothing is beautiful but the true, the true alone is lovable." In the period the true is conceived of as an objective rational order. According to the classical conception of art that dominates in the period, art *imitates* nature, though not nature as given in disordered experience, but the *ideal* nature, the ideal in which we can discern and enjoy "unity in multiplicity." In French classicism, aesthetics is very much under the influence of, and indeed modelled on, systematic, rigorous theoretical science of nature. Just as in Descartes' model of science, where knowledge of all particulars depends on prior knowledge of the principle from which the particulars are deduced, so also in the aesthetics of French classicism, the demand is for systematization under a single, universal principle. The subjection of artistic phenomena to universal rules and principles, the quest for system is expressed, for example, in the title of Charles Batteaux's main work, *The Fine Arts Reduced to a Single Principle* (1746), as well as in Boileau's rules for good versification.

In Germany in the eighteenth century, Christian Wolff's systematic rationalist metaphysics forms the basis for much of the reflection on aesthetics, though sometimes as a set of doctrines to be argued against. For Wolff, the classical dictum that beauty is truth holds good; beauty is truth perceived through the feeling of pleasure. Wolff understands beauty to consist in the perfection in things, which he understands in turn to consist in a harmony or order of a manifold. We judge something beautiful through a feeling of pleasure when we sense in it this harmony or perfection. Beauty is, for Wolff, the sensitive cognition of perfection. Thus, for Wolff, beauty corresponds to objective features of the world, but judgments of beauty are relative to us also, insofar as they are based on the human faculty of sensibility.

Empiricism and Subjectivism

Though philosophical rationalism forms the basis of aesthetics in the early Enlightenment in France and Germany, thinkers in the empiricist tradition in England and Scotland introduce many of the salient themes of Enlightenment aesthetics. In particular, with the rise of empiricism and subjectivism in this domain, attention shifts to the ground and nature of the subject's experience of beauty, the subject's aesthetic response, and this focus is characteristic of Enlightenment aesthetics. Lord Shaftesbury, though not himself an empiricist or subjectivist in aesthetics, makes significant contributions to this development. Shaftesbury re-iterates the classical equation, "all beauty is truth," but the truth that beauty is for Shaftesbury is not an objective rational order that could also be known conceptually. Though beauty is, for Shaftesbury, a kind of harmony that is independent of the human mind, under the influence of Plotinus, he understands the human being's immediate intuition of the beautiful as a kind of participation in the original harmony. Shaftesbury focuses attention on the nature of the subject's response to beauty, as elevating the person, also morally. He maintains that aesthetic response consists in a *disinterested* unegoistic pleasure; the discovery of this capacity for disinterested pleasure in harmony shows the way for the development of his ethics that has a similar grounding. And, in fact, in seeing aesthetic response as elevating oneself above self-interested pursuits, through cultivating one's receptivity to disinterested pleasure, Shaftesbury ties tightly together aesthetics and ethics, morality and beauty, and in that respect also contributes to a trend of the period. Also, in placing the emphasis on the subject's response to beauty, rather than on the objective characteristics of the beautiful, Shaftesbury makes aesthetics belong to the general Enlightenment interest in human nature. Thinkers of the period find in our receptivity to beauty a key both to understanding distinctively human nature and to its perfection.

Francis Hutcheson follows Shaftesbury in his emphasis on the subject's aesthetic response, on the distinctive sort of pleasure that the beautiful elicits in us. Partly because the Neo-Platonic influence, so pronounced in Shaftesbury's aesthetics, is washed out of Hutcheson's, to be replaced by a more thorough-going empiricism, Hutcheson understands this distinctive aesthetic pleasure as more akin to a secondary quality. Thus, Hutcheson's aesthetic work raises the prominent question whether "beauty" refers to something objective at all or whether beauty is "nothing more" than a human idea or experience. As in the domain of Enlightenment ethics, so with Enlightenment aesthetics too, the step from Shaftesbury to Hutcheson marks a step toward subjectivism. Hutcheson writes in one of his *Two Treatises*, his *Inquiry Concerning Beauty, Order, Harmony, Design* (1725) that "the word 'beauty' is taken for the *idea raised in us*, and a *sense* of beauty for *our power of receiving this idea*" (Section I, Article IX). However, though Hutcheson understands beauty to be an idea in us, he takes this idea to be "excited" or "occasioned" in us by distinctive objective qualities, in particular by objects that display "*uniformity amidst variety*" (ibid., Section II, Article III). In the very title of Hutcheson's work above, we see the importance of the classical ideas of (rational) order and harmony in Hutcheson's aesthetic theory, even as he sets the tenor for much Enlightenment discussion of aesthetics through placing the emphasis on the subjective idea and aesthetic response.

David Hume's famous essay on "the standard of taste" raises and addresses the epistemological problem raised by subjectivism in aesthetics. If beauty is an idea in us, rather than a feature of objects independent of us, then how do we understand the possibility of correctness and incorrectness – how do we understand the possibility of standards of judgment – in this domain? The problem is posed more clearly for Hume because he intensifies Hutcheson's subjectivism. He writes in the *Treatise* that "pleasure and pain….are not only necessary attendants of beauty and deformity, but constitute their very essence" (*Treatise,* Book II, part I, section viii). But if a judgment of taste is based on, or expresses, subjective sentiments, how can it be incorrect? In his response to this question, Hume accounts for the expectation of agreement in judgments of taste by appealing to the fact that we share a common human nature, and he accounts for 'objectivity' or expertise in judgments of taste, within the context of his subjectivism, by appealing to the normative responses of well-placed observers. Both of these points (the commonality of human nature and the securing of 'objectivity' in judgments based on sentiments by appeal to the normative responses of appropriately placed observers) are typical of the period more generally, and especially of the strong empiricist strain in the Enlightenment. Hume develops the empiricist line in aesthetics to the point where little remains of the classical emphasis on the order or harmony or truth that is, according to the French classicists, apprehended and appreciated in our aesthetic responses to the beautiful, and thus, according to the classicists, the ground of aesthetic responses.

Late Enlightenment Aesthetics

Immanuel Kant faces squarely the problem of the normativity of judgments of taste. Influenced by Hutcheson and the British empiricist tradition in general, Kant understands judgments of taste to be founded on a distinctive sort of feeling, a *disinterested* pleasure. In taking judgments of taste to be subjective (they are founded on the subject's feeling of pleasure) and non-cognitive (such judgments do not subsume representations under concepts and thus do not ascribe properties to objects), Kant breaks with the German rationalist school. However Kant continues to maintain that judgments of beauty are like cognitive judgments in making a legitimate claim to universal agreement – in contrast to judgments of the agreeable. The question is how to vindicate the legitimacy of this demand. Kant argues that the distinctive pleasure underlying judgments of taste is the experience of the harmony of the faculties of the imagination and the understanding, a harmony that arises through their "free play" in the process of cognizing objects on the basis of given sensible intuition. The harmony is "free" in an experience of beauty in the sense that it is not forced by rules of the understanding, as is the agreement among the faculties in acts of cognition. The order and harmony that we experience in the face of the beautiful is subjective, according to Kant; but it is at the same time universal and normative, by virtue of its relation to the conditions of human cognition.

The emphasis Kant places on the role of the activity of the imagination in aesthetic pleasure and discernment typifies a trend in Enlightenment thought. Whereas early in the Enlightenment, in French classicism, and to some extent in Christian Wolff and other figures of German rationalism, the emphasis is on the more-or-less static rational order and proportion and on rigid universal rules or laws of reason, the trend during the development of Enlightenment aesthetics is toward emphasis on the *play* of the imagination and its fecundity in generating associations.

Denis Diderot is an important and influential author on aesthetics. He wrote the entry "On the Origin and Nature of the Beautiful" for the *Encyclopedia* (1752). Like Lessing in Germany, Diderot not only philosophized about art and beauty, but also wrote plays and influential art criticism. Diderot is strongly influenced in his writings on aesthetics by the empiricism in England and Scotland, but his writing is not limited to that standpoint. Diderot repeats the classical dictum that art should imitate nature, but, whereas, for French classicists, the nature that art should imitate is *ideal* nature – a static, universal rational order – for Diderot, nature is dynamic and productive. For Diderot, the nature the artist ought to imitate is the *real* nature we experience, warts and all (as it were), in its particularity. The particularism and realism of Diderot's aesthetics is based on a critique of the standpoint of French classicism. According to this critique, the artistic rules that the French classicists represent as universal rules of reason are exposed as being nothing more than *conventions* marking what is considered *proper* within a certain tradition; in other words, the prescriptions within the French classical tradition are *artificial*, not *natural*, and the means of liberation from the fetters which Diderot takes them to represent to artistic genius is exactly to turn to the task of observing and imitating *actual nature*. Diderot's emphasis on the primeval productive power and abundance of nature in his aesthetic writings contributes to the trend toward focus on artistic creation and expression (as opposed to artistic appreciation and discernment) that is a characteristic of the late Enlightenment and the transition to Romanticism.

Lessing's aesthetic writings play an important role in elevating the aesthetic category of expressiveness. In his famous *Laocoön: An Essay on the Limits of Painting and Poetry* (1766), Lessing argues, by comparing the famous Greek statue with the representation of Laocoön's suffering in Virgil's poetry, that the aims of poetry and of the visual arts are not the same; he argues that the aim of poetry is not beauty, but expression. In elevating the aesthetic category of expressiveness, Lessing challenges the notion that all art is imitation of nature. His argument also challenges the notion that all the various arts can be deduced from a single principle. Lessing's argument in *Laocoön* supports the contrary thesis that the distinct arts have distinct aims and methods, and that each should be understood on its own terms, not in terms of an abstract general principle from which all arts are to be deduced. For some, especially for critics of the Enlightenment, in this point Lessing is already beyond the Enlightenment, given that it is characteristic of the Enlightenment to know the particular through its subsumption under the universal law (of reason). Certainly it is true that the emphasis on the individual or particular, over against the universal, which one finds in other late Enlightenment thinkers, is in tension with Enlightenment tenets. Herder (following Hamann to some extent) argues that each individual art *object* has to be understood in its own terms, as a totality complete unto itself. With Herder's stark emphasis on individuality in aesthetics, over against universality, the supplanting of the Enlightenment with Romanticism and Historicism is well advanced.

But, according to the point of view taken in this entry, the conception of the Enlightenment according to which it is distinguished by its prioritization of the order of abstract, universal laws and principles, over against concrete particulars and the differences amongst them, is too narrow; it fails to account for much of the characteristic richness in the thought of the period. Indeed aesthetics itself, as a discipline, which, as noted, is founded in the Enlightenment by the German rationalist, Alexander Baumgarten, owes its existence to the tendency in the Enlightenment to search for and discover distinct laws for distinct kinds of phenomena (as opposed to insisting that all phenomena be made intelligible through the same set of general laws and principles). Baumgarten founds aesthetics as a 'science' through the attempt to establish the sensible domain as cognizable in a way different from that which prevails in metaphysics. Aesthetics in Germany in the eighteenth century, from Wolff to Herder, both typifies many of the trends of the Enlightenment and marks the field where the Enlightenment yields to competing worldviews.

Counter-Enlightenment

The Counter-Enlightenment was a term that some 20th century commentators have used to describe multiple strains of thought that arose in the late-18th and early-19th centuries in opposition to the 18th century Enlightenment. The term is usually associated with Isaiah Berlin, who is often credited with coining it, perhaps taking up a passing remark of the German philosopher Friedrich Nietzsche, who used the term *Gegenaufklärung* at the end of the 19th century. The first known use of the term 'counter-enlightenment' in English was in 1949. Berlin published widely about the Enlightenment and its enemies and did much to popularise the concept of a Counter-Enlightenment movement that he characterised as relativist, anti-rationalist, vitalist, and organic, and which he associated most closely with German Romanticism. Some recent scholarship has challenged this view for focusing too narrowly on Germany and stopping abruptly in the early 19th century, thereby ignoring the Enlightenment's many subsequent critics, particularly in the 20th century. Some scholars reject the use of the term 'the Counter-Enlightenment' on the grounds that there was no single Enlightenment for its alleged enemies to oppose.

The Counter-Enlightenment Movement vs Enlightenment Thinkers

Although the term 'the Counter-Enlightenment' was first used in English (in passing) by William Barrett in a 1949 article ("Art, Aristocracy and Reason") in *Partisan Review*, it was Isaiah Berlin who established its place in the history of ideas. He used the term to refer to a movement that arose primarily in late 18th and early 19th century Germany against the rationalism, universalism and empiricism commonly associated with the Enlightenment. Berlin's widely read essay "The Counter-Enlightenment" was first published in 1973, and later reprinted in a popular collection of his essays, *Against the Current*, in 1981. The term has had wide currency since.

Berlin argues that, while there were enemies of the Enlightenment outside of Germany (e.g. Joseph de Maistre) and before the 1770s (e.g. Giambattista Vico), Counter-Enlightenment thought did not really 'take off' until the Germans 'rebelled against the dead hand of France in the realms of culture, art and philosophy, and avenged themselves by launching the great counter-attack against the Enlightenment.' This reaction was led by the Königsberg philosopher J. G. Hamann, 'the most passionate, consistent, extreme and implacable enemy of the Enlightenment', according to Berlin.

This German reaction to the imperialistic universalism of the French Enlightenment and Revolution, which had been forced on them first by the francophile Frederick II of Prussia, then by the armies of Revolutionary France, and finally by Napoleon, was crucial to the epochal shift of consciousness that occurred in Europe at this time, leading eventually to Romanticism. According to Berlin, the surprising and unintended consequence of this revolt against the Enlightenment has been pluralism, which owes more to the Enlightenment's enemies than it does to its proponents, most of whom were monists whose political, intellectual and ideological offspring have often been terror and totalitarianism. Richard Wolin (*The Seduction of Unreason* 2004) has traced the modern descendants of the Counter-Enlightenment in postmodernism's deep suspicion of universalism, paralleled by its endorsement of identity politics, and concludes that it has worked against the values of toleration and mutual recognition, not merely of diversity but of commonality.

In his book *Enemies of the Enlightenment* (2001), historian Darrin McMahon extends the Counter-Enlightenment both back to pre-Revolutionary France and down to the level of 'Grub Street,' thereby marking a major advance on Berlin's intellectual and Germanocentric view. McMahon focuses on the early enemies of the Enlightenment in France, unearthing a long-forgotten 'Grub Street' literature in the late-18th and early 19th centuries aimed at the *philosophes*. He delves into the obscure and at times unseemly world of the 'low Counter-Enlightenment' that attacked the *encyclopédistes* and fought an often dirty battle to prevent the dissemination of Enlightenment ideas in the second half of the century. A great many of these early opponents of the Enlightenment attacked it for undermining religion and the social and political order. This later became a major theme of conservative criticism of the Enlightenment after the French Revolution appeared to vindicate the warnings of the *anti-philosophes* in the decades prior to 1789.

In his 1996 article in the *American Political Science Review* (Vol. 90, No. 2), Arthur M. Melzer identifies the origin of the Counter-Enlightenment in the religious writings of Jean-Jacques Rousseau, showing Rousseau as the man who fired the first shot in the war between the Enlightenment and its enemies. Graeme Garrard follows Melzer in his "Rousseau's Counter-Enlightenment" (2003). This contradicts Berlin's depiction of Rousseau as a *philosophe* (albeit an erratic one) who shared the basic beliefs of his Enlightenment contemporaries. Also, like McMahon, it traces the beginning of Counter-Enlightenment thought back to France and prior to the German *Sturm und Drang* movement of the 1770s. Garrard's book *Counter-Enlightenments* (2006) broadens the term even further, arguing against Berlin that there was no single 'movement' called 'The Counter-Enlightenment'. Rather, there have been many Counter-Enlightenments, from the middle of the 18th century through to 20th century Enlightenment critics among critical theorists, postmodernists and feminists. The Enlightenment has enemies on all points of the ideological compass, from the far left to the far right, and all points in between. Each of the Enlightenment's enemies depicted it as they saw it or wanted others to see it, resulting in a vast range of portraits, many of which are not only different but incompatible.

This argument has been taken a step further by some, like intellectual historian James Schmidt, who question the idea of the 'Enlightenment' and therefore of the existence of a movement opposing it. As our conception of the 'Enlightenment' has become more complex and difficult to maintain, so too has the idea of the 'Counter-Enlightenment'. Advances in Enlightenment scholarship in the last quarter-century have challenged the stereotypical view of the 18th century as an 'Age of Reason', leading Schmidt to speculate on whether the Enlightenment might not actually be a creation of its enemies, rather than the other way round. The fact that the term 'Enlightenment' was first used in 1894 in English to refer to a historical period lends support to the argument that it was a late construction projected back onto the 18th century.

Counter-Enlightenment and Counter-Revolution

Although serious doubts were raised about the Enlightenment prior to the 1790s (e.g. in the works of Jean-Jacques Rousseau in France and J.G. Hamann in Germany in particular), the Reign of Terror during the French Revolution fuelled a major reaction against the Enlightenment, which many writers blamed for undermining traditional beliefs that sustained the ancien regime, thereby fomenting revolution. Counter-revolutionary writings like those of Edmund Burke, Joseph de Maistre and Augustin Barruel all asserted a close link between the Enlightenment and the Revolution, as did many of the revolutionary leaders themselves, so that the Enlightenment became increasingly discredited as the Revolution became increasingly bloody. That is why the French Revolution and its aftermath was also a major phase in the development of Counter-Enlightenment thought. For example, while Edmund Burke's *Reflections on the Revolution in France* (1790) contains no systematic account of the connection between the Enlightenment and the Revolution, it is heavily spiced with hostile references to the French revolutionaries as merely politicised *philosophes*. Barruel argues in *Memoirs Illustrating the History of Jacobinism* (1797) — one of the most widely read books of its period — that the Revolution was the consequence of a conspiracy of *philosophes* and freemasons. In *Considerations on France* (1797), Maistre interprets the Revolution as divine punishment for the sins of the Enlightenment.

The Romantic Revolt against the Eighteenth Century

Many early Romantic writers such as Chateaubriand, Novalis and Samuel Taylor Coleridge inherited this Counter-Revolutionary antipathy towards the philosophes. All three directly blamed the *philosophes* in France and the *Aufklärer* in Germany for devaluing beauty, spirit and history in favour of a view of man as a soulless machine and a view of the universe as a meaningless, disenchanted void lacking richness and beauty. Of particular concern to early Romantic writers was the allegedly anti-religious nature of the Enlightenment since the *philosophes* and *Aufklarer* were generally deists, opposed to revealed religion. Yet many Romantic poets were either Deists or Pantheists, and neither they nor the Enlightenment Deists can be considered anti-religious, unless in a fundamentalist sense. Rather, they questioned the idea of a personal anthropomorphic God who interfered with the laws of nature. Some historians nevertheless contend that this view of the Enlightenment as an age hostile to religion is common ground between these Romantic writers and many of their conservative Counter-Revolutionary predecessors. However, Chateaubriand, Novalis and Coleridge are exceptions here: few Romantic writers had much to say for or against the Enlightenment and the term itself did not exist at the time. For the most part, they ignored it.

The philosopher Jacques Barzun argues that Romanticism had its roots in the Enlightenment. It was not anti-rational, but rather it balanced rationality against the competing claims of intuition and the sense of justice. This view is expressed in Goya's *Sleep of Reason* (left), in which the nightmarish owl offers the dozing social critic of *Los Caprichos* a piece of drawing chalk. Even the rational critic is inspired by irrational dream-content under the gaze of the sharp-eyed lynx. Marshall Brown makes much the same argument as Barzun in *Romanticism and Enlightenment*, questioning the stark opposition between these two periods.

By the middle of the 19th century, the memory of the French Revolution was fading and Romanticism had more or less run its course. In this optimistic age of science and industry, there were few critics of the Enlightenment, and few explicit defenders. Friedrich Nietzsche is a notable and highly influential exception. After an initial defence of the Enlightenment in his so-called 'middle period' (late-1870s to early 1880s), Nietzsche turned vehemently against it and subscribed to the earlier view of conservative Counter-Revolutionaries like Burke and Maistre who attributed the French Revolution (which Nietzsche always hated) to the Enlightenment.

Enlightened Totalitarianism

It was not until after World War II that 'the Enlightenment' re-emerged as a key organising concept in social and political thought and the history of ideas. Shadowing it has been a resurgent Counter-Enlightenment literature blaming the 18th century trust in reason for 20th century totalitarianism. The *locus classicus* of this view is Max Horkheimer and Theodor Adorno's *Dialectic of Enlightenment* (1947), which traces the degeneration of the general concept of enlightenment from ancient Greece (epitomised by the cunning 'bourgeois' hero Odysseus) to 20th century fascism. (They say little about Soviet communism, referring to it as a regressive totalitarianism that "clung all too desperately to the heritage of bourgeois philosophy").

While this influential book takes 'enlightenment' as its target, this includes its 18th century form – which we now call 'the Enlightenment' – epitomised by the Marquis de Sade. Many postmodern writers and some feminists (e.g. Jane Flax) have made similar arguments, likewise seeing *the* Enlightenment conception of reason as totalitarian, and as not having been enlightened enough since, for Adorno and Horkheimer, though it banishes myth it falls back into a further myth, that of individualism and formal (or mythic) equality under instrumental reason.

Michel Foucault, for example, argued that attitudes towards the "insane" during the late-18th and early 19th centuries show that supposedly enlightened notions of humane treatment were not universally adhered to, but instead, that the Age of Reason had to construct an image of "Unreason" against which to take an opposing stand. Berlin himself, although no postmodernist, argues that the Enlightenment's legacy in the 20th century has been monism (which he claims favours political authoritarianism), whereas the legacy of the Counter-Enlightenment has been pluralism (something he associates with liberalism). These are two of the 'strange reversals' of modern intellectual history.

The Enlightenment's "Perversion of Reason"

What seems to unite all of the Enlightenment's disparate critics (from 18th century religious opponents, counter-revolutionaries and Romantics to 20th century conservatives, feminists, critical theorists and environmentalists) is a rejection of what they consider to be the Enlightenment's perversion of reason: the distorted conceptions of reason of the kind each associates with the Enlightenment in favour of a more restricted view of the nature, scope and limits of human rationality.

However, very few of the enemies of the Enlightenment have abandoned reason entirely. The battle has been over the scope, meaning and application of reason, not over whether it is good or bad, desirable or undesirable, essential or inessential per se. The conflict between the Enlightenment and the Counter-Enlightenment is not a conflict between friends and enemies of reason, any more than it is between friends and enemies of the notion of enlightenment.

Although objections have consistently been raised against what has been taken as the typical Enlightenment view of reason by its opponents (on all points of the ideological spectrum, left, right, and centre), this has almost never been generalised to reason as such by Counter-Enlightenment thinkers. Some charge that the Enlightenment inflated the power and scope of reason, while others claim that it narrowed it.

Critical Theory and the Crisis of Social Theory

Social theory today is in crisis. During the 1960s, a variety of new theoretical paradigms emerged which put in question the prevailing quantitative, empiricist, and positivist conceptions of social theory and social research. Growing dissatisfaction with the dominant methodologies and theories produced by the mainstream promoted a search for alternative methodologies and conceptions of social theory and research. The new paradigms of phenomenology, enthno-methodology, structuralism, Marxism, feminism, and other critical theories offered new conceptions which claimed to be more adequate in characterizing contemporary society and in providing inspiration and guidance for transforming it. These theories have caused much ferment in the field of social theory and have inspired heated debates over the nature, methods, and goals of critical social theory.

More recently, poststructuralist and postmodern social theory have further challenged mainstream social theory and science, attacking their basic presuppositions. In addition, these new critical discourses have sharply criticized Marxism, structuralism, phenomenology, and other critical paradigms for participating too staunchly in the premises and methods of modern, enlightenment rationality and traditional social theory (Kellner 1988 and 1989b). While debates have emerged between advocates of critical theory and the newer, postmodern approaches which I shall discuss later in the paper, there are also common positions. Like some of the new French theories, the critical theory of the so-called Frankfurt school offers a multi-disciplinary approach for social theory which combines perspectives drawn from political economy, sociology, cultural theory, philosophy, anthropology, and history. It thus overcomes the fragmentation endemic to established academic disciplines in order to address issues of broader interest.

Both new French theory and critical theory therefore put in question the boundaries established by the academic division of labour which separates social theory from other disciplines. Both claim that there are epistemological and metaphysical problems with abstracting from the interconnectedness of phenomena in the world, or from our experience of it. On this view, philosophy, for example, that abstracts from sociology and economics, or political science that excludes, say, economics or culture from its conceptual boundaries, is by nature one-sided, limited, and flawed. Both critical theory and new French theory therefore transgress established disciplinary boundaries and create new theories and discourses that avoid the deficiencies of the traditional academic division of labour.

In this paper, I shall argue that as an antidote to the frequently non-critical quantitative approaches within mainstream social science and theory, critical theory provides a potentially more useful and politically relevant alternative than poststructuralist and postmodernist theory. In opposition to the subjectivism and relativism, often bordering on nihilism, advanced by some of these postmodernist perspectives, critical theory, by contrast, advances the conception of a critical and normative theory which is committed to emancipation from all forms of oppression, as well as to freedom, happiness, and a rational ordering of society. In contrast to the often hypertheoretical and apolitical discourse of postmodern theory, critical theory seeks a connection with empirical analysis of the contemporary world and social movements which are attempting to transform society in progressive ways.

To highlight the contributions of critical theory to contemporary social theory, I shall therefore, first, present the conception of dialectical social theory contained in the notion of a critical theory of society. Next, I articulate what I consider to be among its most substantive contributions to contemporary social theory, and then I shall criticize some of its limitations and provide some new perspectives for critical theory today. To begin, however, I wish to briefly describe the origins and development of critical theory.

Historical Background

Critical theory is often associated with the so-called "Frankfurt School," a term which refers to the work of members of the Institut fur Sozialforschung (Institute for Social Research). [1] The Institute was established in Frankfurt, Germany during 1923 as the first Marxist-oriented research centre affiliated with a major German university. The Institute's work in the 1920's was directed by Carl Grunberg, and tended to be empirical, historical, and oriented toward problems of the European working class movement, although theoretical works by Karl Korsch, Georg Lukacs, and others were also published in its journal, Archiv fur die Geschichte des Sozialismus und der Arbeiterbewegung.

After Grunberg's retirement in 1930, Max Horkheimer became Director of the Instutute. Horkheimer gathered around him such talented theorists as Leo Lowenthal, Friedrich Pollock, Erich Fromm, Henryk Grossman, and Herbert Marcuse. Later T.W. Adorno, Otto Kirchheimer, Franz Neumann and others joined the Institute, which also supported theorists like Korsch and Walter Benjamin. Under Horkheimer's directorship, the Institute sought to develop an interdisciplinary social theory which could serve as an instrument of social transformation. During the Horkheimer era, Institute work was characterized by a synthesis of philosophy and social theory and research. The results of Institute work were published in its journal, Zeitschrift fur Sozialforschung (1932-1941), which contains a rich collection of articles and book reviews still worth reading.

Upon assuming the position of Director, Horkheimer delivered an inaugural address on January 24, 1931, entitled "The State of Social Philosophy and the Tasks of an Institute for Social Research" (Bronner and Kellner 1989:25-36). In this text, Horkheimer defines social philosophy as an attempt to elucidate the "fate of human beings, insofar as they are parts of a community, and not mere individuals. It concerns itself above all with the social life of people: state, law, economy, religion, in short, with the entire material and spiritual culture of humanity" (ibid:33). Horkheimer's lecture provides the first major conception of his view of critical social theory as a synthesis of social science and philosophy, and therefore provides a useful introduction to the Institute's project.

Horkheimer begins by pointing to the limitations of the classical German social theories of Kant and Hegel, and the limitations of contemporary metaphysical and positivist philosophies. This exercise typifies Horkheimer's method of clarifying his own position through criticism of opposing positions. Kant is criticized for grounding social philosophy in the experience and faculties of the particular individual (ibid:33ff). Hegel's attempt to situate philosophy within society and history is presented as an improvement over Kant, yet Hegel's idealism and tendency to justify the existing order is rejected (ibid:34-37). Then Horkheimer criticizes the current forms of idealism in the neo-Kantian, neo-Hegelian, phenomenological, and existential philosophies for their questionable speculative metaphysics and for their tendencies to celebrate a higher transcendental sphere of Being (Sein) and meaning (Sinn) over concrete existence (ibid:38-39). The positivist schools which root their theories in isolated facts are also criticized for their unsupportable metaphysical presuppositions and methodological limitations (ibid:39).

Horkheimer concludes that none of the dominant philosophical schools contain an adequate social philosophy. He assumes that social philosophy encompasses "the entire material and spiritual culture of humanity." Consequently, he rejects the claims of the specific social sciences such as "material sociology" to provide adequate knowledge since the specialized sciences abstract from the structure and organization of society as a whole to describe limited domains of social experience. In opposing the separation between social theory, science, and philosophy which was dominant at the time, and which continues to be dominant today, Horkheimer calls for a new sort of synthesis between philosophy and the specialized sciences.

Consequently, while Comte, Durkheim, positivists, and others want to purge philosophy from social theory, Horkheimer defends its importance for critical social theory. He claims that the positivist conception that philosophy "is perhaps beautiful, but scientifically fruitless because it is not subject to controls," verification, experiments and the like, must be rejected, as must as well the philosopher's prejudice that he or she is dealing with the essential while the scientist is dealing with bare, trival facts (ibid:40). These conflicting claims to the primacy of science and philosophy must be overcome in favour of a "dialectical penetration and development of philosophical theory and the praxis of the individual disciplines" (ibid:40). For Horkheimer, the philosophical drive toward the universal and essential should be the animating spirit for social research, but philosophy must be at the same time "sufficiently open to the world to allow itself to be impressed with, and transformed by, progress in concrete studies" (ibid:41).

To fulfill these goals, Horkheimer envisaged a program of supradisciplinary research which would investigate current social and political problems. This project would unite "philosophers, sociologists, economists, historians, and psychologists in an ongoing research community who would do together what in other disciplines one individual does alone in the laboratory, — which is what genuine scientists have always done: namely, to pursue the great philosophical questions using the most refined scientific methods; to reformulate and to make more precise the questions in the course of work as demanded by the object; and to develop new methods without losing sight of the universal" (ibid:41).

After praising his predecessor Carl Grundberg's legacy and contributions, Horkheimer stresses that the Institute will now undertake a "new start" directed at "new tasks" (ibid:42). He claims that the Institute's new multidisciplinary program will allow its members to raise the question of "the interconnections between the economic life of society, the psychic development of the individual and transformations in the realm of culture... including not only the so-called spiritual contents of science, art and religion, but also law, ethics, fashion, public opinion, sport, amusement, life style, etc." (ibid:43). This research program is somewhat unorthodox for a Marxian social theory which in the past tended to neglect the dimension of individual and social psychology, and which also downplayed the study of culture and leisure. Attention to these topics would eventually produce many of the distinctive contributions of critical theory.

In his inaugural address, Horkheimer distances his conception of social theory from a crude Marxian materialism. He proclaims that the Institute will not subscribe to any metaphysical theses, such as idealism or materialism, on the relation between the economy, society, culture, and consciousness. Horkheimer notes that the attempt to derive all forms of life from one metaphysical substance is "bad Spinozaism." From the very beginning, therefore, Horkheimer rejects all metaphysical absolutism and all philosophical reductionism. He argues that an illusory idealism that derives everything from the Idea is "an abstract and therefore badly understood Hegel," just as the attempt to derive everything from an economy which is understood merely as material being is "an abstract and therefore badly understood Marx" (ibid:43). Such theses posit an "uncritical, obsolete and highly problematic cleavage of spirit and reality into naive absolutes" and must be dialectically overcome (ibid:43).

Critical social philosophy, by contrast, describes the complex set of mediations that interconnect consciousness and society, culture and economy, state and citizens. These relations can best be clarified and developed in concrete historical contexts in which one asks: "which interconnections exist in a definite social group, in a definite period of time and in a definite country, between the role of this group in the economic process, the transformation of the psychic structures of its individual members, and the totality of the system that affects and produces its thoughts and mechanism" (ibid:44).

To begin this task, the Institute proposed to study technically qualified workers and employees in Germany by gathering empirical material on their psychological, social, and political attitudes which would be interpreted in a theoretical framework that encompasses economic theory, sociology, and psychology. Horkheimer illustrated the project of the Institute's social theory by indicating that an empirical study of the white-collar working class would be its first research project. In addition, he indicated that his colleagues would predominantly undertake studies in "theoretical economics, economic history, and the history of the working class movement" (ibid:45). Thus, at least during the early Horkheimer years, the Institute sought to continue many of Grunberg's projects with regard to topics central to classical Marxism and socialist politics, but from a more comprehensive theoretical vantage point.

Materialism and Dialectics

The Institute began publishing its research and studies in its journal Zeitschrift fur Sozialforschung. In the first issue, Horkheimer described the goal of their work as developing a "theory of contemporary society as a whole," aiming at "the entirety of the social process. It presupposes that beneath the chaotic surface of events one can grasp and conceptualize a structure of the effective powers" (Horkheimer

1932:1). This theory would be based on the results of historical studies and the individual sciences and would therefore strive for the status of "science" (ibid:1 and 4). Yet these investigations would not exclude philosophy, "for it is not affiliation to a specific discipline but its importance for the theory of society which determines the choice of material" (ibid:1).

Although Horkheimer and his colleagues were basically inspired by Marxism, from 1930 through 1936, members of the Institute used code words like "materialism" and the "economic theory of society" for their version of the Marxian theory (Dubiel 1985). The Institute developed a supradisciplinary, materialist social theory as a response both to inadequacies within classical Marxism and within the dominant forms of bourgeois science and philosophy. Orthodox Marxism had congealed into a dogmatic, reductionist, and objectivist metaphysical materialism, while bourgeois social science was characterized by a fragmentation of the sciences, each cut off from the other and pursuing its own investigations isolated from other disciplines. Both bourgeois science and scientistic Marxism utilized excessively objectivist methods, and thus were not able to conceptualize current problems such as the ways that social and cultural conditions were inclining strata of the working class and other social groups toward fascism. Lacking a theory of the subject, orthodox Marxism could not really explain why revolutionary consciousness failed to develop, and could not point to how revolutionary consciousness and struggle could be produced.

The Institute theorists created a new variety of materialism against all idealist modes of thought. Rejecting both the mechanistic metaphysical materialism already criticized by Marx and Engels in The Holy Family, as well as the current positivist forms of materialism, Horkheimer and his colleagues defined the objects of materialist theory in terms of material conditions, human needs, and social struggles against oppression. Furthermore, materialism did not signify for the Institute a specific metaphysical doctrine but stood instead for a whole series of ideas and practical attitudes, taking different forms in different contexts.

Their materialist social theory during the early 1930s developed a particular style of "ideology critique" which analyzes the social interests ideologies serve by exposing their historical roots and assumptions, including the distortions and mystifications which they perpetuate. The Institute also developed a materialist approach to "cultural critiqu and produced one of the first systematic critical theories of mass culture.

In "Materialism and Metaphysics," Horkheimer spells out what is involved for him in a materialist view of the world, and what sort of thought, research, and action it involves (Horkheimer 1972:10ff). [2] He begins by criticizing metaphysical materialism which attempts to capture the totality of being in a universal philosophical system. In these remarks, Horkheimer makes evident his hostility to metaphysical systems, absolutism, and all foundationalist theories that attempt to discover a metaphysical foundation for knowledge. He then argues that the specific views that a materialist holds at a given moment are not dictated by any unchanging metaphysical theses, but rather by the:

"tasks which at any given period are to be mastered with the help of the theory. Thus, for example, criticism of a dogma of religious faith may, at a particular time and place, play a decisive role within the complex of materialist views, while under other circumstances such criticism may be unimportant. Today the knowledge of movements and tendencies affecting society as a whole is immensely important for materialist theory, but in the eighteenth century the need for knowledge of the social totality was overshadowed by questions of epistemology, of natural science, and of politics" (ibid:20-21).

Horkheimer claims that while idealist views generally aim at justification, and are advanced by ruling class ideologues to affirm dominant class interests, materialist theories aim at explanation with references to material conditions, classes, and specific historical situations (ibid:22ff.). He especially objects to notions of metaphysical cognition and absolute truth, and argues that there is "an irreducible tension between concept and being" (ibid:27). Horkheimer here rejects metaphysical theses of the identity of thought and being, of knowledge and the known. He argues, instead, that concepts are not organs of absolute knowledge, but are simply instruments for achieving certain goals which are to be constantly developed and modified in the course of experience.

Horkheimer thus proposes a post-metaphysical conception of materialism, and stresses the different content that materialist theories have in different contexts. He and his colleagues rejected both Hegel's identity theory which posits an identity between thought and being within an idealist ontology, as well as the forms of epistemological realism held by many positivist materialists then and now which maintained that correct thought simply mirrors or reflects the object of thought. In addition, the Institute stressed the historical nature of all theories and their subject matter: "The theoretical activity of humans, like the practical, is not the independent knowledge of a fixed object, but a product of ever-changing reality" (ibid:29). As historical conditions change, concepts and theories must also change; thus, there is no stable foundation for absolutist metaphysical views.

For Horkheimer, concepts and theories therefore provide representations of the socio-material world and not any absolute or indubitable knowledge. Horkheimer also criticizes theories which operate with a subject/object model that rigidly distinguishes between subject and object, arguing that "the subject-object relation is not accurately described by the picture of two fixed realities which are conceptually fully transparent and move towards each other. Rather, in what we call objective, subjective factors are at work; and in what we call subjective, objective factors are at work" (ibid:29). Horkheimer's materialism is thus dialectical, utilizing a subject/object dialectic in which objective conditions help constitute the subject, while the subject in turn helps constitute objective (material, historical) conditions. For Horkheimer:

"A dialectical process is negatively characterized by the fact that it is not to be conceived as the result of individual unchanging factors. To put it positively, its elements continuously change in relation to each other within the process, so that they are not even to be radically distinguished from each other. Thus the development of human character, for example, is conditioned both by the economic situation and by the individual powers of the person in question. But both these elements determine each other continuously, so that in the total development neither of them is to be presented as an effective factor without giving the other its role" (ibid:28).

Horkheimer and his colleagues consistently followed this dialectical conception which stressed the relative autonomy of thought, culture, and all other "superstructural" phenomena in a process of reciprocal interaction with a socio-economic "base." They thereby rejected all versions of economic determinism and reductionism and provided conceptual space for analyzing the often important causal role of cultural factors in history and society. A dialectical social theory thus analyzes the relationships between different aspects of society rather than providing a unidimensional determinist model that appeals to the economic dimension of society as the sole causal factor in explaining social development and structure.

Furthermore, the Institute's version of "dialectical materialism" is thoroughly historical because it stresses that our experience, views of the world, and concepts change in relation to historical development, and that therefore both our theories and perceptual apparatuses, as well as the objects of knowledge, are historical: "Materialism, unlike idealism, always understands thinking to be the thinking of particular men within a particular period of time. It challenges every claim to the autonomy of thought" (ibid:32).

In sum, for Horkheimer, "materialism is not interested in a worldview or in the souls of men. It is concerned with changing the concrete conditions under which humans suffer and in which, of course, their souls must become stunted. This concern may be comprehended historically and psychologically; it cannot be grounded in general principles" (ibid:32). Horkheimer believes that it is primarily materialist theories which are currently concerned with human suffering, and with transforming the material conditions which produce human suffering to produce a more rational society and a more humane form of existence. This analysis assumes that "the wretchedness of our own time is connected with the structure of society; social theory therefore forms the main content of contemporary materialism" (ibid, p. 24). In particular, "the fundamental historical role of economic relations is characteristic of the materialist position... Understanding of the present becomes more idealist, the more it avoids the economic causes of material need and looks to a psychologically naive elaboration of so-called 'basic elements of human existence'" (ibid:25-26).

Horkheimer's materialist social theory thus focuses on human needs and suffering, the ways that economic conditions produce suffering, and the changes necessary to eliminate human suffering and to increase human well-being. Such a project requires a critical social theory which confronts the social problems of the present age: "If materialist theory is an aspect of efforts to improve the human situation, it inevitably opposes every attempt to reduce social problems to second place" (ibid:26). The social theory in turn is produced by a synthesis of philosophy and the sciences (ibid:34ff).

For the Institute, philosophy without empirical scientific research is empty, just as science without philosophy is blind. In the mid-1930s, Horkheimer's unification of science and philosophy seemed to involve a dialectical interpenetration and mediation of science and philosophy, without making one superordinate to the other. [3] Consequently, Horkheimer rejects both metaphysics and positivist concepts of science which profess "'the dogma of the invariability of natural laws'" (ibid, p. 36). Dominant positivist conceptions of science, according to Horkheimer, are "unhistorical," and "science" for critical theory will not be privileged above philosophy and social theory. Yet Horkheimer maintains that: "materialism has in common with positivism that it acknowledges as real only what is given in sense experience, and it has done so since its beginnings" (ibid:42). Sense experience, however, is mediated through concepts, and both sense perception and cognition are subject to social conditions and historical change.

Thus, notions of absolute intuition, whether through the senses or cognition, are to be rejected. Horkheimer and his colleagues therefore subscribe to a non-transcendental materialist theory of knowledge which acknowledges, with Kant and the idealists, that forms of cognition and theories determine our experience of the external world, but which acknowledges as well that objective material conditions in turn condition forms of thought and knowledge. The results of post-metaphysical, materialist social theory are thus always provisional, contextual, and subject to revision.

Critical Theory

The term "critical theory" was first coined in 1937 after the majority of the Institute's members had already emigrated to the United States following the triumph of Hitler. For many years, "critical theory" stood as a codeword for the Institute's Marxism and for its attempt to found a radical supradisciplinary social theory rooted in Hegelian-Marxian dialectics, historical materialism, and the Marxian critique of political economy and theory of revolution. Note that I said supradisciplinary and not "interdisciplinary." The critical theory project initially involved attempts of individuals from various disciplines to work together collectively to develop a historical and systematic theory of contemporary society rather than just bringing individuals from separate disciplines together to chat, or assigning various specialists different topics for research and inquiry. As Lowenthal (1980:109) put it:

The term "interdisciplinary work" simply "means nothing more than to leave the disciplines as they are while developing certain techniques which foster a kind of acquaintance between them without forcing them to give up their self-sufficiency or individual claims." Critical theory, on the contrary, criticized the validity claims of the separate disciplines and attempted to create a new kind of social theory.

Critical theorists privileged Marxian categories in their supradisciplinary discourse, arguing that Marx's concepts of commodity, money, value, exchange, and fetishism characterize not only the capitalist economy but also social relations under capitalism where human relations and all forms of life are governed by commodity and exchange relations and values. Building on Lukacs' theory of reification (1971), they argued that capitalist society produced a rigid, reified structure wherein human beings were transformed into things. On this theory, through the process of reification, the unnatural conditions of the capitalist economy and labour process, the commodification of all goods, services, and objects, and the new modes of thought promoted by the mass media and positivist science appear to be "natural" and to form a system impervious to human control or intervention.

Horkheimer's essay "Traditional and Critical Theory" (1972) provides the most systematic and comprehensive presentation of the Institute's conception of social theory, while spelling out the presuppositions of their project and its relation to traditional theory. Traditional theory from Descartes through positivism is characterized by what is now called "foundationalism" i.e the attempt to ground theory in theoretical postulates which form the foundation of its theory upon which the traditional theorist builds its theoretical constructions. Traditional theory tends to be deductive, privileging natural science and mathematics; its goal, Horkheimer claims, is unity and harmony, with mathematics as its model (1972:190).

Horkheimer suggests that traditional theory is thus a projection of the bourgeois ideal of the harmonious capitalist market unified by calculable laws of supply and demand. Critical theory frequently shows the relationships between ideas and theoretical positions and their social environment, and thus attempts to contextualize or historicize ideas in terms of their roots within social processes. Following this line of inquiry, Horkheimer suggests that traditional theory is itself part of the social practices that constituted capitalism and bourgeois society. Its tendencies toward mechanistic materialism reproduced the mechanistic thought and practice of the industrial revolution according to which the world was conceptualized as a machine during an era in which machines came to dominate human beings.

The dominant bourgeois trends of abstract and quantitative thought which informed traditional theory reproduced the tendencies toward abstraction and a mode of quantification that was based on exchange in the capitalist market where value was expressed in abstract, quantitative terms. Just as a bourgeois society governed by exchange value abstracted from values, goals, sentiments, and qualities, so too did traditional theory. And, finally, the fragmentation and division of the sciences reproduces the bourgeois division of labour under capitalism whereby specialization and fragmentation are dominant features of the structure of society.

Social theories, for critical theory, are thus forms of social practice which reproduce dominant forms of social activity. [4] Traditional theory is, Horkheimer claims, unaware of the ways in which it is bound together with social processes and thus fails to see its lack of autonomy and social determination. As it became increasingly involved in social processes of production and reproduction, it became increasingly conformist, uncritically submitting to the dominant instrumental, quantitative, and capitalist values. Unaware of its social determination, "theory was absolutized...and became a reified, ideological category" (ibid:194). Consequently, "The scholar and his science are incorporated into the apparatus of society; his achievements are a factor in the conservation and continuous renewal of the existing state of affairs, no matter what fine names he gives to what he does" (ibid:196).

Traditional theory uncritically reproduces the existing society, while critical theory articulates activity striving to transform society. As Horkheimer put it:

"There is a human activity that has society itself for its object. The aim of this activity is not simply to eliminate one or another abuse, for it regards such abuses as necessarily connected with the way in which the social structure is organized. Although it itself emerges from the social structure, its purpose is not, either in its conscious intention, or in its objective significance, the better functioning of any element in the structure. On the contrary, it is suspicious of the very categories of better, useful, appropriate, productive, and valuable, as these are understood in the present order" (ibid:206-207).

Critical theory is thus rooted in "critical activity" which is oppositional and which is involved in a struggle for social change and the unification of theory and practice. "Critique," in this context, therefore involves criticism of oppression and exploitation and the struggle for a better society. Yet, in addition to its critique of vulgarized Marxian mechanistic materialism and economic reductionism and determinism, critical theory also rejects the efforts to ground Marxism in proletarian class-consciousness and its embodiment in a communist party —a concept that governed Lukacs' earlier work. Horkheimer argues that "even the situation of the proletariat is, in this society, no guarantee of correct knowledge" (ibid:213). While the proletariat may have knowledge of its exploitation and wretchedness, the fragmentation of the working class and the fact that many of its members are brutalized and undereducated indicates that some workers will fall prey to conservative or reformist tendencies; thus, there is no guarantee that its consciousness will be either theoretically correct or revolutionary.

Nonetheless, a careful reading of Horkheimer's "manifesto" makes it clear that the Institute conceived of itself at the time as part of the tradition of Hegelian Marxism, and grounded its theory in the Marxian critique of political economy. Horkheimer and his associates firmly adhere to the Marxian standpoint that the economy is the crucial determining factor for all social life and individual activity. Moreover, critical theory accepts the Marxian critique of capitalism which sees all social problems as ultimately rooted in the irrationality and contradictions of the capitalist mode of production. For example, Horkheimer writes: "The categories which have arisen under its influence criticize the present. The Marxian categories of class, exploitation, surplus value, profit, impoverishment and collapse are moments of a conceptual whole whose meaning is to be sought, not in the reproduction of the present society, but in its transformation to a correct society" (ibid:218).

System, Totality, and Critical Global Theory

Critical theory insists that one needs a theory of society grounded in a theory of capitalism to make sense of socio-historical processes and developments because the dynamics of capitalism play such a constitutive role in social life. Furthermore, to understand and explain social phenomena, one needs to contextualize one's topic of inquiry within a comprehensive theoretical framework for social analysis and critique in order to avoid illegitimate abstraction which would, for instance, analyze a political or cultural phenomena apart from its constitution in socio-economic processes. Yet while critics of totalizing modes of thought often attack critical theory's use of Hegelian-Marxian concepts of totality, I would argue that critical theory does not operate with either a fetishized or reified concept of totality. Indeed, polemics against the concept of totality, or totalizing modes of thought, generally do not distinguish between varying senses and types of "totality." [5] Often "totality" is identified with a harmonizing metaphysical mode of thought which stresses coherence, unity, and order in which all parts are seen as elements of a whole in which holistic harmony is posited as a normative value. The Institute sharply rejected such metaphysical concepts of totality, and they use the term "totality" in different ways in different contexts.

Frequently, critical theorists use the term "totality" in a synchronic sense to refer to the structure of society, defined by the Marxian critique of political economy, which provides the framework and context of inquiry, and which constitutes many social facts. For the Marxian theory, the relations of production provide the framework for development of a capitalist system; the economy thus constitutes a form of society. The critical theorists begin with the categories of economics and the Marxian critique of political economy precisely because the economy continues to play a constitutive role within all areas of social life and thus provides the framework for developing a theory of society. Marx's concepts of commodity, money, value, and exchange characterize not only economics, but also social relations because social relations and everyday life are governed by commodity and exchange relations and values. In this sense, critical theory utilizes totalizing concepts to describe a totalizing capitalist system which attempts to impose its values, structures, and practices throughout social life.

The concept of totality refers in other contexts to the diachronic, or historical, perspectives of critical theory which both characterize the historical conditions which have produced the existing capitalist society, and which conceptualize the vicissitudes of capitalist development and the (hoped for) transition to socialism. Thus, rather than operating with a static or metaphysical notion of totality, the Institute utilized dynamic and historical modes of totalizing thought. The Institute's justifications for its macro, or global, theory of society were thus: 1) capitalist society is organized as a system and requires systemic theory to grasp its social organization; 2) the logic and social processes of capitalism penetrate into ever more domains of social life requiring a theory of capitalist society as a whole to explain developments and processes in every domain of social reality. Consequently, since capitalist society is totalizing, so too must social theory; 3) capitalist society constantly changes and develops, and requires global historical analysis of its various stages and transformations; and 4) social critique and transformation require delineation of historical alternatives and normative values which can be used to criticize existing states of affairs and to argue for alternative values and organization of society.

Critical theory is thus intrinsically global and historical, and attempts to provide the "Big Picture" that sketches the fundamental outlines of socio-economic development and the ways in which capitalism structures social life, as well as the dynamics through which a capitalist society can be replaced by a socialist one. Yet the Institute was constantly on the alert to avoid any sort of economic reductionism and was especially concerned to trace the linkages between the economy and the political, social, cultural, and psychic realms while stressing the relative autonomy of the superstructures. The critical theorists thus described the mediations, or interconnections, between these spheres as well as the contradictions, and thus produced what might be called a "mediated totality." That is, the critical theorists believed that the boundaries between the various realms of existence reproduced in the fragmentation of the disciplinary sciences are artificial and abstract. Consequently, to intelligently pursue theoretical and political issues requires supradisciplinary research and a dialectical method of presentation that demonstrates in concrete detail the interconnections and conflicts between the primary areas of the socio-historical system that constitutes the context and framework for thought and action. Dialectics for the Institute involved model-building and the making of connections or mediations. Social theory therefore involves construction of a model of the current society and a demonstration of the fundamental connections — as well as of the contradictions and conflicts — among the various domains of the current social system. Consequently, critical theory provides analyses of a mediated social totality that describe various relations among spheres of reality, rather than reducing all of society to the dynamics of the economy.

Critical theory is thus systemic, totalizing, integrating, and global. Social theory therefore has a mediating function for the critical theorists, integrating science and philosophy and mediating between research (Forschung) and theoretical construction and presentation (Darstellung) (Dubiel 1985). Critical theory mediates between various domains of reality, between parts and whole, between appearance and essence, and between theory and practice. The now "classical" 1930s model of critical theory thus synthesizes social theory, research, and radical politics in a critical global theory of the present age. Critical theory today, as I shall argue in the remainder of this essay, confronts the challenge of reconstructing its theory of capitalist society in the light of new social conditions and developments.

Conflicting Paradigms and the Critical Theory of Society

In discussions within the Institute, Marcuse argued that Horkheimer's "manifesto" underplayed the importance of philosophy and consequently he wrote a systematic essay on "Philosophy and Critical Theory" (1968). Horkheimer seemed to agree with this position and himself contributed a "Postscript" which highlighted the role of philosophy (1972:244ff). Critical theory's goal of helping to create a rational society, Horkheimer suggests, follows rationalist philosophy's demand that reason should shape the totality of life and follows as well its activist concept of rational/critical activity (ibid:244ff.). Yet critical theory "never aims simply at an increase of knowledge as such. Its goal is man's emancipation from slavery" (ibid:245).

Philosophy's role in critical theory is to analyze the presuppositions of a critical social theory and to criticize the presuppositions and effects of competing theories. For the Institute, philosophy provided a critical perspective on the nature and social function of social theories that was constitutive for the development of a critical theory of society. Rejecting dichotomies between fact and values and the Weberian/ positivist notion of a value-free social science, critical theory urged reflection on the values and interests underlying any specific social theory and urged scrutiny and defence of its presuppositions. Critical theory is thus deeply self-reflexive and self-critical, forcing critical theorists to continually concern themselves with reflections on method and the nature and effects of a critical social theory.

Horkheimer and Marcuse generally agreed on the project of developing a synthesis of philosophy, social theory, and research in a supradisciplinary project. There were some differences, however, with the models developed by Adorno and Benjamin (Buck-Morss 1977; Breuer 1985). While Horkheimer believed that critical social sciences would provide indispensible material for the theory, Adorno and Benjamin put more faith in philosophy and cultural theory as providing privileged sources of knowledge of contemporary society. For both, constellations of certain cultural artifacts contained "dialectical images" which would illuminate contemporary social conditions. They were more mistrustful of the social sciences than Horkheimer and tended to focus on cultural and philosophical criticism and ideology critique -emphases that would increasingly come to dominate the Institute's work and which would frequently displace their project of developing a social theory of the contemporary era.

During the 1930s and early 1940s, the Institute attempted to develop a theory of capitalist society which would build upon, update, and go beyond classical Marxism. Thus, it is important to discern that critical theory strives to provide both a substantive social theory of the present age and a meta-theory of its theoretical presuppositions and method. On one hand, critical theory contains a set of ways of looking at theory and at the world and a set of investigative, research, textual, and political practices. Yet, critical theory also provides a substantive, comprehensive theory of the present age in addition to its methodological orientation for doing social theory and research and for relating theoretical work to radical politics. Its substantive theory contains one of the first attempts to develop a synthesis of Marx and Freud and to incorporate psychoanalytic perspectives into its research. The critical theorists undertook projects which attempted to discern why individuals submitted to irrational authority and what psychological conditions produced authoritarian personalities who would submit to fascism. [6] Later, the critical theorists analyzed changes in socialization processes which were producing a weakness of the ego and "the decline of the individual." They also analyzed the new relationships between the state and economy, the role of new technologies and mass communication as new modes of social control, and new class stratifications and the integration of the proletariat which was diminishing class conflict in a new consumer society.

In general, the critical theorists hoped to produce aspects of a theory of the transformation of competitive capitalism into monopoly capitalism and fascism, and hoped to be part of a historical process through which capitalism would be replaced by socialism. Their categories were intended to criticize the existing organization of society and to provide utopian sketches of a better society. Critical theory is thus motivated by an interest in emancipation from capitalism and provides a philosophy of social practice engaged in "the struggle for the future." Critical theory, Horkheimer argued, must remain loyal to the "idea of a future society as the community of free human beings, insofar as such a society is possible, given the present technical means" (1972:245).

Pollock's "State Capitalism" (Bronner and Kellner 1989:95-118) established a framework for the Institute's later analysis of the new relations between the state and the economy during the postwar era. Pollock claims that state capitalism — in both its "democratic" and "totalitarian" forms — produces a "command economy" exhibiting a "primacy of the political" whereby the state comes to manage the economy. Against Neumann's analysis of fascism in Behemoth (1941), Pollock maintained that "the profit motive is superseded by the power motive." Indeed, the Institute members never agreed about whether economic or political imperatives were primary for the new fascist state. Building on the Austrian Social Democrat Rudolf's Hilferding's Finance Capital (1910), Pollock's essay laid the foundation for later claims regarding the integration of the economy, the state, and the public sphere. It also maintained that capitalism had discovered new strategies to avoid economic crisis and provided the basis for the burgeoning belief that capitalism could henceforth stabilize itself and prevent the realization of socialism. Thus, it raised new doubts concerning the revolutionary role of the working class which was so central to the classical Marxian theory.

For Marx, the industrial proletariat was to serve as the agent of socialist revolution because it was the largest, most exploited, and the most militant class. Bearing the burden of industrial production, the working class was seen as the logical subject of revolution due to its crucial position in the production process and its potential for organization in highly centralized, large-scale industries. The Marxian theory of revolution also predicted severe capitalist economic crises which would lead the working class to revolt against poverty-stricken conditions where it had "nothing to lose but its chains." Even as capitalism was undergoing one of its most intense crises in the 1930s, however, the powerful parties and unions of the European working classes were defeated by the forces of fascism. Indeed, following that defeat, the prospects for socialist revolution looked ever bleaker to the Institute theorists.

As a consequence, the critical theorists increasingly distanced themselves from the traditional Marxist position which claimed that socialist revolution was inevitable and that historical progress would necessarily lead from capitalism to socialism. Henceforth, their relation to Marxism would become more ambivalent and complex. While individuals like Horkheimer would eventually abandon Marxism altogether for a form of mystical irrationalism derived from Schopenhauer and Nietzsche, Marcuse and others would continue to develop their own particular versions of the Marxian theory.

One-Dimensional Society and the Crisis of Critical Theory

One of the key Institute positions was that the "culture industries" were now playing an increasingly important role in managing consciousness and obscuring social conflict. First sketched out in Horkheimer and Adorno's Dialectic of Enlightenment (1972), originally written during the early 1940s, this standpoint became an essential component of critical theory and inaugurated a new discourse about the role of mass communication and culture in the constitution of contemporary societies. According to Adorno and Horkheimer, the culture industries were organs of mass deception which manipulated individuals into accepting the current organization of society. In their view, the culture industries were engaging in sophisticated forms of ideological indoctrination, using "entertainment" to sugarcoat oppression while eroding cultural standards in order to quell any forms of expression which might contest the given order.

During World War II, the Institute split up due to pressures of the war. Horkheimer and Adorno moved to California, while Lowenthal, Marcuse, Neumann, and others worked for the U.S. government as their contribution in the fight against fascism. Horkheimer and Adorno worked on their book, Dialectic of Enlightenment, which contains implicit critiques of Marxism, as well as of fascism and consumer capitalism. Departing from the Marxian theory of history, they presented a philosophy of history that traced the fate of the Enlightenment from the beginnings of scientific thought among the Greeks to fascist concentration camps and the cultural industries of U.S. capitalism. They showed how Western rationality served as an instrument of domination and how "enlightenment" turned into its opposite: mystification and oppression. The book criticized enlightenment scientism and rationalism, and implicitly implicated Marxism within the "dialectic of Enlightenment."

After World War II, Adorno, Horkheimer, and Pollock returned to Frankfurt to reestablish the Institute in Germany, while Lowenthal, Marcuse, and others remained in the United States. In Germany, Adorno, Horkheimer, and their associates published a series of books and became a major intellectual force in their native land. At this time, the term "Frankfurt School" became widespread as a characterization of its version of supradisciplinary social research and of the particular social theory developed by Adorno, Horkheimer, and their associates. The Frankfurt school engaged in frequent methodological and substantive debates with other social theorists, most notably, in the "positivist dispute" in which they criticized more empirical and quantatitive approaches to social theory and defended their own more speculative and critical brand of social theory. The German group around Horkheimer and Adorno was also increasingly hostile toward orthodox Marxism and in turn were criticized by a variety of "Marxist-Leninists" and "scientific Marxists" for their alleged surrender of revolutionary and scientific Marxian perspectives.

The Frankfurt School eventually became best known for its theories of "the totally administered society," or "one-dimensional society," which theorized the increasing power of capitalism over all aspects of social life and the development of new forms of social control. This theory included analyses of working class integration within contemporary capitalist societies and new techniques of capitalist stabilization which severely questioned the Marxian theory of revolution. According to many critical theorists, new forms of technology, new modes of organizing production, new configurations of class, and new methods of social control were producing a "one-dimensional" society without opposition. It also seemed that new forms of political, social, and especially cultural conformity, were becoming institutionalized (Marcuse 1964; Kellner 1984).

The development of a "totally administered society" led Adorno and Horkheimer to theorize "the end of the individual" and to stress the importance of preserving subjectivity in order to fulfill the goals of liberalism and socialism alike. The erosion of subjectivity, they believed, betrayed the promise of modernity which was itself predicated on the belief that the augmentation of science and technology would improve human control over nature and produce greater freedom, individuality, and happiness. Instead, the critical theorists argued, the institutions and practices of "advanced industrial society" were producing ever greater conformity and social domination. Ultimately, in his highly esoteric Negative Dialectics and Aesthetic Theory this situation led Adorno to attempt the resurrection of a repressed subjectivity against mass society and its philosophical expressions like existentialism and positivism.

It was ultimately Marcuse who provided the most comprehensive formulation of the theory of one-dimensional society in One Dimensional Man (1964). In his now-classic analysis, advanced industrial society integrates and absorbs all forces of opposition so that the "subjective" conditions for conflict between classes, as well as between the individual and society vanish at the very time that the "objective" reality of exploitation and injustice intensifies. Marcuse analyzes the new forms of social control in "one-dimensional society" and the diminution of the "other dimension" of social critique, rebellion, and utopian thinking, which presents alternatives to the existing order. Against "one-dimensionality," he advocated the "power of negative thinking" and the "great refusal." These slogans found empirical referents during the 1960s in the New Left and the counterculture which, to some extent, embraced Marcuse as a theoretical spokesperson (Kellner 1984).

During the 1950s, however, there were divergences between the work of the Institute relocated in Frankfurt and Fromm, Lowenthal, Marcuse, and others who did not return to Germany and who frequently developed theories that were at odds with both the current and earlier work of Horkheimer and Adorno. Thus, it is misleading to consider the work of various critical theorists during the postWar period as members of a monolithic "Frankfurt School." Whereas there was both a shared sense of purpose and collective work on supradisciplinary social theory from 1930 to the early 1940s, thereafter critical theorists frequently diverge and during the 1950s and 1960s the term the "Frankfurt School" can really only be applied to the work of those associated with the Institute in Germany.

It is therefore impossible to characterize the "Frankfurt School" as a whole since its work spanned several decades and involved a variety of thinkers who later engaged in sharp debates with each other. Rather, one should perceive various phases of Institute work: 1) the empirical-historical studies of the Grunberg era; 2) the attempts in the early to mid-1930s to establish a materialist supradisciplinary social theory under Horkheimer's directorship; 3) the attempts to develop a critical theory of society during the exile period from about 1937 to the early 1940s; 4) the dispersion of Institute members in the 1940s and the new directions sketched out by Horkheimer and Adorno; 5) the return of the Institute to Germany and its work in Frankfurt during the 1950s and 1960s; 6) the development of critical theory in various directions by Fromm, Lowenthal, Marcuse, and others who remained in the U.S.; 7) the continuation of Institute projects and development of critical theory in Germany by Jurgen Habermas, Oskar Negt, Alfred Schmidt, and others in the 1970s and 1980s; and, finally, 8) contributions to critical theory by a variety of younger theorists and scholars currently active in Europe and the United States.

In retrospect, one can see that a crisis of critical theory emerged with its fragmentation after World War II (Kellner 1989a). In effect, its social theory stopped developing, despite some empirical research projects and sustained metatheoretical analyses by certain of its members, especially Adorno. Consequently, while I believe that critical theory provides the most advanced theoretical perspectives within contemporary social theory from the 1930s through the early 1960s (Kellner 1989a), new socio-cultural developments since then have rendered obsolete some of its theses concerning one-dimensional society, the media, technology, and so on. In particular, critical theory has not continued to theorize new technologies, new developments in the media, changes in socialization practices, and new cultural developments. This is somewhat surprising since its earlier contributions were precisely in these areas. [8]

The reasons for the failure of most critical theorists to update and develop their substantive social theory are many and complex. Horkheimer seems to have burned out by the 1950s and provided few important contributions during his later years. Adorno did a great deal of work in social theory in the 1950s and 1960s, as well as turning out an incredible profusion of texts in the areas of literary criticism, cultural critique, philosophy, and aesthetics. But his work turned more and more from supradisciplinary research to philosophical reflections. Habermas also tended to focus his attention increasingly on philosophical theorizing, although his book Legitimation Crisis (1975) provides some important new perspectives for critical social theory, as do many of his later texts, especially Theory of Communicative Action (two volumes, 1984, 1987) and The Philosophical Discourse of Modernity (1987).

In Germany and the United States, most of the work in critical theory during the last decade has followed Habermas in attempting to develop more adequate philosophical foundations for critical theory (see, especially, Benhabib 1986), or to delineate philosophical aspects of critical theory. Thus, there has been a deficit of social research and elaboration of new theoretical perspectives in the domain of social theory. Contributions of this sort have come, by contrast, from members of the postmodern camp who have attempted to theorize the impact of new technologies, new media, and other socio-cultural developments. The response of critical theory has been by and large to polemicize against postmodern theory as a new form of irrationalism (Habermas 1987 and the discussion in Kellner 1989a). Yet if critical theory wishes to meet the postmodern challenge and win back its role as the cutting edge of radical social theory, it must seek new directions and provide theoretical accounts of contemporary developments in a wide range of domains.

New Directions; New Perspectives

With its fragmentation, trivialization, and academicization, social theory today is in acute crisis and needs new directions and new perspectives to which critical theory can contribute. While critical theory stopped developing and articulating new social conditions and developments, postmodern social theory and theories of postindustrial society lack the sustained commitment to social research, social critique, and political practice found in the best contributors to critical theory. While both schools provide a powerful challenge to mainstream theory, I believe that critical theory's sustained criticism of mainstream theory's presuppositions, methodologies, and lack of critical reflexivity, provides a more sustained critique than postmodern theory. Moreover, I believe that critical theory's traditional goal of providing a theory of the present age and radical politics provides superior perspectives to the often corrosive skepticism and nihilism found in much postmodern theory which disables both theoretical inquiry and political practice (Kellner 1989b).

But if critical theory seeks to contribute to finding the way out of the contemporary crisis of social theory, it must itself develop new perspectives. In opposition to the previous model of "one-dimensional society," critical theorists today should focus on the contradictions, conflicts, and crisis tendencies within contemporary capitalist societies. To the neglect of political economy and empirical research found in much critical theory, we should respond with theoretical analyses of developments within the capitalist economy and of changes in class stratification, the labour process, new technologies, the media, and politics. In opposition to the apolitical and even depoliticized versions of critical theory that continue to circulate, those who wish to revitalize critical theory should attempt to politicize it, to connect it with new social movements and existing political struggles. As we move into the 1990s and toward the end of the century, many theoretical and political tasks stand before us. If critical theory wishes to participate in the Left Turn needed to eliminate the current hegemony of the Right and to help to build a better society, it needs to develop both its analysis of the present situation and a new politics in order to become once again the cutting edge of radical social theory. [10]

Ethnomethodology

Ethnomethodology is an approach to sociological inquiry introduced by the American sociologist Harold Garfinkel' and 'Harvey Sacks. Ethnomethodology's research interest is the study of the everyday methods that people use for the production of social order (Garfinkel:2002). Ethnomethodology's goal is to document the methods and practices through which society's members make sense of their world.

Definition

This particular approach in sociology is closely related to applications and approaches employed by researchers of ethnology, ethnobotany, ethnophysiology, and ethnomusicology. According to Garfinkel, ethnomethodology is an appropriate term for the study of, "a member's knowledge of his ordinary affairs, of his own organised enterprises, where that knowledge is treated by us [as researchers] as part of the same setting that makes it orderable." According to Anne Rawls [editor of Garfinkel's *Nachlass*] ethno+method+ology means the study of members' methods for producing recognisable social order/s.

Example

Investigating the conduct of jury members, an ethnomethodologist would seek to describe the common sense methods through which members of a jury produce themselves in a jury room as jurors: methods for establishing matters of fact; methods for developing evidence chains; methods for determining the reliability of witness testimony; methods for establishing the hierarchy of speakers in the jury room; methods for determining the guilt or innocence of defendants, etc. Such methods, taken individually, or in combination, depending on the scope of the investigation, would serve to constitute the social order of being a juror for the participants, and researcher(s), in that specific social setting. For the ethnomethodologist, participants bring order to social settings - make them orderable - through the sense making activities of their shared methods and practices as witnessably enacted in those settings.

In this way, ethnomethodology points to a broad and multi-faceted area of inquiry. John Heritage writes, "In it's open-ended reference to [the study of] any kind of sense-making procedure, the term represents a signpost to a domain of uncharted dimensions rather than a staking out of a clearly delineated territory."

Origins of Ethnomethodology

Theoretical concerns, influences and resources used in the development of ethnomethodology include: traditional sociological concerns, especially the Parsonian [Talcott Parsons], "Problem of Order"; traditional sociological theory and methods, primarily Parsons, Emile Durkheim, and Max Weber; Aron Gurwitsch's phenomenological field theory of consciousness / Gestalt Psychology; the Transcendental Phenomenology of Edmund Husserl; Alfred Schutz's Phenomenology of the Natural Attitude; Maurice Merleau-Ponty's phenomenology of embodiment, Martin Heidegger's phenomenology of being / Existential Phenomenology; and Ludwig Wittgenstein's investigations regarding ordinary language use (Heritage: 1986; Garfinkel: 2002).

Anne Rawls provides a brief developmental history of Garfinkel, and ethnomethodology, in "Ethnomethodology's Program" (Rawls/ Garfinkel: 2002).

Theory and Methods

One of the most perplexing problems for those new to ethnomethodology is the discovery that it lacks both a formally stated theory and a formal methodology. As serious as these problems might appear on the face of it, neither has prevented ethnomethodologists from doing ethnomethodological studies, and generating a substantial literature of "findings".

John Heritage has noted the, "off-stage role of theory", in ethnomethodological writings, and the concern that there is nowhere in the ethnomethodological corpus a systematic theoretical statement that would serve as a touchstone for ethnomethodological inquiries.

Instead, as in the case of, Studies in Ethnomethodology (1967), we are given oblique theoretical references to: Wittgenstein [Ordinary Language Philosophy]; Husserl [Transcendental Phenomenology]; Gurwitsch [Phenomenology/Gestalt Theory]; the works of the social phenomenologist Alfred Schutz [Phenomenology of the Natural Attitude]; and an assortment of traditional social theorists generally appearing as antipodes and/or sounding boards for ethnomethodological ideas.

Likewise in, Ethnomethodology's Program (2002), we again find a multiplicity of theoretical references, including the usual suspects from Studies, and introducing among others [Heidegger, Merleau-Ponty, etc.], a key theoretical statement by Emile Durkheim regarding the objectivity of social facts, and a key insight into ethomethodology's way of doing theory.

This statement by Durkheim, although not a fully worked out theory or directive in its original form, or conceived as an aphorism for that matter, becomes, in the hands of Garfinkel, a theoretical directive - an "aphorism" - regarding both the object of ethnomethodological studies, and the focus of ethnomethodological description.

For this interpretation, Garfinkel "appropriates" Durkheim's statement, "misreads" it ethnomethodologically (2002:" Some leading policies...": "Misreading [A text]"), and transforms its meaning through its "respecification" into an ethnomethodologically useful directive for ethnomethodological studies.

Durkheim's statement: "...our basic principle, that of the objective reality of social facts. It is...upon this principle that in the end everything rests, and everything comes back to it" (Durkheim:1895:45 - as cited from Rawls/Garfinkel:2002:2:fn#2).

Rawls/Garfinkel's characterisation: "Durkheim's aphorism refers to Durkheim's statement in, The Rules of Sociological Method, to the effect that, 'The objective reality of social facts is sociology's fundamental principle'" (2002:9,119).

"Misreading" Durkheim's statement in the context of, as juxtaposed to, or read against, the fundamental assumption of ethnomethodological studies, produces an ethnomethodological "respecification" of Durkheim's statement [a rationale w/a strictly textual reading is also offered (Rawls/Garfinkel:2002:19-22; Garfinkel:2002:118-119:fn#46)].

Garfinkel writes: "Ethnomethodology's fundamental phenomenon and it's standing technical preoccupation in its studies is to find, collect, specify, and make instructably observable the local endogenous production and natural accountability of immortal familiar society's most ordinary organisational things in the world, and to provide for them both and simultaneously, as objects, and procedurally, as alternate methods" (Garfinkel:2002:124).

"Durkheim's aphorism", now ethnomethodologically respecified, directs us to account for this, "objective reality of social facts" (Durkheim), these, "organizational things in the world" (Garfinkel), as, social "objects", and their, *in situ* "methods" of production; that is, in terms of their factual status as, "organizational things in the world", and simultaneously, as methodic achievements by real individuals in actual social settings.

This, in a nutshell, becomes the central tenet of ethnomethodology's research program: "working out Durkheim's aphorism" (2002:118-119:fn#46). Rawls states: "According to Garfinkel, the result of Ethnomethodological studies is the fulfillment of Durkheim's promise that the objective reality of social facts is sociology's fundamental principle" (Rawls/Garfinkel:2002:9). As such, ethnomethodology's programmatic directive becomes,"...to restore Sociology to the pursuit of Durkheim's aphorism, through an insistence on the concreteness of things [as opposed to theoretical and conceptual constructionism], and on the claim that the concreteness of things necessarily depends on, and is produced in and through, complex mutually recognisable practices enacted by participants in social scenes" (Rawls/Garfinkel:2002:2).

Such a reading serves to locate ethnomethodology firmly in the sociological tradition, if not *de facto* serving to appropriate that tradition [despite periodic declarations to the contrary], and serves as an example of ethnomethodological theorising, but it does not in itself, or combined with any or all of the other references, constitute a unified theoretical statement in any traditional sense.

The larger point here is that the authors and theoretical references cited in Garfinkel's work do not themselves serve as a rigorous theoretical underpinning for ethnomethodology, in whole or in part. Ethnomethodology is not Durkheimian, although it shares some of the interests of Durkheim; it is not a form of phenomenology, although it borrows from Husserl and Schutz's studies of the Lifeworld [*Lebenswelt*]; it is not a form of Gestalt theory, although it describes social orders as having Gestalt-like properties; and, it is not a version of Wittgenstein's Ordinary Language Analysis, although it makes use of Wittgenstein's understanding of rule-use, etc.

Instead, these borrowings are only fragmentary references to theoretical works from which ethnomethodology has "appropriated", "misread", and/or, "respecified", the theoretical ideas of others for the expressed purposes of doing ethnomethodological investigations.

In terms of the question of ethnomethodological methods, it is the position of Anne Rawls, speaking for Garfinkel, that ethnomethodology is itself not a method. That is, it does not have a set of formal research methods or procedures. Instead, the position taken is that ethnomethodologists have conducted their studies in a variety of ways, and that the point of these investigations is, " ...to discover the things that persons in particular situations do, the methods they use, to create the patterned orderliness of social life".

As Rawls states: "Ethnomethodology...is not a methodology, but rather a study of methodology" (Rawls/Garfinkel:2002:122:fn.#3). That is, it does not have a formal methodology, but is the study of, "member's methods", the methods of others (Garfinkel:2002:72-73). Michael Lynch has also noted that: "Leading figures in the field have repeatedly emphasised that there is no obligatory set of methods [employed by ethnomethodologists], and no prohibition against using any research procedure whatsoever, if it is *adequate* to the particular phenomena under study".

Again, as perplexing as this position might seem to a traditional social scientist, such a proposition is consistent with ethnomethodology's understanding of "member's methods", and has philosophical standing when looked at in terms of certain lines of philosophical thought regarding the philosophy of science (Polyani:1974; Kuhn:1996; Feyerabend:1975/2010), and the study of the actual practices of scientific procedure (Lynch:1993).

Some Leading Policies, Methods and Definitions

- The Fundamental Assumption of Ethnomethodological Studies. As characterised by Anne Rawls, speaking for Garfinkel: "If one assumes, as Garfinkel does, that the meaningful, patterned, and orderly character of everyday life is something that people must work to achieve, then one must also assume that they have some methods for doing so". That is, "...members of society must have some shared methods that they use to mutually construct the meaningful orderliness of social situations" (Rawls/Garfinkel: 2002:6).
- Ethnomethodology is an Empirical Enterprise. Rawls states: "Ethnomethodology is a thoroughly empirical enterprise devoted to the discovery of social order and intelligibility [sense making] as witnessable collective achievements." "The keystone of the [Ethnomethodological] argument is that local [social] orders exist; that these orders are witnessable in the scenes in which they are produced; and that the possibility of [their] intelligibility is based on the actual existence and detailed enactment of these orders" (Rawls:2000:146).
- Ethnomethodological Indifference. This is the policy of deliberate agnosticism, or indifference, towards the dictates, prejudices, methods and practices of sociological analysis as traditionally conceived (examples: theories of "deviance", analysis of behaviour as rule governed, role theory, institutional (de)formations, theories of social stratification, etc.). Dictates and prejudices which serve to pre-structure traditional social scientific investigations independently of the subject matter taken as a topic of study, or the investigatory setting being subjected to scrutiny. The policy of ethnomethodological indifference is specifically not to be conceived of as indifference to the problem of social order taken as a group [member's] concern.
- First Time Through. This is the practice of attempting to describe any social activity, regardless of its routine or mundane appearance, as if it were happening for the very first time. This is in an effort to expose how the observer of the activity assembles, or constitutes, the activity for the purposes of formulating any particular description. The point of such an exercise is to make available and underline the complexities of sociological analysis and description, particularly the indexical and reflexive properties of the actors', or observer's,

own descriptions of what is taking place in any given situation. Such an activity will also reveal the observer's inescapable reliance on the hermeneutic circle as the defining "methodology" of social understanding for both lay persons and social scientists.

- Breaching Experiment. A method for revealing, or exposing, the common work that is performed by members of particular social groups in maintaining a clearly recognisable and shared social order. For example, driving the wrong way down a busy one-way street can reveal myriads of useful insights into the patterned social practices, and moral order, of the community of road users. The point of such an exercise is to demonstrate that gaining insight into the work involved in maintaining any given social order can often best be revealed by breaching that social order and observing the results of that breach - especially those activities related to the reassembly of that social order, and the normalisation of that social setting.
- Member's Methods. [Coming Soon].
- Sacks' Gloss. A question about an aspect of the social order that recommends, as a method of answering it, that the researcher should seek out members of society who, in their daily lives, are responsible for the maintenance of that aspect of the social order. This is in opposition to the idea that such questions are best answered by a sociologist. Sacks' original question concerned objects in public places and how it was possible to see that such objects did or did not belong to somebody. He found his answer in the activities of police officers who had to decide whether cars were abandoned.
- Durkheim's Aphorism. Durkheim famously recommended: "...our basic principle, that of the objectivity of social facts" (Durkheim:1895/1982:S.45 - as cited in Garfinkel/ Rawls:2002:2:fn#2). This is usually taken to mean that we should assume the objectivity of social facts as a principle of study (thus providing the basis of sociology as a science). Garfinkel's alternative reading of Durkheim is that we should treat the objectivity of social facts as an achievement of society's members, and make the achievement process itself the focus of study. An ethnomethodological respecification of Durkheim's statement via a "misreading" of his quote appears above. There is also a textual link/rationale provided in the literature (Rawls/ Garfinkel:2002:ppgs.19-22). Both links involve a leap of faith on the part of the reader; that is, we don't believe that one

method for this interpretation is necessarily better than the other, or that one form of justification for such an interpretation outweighs its competitor.

- Accounts. Accounts are the ways members signify, describe or explain the properties of a specific social situation. They can consist of both verbal and non-verbal objectifications. They are always both indexical to the situation in which they occur, and, simultaneously reflexive - they serve to constitute that situation. An account can consist of something as simple as a wink of the eye, a material object evidencing a state of affairs [documents, etc.], or something as complex as a story detailing the boundaries of the universe.
- Indexicality. The concept of Indexicality is a key core concept for Ethnomethodology. Garfinkel states that it was derived from the concept of indexical expressions appearing in ordinary language philosophy (1967), wherein a statement is considered to be indexical insofar as it is dependent for its sense upon the context in which it is embedded (Bar-Hillel:1954:359-379). The phenomenon is acknowledged in various forms of analytical philosophy, and sociological theory and methods, but is considered to be both limited in scope and remedied through specification [operationalisation]. In ethnomethodology, the phenomenon is universalised to all forms of language and behaviour, and is deemed to be beyond remedy for the purposes of establishing a scientific description and explanation of social behaviour. The consequence of the degree of contextual dependence for a "segment" of talk or behaviour can range from the problem of establishing a "working consensus" regarding the description of a phrase, concept or behaviour, to the end-game of social scientific description itself. Note that any serious development of the concept must eventually assume a theory of meaning as its foundation. Without such a foundational underpinning, both the traditional social scientist and the ethnomethodologist are relegated to merely telling stories around the campfire.
- Misreading [A text]. Misreading a text, or fragments of a text, does not denote making an erroneous reading of a text in whole or in part. As Garfinkel states, it means to denote an, "alternate reading", of a text or fragment of a text. As such, the original and its misreading do not, "...translate point to point", but, "...instead, they go together" (Garfinkel:2002:112:fn#36).

No criteria are offered for the translation of an original text and its misreading - the outcome of such translations are in Garfinkel's term: "incommensurable" (Garfinkel:2002:112:fn#36). The misreading of texts or fragments of texts is a standard feature of ethnomethodology's way of doing theory, especially in regards to topics in phenomenology.

- Reflexivity. Despite the fact that many sociologists use "reflexivity" as a synonym for "self-reflection," the way the term is used in ethnomethodology is different: it is meant "to describe the acausal and non-mentalistic determination of meaningful action-in-context."
- Documentary Method of Interpretation. The Documentary Method is the method of understanding utilised by everyone engaged in trying to make sense of their social world - this includes the ethnomethodologist. Garfinkel recovered the concept from the work of Karl Mannheim and repeatedly demonstrates the use of the method in the case studies appearing in his central text, Studies in Ethnomethodology (1967). Mannheim defined the term as a search for an identical homologous pattern of meaning underlying a variety of totally different realisations of that meaning. Garfinkel states that the documentary method of interpretation consists of treating an actual appearance as the "document of", "as pointing to", as "standing on behalf of", a presupposed underlying pattern. These "documents" serve to constitute the underlying pattern, but are themselves interpreted on the basis of what is already known about that underlying pattern. This seeming paradox is quite familiar to hermeneuticians who understand this phenomenon as a version of the hemeneutic circle. This phenomenon is also subject to analysis from the perspective of Gestalt theory [part/whole relationships], and the phenomenological theory of perception.
- Social Orders. Theoretically speaking, the object of ethnomethodological research is social order taken as a group members' concern. Methodologically, social order is made available for description in any specific social setting as an accounting of specific social orders: the sensible coherencies of accounts that order a specific social setting for the participants relative to a specific social project to be realised in that setting. Social orders themselves are made available for both participants

and researchers through phenomena of order: the actual accounting of the partial [adumbrated] appearances of these sensibly coherent social orders. These appearances [parts, adumbrates] of social orders are embodied in specific accounts, and employed in a particular social setting by the members of the particular group of individuals party to that setting. Specific social orders have the same formal properties as identified by A. Gurwitsch in his discussion of the constituent features of perceptual *noema*, and, by extension, the same relationships of meaning described in his account of Gestalt Contextures. As such, it is little wonder that Garfinkel states: "you can't do anything unless you do read his texts" (Garfinkel:2002:167).

- Ethnomethodology's Field of Investigation. For ethnomethodology the topic of study is the social practices of real people in real settings, and the methods by which these people produce and maintain a shared sense of social order.

Ethnomethodology and Phenomenology

Even though ethnomethodology has been characterised as having a "phenomenological sensibility", and reliable commentators have acknowledged that, "there is a strong influence of phenomenology on ethnomethodology..." , orthodox adherents to the discipline - those who follow the teachings of Garfinkel - know better than to represent it as a branch, or form, of phenomenology, or phenomenological sociology.

The confusion between the two disciplines stems, in part, from the practices of some ethnomethodologists [including Garfinkel], who sift through phenomenological texts, recovering phenomenological concepts and findings relevant to their interests, and then transpose these concepts and findings to topics in the study of social order. Such interpretive transpositions do not make the ethnomethodologist a phenomenologist, or ethnomethodology a form of phenomenology.

To further muddy the waters, some phenomenological sociologists seize upon ethnomethodological findings as examples of applied phenomenology; this even when the results of these ethnomethodological investigations clearly do not make use of phenomenological methods, or formulate their findings in the language of phenomenology. So called phenomenological analyses of social structures that do not have prima facie reference to any of the structures of intentional consciousness should raise questions as to the phenomenological status of such analyses.

Another way of convincing yourself of the difference between these two disciplines is to read, Studies in Ethnomethodology (1967), and try to find any reference to: a subject [other than experimental], consciousness, intentionality, or phenomenological methodology, etc. There are no such references. A phenomenological analysis should reflect phenomenological methods. This text clearly does not. In, Ethnomethodology's Program (2002), Garfinkel speaks of phenomenological texts and findings as being, "appropriated", and intentionally, "misread" (2002:112:fn#36), for the purposes of exploring topics in the study of social order (2002:176-179; 255-258). These appropriations and methodical "misreadings" of phenomenological texts and findings are clearly made for the purposes of furthering ethnomethodological analyses (2002:177), and should not be mistaken for logical extensions of these phenomenological texts and findings (2002:112:fn.#36).

Lastly, there is no claim in any of Garfinkel's work that ethnomethodology is a form of phenomenology, or phenomenological sociology. To state that ethnomethodology has a, "phenomenological sensibility", or that, "there is a strong influence of phenomenology on ethnomethodology", is not the equivalent of describing ethnomethodology as a form of phenomenology.

This having been said, one should also note that even though ethnomethodology is not a form of phenomenology, the reading and understanding of phenomenological texts, and developing the capability of seeing phenomenologically is essential to the actual doing of ethnomethodological studies. As Garfinkel states in regard to the work of the phenomenologist Aron Gurwitsch, especially his, "Field of Consciousness" (1964/2010: ethnomethodology's phenomenological *urtext*): "you can't do anything unless you do read his texts" (Garfinkel:2002:167).

7

Sociology of Science: From Marx to Merton and Beyond

Marxist Sociology

Marxist sociology refers to the conduct of sociology from a Marxist perspective. Marxism itself can be recognized as both a political philosophy and a sociology, particularly to the extent it attempts to remain scientific, systematic and objective rather than purely normative and prescriptive. Marxist sociology may be defined as "a form of conflict theory associated with ... Marxism's objective of developing a positive (empirical) science of capitalist society as part of the mobilization of a revolutionary working class."

The American Sociological Association has a section dedicated to the issues of Marxist sociology; the section is "interested in examining how insights from Marxist methodology and Marxist analysis can help explain the complex dynamics of modern society". Marxist sociology would come to facilitate the developments of critical theory and cultural studies as loosely-distinct disciplines.

Concepts and Issues

Key concepts of Marxist sociology include: historical materialism, mode of production, the relation between capital and labour. Marxist sociology is significantly concerned, but not limited to, the relations between society and economics. Key questions asked by Marxist sociology include:

- how does the capital control the workers?
- how does the mode of production influence the social class?

- what is the relation between workers, capital, the state and our culture?
- how do economic factors influence inequalities, including those related to gender and race?

Within the field of sociological theory, Marxist sociology, recognized as one of the major sociological paradigms, is associated with conflict and critical theories.

Compared to Marxism, Marxist sociology has proven to put relatively little weight on making class revolution.

Compared with Marxist philosophy, Marxist sociology aims to develop an objective, political economic science of society instead of a critical philosophy of praxis.

Compared with economic sociology, Marxist sociology can be seen as a subset of that field, influenced by Marxism.

Historical Development

Marxist sociology emerged around late 19th/early 20th century, influenced by the thought of Karl Marx. Marx is seen as one of the most influential thinkers in early sociology, alongside thinkers such as Max Weber and Émile Durkheim. The first Marxist school of sociology was known as the Austro-Marxism and notable Marxist thinkers of that period included Carl Grünberg and Antonio Labriola. Much of the development in the field of Marxist sociology occurred on the outskirts of academia, and some pitted Marxist sociology against the "bourgeois sociology".

For a while, this division was reinforced by the Marxism-inspired Russian Revolution, which led to the creation of the Soviet Union; soon, however, sociology found itself a victim of the suppression of "bourgeois" science in the communist states. While after several decades sociology was reestablished under communist states, two separate currents of thought evolved within Marxist sociology: the Soviet Marxism, developed in the 20th century communist states (primarily in the Soviet Union), serving the state's interests, and significantly crippled by forced adherence to the dogma of historical materialism, and the more independent school centred around the studies of Marxism in the West.

The Western Marxist school (around 1940s) became accepted within Western academia, and over time fractured into several different perspectives, such as the Frankfurt School or the school of critical theory.

In post-communist states there has been a backlash against the Marxist thought due to its former state-supported favoured position, but the Marxist thought is still dominant in the sociological research in the remaining communist countries.

Strong Programme

The strong programme or Strong Sociology is a variety of the sociology of scientific knowledge (SSK) particularly associated with David Bloor, Barry Barnes, Harry Collins, Donald A. MacKenzie, and John Henry. The strong programme's influence on Science and Technology Studies is credited as being unparalleled (Latour 1999). The largely Edinburgh-based school of thought has illustrated how the existence of a scientific community, bound together by allegiance to a shared paradigm, is a pre-requisite for normal scientific activity.

The strong programme is a reaction against 'weak' sociologies of science, which restricted the application of sociology to "failed" or "false" theories, such as phrenology. Failed theories would be explained by citing the researchers' biases, such as covert political or economic interests. Sociology would be only marginally relevant to successful theories, which succeeded because they had revealed a true fact of nature. The strong programme proposed that both 'true' and 'false' scientific theories should be treated the same way. Both are caused by social factors or conditions, such as cultural context and self-interest. All human knowledge, as something that exists in the human cognition, must contain some social components in its formation process.

Characteristics

As formulated by David Bloor in *Knowledge and Social Imagery* (1976), the strong programme has four indispensable components:

1. *Causality*: it examines the conditions (psychological, social, and cultural) that bring about claims to a certain kind of knowledge.
2. *Impartiality*: it examines successful as well as unsuccessful knowledge claims.
3. *Symmetry*: the same types of explanations are used for successful and unsuccessful knowledge claims alike.
4. *Reflexivity*: it must be applicable to sociology itself.

History

Because the strong programme originated at the 'Science Studies Unit,' University of Edinburgh, it is sometimes termed the Edinburgh

School. However, there is also a Bath School associated with Harry Collins that makes similar proposals. In contrast to the Edinburgh School, which emphasizes historical approaches, the Bath School emphasizes microsocial studies of laboratories and experiments. The Bath school, however, does depart from the strong programme on some fundamental issues. In the social construction of technology (SCOT) approach developed by Collins' student Trevor Pinch, as well as by the Dutch sociologist Wiebe Bijker, the strong programme was extended to technology. There are SSK-influenced scholars working in science and technology studies programs throughout the world.

Externalism

Externalism is a group of positions in the philosophy of mind which hold that the mind is not only the result of what is going on inside the nervous system (or the brain) but also of what either occurs or exists outside the subject. It is often contrasted with internalism which holds that the mind emerges from neural activity alone. Externalism articulates the belief that the mind is not just the brain or what the brain does.

There are different versions of externalism based both on the strength of the relation, and on what the mind is taken to be. Externalism stresses the importance of factors external to the nervous system. At one extreme, the mind could possibly depend on external factors. At the opposite extreme, the mind depends necessarily on external factors. The most extreme form of externalism maintains that the mind is either constituted by or identical with physical processes partially or totally external to the nervous system.

Another important criterion is which aspect of the mind is addressed. Some externalists focus on purely cognitive aspects of the mind – such as Andy Clark and David Chalmers, Shaun Gallagher and many others – while some tackle either the phenomenal aspect of the mind or the conscious mind itself. A few consider only the phenomenal content, such as William Lycan, Alex Byrne or Francois Tonneau; while others also argue the role of the mind as a vehicle of [mental phenomenal] activity, such as Teed Rockwell or Riccardo Manzotti. One last important differentiating factor is whether what is external to the mind is the content or the vehicle of the mind.

Proto-Externalists

To this group belong many authors who weren't dubbed as externalist but whose work suggested views not too far from current forms of externalism.

The first group of protexternalists to consider is the group of neorealists active at the beginning of 1900. In particular, Edwin Holt suggested a view of perception that considered the external world as constitutive of mental content. His rejection of representation paved the way to consider the external object as being somehow directly perceived: "Nothing can represent a thing but that thing itself". Holt's words anticipated by almost a century the famous anti-representationalist slogan by Rodney Brooks: "The world is its best representation". Recently, neorealist views were refreshed by Francois Tonneau, who wrote that "According to neorealism, consciousness is merely a part, or cross-section, of the environment. Neorealism implies that all conscious experiences, veridical or otherwise." (Tonneau 2004, p. 97)

Another author to be taken into account is Alfred North Whitehead, whose process ontology is a form of externalism since it endorses a neutral ontology, whose basic elements (prehension, actual occasions, events, and processes) seamlessly proceeded from microscopic activity up to the highest level of psychological and emotional life. Although the main Whitehead text is rather difficult, David Ray Griffin recently wrote an interesting update on Whitehead's thought.

John Dewey also expressed a conception of the mind and its role in the world which is very sympathetic with externalism (Dewey 1925).

More recently, James J. Gibson defended an ecological view of perception and thus of many aspects of the mind. He re-formulated several notions of various cognitive processes which are customarily internal to the brain. Two clear examples are optical flow and information. For Gibson the optical flow is not the computation of the spatial derivatives of the images acquired by the retina as in the classic computational view of the mind championed by David Marr and many others, rather the optical flow is an environmental dynamic manifold into which the agent is moving. In Gibson's system, information gets a twist, too, and it is relocated at an ecological level. Gibson introduced the notion of affordance which is external to the agent as such being the potential causal engagement between the body of the agent and some other object.

Gregory Bateson also outlined an ecological view of the mind. Because of his background in cybernetics, he was familiar with the notion of feedback that somehow hampers the traditional separation between the inside and the outside of a system. He questioned the traditional boundary of the mind and tried to express an ecological view of it, attempting to show that the chasm between mind and nature is much less obvious than it seems.

Semantic Externalism

Semantic externalism is the first form of externalism which was dubbed so. As the name suggests it focuses on mental content of semantic nature.

Semantic externalism suggests that the mental content does not supervene on what is in the head. Yet the physical basis and mechanisms of the mind remain inside the head. This is a relatively safe move since it does not jeopardize our beliefs of being located inside our cranium. Hilary Putnam focused particularly on intentionality between our thoughts and external state of affairs – whether concepts or objects. To defend his position, Putnam developed the famous Twin Earth thought experiment. Putnam expressed his view with the slogan "'meanings' just ain't in the *head*."

In contrast, Tyler Burge emphasized the social nature of the external world suggesting that semantic content is externally constituted by means of social, cultural, and linguistic interactions.

Phenomenal Externalism

Phenomenal externalism extends the externalist gist to phenomenal content. Fred Dretske (Dretske 1996) suggested that "The experiences themselves are in the head (why else would closing one's eyes or stopping one's ears extinguish them?), but nothing in the head (indeed, at the time one is having the experiences, nothing outside the head) need have the qualities that distinguish these experiences." (Dretske 1996, p. 144-145). So, although experiences remain in the head, their phenomenal content could depend on something elsewhere.

In similar way, William Lycan defended an externalist and representationalist view of phenomenal experience. In particular, he objected to the tenet that qualia are narrow.

It has been often held that some, if not all, of mental states must have a broad content, that is an external content to their vehicles. For instance, Frank Jackson and Philip Pettit stated that "The contents of certain intentional states are broad or context-bound. The contents of some beliefs depend on how things are outside the subject" (Jackson and Pettit 1988, p. 381)

However, neither Dretske nor Lycan go far as to claim that the phenomenal mind extends literally and physically beyond the skin.

In sum they suggest that phenomenal contents could depend on phenomena external to the body, while their vehicles remains inside.

The Extended Mind

The extended mind model suggests that cognition is larger than the body of the subject. According to such a model, the boundaries of cognitive processes are not always inside the skin. "Minds are composed of tools for thinking" (Dennett 2000, p. 21). According to Andy Clark, "cognition leaks out into body and world". The mind then is no longer inside the skull, but it is extended to comprehend whatever tools are useful (ranging from notepad and pencils up to smartphones and USB memories). This, in a nutshell, is the model of the extended mind. When someone uses pencil and paper to compute large sums, cognitive processes extend to the pencil and paper themselves. In a loose sense, nobody would deny it. In a stronger sense, it is rather controversial whether the boundaries of the cognitive mind would extend to the pencil and paper. For most of the proponents of the extended mind, the phenomenal mind remains inside the brain. While commenting on Andy Clark's last book *Supersizing the Mind,* David Chalmers asks "what about the big question: extended consciousness? The dispositional beliefs, cognitive processes, perceptual mechanisms, and moods [...] extend beyond the borders of consciousness, and it is plausible that it is precisely the nonconscious part of them that is extended." (Chalmers 2009, p. xiv)

Enactivism and Embodied Cognition

Enactivism and embodied cognition stress the tight coupling between the cognitive processes, the body, and the environment. Enactivism builds upon the work of other scholars who could be considered as proto externalists; these include Gregory Bateson, James J. Gibson, Maurice Merleau-Ponty, Eleanor Rosch and many others. These thinkers suggest that the mind is either dependent on or identical with the interactions between the world and the agents. For instance, Kevin O'Regan and Alva Noe suggested in a seminal paper that the mind is constituted by the sensory-motor contingency between the agent and the world. A sensory-motor contingency is an occasion to act in a certain way and it results from the matching between environmental and bodily properties. To a certain extent a sensory-motor contingencies strongly resembles Gibson's affordances. Eventually, Noe developed a more epistemic version of enactivism where the content is the knowledge the agent has as to what it can do in a certain situation. In any case he is an externalist when he claims that "What perception is, however, is not a process in the brain, but a kind of skilful activity on the part of the animal as a whole. The enactive view challenges neuroscience to devise new ways of understanding the neural basis of perception and consciousness" (Noë 2004, p. 2). Recently, Noe published a more popular and shorter version of his position.

Enactivism receives support from various other correlated views such as embodied cognition or situated cognition. These views are usually the result of the rejection of the classic computational view of the mind which is centred on the notion of internal representations. Enactivism receives its share of negative comments, particularly from neuroscientists such as Christof Koch (Koch 2004, p. 9): "While proponents of the enactive point of view rightly emphasize that perception usually takes place within the context of action, I have little patience for their neglect of the neural basis of perception. If there is one thing that scientists are reasonably sure of, it is that brain activity is both necessary and sufficient for biological sentience."

To recap, enactivism is a case of externalism, sometimes restricted to cognitive or semantic aspects, some other times striving to encompass phenomenal aspects. Something that no enactivist has so far claimed is that all phenomenal content is the result of the interaction with the environment.

Recent Forms of Phenomenal Externalism

Some externalists suggest explicitly that phenomenal content as well as the mental process are partially external to the body of the subject. The authors considering these views wonder whether not only cognition but also the conscious mind could be extended in the environment. While enactivism, at the end of the day, accepts the standard physicalist ontology that conceives the world as made of interacting objects, these more radical externalists consider the possibility that there is some fundamental flaw in our way to conceive reality and that some ontological revision is indeed unavoidable.

Teed Rockwell recently published a wholehearted attack against all forms of dualism and internalism. He proposed that the mind emerges not entirely from brain activity but from an interacting nexus of brain, body, and world. He therefore endorses embodied cognition, holding that neuroscience wrongly endorses a form of *Cartesian materialism*, an indictment also issued by many others. Dwelling on John Dewey's heritage, he argues that the brain and the body bring into existence the mind as a "behavioural field" in the environment.

Ted Honderich is perhaps the philosopher with the greatest experience in the field. He defends a position he himself dubbed "radical externalism" perhaps because of its ontological consequences. One of his main examples is that "what it actually is for you to be aware of the room you are in, it is for the room a way to exist." According to him, "Phenomenologically, what it is for you to be perceptually conscious is for a world somehow to exist". Therefore he identifies existence with consciousness.

Another radical form of phenomenal externalism is the view called the *spread mind* by Riccardo Manzotti. He questions the separation between subject and object, seeing these as only two incomplete perspectives and descriptions of the same physical process. He supports a process ontology that endorses a mind spread physically and spatio-temporally beyond the skin. Objects are not autonomous as we know them, but rather actual processes framing our reality.

Structure and Agency

In the social sciences there is a standing debate over the primacy of structure or agency in shaping human behaviour. Agency is the capacity of individuals to act independently and to make their own free choices. Structure is the recurrent patterned arrangements which influence or limit the choices and opportunities available. The structure versus agency debate may be understood as an issue of socialization against autonomy in determining whether an individual acts as a free agent or in a manner dictated by social structure.

Structure, Socialisation and Autonomy

The debate over the primacy of structure or agency relates to an issue at the heart of both classical and contemporary sociological theory: the question of social ontology: "What is the social world made of?" "What is a cause of the social world, and what is an effect?" "Do social structures determine an individual's behaviour or does human agency?"

For functionalists such as Émile Durkheim, structure and hierarchy are essential in stabilising the very existence of society. Theorists such as Karl Marx, by contrast, emphasise that the social structure can act to the detriment of the majority of individuals in a society. In both these instances "structure" may refer to something both material (or "economic") and cultural (e.g. related to norms, customs, traditions and ideologies). Some theorists put forward that what we know as our social existence is largely determined by the overall structure of society. The perceived agency of individuals can also mostly be explained by the operation of this structure. Theoretical systems aligned with this view include: structuralism, and some forms of functionalism and Marxism (all of which in this context can be seen as forms of holism—the notion that "the whole is greater than the sum of its parts"). In the reverse of the first position, other theorists stress the capacity of individual "agents" to construct and reconstruct their worlds. Theoretical systems aligned with this view include: methodological individualism, social phenomenology, interactionism and ethnomethodology.

Lastly, a third option, taken by many modern social theorists (Bourdieu, 1977, 1990), is to attempt to find a point of balance between the two previous positions. They see structure and agency as complementary forces - structure influences human behaviour, and humans are capable of changing the social structures they inhabit. Structuration is one prominent example of this view.

The first approach (emphasizing the importance of societal structure) was dominant in classical sociology. Theorists saw unique aspects of the social world that could not be explained simply by the sum of the individuals present. Émile Durkheim strongly believed that the collective had emergent properties of its own and that there was a need for a science which would deal with this emergence. The second approach (methodological individualism, etc.), however, also has a well-established position in social science. Many theorists still follow this course (e.g., economists are very prone to disregarding any kind of holism).

The central debate, therefore, is between theorists committed to the notions of methodological holism and those committed to methodological individualism. The first notion, methodological holism, is the idea that actors are socialised and embedded into social structures and institutions that constrain, or enable, and generally shape the individuals' dispositions towards, and capacities for, action, and that this social structure should be taken as primary and most significant. The second notion, methodological individualism, is the idea that actors are the central theoretical and ontological elements in social systems, and social structure is an epiphenomenon, a result and consequence of the actions and activities of interacting individuals.

Major Theorists

Georg Simmel: Georg Simmel (March 1, 1858 – September 28, 1918, Berlin, Germany) was one of the first generation of German nonpositivist sociologists. His studies pioneered the concepts of social structure and agency. His most famous works today include *The Metropolis and Mental Life* and *The Philosophy of Money*.

Norbert Elias

Norbert Elias (June 22, 1897 — August 1, 1990) was a German sociologist whose work focused on the relationship between power, behaviour, emotion, and knowledge over time. He significantly shaped what is called "process sociology" or "figurational sociology."

Talcott Parsons

Talcott Parsons (December 13, 1902 – May 8, 1979) was an American sociologist and the main theorist of action theory (misleadingly called "structural functionalism") in sociology from the 1930s in the United States. His works analyze social structure but in terms of voluntary action and through patterns of normative institutionalisation by codifying its theoretical gestalt into a system-theoretical framework based on the idea of living systems and cybernetichierarchy. For Parsons there is no "structure"- "agency" problem. It is a pseudo-problem.

Pierre Bourdieu

Pierre Bourdieu (1 August 1930 – 23 January 2002) was a French theorist who presented his *theory of practice* on the dichotomical understanding of the relation between agency and structure in a great number of published articles, beginning with *An Outline of the Theory of Practice* in 1972, where he presented the concept of habitus. His book *Distinction: A Social Critique of the Judgement of Taste* (1979), was named as one of the 20th century's 10 most important works of sociology by the International Sociological Association. The key concepts in Bourdieu's work are habitus, field, and capital. The agent is socialized in a "field", an evolving set of roles and relationships in a social domain, where various forms of "capital" such as prestige or financial resources are at stake. As the agent accommodates to his or her roles and relationships in the context of his or her position in the field, the agent internalises relationships and expectations for operating in that domain. These internalised relationships and habitual expectations and relationships form, over time, the *habitus*.

Bourdieu's work attempts to reconcile structure and agency, as external structures are internalised into the habitus while the actions of the agent externalise interactions between actors into the social relationships in the field. Bourdieu's theory, therefore, is a dialectic between "externalising the internal", and "internalising the external."

Berger and Luckmann

Peter L. Berger and Thomas Luckmann in their *Social Construction of Reality* (1966) saw the relationships between structure and agency as a dialectical one. Society forms the individuals who create society - forming a continuous loop.

James Coleman

James Samuel Coleman's *Coleman boat* provides a link between macrosociological phenomena and individual behaviour. A macro-level phenomenon is described as instigating particular actions by individuals, which results in a subsequent macro-level phenomenon.

In this way, individual action is taken in reference to a macrosociological structure, and that action (by many individuals) results in change to that macro structure.

Anthony Giddens

Contemporary sociology has generally aimed toward a reconciliation of structure and agency as concepts. Anthony Giddens's developed "Structuration Theory" in such works as *The Constitution of Society* (1984).

He presents a developed attempt to move beyond the dualism of structure and agency and argues for the "duality of structure" - where social structure is both the medium and the outcome of social action, and agents and structures as mutually constitutive entities with 'equal ontological status." For Giddens, an agent's common interaction with structure, as a system of norms, is described as "structuration".

The term "reflexivity" is used to refer to the ability of an agent to consciously alter his or her place in the social structure; thus globalization and the emergence of the 'post-traditional' society might be said to allow for "greater social reflexivity". Social and political sciences are therefore important because social knowledge, as self-knowledge, is potentially emancipatory.

Roberto Unger

Social theorist and legal philosopher Roberto Mangabeira Unger developed the thesis of negative capability to address this problem of agency in relation to structure. In his work on false necessity — or anti-necessitarian social theory — Unger recognizes the constraints of structure and its molding influence upon the individual, but at the same time finds the individual able to resist, deny, and transcend their context. The varieties of this resistance are negative capability.

Unlike other theories of structure and agency, *negative capability* does not reduce the individual to a simple actor possessing only the dual capacity of compliance or rebellion, but rather sees him as able to partake in a variety of activities of self empowerment.

Recent Developments

The critical realist structure/agency perspective embodied in the Transformational Model of Social Action (TMSA) has been further advocated and applied in other social science fields by additional authors, for example in economics by Tony Lawson and in sociology by Margaret Archer. In 2005, the Journal of Management Studies debated the merits of critical realism.

Kenneth Wilkinson in the *Community in Rural America* took an interactional/field theoretical perspective focusing on the role of community agency in contributing to the emergence of community.

With Critical Psychology as a framework, the Danish psychologist Ole Dreier, proposes in his book *Psychotherapy in Everyday Life* that we may best conceptualize persons as participants in social practices (that constitute social structures) who can either reproduce or change these social practices. This indicates that neither participants, nor social practices can be understood when looked at in isolation (in fact, this undermines the very idea of trying to do so), since practice and structure is co-created by participants and since the participants can only be called so, if they *participate* in a social practice.

The structure/agency debate continues to evolve, with contributions such as Nicos Mouzelis's *Sociological Theory: What Went Wrong?* and Margaret Archer's *Realist Social Theory: The Morphogenetic Approach* continuing to push the ongoing development of structure/agency theory. Work in information systems by Mutch (2010) has emphasized Archer's Realist Social Theory. In entrepreneurship a discussion between Sarason *et al.* and Mole and Mole (2010) used Archer's theory to critique structuration by arguing that starting a new business organization needs to be understood in the context of social structure and agency.

However, this depends upon one's view of structure, which differs between Giddens and Archer. Hence if strata in social reality have different ontologies, then they must be viewed as a dualism. Moreover, agents have causal power, and ultimate concerns which they try to fallibly put into practice. Mole and Mole propose entrepreneurship as the study of the interplay between the structures of a society and the agents within it.

A European Problem?

While the structure/agency debate has been a central issue in social theory, and recent theoretical reconciliation attempts have been made, structure/agency theory has tended to develop more in European countries by European theorists, while social theorists from the United States have tended to focus instead on the issue of integration between macrosociological and microsociological perspectives. George Ritzer examines these issues (and surveys the structure agency debate) in greater detail in his book *Modern Sociological Theory* (2000).

8

The Constructivist-Relativist Sociology of Science

Constructivism (Philosophy of Education)

Constructivism, as perspective in education, is based on experiential learning through real life experience to construct and conditionalize knowledge. It is problem-based, adaptive learning that challenges faulty schema, integrates new knowledge with existing knowledge, and allows for creation of original work or innovative procedures. The types of learners are self-directed, creative, innovative, drawing upon visual/spatial, musical/rhythmic, bodily kinesthetic, verbal/linguistic, logical/mathematical, interpersonal, intrapersonal, and naturalistic intelligences. The purpose in education is to become creative and innovative through analysis, conceptualizations, and synthesis of prior experience to create new knowledge. The educator's role is to mentor the learner during heuristic problem solving of ill-defined problems by enabling quested learning. The learning goal is the highest order of learning: heuristic problem solving, metacognitive knowledge, creativity, and originality that may modify existing knowledge and allow for creation of new knowledge. Exemplars of constructivist perspective may be found in the works of John Dewey, Maria Montessori, and David Kolb.

Constructivism influences Instructional theory by encouraging discovery learning, hands-on learning, experiential learning, collaborative learning, project-based learning, and task-based learning. Constructivist epistemology, as a branch of the philosophy of science, offers an explanation of how human beings construct knowledge from information generated by previous experiences (heuristic knowledge).

It has roots in cognitive psychology and biology and is an approach to education that lays emphasis on the ways knowledge is created while exploring the world.

Historical and Theoretical Roots

There are multiple strands of the Constructivist epistemology. Two of these strands, Cognitive constructivism and Social constructivism, are different in emphasis, but they share common perspectives about teaching and learning. Before looking at the differences between cognitive and social constructivists, it might be worthwhile to look at what they have in common. Jonassen's (1994) description of the general characteristics of constructivist learning environments is a succinct summary of the constructivist perspective. Jonassen proposed that there are eight characteristics that differentiate constructivist learning environments:

1. Constructivist learning environments provide multiple representations of reality.
2. Multiple representations avoid oversimplification and represent the complexity of the real world.
3. Constructivist learning environments emphasize knowledge construction instead of knowledge reproduction.
4. Constructivist learning environments emphasize authentic tasks in a meaningful context rather than abstract instruction out of context.
5. Constructivist learning environments provide learning environments such as real-world settings or case-based learning instead of predetermined sequences of instruction.
6. Constructivist learning environments encourage thoughtful reflection on experience.
7. Constructivist learning environments "enable context- and content- dependent knowledge construction."
8. Constructivist learning environments support "collaborative construction of knowledge through social negotiation, not competition among learners for recognition.

Jonassen's eight characteristics would be supported by both social and cognitive constructivists; however, there is a difference in the emphasis each strand places on the characteristics.

According to Kliebard, John Dewey created an active intellectual learning environment in his laboratory school, which existed between 1896 and 1904. The neuroscientist James Zull has argued that the sort of active learning Dewey fostered is the way people naturally learn. Active learning conditionalizes knowledge through experiential learning. Smith writes that John Dewey believed education must engage with and expand experience; those methods used to educate must provide for exploration, thinking, and reflection; and that interaction with the environment is necessary for learning; also, that democracy should be upheld in the educational process. Dewey advocates the learning process of experiential learning through real life experience to construct and conditionalize knowledge, which is consistent with the Constructivists. Dewey re-imagined the way that the learning process should take place as well as the role that the teacher should play within that process. According to Dewey, the teacher should not stand at the front of the room doling out bits of information to be absorbed by passive students. Instead, the teacher's role should be that of facilitator and guide. As Dewey explains it:

The teacher is not in the school to impose certain ideas or to form certain habits in the child, but is there as a member of the community to select the influences which shall affect the child and to assist him in properly responding to these. Thus the teacher becomes a partner in the learning process, guiding students to independently discover meaning within the subject area.

John Dewey was actively and directly involved in setting up educational institutions such as the University of Chicago Laboratory Schools and The New School for Social Research. Many of Dewey's ideas influenced the founding of Bennington College and Goddard College where he served on the Board of Trustees. Dewey's works and philosophy also held great influence in the creation of the Black Mountain College in North Carolina, an experimental college focused on interdisciplinary study. Faculty at the Black Mountain College included Buckminster Fuller, Willem de Kooning, Charles Olson, Franz Kline, Robert Duncan, Robert Creeley, and Paul Goodman.

Maria Montessori's key points contribute to both Humanism and Constructivism. However, she emphasizes the value of experiential learning to conditionalize knowledge:

Scientific observation has established that education is not what the teacher gives; education is a natural process spontaneously carried out by the human individual, and is acquired not by listening to words but by experiences upon the environment. The task of the teacher becomes that of preparing a series of motives of cultural activity, spread over a specially prepared environment, and then refraining from obtrusive interference. Human teachers can only help the great work that is being done, as servants help the master. Doing so, they will be witnesses to the unfolding of the human soul and to the rising of a New Man who will not be a victim of events, but will have the clarity of vision to direct and shape the future of human society.

Montessori's beliefs are consistent with the Constructivists in that she advocates a learning process which allows a student to experience an environment first-hand; thereby, giving the student reliable, trust-worthy knowledge. While working with children in the *Casa dei Bambini* in 1907, Montessori began to develop her own instructional theory. The essential elements of her educational theory are described in *The Montessori Method* in 1912 and in *The Discovery of the Child* in 1948. Her method was founded on the observation of children at liberty to act freely in an environment that was prepared to meet their needs. Montessori came to the conclusion that the children's spontaneous activity in this environment revealed an internal program of development that an educator could enhance by removing obstacles to their natural development; thereby, providing opportunities for their natural development to proceed and flourish. Accordingly, the school-room was quipped with child-sized furnishings; included practical life activities such as sweeping and washing tables; and included teaching material developed by Montessori. Children were given the freedom to choose and carry out their own activities, at their own paces, and following their own inclinations. In these conditions, Montessori made a number of observations which became the foundation of her work. First, she observed great concentration in the children and spontaneous repetition of chosen activities. She also observed a strong tendency in the children to order their own environment, straightening tables and shelves, and ordering materials. As children chose some activities over others, Montessori refined the materials she offered to them. Over time, the children began to exhibit what she called "spontaneous discipline".

David Kolb, in his books *Learning Style Inventory Technical Manual* and *Experiential Learning*, emphasizes the importance of conditionalized knowledge through experiential learning.

David A. Kolb and Roger Fry created the Kolb & Fry Model out of four elements: concrete experience, observation-reflection, the formation of abstract concepts, and testing in new situations. They represented these in the famous experiential learning circle (after Kurt Lewin). Kolb and Fry argue that the learning cycle can begin at any point, and that it should really be approached as a continuous spiral. Kolb's beliefs are consistent with the Constructivists in that he includes Concrete Experience as part of the learning process and requires a student to test knowledge by acting upon the environment; thereby, giving the student reliable, trust-worthy [conditionalized] knowledge.

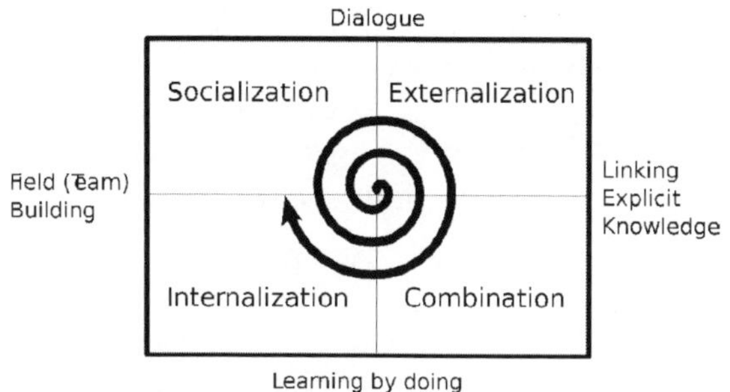

The Kolb & Fry model complements other models and parallels research done by neuroscientist. They suggest that the learning process often begins with a person carrying out a particular action and then seeing the effect of the action in this situation. Following this, the second step is to understand these effects in the particular instance, so that, if the same action were taken in the same circumstances, it would be possible to anticipate what would follow from the action. In this pattern, the third step would be to understand the general principle under which the particular instance falls. Kolb's beliefs are consistent with the Constructivists in that he includes Concrete Experience as part of the learning process and requires a student to test knowledge by acting upon the environment, thereby, giving the student reliable, trust-worthy [conditionalized] knowledge. Kolb's work closely parallels recent work in the field of neuroscience.

The Nature of the Learner

The type of learner is self-directed, creative, and innovative. The purpose in education is to become creative and innovative through analysis, conceptualizations, and synthesis of prior experience to create new knowledge. The learning goals are proficiency in higher-order cognitive functions: heuristic problem solving, metacognitive knowledge, creativity, and originality. Constructivism not only acknowledges the uniqueness and complexity of the learner, but actually encourages, utilizes, and rewards it as an integral part of the learning process. Constructivism encourages the learner to arrive at his or her version of the truth, influenced by his or her background, culture, or embedded worldview. Historical developments and symbol systems, such as language, logic, and mathematical systems, are inherited by the learner as a member of a particular culture and these life experiences influence a learner's schema. Constructivism emphasizes the importance of the learner being actively involved in the learning process . Another crucial assumption regarding the nature of the learner concerns the level and source of motivation for learning. According to Von Glasersfeld sustaining motivation to learn is strongly dependent on the learner's confidence in his or her potential for learning. The belief in their own potential to solve new problems, a feelings of competence, is derived from first-hand experience mastering problem solving, which is more powerful than any external motivator.

In adult learning, methods must take account of differences in learning due to the adults' well developed schema (adults have more life experiences) resulting in well developed neurological structures. Personal relevance of the content, involvement of the learner in the process, and deep understanding of underlying concepts are some of the aspects of constructivism relevant to the advanced instructional theories of and ragogy or heutagogy . In contrast, controlled studies uniformly supports direct, strong instructional guidance rather than minimal guidance during the instruction of novice to intermediate learners. Young students with considerable prior knowledge may require strong guidance while learning. Even though constructivist methods are often found to be *equally* effective to other approaches there is evidence that unguided approaches may have negative results when students acquire misconceptions or incomplete or disorganized knowledge.

Mayer's arguments against pure discovery are not specifically aimed at constructivism:

"Nothing in this article should be construed as arguing against the view of learning as knowledge construction or against using hands-on inquiry or group discussion that promotes the process of knowledge construction in learners. The main conclusion I draw from the *three* research literatures I have reviewed is that it would be a mistake to interpret the current constructivist view of learning as a rationale for reviving *pure* discovery as a method of instruction."

Mayer's concern is how one applies discovery-based teaching techniques. Students learn to become better at solving mathematics problems when they study worked-out examples rather than when they solely engage in hands-on problem solving. Today's proponents of discovery methods, who *claim* to draw their support from constructivist philosophy, are making inroads into educational practice, but Mayer's point is that people often misuse constructivism to promote pure discovery-based teaching techniques. Sweller found evidence that practice by novices during early schema acquisition, distracts these learners with unnecessary search-based activity, when the learner's attention should be focused on understanding (acquiring schemas).

The Role of the Instructor

The educator's role is to mentor the learner during heuristic problem solving of ill-defined problems by enabling quested learning that may modify existing knowledge and allow for creation of new knowledge. Instructors are facilitators rather than teachers. Where a teacher gives a didactic lecture that covers the subject matter, a facilitator helps the learner to get to his or her own understanding of the content. In the former scenario the learner plays a passive role and in the latter scenario the learner plays an active role in the learning process. The emphasis thus turns away from the instructor or the content and towards the learner. This change of role implies that a facilitator needs to display a different set of skills than a traditional teacher. A teacher tells, a facilitator asks; a teacher lectures from the front, a facilitator supports from the back; a teacher gives answers according to a set curriculum, a facilitator provides guidelines and creates the environment for the learner to arrive at his or her own conclusions; a teacher mostly gives a monologue, a facilitator is in continuous dialogue with the learners.

The Learning Environment

The learning environments (e.g. laboratories, studios, and workshops) are designed to support and challenge the learner's thinking. According to Montessori, the task of the instructor is to prepare a series of motives of cultural activity, spread over a specially prepared environment, and then refrain from obtrusive interference. Savery contends that the more structured the learning environment, the harder it is for the learners to construct meaning based on their conceptual understandings. A facilitator structures the learning experience to make certain that the students receive clear guidance and parameters to achieve the learning objectives, yet the learning experience should be open and free to allow the learners to discover, enjoy, interact, and arrive at their own socially verified version of truth.

The Nature of the Learning Process

Approaches based on constructivism stress the importance of mechanisms for mutual planning, identifying learner needs and interests, a cooperative learning climate, sequential activities for achieving objectives, then the formulation of learning objectives based on the diagnosed needs and interests. Some strategies for cooperative learning include: Reciprocal Questioning where students work together to ask and answer questions, Jigsaw Classroom where students become "experts" on one part of a group project and teach it to the others in their group, and Structured Controversies where students work together to research a particular controversy. A premise of Constructivism is the ability to construct person-centred messages to accomplish one's goal. Griffin explains a person-centred message is a "tailor-made message for a specific individual and context." If one is able to carry through with their person-centred message then they are able to manipulate their original message in mind and adjust it to whatever level the person they are talking to will best understand it. Problem-based learning Problem-based learning follows a constructivist perspective in learning since the role of the instructor is to guide and challenge the learning process. Students learn about a subject through the experience of problem solving. It is important to achieve the right balance between the degree of structure and flexibility that is built into the learning process. Learners should learn to discover principles, concepts, and facts for themselves. Learning is viewed as active, where guesswork and intuitive thinking are encouraged. Learners with different skills and backgrounds are encouraged to collaborate in tasks and discussions to arrive at a shared understanding of the truth. Students also Learning by teaching. Philosophically, the real is not there to be found, it does not pre-exist, the learner's reality exits only in the context of the learner's experiences. Kukla posits that people, together, construct what is real through actions as members of a group; thereby, inventing the properties of the world. Other constructivist scholars agree with this and hold that we make meanings through acting with each other and the environment. Knowledge is thus a product of humans, a product of our social nature, and a product of our culture. Another characteristic of the learning process is that the instructor and the learners are equally involved in learning from one another. The learning experience is both subjective and objective requiring the instructor's culture, values, and background to become an essential element in associating learners and tasks. To get to a new, socially tested, version of truth learners compare their version of the truth with that of the instructor and fellow learners. The task or problem is thus the interface between the instructor and the learner, creating a dynamic interaction between task, instructor, and learner. Learners and instructors develop an awareness of each others viewpoints, looking to their own beliefs, standards and values, becoming both subjective and objective. Some interactive learning approaches include reciprocal teaching, peer collaboration, cognitive apprenticeship, problem-based instruction, web quests, and anchored instruction. Holt and Willard-Holt emphasize the concept of dynamic assessment, which is a way of assessing the true potential of learners that differs significantly from conventional tests. Here the essentially interactive nature of learning is extended to the process of assessment. Rather than viewing assessment as a process carried out by a single person, such as an instructor, it is seen as a two-way process involving interaction between both instructor and learner.

The role of the assessor becomes one of dialogue with the persons being assessed to establish their current level of performance and share with them ways that performance might be improved. Assessment and learning are seen as inextricably linked and not separate processes. According to this viewpoint, instructors should see assessment as a continuous and interactive process that measures the achievement of the learner, the quality of the learning experience, and the quality of the course ware. Knowledge is discovered as an integrated whole and not divided into different subjects or compartments but discovered as an integrated whole. Emphasizing the importance of the context in which learning is presented. The world, in which the learner needs to operate, does not approach one in the form of different subjects but as a complex myriad of facts, problems, dimensions, and perceptions. Learners are constantly challenged with tasks that refer to skills and knowledge just beyond their current level of mastery.

This captures their motivation and builds on previous successes to enhance learner confidence. Where the sequencing of subject matter is concerned, it is the constructivist viewpoint that the foundations of any subject may be taught to anybody at any stage in some form. This means that instructors should first introduce the basic ideas that give life and form to any topic or subject area, and then revisit and build upon these repeatedly. It is also important for instructors to realize that although a curriculum may be set down for them, it inevitably becomes shaped by them into something personal that reflects their own belief systems, their thoughts and feelings about both the content of their instruction and their learners. Thus, the learning experience becomes a shared enterprise. The emotions and life contexts of those involved in the learning process must therefore be considered as an integral part of learning. The goal of the learner is central in considering what is learned.

Applications of Constructivism

Hmelo-Silver, Duncan, & Chinn cite several studies supporting the success of the constructivist methods of problem-based and inquiry learning

GenScope

For example, they describe a project called GenScope, an inquiry-based science software application. Students using the GenScope software showed significant gains over the control groups, with the largest gains shown in students from basic courses. Hmelo-Silver et al. also cite a large study by Geier on the effectiveness of inquiry-based science for middle school students, as demonstrated by their performance on high-stakes standardized tests. The improvement was 14% for the first cohort of students and 13% for the second cohort. This study also found that inquiry-based teaching methods greatly reduced the achievement gap for African-American students. Guthrie et al. (2004) compared three instructional methods for third-grade reading: a traditional approach, a strategies instruction only approach, and an approach with strategies instruction and constructivist motivation techniques including student choices, collaboration, and hands-on activities. The constructivist approach, called CORI (Concept-Oriented Reading Instruction), resulted in better student reading comprehension, cognitive strategies, and motivation. Jong Suk Kim found that using constructivist teaching methods for 6th graders resulted in better student achievement than traditional teaching methods. This study also found that students preferred constructivist methods over traditional ones. However, Kim did not find any difference in student self-concept or learning strategies between those taught by constructivist or traditional methods. Doðru and Kalender compared science classrooms using traditional teacher-centred approaches to those using student-centred, constructivist methods. In their initial test of student performance immediately following the lessons, they found no significant difference between traditional and constructivist methods. However, in the follow-up assessment 15 days later, students who learned through constructivist methods showed better retention of knowledge than those who learned through traditional methods.

Role Category Questionnaire

An important key in Constructivism is the idea of the RCQ which stands for Role Category Questionnaire. This tool is a questionnaire or survey that is designed to reveal individual's cognitive complexity in accordance to their interpersonal perception. To take this one step further it is important to define exactly what cognitive complexity is. In this case cognitive complexity is the degree of ability to distinguish between personalities, no matter how obvious the personality difference may be or how minute the personality difference may be. When someone has a high level of cognitive complexity they are able to put themselves in that person's shoes and relate to them on their level, as well as better understanding the events happening around them. Researchers believe that those with more sets of constructs have an advantage of social perception skills compared to those who have only a small amount of constructs to interpret people with (Griffin 99). Delia and Burleson (constructivist theorists) define two types of people: those who think there are two kinds of people in the world and those who don't (Griffin 100). If we use this as our base then those who only view the world made up of one type of person can be coined as lackluster. Those who view more than one type of person in the world are a notch above the rest, elevated human beings able to distinguish the different characteristics amongst those they interact with. It is the degree of differences that are tested upon with the RCQ, revealing how intricate and complicated the person's mind is (Griffin 100).

Criticism of Discovery-Based Teaching Techniques

Controlled studies uniformly supports direct, strong instructional guidance rather than minimal guidance during the instruction of novice to intermediate learners. Even for students with considerable prior knowledge, strong guidance while learning is most often found to be *equally* effective as unguided approaches. However, there is evidence that unguided approaches may have negative results when student acquire misconceptions or incomplete or disorganized knowledge Mayer argues against discovery-based teaching techniques and provides an extensive review to support his argument. Mayer's arguments are against pure discovery, and are not specifically aimed at constructivism: "Nothing in this article should be construed as arguing against the view of learning as knowledge construction or against using hands-on inquiry or group discussion that promotes the process of knowledge construction in learners. The main conclusion I draw from the *three* research literatures I have reviewed is that it would be a mistake to interpret the current constructivist view of learning as a rationale for reviving pure discovery as a method of instruction." Mayer's concern is how one applies discovery-based teaching techniques. Students learn to become better at solving mathematics problems when they study worked-out examples rather than when they solely engage in hands-on problem solving. Today's proponents of discovery methods, who *claim* to draw their support from constructivist philosophy, are making inroads into educational practice. Mayer's point is that people often misuse constructivism to promote pure discovery-based teaching techniques. He proposes that the instructional design recommendations of constructivism are too often aimed at discovery-based practice. Sweller found evidence that practice by novices during early schema acquisition, distracts these learners with unnecessary search-based activity, when the learner's attention should be focused on understanding (acquiring schemas). The study by Kirschner et al. from which the quote at the beginning of this section was taken has been widely cited and is important for showing the limits of minimally guided instruction. Hmelo-Silver et al. responded, pointing out that Kirschner et al. conflated constructivist teaching techniques such as inquiry learning with "discovery learning". This would agree with Mayer's viewpoint that even though constructivism as a theory and teaching techniques incorporating guidance are likely valid applications of this theory, nevertheless a tradition of misunderstanding has led to some question "pure discovery" techniques. The argument between the use or working memory and long term memory is also important to focus on in this reference, as it argues one of the main beliefs of constructivism itself that one derives new ideas from past knowledge. "Any instructional theory that ignores the limits of working memory when dealing with novel information or ignores the disappearance of those limits when dealing with familiar information is unlikely to be effective." This contrasts the belief that one can build upon ideas that are recently attained, yet also rejects the idea that one can't combine the two.

Criticism by Cognitive Psychologists

Several cognitive psychologists and educators have questioned the central claims of constructivism. It is argued that constructivist theories are misleading or contradict known findings. Matthews (1993) attempts to sketch the influence of constructivism in current mathematics and science education, aiming to indicate how pervasive Aristotle's empiricist epistemology is within it and what problems constructivism faces on that account. In the neo-Piagetian theories of cognitive development it is maintained that learning at any age depends upon the processing and representational resources available at this particular age. That is, it is maintained that if the requirements of the concept to be understood exceeds the available processing efficiency and working memory resources then the concept is by definition not learnable. This attitude toward learning impedes the learner from understanding essential theoretical concepts or, in other words, reasoning. Therefore, no matter how active a child is during learning, to learn the child must operate in a learning environment that meets the developmental and individual learning constraints that are characteristic for the child's age and this child's possible deviations from her age's norm.

If this condition is not met, construction goes astray. Several educators have also questioned the effectiveness of this approach toward instructional design, especially as it applies to the development of instruction for novices (Mayer, 2004; Kirschner, Sweller, and Clark, 2006). While some constructivists argue that "learning by doing" enhances learning, critics of this instructional strategy argue that little empirical evidence exists to support this statement given novice learners (Mayer, 2004; Kirschner, Sweller, and Clark, 2006). Sweller and his colleagues argue that novices do not possess the underlying mental models, or "schemas" necessary for "learning by doing" (e.g. Sweller, 1988). Indeed, Mayer (2004) reviewed the literature and found that fifty years of empirical data do not support using the constructivist teaching technique of pure discovery; in those situations requiring discovery, he argues for the use of guided discovery instead. Mayer (2004) argues that not all teaching techniques based on constructivism are efficient or effective for all learners, suggesting many educators misapply constructivism to use teaching techniques that require learners to be behaviourally active. He describes this inappropriate use of constructivism as the "constructivist teaching fallacy". "I refer to this interpretation as the constructivist teaching fallacy because it equates active learning with active teaching." (Mayer, 2004, p. 15). Instead Mayer proposes learners should be "cognitively active" during learning and that instructors use "guided practice." In contrast, Kirschner *et al.* (2006) describe constructivist teaching methods as "unguided methods of instruction."

They suggest more structured learning activities for learners with little to no prior knowledge. Slezak states that constructivism "is an example of fashionable but thoroughly problematic doctrines that can have little benefit for practical pedagogy or teacher education." and similar views have been stated by Meyer, Boden, Quale and others. Kirschner *et al.* group a number of learning theories together (Discovery, Problem-Based, Experiential, and Inquiry-Based learning) and stated that highly scaffolded constructivist methods like problem-based learning and inquiry learning are ineffective. Kirschner *et al.* described several research studies that were favourable to problem-based learning given learners were provide some level of guidance and support. Guidance as a strategy While there are critics of the Kirschner, Sweller, and Clark article, Sweller and his associates cover:

1. instructional designs for producing procedural learning (learning as behaviour change) (Sweller, 1988);
2. their grouping of seemingly disparate learning theories (Kirschner *et al.*, 2006) and;
3. a continuum of guidance beginning with worked examples that may be followed by practice, or transitioned to practice (Kalyuga, Ayres, Chandler, and Sweller, 2003; Renkl, Atkinson, Maier, and Staley, 2002) Kirschner *et al.* (2006) describe worked examples as an instructional design solution for procedural learning. Clark, Nguyen, and Sweller (2006) describe this as a very effective, empirically validated method of teaching learners procedural skill acquisition. Evidence for learning by studying worked-examples, is known as the worked-example effect and has been found to be useful in many domains e.g. music, chess, athletics (Atkinson, Derry, Renkl, & Wortham, 2000); concept mapping (Hilbert & Renkl, 2007); geometry (Tarmizi and Sweller, 1988); physics, mathematics, or programming (Gerjets, Scheiter, and Catrambone, 2004).

Kirschner *et al.* (2006) describe why they group a series of seemingly disparate learning theories (Discovery, Problem-Based, Experiential, and Inquiry-Based learning). The reasoning for this grouping is because each learning theory promotes the same constructivist teaching technique—"learning by doing." While they argue "learning by doing" is useful for more knowledgeable learners, they argue this teaching technique is not useful for novices. Mayer states that it promotes behavioural activity too early in the learning process, when learners should be cognitively active (Mayer, 2004). In addition, Sweller and his associates describe a continuum of guidance, starting with worked examples to slowly fade guidance. This continuum of faded guidance has been tested empirically to produce a series of learning effects: the worked-example effect (Sweller and Cooper, 1985), the guidance fading effect (Renkl, Atkinson, Maier, and Staley, 2002), and the expertise-reversal effect (Kalyuga, Ayres, Chandler, and Sweller, 2003).

The Math Wars and Discovery-Based Teaching Techniques and Technology

The math wars controversy in the United States is an example of the type of heated debate that sometimes follows the implementation of constructivist-inspired curricula in schools. In the 1990s, mathematics textbooks based on new standards largely informed by constructivism were developed and promoted with government support. Although constructivist theory does not require eliminating instruction entirely, some textbooks seemed to recommend this extreme. Some parents and mathematicians protested the design of textbooks that omitted or de-emphasized instruction of standard mathematical methods. Supporters responded that the methods were to be eventually discovered under direction by the teacher, but since this was missing or unclear, many insisted the textbooks were designed to deliberately eliminate instruction of standard methods. In one commonly adopted text, the standard formula for the area of a circle is to be derived in the classroom, but not actually printed in the student textbook as is explained by the developers of CMP: "The student role of formulating, representing, clarifying, communicating, and reflecting on ideas leads to an increase in learning. If the format of the texts included many worked examples, the student role would then become merely reproducing these examples with small modifications." Similarly, this approach has been applied to reading with whole language and inquiry-based science that emphasizes the importance of *devising* rather than just performing hands-on experiments as early as the elementary grades, rather than studying facts. In other areas of curriculum such as social studies and writing are relying more on "higher order thinking skills" rather than memorization of dates, grammar or spelling rules or reciting correct answers. Advocates of this approach counter that the constructivism does not require going to extremes, that in fact teachable moments should regularly infuse the experience with the more traditional teaching. The primary differentiation from the traditional approach being that the engagement of the students in their learning makes them more receptive to learning things at an appropriate time, rather than on a preset schedule.

Constructivist Learning Environments? ...for Which Learners?

During the 1990s, several theorists began to study the cognitive load of novices (those with little or no prior knowledge of the subject matter) during problem solving. Cognitive load theory was applied in several contexts (Paas, 1992; Moreno & Mayer, 1999; Mousavi, Low, & Sweller, 1995; Chandler and Sweller, 1992; Sweller & Cooper, 1985; Cooper & Sweller, 1987). Based on the results of their research, these authors do not support the idea of allowing novices to interact with ill-structured learning environments. Ill-structured learning environments rely on the learner to discover problem solutions

(Jonassen, 1997). Jonassen (1997) also suggested that novices be taught with "well-structured" learning environments. Jonassen (1997) also proposed well-designed, well-structured learning environments provide scaffolding for problem-solving. Finally both Sweller and Jonassen support problem-solving scenarios for more advanced learners (Jonassen, 1997; luga, Ayres, Chandler, and Sweller, 2003). Sweller and his associates even suggest well-structured learning environments, like those provided by worked examples, are not effective for those with more experience—this was later described as the "expertise reversal effect" (Kalyuga et al., 2003). Cognitive load theorists suggest worked examples initially, with a gradual introduction of problem solving scenarios; this is described as the "guidance fading effect" (Renkl, Atkinson, Maier, and Staley, 2002; Sweller, 2003). Each of these ideas provides more evidence for Anderson's ACT-R framework (Clark & Elen, 2006). This ACT-R framework suggests learning can begin with studying examples. Finally Mayer states: "Thus, the contribution of psychology is to help move educational reform efforts from the fuzzy and unproductive world of educational ideology—which sometimes hides under the banner of various versions of constructivism—to the sharp and productive world of theory-based research on how people learn." (Mayer, 2004, p. 18).

Confusion between Views

Many people confuse Constructivist (learning theory) with social constructivism. Constructivist learning theory is associated with high order learning of mature learners, androgogy or heutagogy, not early learning as discussed by the Cognitivist, Piaget or Vygotsky, whose research focused on children and sequential learning. Social constructivism is not congruent with the Constructivist learning theory. Dewey, Montessori, and Kolb represent the Constructivist learning theory where experiential learning occurs through real life experience to construct and conditionalize knowledge, and a mentor guides the mature learner. Piaget, Bruner, and Vygotsky are Cognitivists who work with young children and base their learning theories upon sequential development of mental processes scaffolded by an instructor. In recent decades, theorists have extended the traditional focus on individual learning to address collaborative and social dimensions of learning. It is possible to see *social constructivism* as a bringing together of aspects of the work of Piaget with that of Bruner and Vygotsky (Wood 1998: 39). The term *Communal constructivism* was developed by Leask and Younie (2001) through their research on the European School Net project which demonstrated the value of peer to peer learning i.e. communal construction of new knowledge rather than social construction of knowledge as described by Vygotsky where there is a learner to teacher scaffolding relationship. Bryn Holmes in 2001 applied this to student learning as described in an early paper, "in this model, students will not simply pass through a course like water through a sieve but instead leave their own imprint in the learning process."

Relativism

Relativism is not a single doctrine but a family of views whose common theme is that some central aspect of experience, thought, evaluation, or even reality is somehow relative to something else. For example standards of justification, moral principles or truth are sometimes said to be relative to language, culture, or biological makeup. Although relativistic lines of thought often lead to very implausible conclusions, there is something seductive about them, and they have captivated a wide range of thinkers from a wide range of traditions.

Relativistic motifs turn up in virtually every area of philosophy. Many versions of descriptive relativism (described below) bear on issues in the philosophy of social science concerning the understanding and interpretation of alien cultures or distant historical epochs. Other versions bear on issues in the philosophy of mind about mental content. Still others bear on issues in the philosophy of science about conceptual change and incommensurability.

Relativistic themes have also spilled over into areas outside of philosophy; for example, they play a large role in today's "culture wars." Some strains of ethical relativism (also described below) even pose threats to our standards and practices of evaluation and, through this, to many of our social and legal institutions. And the suggestion that truth or justification are somehow relative would, if correct, have a dramatic impact on the most fundamental issues about objectivity, knowledge, and intellectual progress.

Relativistic arguments often begin with plausible, even truistic premises—e.g., that we are culturally and historically situated creatures, that justification cannot go on forever, that we cannot talk without using language or think without using concepts—only to end up with implausible, even inconsistent, conclusions. There is little consensus, however, about how to block the slide from inviting points of departure to uninviting destinations.

Both sides in debates over relativism tend to oversimplify the views of the other side. The problem is exacerbated by the fact that relativistic theses often come in two forms: a bold and arresting version, which is proclaimed, and a weaker, less vulnerable version, which is defended—with the first having a tendency to morph into the second when under attack. Relativism also often sounds better in the abstract than it does when we get down to actual cases, which often turn out to be rather trivial, on the one hand, or quite implausible, on the other.

But it is also true that most academic philosophers in the English-speaking world see the label 'relativist' as the kiss of death, so few have been willing to defend any version of the doctrine (there is less reluctance in some other disciplines). Indeed, many explicit characterizations of relativism are to be found in the writings of unsympathetic opponents, who sketch flimsy versions to provide easy targets for criticism.

Discussions of relativism are also frequently marred by all-or-none thinking. Phrases like "everything is relative" and "anything goes" suggest versions of relativism that, as we will see, often are inconsistent.

But to conclude that there are no interesting versions of relativism is to err in the opposite direction. Often the important question is whether there is a space for an interesting and plausible version of relativism between strong but implausible versions (e.g., all truth is relative), on the one hand, and plausible but trivial versions (e.g., some standards of etiquette are relative), on the other.

Finally, relativistic themes are frequently defended under alternative banners like 'pluralism' or 'constructivism' (with a particular author's line between relativism and pluralism typically marking off those views he likes from those he doesn't). I will use the label 'relativist' for all such views, with the understanding that many species of relativism may be plausible or even true. But it is the views, not the labels, that are important.

Section one contains a sketch of the general form of many relativistic claims and maps the general terrain. Section two explores the main things that have been thought to be relative and section three the main things they have been relativized to. Section four presents the chief motivations and arguments for relativism, and section five is devoted to the major responses to the major relativistic themes. After section one the sections, and in many cases subsections, are relatively modular, and readers can use the detailed tables of contents, an index, and hyperlinks in the text to locate the topics of most interest to them.

A Framework for Relativism

In this section we consider the general form of the major relativistic claims and introduce some distinctions to map the terrain. We then note the major candidates for things that have been claimed to be relative and the things to which they are often relativized. We also distinguish descriptive and normative versions of relativism and see that normative relativism has two faces, an anti-realist face (there are *no* framework-*in*dependent facts of certain sorts) and a realist face (but there *are* framework-dependent facts of those sorts). It will save qualifications if we view the relativist as an ideal type that a number of thinkers approach rather closely, even when they disavow that label 'relativist'.

Y *is Relative to* X

One is not a relativist, or a descriptive or normative relativist, *simpliciter*. Both descriptive and normative relativism are families of views, each member of which holds that one or more things (e.g., epistemic standards, moral principles) is relative to something else (e.g., language, culture), and it is possible to be a relativist about some of these things but not about others.

It is often useful to think about relativism in terms of a general relativistic schema:

Relativistic Schema:Y is relative to *X*.

Different versions of relativism result from replacing *Y* by different features of thought, experience, evaluation, or even reality (e.g., modes of perception, standards of rationality), replacing *X* by something that is thought to lead to differences in the value of *Y* (e.g., language, historical period), and explaining what the phrase *relative to* amounts to in the case at hand. Each choice of *Y* and *X* yields both a version of descriptive relativism and a version of normative relativism (we turn to these below). Many variations are possible, but for a relativistic thesis to be of much interest, *Y* needs to be something that is important and that is often regarded as non-relative across groups. It will be useful to have a generic, catch-all label for the *X* slot—what things are *relativized to*—and following a common usage we will speak of relativization to *conceptual frameworks* or simply *frameworks*. Cover terms that have been used in related ways include 'worldview' (*Weltanschauung*), 'categorial scheme' and, more distantly, 'form of life', 'paradigm', and 'life world' (*Lebenswelt*). Conceptual frameworks themselves are almost always thought to be determined by something else. Hence labels like 'framework' are really just placeholders, with the real work being done by concrete instantiations of *X* with notions like language, culture, historical epoch, or some other parameter.

In the general schema *Y* is a *dependent variable* (depending on frameworks), and *X* is the *independent variable* (that influences one or more dependent variables). When people speak of relativism of a given sort they sometimes focus on factors that typically function as dependent variables (as with conceptual relativism or moral relativism); other times they focus on factors that typically function as independent variables (cultural relativism, the linguistic relativity hypothesis). But a complete version of relativism requires the specification of both (along with an account of the relationship between them).

It is easy to over-intellectualize the notion of a conceptual framework. On most accounts frameworks are not tidy and precise cognitive artifacts like road maps or axiomatic formal systems. They are often messy, indefinite, and may include vague intuitions or cognitive habits as well as specific principles and standards. For example, we form various cognitive habits so that certain things automatically count, with little need for argument or reflection, as strong evidence for certain other things. Nor are frameworks cognitive artifacts that we can abandon or change at will. We inhabit them. They permeate many aspects of our thought and experience, providing much of the texture of our lives, and when they do they are central to who we are, what matters to us most, and what we can see as making sense. We return to frameworks in §3.7.

Descriptive Relativism and Normative Relativism

It will be useful to generalize a distinction familiar from discussions of ethical relativism and to distinguish *descriptive relativism* and *normative relativism* with respect to anything that is claimed to be relative (e.g., descriptive relativism about concepts, normative relativism about truth).

Descriptive relativism is a family of *empirical claims* to the effect that certain groups in fact have different modes of thought, standards of reasoning, or the like. Such claims are meant to *describe* (but not evaluate) the principles and practices of the two groups, and they are compatible with the claims that both groups are right (in their different ways), that only one is, that neither is, or even that (in the case at hand) there is no such thing as getting things right (e.g., there is no ultimate fact of the matter as to which epistemic principles or ethical principles are correct). It is possible to be a descriptive relativist about some things (e.g., ethical principles) but not about others (e.g., logical principles).

The claim that a person's culture, language, or the like influences his modes of thought does not mean that they completely determine how she thinks. Smoking is a causal factor for lung cancer; other things being equal, smokers are more likely to get cancer, and to do so *because* they smoke. But many other things, from genetic make-up to exposure to asbestos, are causal factors as well. Similarly, a claim that culture or language or some other independent variable affects a particular facet of experience or thought allows for other influences as well, and descriptive versions of relativism come in stronger and weaker forms, depending on the hypothesized strength of an independent variable's influence.

The descriptive relativist's claims about epistemic principles, moral ideals and the like are often countered by arguments that such things are universal, and much of the recent literature on these matters is explicitly concerned with the extent of, and evidence for, cultural or moral or linguistic or human universals.

The fact that the various species of descriptive relativisms are empirical claims may tempt us to conclude that they are of little philosophical interest, but there are several reasons why this isn't so.

First, some philosophers, including Kant, argue that certain sorts of cognitive differences between human beings (or even all rational beings) are impossible, so such differences could never be found to obtain in fact. This claim is interesting, because it places *a priori* limits on what empirical inquiry could discover and on what versions of descriptive relativism could be true. Second, claims about actual differences between groups play a central role in several arguments for various types of normative relativism; for example, arguments for normative ethical relativism often begin with claims that different groups in fact have different moral codes or ideals. Finally, descriptive versions of relativism help us to separate the fixed aspects of human nature from those that can vary, and so a descriptive claim that some important aspect of experience or thought does (or does not) vary across groups of human beings tells us something important about human nature and the human condition.

Normative relativism is a family of non-empirical *normative* or *evaluative claims* to the effect that modes of thought, standards of reasoning, or the like are only right or wrong, correct or incorrect, veridical or non-veridical, *relative to* a framework. The adjective 'normative' is meant in a generic and untendentious sense that can apply to a wide range of views. Like the notion of a framework, the real work is done by the specific form that normativity takes with a specific species of relativism. In the case of beliefs, for example, being normatively correct amounts to being true. This does not mean, of course, that the normative relativist's notion of framework-relative correctness or truth is always clear, and her first challenge is to explain what it amounts to in any given case (e.g., with respect to concepts, truth, epistemic norms).

It is possible to think of normative relativism about something, e.g., normative ethical relativism, as the thesis that claims about ethics are not true or false *simpliciter*, but only have truth values relative to moral codes or the like. But many of the normative ethical relativist's arguments run *from* premises about ethics *to* the conclusion that claims in ethics have relative truth values, rather than depending on general claims about the nature of truth. In such cases it is often more illuminating to consider the type of relativism (e.g., normative ethical relativism) directly, without a detour through a discussion of relative truth, and it also can make it easier to align discussion with much of the literature on various kinds of relativism. We will take this approach here, but this is not to deny that in some contexts it may be more illuminating to examine various kinds of normative relativism as species of truth-value relativism.

It is possible to be a descriptive relativist about something without being a normative relativist about it. In contexts where a point applies to all species of normative relativism, or where it is clear which species are at issue, I will often simply speak of normative relativism, without modifiers like 'conceptual' or 'epistemic', and similarly for descriptive relativism.

The Two Faces of Normative Relativism

Each species of normative relativism is a Janus-faced view. First there is an *anti-realist face*. The normative relativist about morality, for example, agrees with the anti-realist about morality that there are no absolute, completely objective, framework-independent facts about moral truth or moral justification. Similar points hold for normative relativism and anti-realism about other things like epistemic standards or truth. But, second, each species of normative relativism also has a *realist face*. Its message is that *once we relativize things to frameworks*, there *are* facts about morality, epistemic justification, truth, or the like.

The existence of the two faces means that the normative relativist must fight on two very different fronts. On the first front, the normative relativist must defend anti-realist claims to the effect that there are *no* framework-*independent* facts about which beliefs, standards, or the like are correct. Sometimes the normative relativist can adapt standard anti-realist arguments to relativistic ends. But in many cases these arguments will be too strong, since they aim to show that there are no facts about which things are correct in *any* sense, even a framework-relative one.

On the second front the normative relativist must defend (relativized) realist claims that there *are* framework-*relative*, or framework-*dependent*, facts about what is right, justified, or true. This front is more treacherous than the first. In some cases it is difficult even to explain what framework-relative correctness amounts to. Then, assuming such an explanation has been given, the normative relativist must go on to show that there really are framework-relative facts or norms of the relevant sort. Sometimes she can reinterpret or reconstrue standard realist arguments and positions in a way that allows her to adapt or co-opt them, but this is not always the case.

Relativistic Reconstrual

In defending the (relativized) realist face of some species of normative relativism—particularly the more global versions like normative relativism with respect to epistemic standards, truth, or reality—the relativist can sometimes reconstrue or reinterpret realist views about these things with a relativistic spin. This *relativistic reconstrual*, like Berkeley's account of physical objects, is intended to save most of the phenomena of commonsense—to treat as many of the things that we normally think are true or justified or right as indeed being true or justified or right—while giving them a new and arresting philosophical interpretation. Thus, the normative relativist can agree that at least most events have causes, that inference to the best explanation is a legitimate pattern of inference, and that murder is wrong. But he offers a new and arresting philosophical account about the ultimate *nature* of—though not necessarily the criteria for—

truth, justification, or rightness, relativizing these to frameworks. No one thinks that believing something true can always make it true, so the normative relativist also needs to provide accounts of belief and truth that allow the him to explain the difference between the two, that enable him to draw a principled distinction between what the users of a framework *believe* to be the case and what really *is* the case (relative to that framework).

There are various ways to attempt this, e.g., by arguing that there is some sort of neutral input that constrains our experience and determines, in concert with our concepts and other aspect of our framework, what is true in that framework. On such an account our beliefs may often be wrong. For example, if I have a concept of a dog and a concept of this room it may be true that there is a dog in the room, even if I don't believe that there is. It is not easy to work out the details of such an approach, but the relativist needs something of the sort to maintain *a descriptive-normative gap*, so that merely thinking something right or true doesn't make it right or true, not even relative to her framework.

Many philosophers will urge that relativistic reconstrual does not give us everything we want. Still, as we will see, this approach yields a more defencible relativism than many alternatives do, since it requires fewer revisions in our concepts and beliefs.

Tensions between the Faces

The two faces are not always of one mind. At key junctures the realist face of normative relativism needs something objective of the sort that the first face is bound to find threatening. For example, without something objective it is difficult for the normative relativist to avoid idealism or to explain how intra-framework objectivity and truth are possible. As we will see, there is a fine line here. If the objective constraints play too large a role, the relativist's view may simply wind up as some sort of pluralistic realism; if they play too small a role, her view may collapse into some sort of idealism or solipsism.

Relativism as Presupposing Realism and Inconceivable without It

Relativism presupposes some measure of realism. If there are no such things as concepts, beliefs, or modes of reasoning, then groups cannot differ with respect to their concepts, beliefs, or modes of reasoning. And if speaking different languages or belonging to different cultures leads to different modes of thought, then there must be objective causal connections between speaking a particular language or belonging to a particular culture, on the one hand, and how one thinks, on the other.

This suggests that any all-embracing relativism will be difficult to defend, and in §5.9 we will see additional reasons for concluding this. But it would be a mistake to conclude, without further examination, that this precludes any interesting versions of relativism. The important question is often whether a version of realism leaves enough space for *interesting* versions of relativism.

A Taxonomy of Positions

Relativism can be divided into subtypes in various ways, with different divisions useful for different purposes. The classification I'll use is geared to the relativistic schema

Y is relative to *X*.

and so involves three things:

1. *Y*: the thing that is relative
2. *X*: what it's relative to
3. Type of connection between *X* and *Y* (reflected in the phrase *is relative to*)

A complete characterization of a species of relativism requires specification of all three things, telling how changes in one or more independent variables lead to changes in one or more dependent variables. The general structure is shown in below in Figure 1.

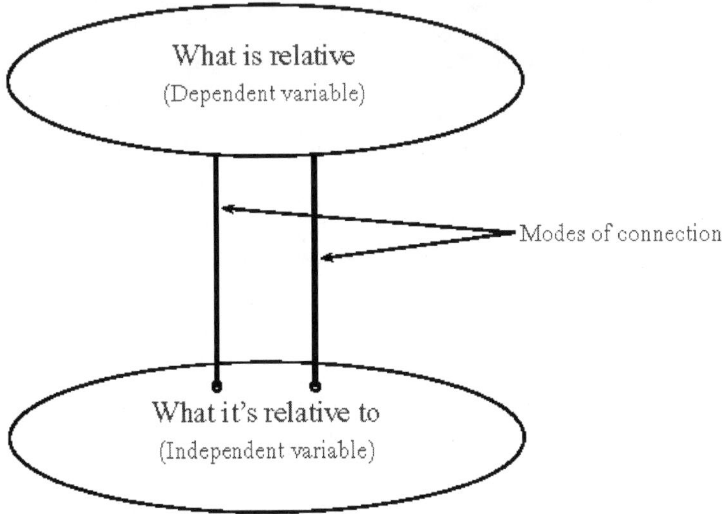

Figure: *General Structure of the Taxonomy*

It is possible to make more distinctions (e.g., by distinguishing various kinds of epistemic relativism), fewer (e.g., by lumping language and culture together), or to add additional categories (e.g., aesthetic relativism). It is also would be possible to have more than two modes of connection (e.g., more than one form of normative relativism). And of course schemes that are not variants of these are possible. The present account aims to distinguish interestingly different views, including those that appear most often in the literature, without endless proliferation (Figure 2).

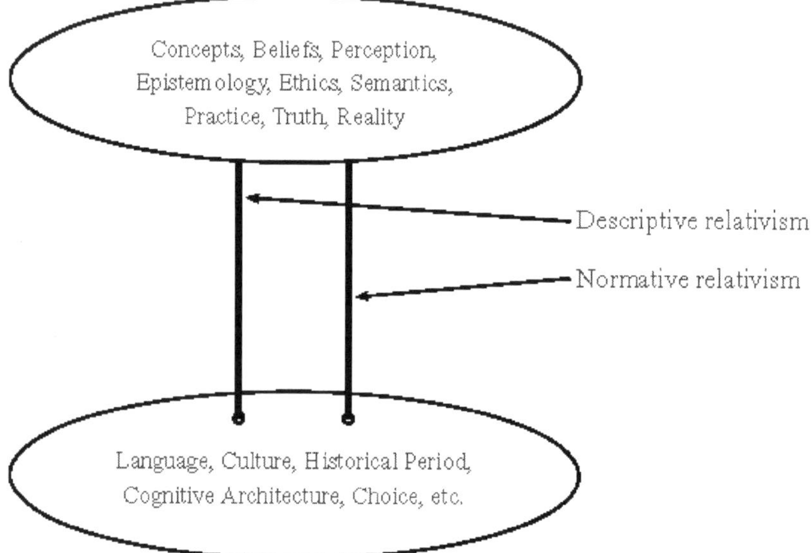

Figure: *The Taxonomy*

I will focus on the variables in Table One. The items in the left column of the table are the most common candidates for *Y*, those in the right the most common candidates for *X*, and there are two modes of connection for each pairing of *X* and *Y*, descriptive and normative. We will consider the major candidates for dependent variables in Section 2 and those for independent variables in Section 3 (the numbers in the table indicate the section where the relevant variable is discussed).

Major Relativistic Variables

- Dependent Variables(What is Relative)
  - 2.1 Central Concepts
  - 2.2 Central Beliefs
  - 2.3 Perception

  - 2.4 Epistemic Appraisal
  - 2.5 Ethics
  - 2.6 Semantics
  - 2.7 Practice
  - 2.8 Truth
  - 2.9 Reality
- Independent Variables(Relative to What)
  - 3.1 Language
  - 3.2 Culture
  - 3.3 Historical Period
  - 3.4 Innate Cognitive Architecture
  - 3.5 Choice
  - 3.6.1 Scientific Frameworks
  - 3.6.2 Religion
  - 3.6.3 Gender, Race, or Social Status
  - 3.6.4 The Individual

Even with our moderately coarse distinctions the above parameters yield (nine times nine =) eighty-one species of relativism, and each comes in a descriptive version and a normative version (= 162). With finer distinctions, or with combinations (e.g., the claim that perception is relative to some interaction between culture and gender), the number climbs well into the thousands. Only someone inordinately fond of splitting hairs could persevere through even a tenth of them, but fortunately many are not particularly interesting or compelling. For example, it is much more plausible to view ethical ideals as relative to culture or religion than as relative to paradigms in high-energy particle physics, and some of the other positions are inconsequential or trivial. We will confine attention to a manageable number of the more interesting packages.

We will explore the relationships among the varieties of relativism in later sections, so here I'll simply note that whether one species of relativism entails, or precludes, another depends on how the details of the relevant variables are filled in and on the background assumptions in play. But even without such detail there seem to be affinities between some positions (e.g., relativism about reality, relativism about truth) and strong tensions among others (e.g., the claim that fundamental modes of cognition are due to culture does not fit easily with the view that they are relative to innate cognitive architecture, i.e., to biological makeup). Although we will consider these matters in more detail below, a few quick examples may help fix ideas. Thus, many American anthropologists in the first part of the twentieth century held that ethical values [2.5] are relative (both in fact and normatively) to culture [3.2], or [2.5]-to-[3.2], for short. Linguistic relativists like Whorf held that concepts, basic beliefs, and some aspects of perception are relative (in fact) to language, i.e., [2.1; 2.2; 2.3]-to-[3.1]. Kuhn's more relativistic passages in the first edition of *The Structure of Scientific Revolutions* suggest that perception, standards of epistemic appraisal, and meaning are relative (both in fact and normatively) to paradigms or scientific frameworks, i.e., [2.3; 2.4; 2.6]-to-[3.6.1] (further passages suggest that truth and even reality are also relativized to paradigms). Although relativism is typically thought of as a social view, we can also treat the individual as an independent variable; for example, many passages in Sartre suggest that moral values are relative (in fact and normatively) to individuals, i.e., [2.5]-to-[3.6.4].

Matters of Degree

Relativistic views can differ along two dimensions.

Large vs. Small Differences

Not just any difference in concepts, beliefs, epistemic standards, or the like justifies talk of alternative frameworks or worldviews. Some concepts, beliefs, and standards are much more *central* than others, and interesting versions of relativism involve these.

Let us call concepts that are especially important to a group, that figure prominently in their most fundamental beliefs, *central concepts* for that group. Central concepts often have much in common with philosophers' lists of *categories*. The notion of centrality is vague, but examples should help fix the idea: our central concepts include *causation*, *physical object*, *person*, *number*, and *time*, but not the concepts of a *pickup truck*, a *large infinite cardinal number*, or (for most of us) *karma*, or *witchcraft*.

A *central belief* is a belief that is so fundamental for a person or group that they could not abandon it without abandoning many other beliefs (and perhaps some epistemic standards) as well. Our central beliefs include the convictions that at least many events have causes, that physical objects exist even when no one perceives them, and that other people have beliefs and desires. But unlike people at certain other times and places, few of us have central beliefs (or any beliefs at all) to the effect that kings rule by divine right or that all of a person's misfortunes result from evil spells or bad karma. Central concepts and central beliefs are intimately related, since concepts are typically central because they figure in central beliefs, and central beliefs often involve central concepts.

Centrality is a *functional*, rather than as intrinsic, *property* of concepts, beliefs, values, standards, and the like. It is a property they have because of the *role* they play in peoples' thought and action, and the same concept or belief might be central for one group, peripheral for a second, and altogether lacking for a third.

Centrality comes in degrees, and it would be unrewarding to try to draw a sharp line between central concepts and beliefs, on the one hand, and all the remaining concepts and beliefs, on the other. Moreover, we typically gain a better understanding of relativistic themes if we evaluate each case on its own merits, note the similarities and differences between cases, see how these matter, and worry less about giving a sharp 'yes' or 'no' to the question of whether a particular concept or belief is fundamental enough to justify talk about alternative frameworks.

Local vs. Global Relativisms

A version of relativism is local if it only applies to limited aspects of a group's cognitive or evaluative life. For example, some ethical relativists claim that moral principles or values are relative to a group but allow that other things, e.g., logic or truth about non-normative matters, are not relative. Again, claims that scientific frameworks or paradigms are relative leave room for a non-relative conception of many other things, e.g., logic or morality. By contrast, relativism about all epistemic standards or about truth in general affect more aspects of a persons life and thought, and so are more global. Locality, like centrality, is a matter of degree.

Exceptions and Dispensations: The Exemption Problem

A completely global version of normative relativism (e.g., normative relativism about truth or about epistemic justification) claims complete, across-the-board coverage, and this would make the relativist's own claims and arguments relative too. This can lead to severe difficulties, including self-refutation, and a recurring danger for relativists is to assume, often tacitly, that the concepts, principles, or standards used to formulate their own relativist theses somehow escape the relativity they insist permeates everything else.

This difficulty, which we might call *the exemptions problem*, turns up in many guises. Here are a few:

- It can be tempting for a global normative relativist to hold that the claim that truth is relative is itself somehow true absolutely or that the claim that justification is relative is justified in some absolute sense.
- Many relativistic arguments employ the premise that it is impossible to think or speak about reality "as it really is"—as it is independently of our modes of thought—because thinking and speaking requires us to use our concepts and words. But in order to explain things like intra-framework objectivity, it can be very tempting to go on to offer minimal descriptions of an extra-mental reality, e.g., as containing objective similarities that guide our classifications or as playing a causal role in our perception.
- Claims that values or truth or rationality are relative to culture, language or the like often assume that there are various absolute truths about culture, language, or the like.
- The claim that ethical (and perhaps other) values are relative to cultures or moral codes plays a key role in some defences of tolerance; all views are equally good, so we should respect them all. But tolerance and open-mindedness are values, and they can hardly be defended by arguing that there are no objective values.

Relativism is not always the most effective topic for promoting consistency in those who discuss it, and as we will see below many relativistic views are unable to give a consistent account of the status of *their own* claims. With care some local versions of relativism can avoid the exemptions problem, but it is an ever-present danger for more global versions.

Dependent Variables: What is Relative?

In this section we examine the chief candidates for relativistic dependent variables. They are not all independent of one another, but they are often singled out for separate treatment, and we begin by following suit.

- 2.1 Central Concepts
- 2.2 Central Beliefs
- 2.3 Perception
- 2.4 Epistemic Appraisal
- 2.5 Ethics
- 2.6 Semantics

- 2.7 Practice
- 2.8 Truth
- 2.9 Reality
- 2.10 Relationships among the Variables

Central Concepts

Conceptual relativism is the view that different groups, e.g., those with very different languages or cultures, may have rather different central concepts and that this can lead their members to rather different conceptions of the world. Conceptual relativism can be quite global, applying to concepts across the board, but it also comes in more local versions that apply to more limited domains like ethics or science; for example, Kuhn tells us that what characterizes scientific revolutions is "change in several of the taxonomic categories prerequisite to scientific descriptions and generalization" (2000, p. 30).

Descriptive conceptual relativism is the empirical thesis that members of at least some different groups, e.g., some cultures, linguistic communities or biological species, have interestingly different sets of central concepts. For example, it is generally agreed our modern concept of individual rights did not exist in the Ancient world. More controversially, Whorf (1959, pp. 59, 147, 215) tells us that where modern speakers of English think of many of the things in the external world as falling under the concept of an enduring object (rocks, horses), the Hopi instead think of the things in their world as falling under the concept of an event or happening.

What about normative conceptual relativism? Concepts have many uses, and there is no single sense in which these can be correct or incorrect; furthermore, some of these senses are uncontroversial. We all misclassify things now and then, and sometimes we do so systematically. For example, if someone is under the misapprehension that the concept of a score applies to a period of fifteen years (so that four score and seven years is sixty-seven years), they simply get things wrong when they deploy the concept of a score.

But when people discuss conceptual relativism they often have a more interesting and more controversial idea in mind. They want to deny that *any* system or framework of concepts is correct in the sense of matching or fitting or corresponding to the structure of the world. There simply are no concepts that divide things up into groups in a way that corresponds to the way things are truly divided up in nature; to adapt Plato's metaphor, there are no concepts that carve reality at its joints (*Phaedrus*, 265e). In this metaphor reality is like a chicken; there are real joints out there, facts about which things there are, independently of how we parcel things out in thought. This is what the conceptual relativist typically wants to deny.

The inability to achieve a match with reality is not a defect in our concepts, however, but arises because the world does not come with prepackaged or preindividuated objects exemplifying prefabricated properties and standing in prefabricated relations. Hence this sort of relativism often goes hand in hand with a general sort of relativism about truth and reality. I have separated it here, however, because discussions of conceptual relativism are common and because some partisans of conceptual pluralism want to defend a view of roughly this sort while rejecting other central species of relativism.

Normative conceptual relativism, in the sense we will use here, is the philosophical thesis that no single set of central concepts is correct in any framework-dependent sense, although a set of concepts may be correct *relative to* a framework. The normative conceptual relativist often adds that our concepts could never be read off from, or even match, the structure of reality, arguing that instead the notions of structure or similarity or kinds are features of our descriptions and thoughts, rather than features of some mind- and language-independent reality "in-itself." To be sure, some schemes of classification strike us as much more natural, simple, or useful than others. But naturalness, simplicity, and usefulness are our values, not the world's.

Concepts do More than Classify

Classification is rarely an end in itself, and concepts underlie all of our higher mental processes, including inference, prediction, planning, learning, and explanation. The use of concepts (and the information we associate with them) to *mediate ampliative inferences* subserves many of these other uses, enabling us to apply what we have learned to new and novel cases. When I see that the creature under the rock is a *rattlesnake*, I immediately infer that it is *dangerous*.

Concepts Give us Things and Kinds

The members of any very large group of items can be classified or sorted in many different ways, and so many different schemes of classification are possible. But our concepts also determine what things we think are out there waiting to be sorted. Whether we think we have the same thing or something new, one thing or more, depends on which sortal concept we have in mind: this is the same *song*, but a different *verse*; same novel, new chapter; same type, different token. In short, different systems of concepts may sort the same group of pre-individuated things in different ways, but they may also divide the world up into different numbers of things. Indeed, the central role of concepts in the individuation and demarcation of things plays a large role in many arguments for reality relativism. Hilary Putnam expresses the general sentiment this way:

'Objects' do not exist independently of conceptual schemes. *We* cut up the world into objects when we introduce one or another scheme of description (1981, p. 52). If, as I maintain, 'objects' themselves are *as much made as discovered*, as much products of our conceptual *invention* as of the 'objective' factor in experience, the factor independent of our will, then of course objects intrinsically belong under certain labels because those labels are just the *tools we use to construct a version* of the world with such objects in the first place (1981, p. 54, italics his).

In such argument we move (by steps that are not always very clear) from the fact that introducing a concept for a kind of thing allows us to individuate things of that kind to a conclusion to the effect that the introduction or use of such concepts plays a role in creating the things in its extension.

Expressibility vs. Usability

It is natural to suppose that if we could come to understand the concepts of some exotic culture or group we could express their concepts in terms we understand—and so their conceptual framework really wouldn't really be very different from our own after all. Even if two groups share certain concepts, however, they may *use* them in quite different ways, and this could lead them to quite different conceptions of the world.

Applying vs. Not Applying

The most obvious conceptual difference between two groups with the same concept occurs when one group applies a concept to a wide range of things they deem important but the other group doesn't apply it to anything at all. Many historians understand what the divine right of kings was supposed to involve, but few people nowadays think that this concept has any instances. Or one group may apply a concept much more widely than another; for example, the concept of a person would be applied more widely in an animistic culture than in our own.

Applying with Ease vs. Applying with Difficulty

Even when two groups have many of the same concepts, there can be differences in how accessible those concepts are to them, how natural it is to use them, whether they are be used by automatically and by default or only with effort and care. Differences in which concepts are applied by default, habitually or automatically could, if large enough, lead to rather different conceptions of the world. Someone who believed in a world full of magic and spirits and witchcraft might automatically think of disease as the result of witchcraft, whereas a mildly superstitious person might only entertain this possibility as a last resort.

Projecting vs. Not Projecting

Two groups might be able to express all of one another's concepts but *project* different concepts. For example, we can imagine a group that projects the concepts grue and bleen rather than our green and blue.

- An object is *grue* just in case it is observed before 2010 and is green, or else is not so observed and is blue.
- An object is *bleen* just in case it is observed before 2010 and is blue, or else is not so observed and is green.

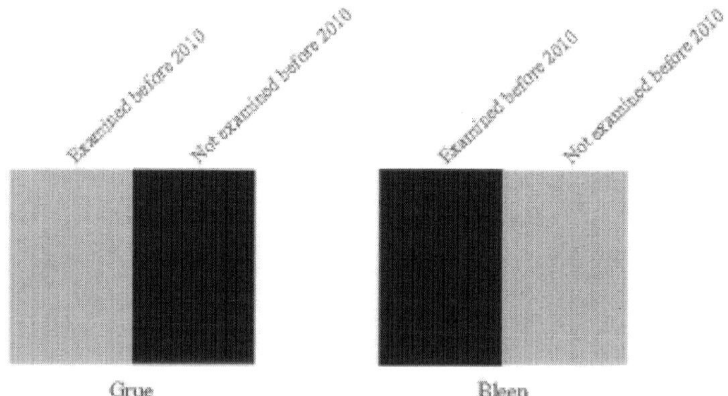

Figure: *Grue and Bleen Defined in Terms of Green and Blue*

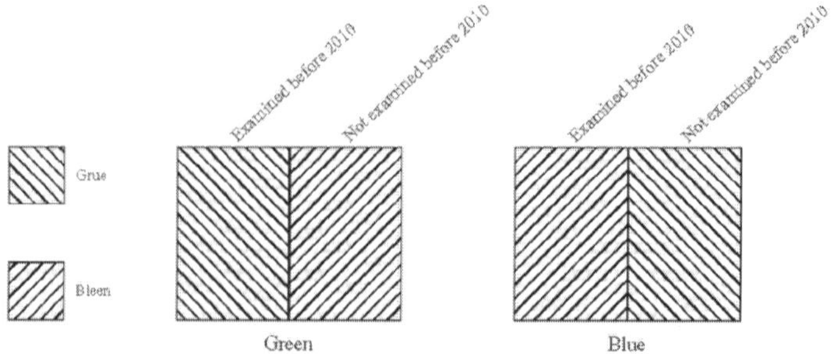

Figure: *Green and Blue Defined in Terms of Grue and Bleen*

We can *express* the other group's concepts in terms of ours and, at the cost of eccentricity and circumlocution, we could even *use* their concepts to classify things. What we cannot do is *project* grue and bleen (at least not without massive, compensatory changes in our overall set of concepts, beliefs, and inductive practices). It is both normatively incorrect for us to project such concepts (it violates our standards for good inductive inferences), and it would in fact be very difficult to bring ourselves to do so, to believe viscerally that grass is grue and the sky is bleen.

In short, it is one thing to be able to *express* a given concept and quite another to be able to use it easily, by default, to project it, or even to apply it to anything at all.

The descriptive claim that different groups in fact employ somewhat different sets of concepts leads only to a conceptual pluralism that is quite compatible with a robust realism about the things the concepts apply to. But our uses of concepts are bound up with our beliefs and practices in many ways, and we will see that conceptual relativism can be used, in conjunction with additional (not always terribly plausible) premises, to defend other types of relativism as well.

The Linguistic Turn

Much twentieth-century philosophy took what is often called the *linguistic turn*, with questions about properties and concepts being replaced by questions about words and linguistic usage. During this period, conceptual relativism was often transformed into a relativism involving linguistic meanings. For example, some philosophers spoke of the role of language or, more generally, systems of symbols in structuring our experience, thought, or even reality itself. One can find strains of this in Wittgenstein (e.g., 1969) and Carnap (1950), and it is explicit in Goodman (e.g., 1978). No one could now seriously suggest that most philosophical problems are at bottom problems about language, and concepts are once again respectable. But there is a substantial philosophical literature in which the points made here about concepts and relativism were translated into a linguistic mode as parallel points about words and relativism.

Central Beliefs

A *central belief* or, to use Kant's term, *principle* is one that a person could not abandon without having to surrender many other beliefs as well. For most of us these include the beliefs that at least some events have causes and that other people have feelings and emotions. Even if we could somehow divest ourselves of such beliefs, doing so would leave us with a very different picture of the world from the one most of us have now. As is often the case in discussions of relativism, a distinction between descriptive and normative considerations is relevant here. We can distinguish beliefs that a person or group would in fact have great difficulty giving up, those they should, by *their* standards, have great difficulty giving up, and even those they should, by *our* standards, have great difficulty giving up.

Descriptive relativism with respect to central beliefs is the empirical thesis that certain groups in fact have different central beliefs. For example, the belief that all of nature is alive may be central in an animistic culture but is not central to, or even held by, many people in the Western world today. The belief in causal determinism may have been central among physicists during the eighteenth century but is not central among physicists now. The belief that all people are of equal moral worth is central to some people now, but wasn't central to many in ancient Sparta.

Normative relativism with respect to central beliefs is the thesis that there is no framework-independent fact about which central beliefs are right, but that such beliefs can be right or wrong relative to a framework. The unqualified claim that any belief, even those that are inconsistent, could be correct relative to *some* framework or other is too strong to be plausible, but more modest versions of normative relativism about belief are possible. For a belief to be correct is for it to be true, so normative relativism about belief amounts to a normative relativism about truth. But since relative truth is the major flash point in discussions of relativism, we will single it out for special attention below.

Perception

Perception is the interface between cognition and reality. *Descriptive perceptual relativism* is the empirical claim that certain groups (e.g., those with different cultures, languages, biological makeup) perceive the world differently. For example, various philosophers of science have argued that theory influences perception to such an extent that partisans of substantially different theories might literally see the world differently.

Descriptive claims about perception are sometimes thought to bear on various versions of normative relativism. For example, some writers have argued that people with different concepts and beliefs will nevertheless perceive the same things in the much same way and that these common perceptions can be used as a fixed point from which to adjudicate the claims of rival frameworks. Most philosophers and vision scientists today now agree, though, that perception is *theory-laden*; our perceptual experiences in a given situation are influenced by the concepts, beliefs, expectations and, perhaps, even the hopes and desires, which we bring to the situation.

Normative perceptual relativism is the claim that there is not just one correct, framework-independent way to perceive things. But different ways are correct relative to different constellations of concepts and beliefs. Given modern medical training and practice, a competent radiologist should see that this spot on the X-ray is a stomach tumor, and anyone with any sensitivity should see that Sam felt humiliated.

As with most versions of normative relativism, the strongest versions of normative perceptual relativism, ones on which "anything goes," are implausible; there clearly are constraints on the perception. But weaker versions of the thesis may be defencible. Perception is theory-laden to some degree; it involves what current vision scientists call *top down processing*.

Epistemic Appraisal

Epistemology (from the Greek *episteme*, 'knowledge', and *logos*, 'theory'), or *the theory of knowledge*, is the area of philosophy that deals with knowledge and related concepts like justification and rationality. On a broad but natural construal, the epistemic realm includes standards or norms for justification and reasoning (e.g., logic, probability theory, guidelines for revising beliefs), ideals of rationality, standards for intelligibility and explanation, epistemic commitments and values (e.g., learning the truth, gaining insight, avoiding error, avoiding ignorance), virtues (e.g., being open-minded) and vices (e.g., having a tendency to jump to conclusions). This is a mixed bag, and one can be a relativist about some of the things in it (e.g., standards of explanation) but not others (e.g., logic).

Many of these things, particularly rationality and justification, are far from clear or univocal. Thus specific beliefs and decisions, ways of arriving at beliefs, policies for making decisions, individuals, groups, and (perhaps) even goals, emotions, and desires are often evaluated as rational or irrational. Moreover, there is intense controversy over what rationality in each of these cases involves; for example, there is debate over whether rational action requires some sort of maximization or optimization, or whether something more modest will suffice. Again, there is debate over whether rationality only involves formal notions like logical consistency and probabilistic coherence, or whether it involves something more substantive. And our concepts of justification are as multifaceted and subject to controversy as our concepts of rationality.

Epistemic Diversity

Many writers have made striking claims about the epistemic diversity among human beings. For example, Jean Piaget and various other developmental psychologists have suggested that children employ a logic unlike that used by adults (1972, p. 163). And C. I. Lewis was inspired to develop several relativistic themes in detail by his work on alternative (in his case modal) logics, which convinced him that the ultimate criteria for selecting a logical system—or any other sort of system of concepts and standards—are pragmatic (e.g., 1923, p. 232; 1929).

Many discussions of relativism in the earlier part of the twentieth century focused on the French anthropologist Lucien Lévy-Bruhl's (1922/1978) claim that members of preliterate (then called "primitive") cultures had a "pre-logical mentality" that led them to reason in ways that differ from modes of reasoning common in modern Western cultures. Lévy-Bruhl's opponents countered with the thesis of the "psychic unity of mankind." Various later writers urged "that standards of rationality in different societies do not always coincide" (Winch, 1970, p. 97), sometimes adding that different cultures have different standards of rationality that make good sense in the rich cultural contexts in which they occur, even if they look odd to us when wrenched out of that context. In a related spirit, the historian and philosopher of science Larry Laudan (1977, p. 187) urges that "*specific canons of rationality are time-dependent.* A mode of argument which one epoch, or 'school of thought,' views as entirely legitimate and reasonable may be viewed by another era or another intellectual tradition as ill-founded and obscurantist."

Epistemic Genealogy

Concepts and beliefs can have histories, and so can epistemic standards and sensibilities, with what counts as justification, evidence, or reasonableness shifting over time. For example, Aristotle's picture of what it takes to justify a scientific theory (roughly deduction from necessary, self-evident premises) differs markedly from our picture today (roughly testing by making predictions and seeing whether they pan out). The precise and formal conception of probability common today only emerged around 1660, and inferential statistics and experimental design, which now play an absolutely central role in the inductive practices in scientific and medical research, are almost exclusively the product of the last hundred years.

Authority and Tradition

Epistemic standards are not limited to the sorts of things codified in normative models like deductive logic, decision theory, or normative philosophy of science. The epistemic individualism, so pronounced in modern philosophers from Descartes to Kant, can lead us to overlook the fact that most of what we know we learned from others. But in many less-secular, more-traditional cultures, tradition and authority may play an especially dominant role, overriding virtually all other epistemic considerations. Thus, a culture or subculture may believe that the most secure basis for knowledge is faith or divine revelation or some authoritative person (e.g., Aristotle, a shaman, the Pope speaking *ex cathedra*), text (e.g., the *Bible*, the *Qur'an*) or practice (e.g., the deliverances of an oracle), and that their pronouncements cannot be overturned by any other methods (e.g., empirical science). For example, modern views about creationism are sometimes based on the view that the *Bible* provides a more accurate account of our origins than geology and biology ever could.

Rules

Standards of justification and norms of rationality are sometimes construed as rules or even algorithms (e.g., *modus ponens* or *existential generalization* for deductive logic; Bayesian conditionalization or Jeffrey conditionalization for updating probabilities of beliefs). But some of our epistemic standards and practices are also more indefinite than the picture of formal rules and procedures might suggest. They are more like rules or thumb or heuristics or even embody procedural knowledge that is difficult to express precisely in words. Indeed, to the extent that connectionist systems provide good models of various aspects of human reasoning, our standards may be quite amorphous and indefinite.

Epistemic Relativism

By analogy with the notions of central concepts and beliefs, we may call a group's more fundamental epistemic standards *central* or *framework standards*; as with their counterparts, centrality here is a matter of degree.

Descriptive epistemic relativism about a given mode of inference or reasoning (e.g., deductive inference, causal reasoning, contingency planning) is an empirical claim to the effect that certain groups in fact employ different central standards for evaluating that type of reasoning.

Much of the literature on descriptive relativism in the first two-thirds of the twentieth century was based on uncritical and poorly supported claims about the patterns of reasoning of educated people in modern Western societies. The last three decades have seen a great deal of empirical work on reasoning in our culture, but although we know more now than we did thirty years ago, many of the most basic matters remain controversial. These difficulties in getting clear about *our own* modes and norms of reasoning suggest a measure of skepticism when we encounter glib descriptions of the exotic reasoning patterns of members of quite alien cultures or groups.

Normative epistemic relativism is the claim that there are no framework-independent facts about which modes of inference, norms of justification, standards of rationality or the like are right, but that there *are* facts about such things relative to particular frameworks. Put another way, people or groups can disagree about what counts as good evidence or strong justification without being inconsistent, irrational, unintelligent, unjustified, or even just obtuse. Epistemic standards have a strong normative dimension—we use our standards of rationality and reasonableness to guide, evaluate, and criticize reasoning, both our own and that of others—so here the label 'normative' applies in a very full-blooded sense. And if knowledge requires justification, as many philosophers suppose, then relativism about justification also leads to relativism about knowledge.

Normative epistemic relativism is one of the most interesting and important species of relativism. The strongest versions, ones that allow *any* epistemic standards or norms, even those that are blatantly inconsistent by their own lights, to be correct relative to *some* framework or other are implausible.

But a number of writers endorse more subtle versions, or at least pay lip service to them, and it is not as easy as one might suppose to show that all of these are false. It is not easy, for example, to devise non-circular defences of some of our more fundamental epistemic standards and practices like induction.

This does not mean that the normative epistemic relativist wins by default, since she must defend a realism account about framework-immanent correctness in addition to an anti-realism about framework-transcendent correctness, but her claims cannot be dismissed out of hand.

Although normative epistemic relativism has attracted numerous proponents, we will see that problems of self-refutation threaten stronger versions of the view that are just as severe as the problems of self-refutation that beset the doctrine of relative truth.

Ethics

Our ethical lives involve principles, rules, commitments, rights, duties, ideals, virtues, modes of justifying and criticizing ethical claims, and doubtless other things as well. It is possible to be a relativist about some of these (e.g., what constitutes a good or worthwhile life) but not about others (e.g., rights).

The phrases 'ethical relativism' and 'moral relativism' are sometimes used interchangeably, but it is useful to distinguish them because morality is often characterized as a part of ethics, that involving obligations, rights, and justice, whereas other parts of ethics concern such things as what constitutes a good life or human flourishing (Aristotle's *eudaimonia*).

Descriptive ethical relativism is the empirical claim that certain groups differ along one or more ethical dimensions. For example, it is often said that modern Western cultures count individualism, autonomy, and personal dignity as key values, where certain other cultures see group solidarity or placating the Gods as more important. Again, one group may view meekness, humility, and submissiveness to the group as virtues, where another emphasizes heroism and pride. Such differences in moral concepts, values, and practices could also give rise to differences in moral perception and moral sensibilities.

Normative ethical relativism is the claim that what is right or just or virtuous or good only holds within, relative to, a particular ethical framework.

Ethical (or moral) relativism is the topic of a separate entry, and we will only advert to it when it is helpful to note its similarities to, or difference from, other species of relativism.

Semantics

There are various ways to be a relativist about the semantics of natural languages, i.e., about the meanings of words, phrases, and sentences in a languages like English or Choctaw. Some of these are fairly trivial, but others are more interesting, in part because they are frequently invoked in defence of other relativistic themes. The distinction between descriptive and normative relativism may be less clear cut here than in other cases, but it can still be usefully drawn.

Descriptive semantic relativism, as we will use the phrase, is the empirical claim that different groups, e.g., people living at different times or in different cultures, sometimes have different beliefs about the meaning of a word (where words are individuated independently of their meanings by such things as pronunciation or spelling). For example, some philosophers of science urge that scientists in the late seventeenth century used the word 'mass' so differently from the way physicists use it today that members of the two groups think of the word as having different meanings.

Normative semantic relativism is the view that the meanings of words *literally are* determined by a linguistic community, culture, or historical period. So if two communities overlap enough to have the same word (individuated without recourse to meanings), it is possible that *it* will have different meanings in the two communities. For example, some philosophers argue that in the Newtonian framework 'mass' has one meaning (e.g., it denotes a physical magnitude that isn't affected by velocity) and in today's physical framework it has a different meaning. Similarly, it is sometimes urged that the meanings of logical connectives (e.g., 'not', 'if', 'some') is relative to alternative logical frameworks like intuitionism or classical logic.

More global versions of normative semantic relativism sometimes arise in debates about the meanings of texts (like novels and epic poems). Originally such concerns involved Biblical interpretation, but in the nineteenth century Schleiermacher, Dilthey and others extended interpretive or hermeneutical concerns to all texts (and some contemporary literary theorists have extended the notion of a text, so that it needn't even involve anything linguistic). Interpretive work needn't involve strong versions of normative semantical relativism, but it sometimes does, particularly in postmodernist literary or cultural theory ("every interpretation is just a *re*interpretation").

Virtually everyone would agree that the meanings of words are in *some way* determined by the practices and beliefs of the members of the linguistic community who uses them. The important point for strong and interesting versions of semantic relativism is the *form* this determination takes. On relativistic accounts it typically involves a semantic holism to the effect that the denotations, or at least the meanings in some more general sense, of linguistic expressions are determined by their overall role in a language (theory, form of life, etc.). Indeed, the semantic relativist often continues, the denotations or meanings of the expressions of one language cannot be expressed in any but the most approximate way in a substantially different language. Semantic relativism, so construed, is more a linguistic thesis than an overt species of relativism, but there are interesting parallels with other species or relativism and, more importantly, it is frequently invoked in defences of other species.

Meaning Holism and the Relativity of Meaning

The notion of linguistic meaning is multifaceted and subject to endless controversy, but most thinkers agree that meaning, denotation (i.e., reference), and truth, are key semantic notions. We will begin with the intuitive but somewhat amorphous notion of meaning, focusing on the ways relativism about it are frequently invoked to defend other relativistic themes. Relativism about truth and relativism about denotation are discussed below.

Incommensurability and Conceptual Change

The most widely-discussed form of semantic relativism in recent decades is the doctrine of the incommensurability of meaning championed by Thomas Kuhn (e.g., 1970b), Paul Feyerabend (e.g., 1962), who cites Whorf in support, and several other philosophers of science in the 1960s. Although their views became more nuanced over the years, their early proposal was that the terms (e.g., 'mass', 'gene', 'temperature', 'electron') of scientific paradigms (Kuhn) or high-level background theories (Feyerabend) draw their meaning from their location or overall role in that paradigm or theory.

When a scientific paradigm or theory changes substantially, as happens during a scientific revolution, scientists change their mind about the truth values of many of the most important sentences or beliefs involving these terms (e.g., "the mass of an object is the same relative to all inertial frames"), and surprising new claims employing such terms many be added to the picture. Hence, the argument continues, the role of such terms changes, and with it so do their meanings. This is a version of *semantic* or *meaning holism*, the view that the meaning of linguistic phrases and sentences is determined by their place in the overall web of beliefs or sentences that comprise a theory or, at the limit, an entire worldview.

If the thesis of meaning holism is right, then substantially different theories cannot contain words or phrases that have the same meanings. It follows, proponents of incommensurability add, that in such cases the claims of competing theorists cannot be compared, because even when they seem to be using the same word, e.g., when Newton and Einstein use the word 'mass', it means different things. Rather than disagreeing, proponents of competing theories simply talk about different things—and past each other. And so it is that their claims and beliefs and theories are incommensurable.

It is also possible to formulate a holistic account of belief or mental content, so that the meaning or content of a belief is determined by its place in a large web of beliefs, and to develop an account of incommensurability and relativism in terms of concepts rather than worlds. Most of the issues that concern us here are similar in either case, however, and much of what follows applies to the content of concepts and beliefs as well as to the meanings of words and sentences.

Sometimes relativism is simply *equated* with the view that there are, or could be, completely incommensurable frameworks. This extreme view, which is rarely defended in any detail, has little to recommend it because it simply dismisses many interesting versions of relativism. Still, incommensurability theses *do* support some varieties of descriptive relativism, since groups with quite different outlooks would have quite different frameworks of concepts, standards, and beliefs.

Incommensurability and Cross-Cultural Comparisons

The meanings, concepts, and beliefs of very different cultures are also sometimes said to be incommensurable. For example, it might be argued that our word 'rights' (or, on more mentalistic accounts, our concept of individual rights) derives its meaning from its relationships to our other words or concepts (e.g., liberty, obligation, autonomy, equality), beliefs (e.g., people should be allowed some control over their own lives), and practices (e.g., our system of laws and sanctions).

The Problem of Conceptual Alignment

But if the meanings and concepts and beliefs and traditions and practices of another culture are substantially different from our own, it follows that none of their words (or complex phrases) *line up* well enough with the meaning of our word 'rights' for us to accurately interpret them as having any phrases or concepts that are genuine counterparts of our word or concept, or as having any beliefs about rights.

Similarly, this line of thought can be continued, another group might have quite different meanings or concepts when it comes to causation, epistemic evaluation, or even logic (cf. Winch, 1970 §1). And if this is so, it leads to a descriptive relativism about concepts, logical principles, or the like, as well as to weak truth-value relativism. (We turn to criticisms of such views below.)

The Inscrutability of Reference and Ontological Relativity

The influential American philosopher W. V. O. Quine is well known for his thesis of the *inscrutability of reference* and its attendant notions of the *indeterminacy of translation* and *ontological relativity*. These labels may conjure up visions of an extreme relativism in which ontology (i.e., what exists) is relative to languages or frameworks. In fact, though, Quine's views are a form of antirealism about both semantic and mentalistic notions that would simply undercut many forms of relativism. The thesis of the inscrutability of reference tells us that it makes no sense to say absolutely, i.e., in any language or framework-independent sense, what objects a speaker is talking about. For example, there is no language-transcendent fact as to whether someone pointing in the direction of a rabbit is speaking of enduring physical objects (rabbits) or events (temporal stages of rabbits).

Hence, far from supporting most varieties of relativism, Quine's views actually undermine them, since there is no longer any absolute fact about what the speakers of different languages or members of different cultures think and talk about, and hence no fact that they think in interestingly different ways. It is not that the native—or anyone else's—mind is inscrutable, Quine tells us, but that there is simply "nothing to scrute" (1969, p. 5; cf. p. 27 and 1960, p. 58 and p. 77). Nor is there any absolute fact to scrute about the denotation of the native's words or the contours of his worldview.

Practice

Much of our thought and action takes place against a background of common but tacit assumptions, understandings, intuition, attitudes, concerns, skills, and other ways of coping with the world around us. These are largely unarticulated, perhaps sometimes not articulable, and often difficult to identify. They include inferential and other cognitive habits, automatic ways of interpreting things, and the concepts it is second nature to project.

The claim that explicit beliefs and reasoning do not tell the whole story about our mental lives is not just some esoteric bit of theory. Few of us see our abilities to speak our native language or to recognize facial expressions in terms of precepts or rules, and cognitive scientists who have tried to write explicit rules to simulate these skills inevitably find it very difficult to do. Some aspects of practice, e.g., the ways we individuate things into physical objects, may be part of our biological heritage, but other aspects differ from one group to another. Practice is in some ways more naturally viewed as an independent variable (e.g., as an aspect of culture or form of life), but in some ways it also works like a dependent variable, so it is useful to introduce it here.

One would expect an emphasis on practice in Marxist writings on praxis and pragmatists' writings on inquiry and education, but many other writers have stressed it as well. Aristotle emphasizes the importance of practical wisdom (*phronesis*), the ability to judge what to do in concrete situations, and because practical wisdom cannot be reduced to formal directives, he emphasizes that education should aim to inculcate habits and promote the internalization of ways of seeing and feeling and acting, rather than simply to impart rules.

Much more recently Michael Polanyi (1958) has argued that we know more than we can tell and that this tacit knowledge underlies all of our more explicit knowledge. Related themes surface in Gilbert Ryle's distinction between knowing-how and knowing-that, in Pierre Bourdieu's notion of *habitus*, in Thomas Kuhn's likening the learning of science to an apprenticeship in which one acquires not just explicit knowledge, but also habits and skills. And various philosophers (e.g., Searle, 1983, Ch. 5) have argued that an inexplicit, unarticulated, and perhaps even non-representational *background* of assumptions, presuppositions, ways of perceiving, and modes of acting underlie our all our knowledge and evaluation.

This emphasis on practice—on engagement, judgment, and action—is a useful corrective to what Dewey excoriated as spectator theories of knowledge that portray human beings in too passive a way and that still mar some treatments of relativism.

Practice and Relativism

Descriptive relativism about practice is the empirical claim that certain groups have different practices of the sort that lead to different modes of thought and evaluation. On such pictures one might think of cultures, say, as determining practices, which in turn determine modes of classification and evaluation. But it would be more accurate to see cultural practices and modes of classification and evaluation as aspects of the same thing that we separate, somewhat artificially, for purposes of discussion.

Normative relativism about practice is the claim that there can be framework-dependent, but no framework-independent, facts as to which practices are right. The notion of a practice being right in some framework-independent sense is not particularly clear, but examples give us some purchase on the idea. Thus Goodman argues that there is no framework-transcendent fact that people should project the concept green rather than grue. Still, it would be incorrect for *us*, with our current inductive practices, to do so. Goodman urges that which predicates are projectible—for us, here, now—depends in part on the inductive practices of our community, on which predicates its members have successfully projected in the past. Indeed, the history of our practices determines which categories are right for a variety of purposes (e.g., Goodman, 1984, pp. 120-124; 1978, p. 138).

Ludwig Wittgenstein's treatment of practice is especially important. He argues that justifications and reasons do not bottom out in arguments or beliefs or principle, but in the fact that we behave in the ways that we do, in our form of life, in the practices we have. For example, at some point our applications of rules and standards rests on the fact that we (typically) agree about what counts as going on in the same way or what makes for a correct application of a rule in a novel situation. Some aspects of our form of life may be common to all normal adult human beings, but others may vary across groups. The first two passages are from Wittgenstein's On Certainty, the next two from the Philosophical Investigations.

110. What counts as its test? "But is this an adequate test? And, if so, must it not be recognizable as such in logic?"—As if giving grounds did not come to an end sometime. But the end is not an ungrounded presupposition: it is an ungrounded way of acting.

204 Giving grounds, however, justifying the evidence, comes to an end;—but the end is not certain propositions' striking us immediately as true, i.e. it is not a kind of seeing on our part; it is our acting, which lies at the bottom of the language-game.

217 If I have exhausted the justifications I have reached bedrock, and my spade is turned. Then I am inclined to say: "This is simply what I do."

What has to be accepted, the given, is—so one could say—*forms of life* (Pt. II, p. 226).

Practice suffuses all aspects of culture and thought and evaluation, but it is worth singling it out because its very ubiquity makes it easy to overlook.

Truth

Truth is important because it is a major goal of inquiry, a central component of knowledge, the thing justification is supposed to track, what valid arguments preserve, perhaps (in the form of truth conditions) a component of linguistic meanings and, for many people, a valuable end in itself. Philosophers call truth and falsity *truth values*, so it is natural to call relativism about truth *truth-value relativism*.

Descriptive truth-value relativism is the empirical claim that in some cases the members of different groups believe different things to be true.

Normative truth-value relativism is the claim that tokens of sentences, beliefs or the like are only true relative to a framework. Thus Kuhn says "If I am right, then 'truth' may, like 'proof', be a term with only intra-theoretical applications" (1970a, p. 266). Normative truth-value relativism comes in two versions. The *weak version* is the claim that there may be things that are true in one framework that are not true in a second simply because they are not expressible in the second.

The *strong version*, which receives the most attention, is the claim that one and the same thing, e.g., one and the same belief, can be true in one framework and false in another.

Relativism about truth boils down to relativism about belief, but rather different sets of issues are typically connected with central beliefs or principles, on the one hand, and issues about relative truth, on the other. The first set of issues involves what I will call *framework principles*, very general principles (e.g., every event has a cause) that guide classification and inquiry. By contrast, the second set of issues involves the strong version of normative truth-value relativism quite explicitly. Since the two sets of issues are rather different, we treat them separately here.

Truth is a major flash point in discussions of relativism. The traditional indictment of the strong version of truth-value relativism is that it is self-refuting. The claim that truth is relative is, by the relativist's own lights, only true relative to some frameworks and it may be false relative to others. Hence, it is argued, the relativist cannot account for the status of his own claims. We examine this objection in §5.9.

Reality

In a phrase so arresting it couldn't help but catch on, Peter Berger and Thomas Luckmann (1966) spoke of the *social construction of reality*. The term suggests that the world, *reality itself*, is in some measure the product of our cognitive activity. Such views have gone by various names, including *metaphysical relativism* and *constructivism*, and they are the most extreme forms of relativism that there are. I will call the general view *reality relativism*.

Descriptive reality relativism is the empirical claim that certain groups think about, or experience, the world as involving certain things (e.g., physical objects) whereas other groups think or experience it differently (e.g., events). This claim overlaps descriptive relativism with respect to concepts, beliefs, and perception, and so is not of great independent interest.

Normative reality relativism is the view that what is *real* is somehow relative to a framework. But what could this mean? Perhaps in some sense we use concepts to construct the world, but no one supposes that the world is *literally* composed of concepts. It is tempting, and often best, to regard talk of social construction as a metaphor that is meant to suggest some less hyperbolic doctrine, e.g., that people with quite different concepts will think about things in different ways.

There is no escaping the fact, however, that some very able thinkers, from Immanuel Kant to Nelson Goodman, have held the stronger view that the mind plays an essential role in the *construction* of the objects of knowledge. This is not to say that it constructs them out of nothing; most thinkers who adopt this line urge that there is some sort of input or raw material that we shape, not with our hands or coping saws or lathes, but with our concepts and beliefs and cognitive practices. Here a common theme, noted above, is that the individuation of the raw material into things requires the imposition of concepts on it.

On the face of it, the view that reality is socially constructed seems so peculiar that it is worth documenting that a wide range of thinkers have said things that at least strongly suggest it. The greatest difficulty with normative reality relativism is making sense of it, with finding a version of it that does some justice to the claims of thinkers sympathetic to it without being incoherent when we turn to the details. We will return to this in §4.

Other Contenders

Other things, including aesthetic standards, emotions, personality structure, memory, strategies for solving problem, motivation, decision making, social cognition, and even sense of humor, have been claimed to be relative in interesting ways. In her famous work, for example, Margaret Mead claimed to find differences in personality structure between adolescents in American and Samoa. But the variables discussed above have received the greatest attention in discussions of relativistic themes. Table One displays these nine independent variables, along with a few illustrative subtypes (qualifiers like 'central' and 'basic' are omitted; not all of the subtypes discussed, much less all of those that might be distinguished, will easily fit into a readable tree). Each type and subtype comes in a descriptive and in a normative version.

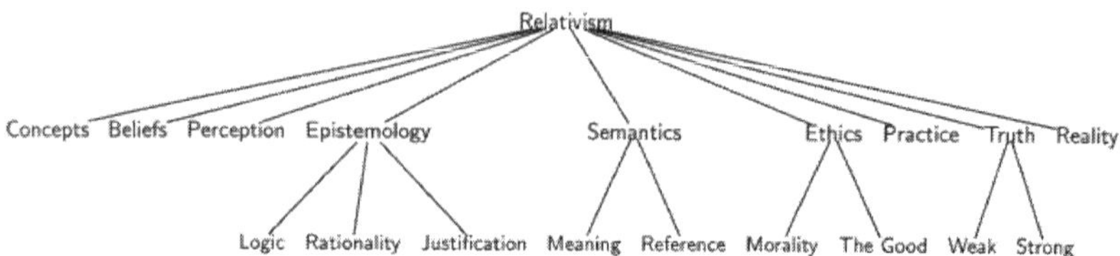

Figure: *Tree Diagram of Dependent Variables with Illustrative Subtypes*

Relationships among the Kinds of Relativism

The goal here is to facilitate discussion rather than to give a taxonomy of mutually exclusive positions, and in fact there are areas of overlap among some of these species of relativism. For example, normative truth-value relativism about ethics overlaps normative ethical relativism. The best way of thinking about a view in the region of overlap often depends on the purposes at hand, e.g., whether we are primarily interested in the ethical aspects of the view or whether we are interested in comparing different types of relativism about truth.

The precise relationships among various types of relativism, e.g., between conceptual relativism and epistemic relativism, depend on the detailed way in which the view is developed, but there are affinities between several types of relativism as they are most commonly construed.

Some connections exist because we have abstracted away from the rich texture of peoples' thought and life. For example, talk of ethical or epistemic or legal or religious realms may suggest a sort of compartmentalization that rarely exists in actual life. People often have a multiplicity of concerns at any given time, and in many cases the boundaries between various sorts of considerations and reasons—e.g., the prudential, the epistemic, the ethical—are blurry. Indeed, it is sometimes even unclear whether some aspect of a person's cognitive life is best construed as a rule, value, or a higher-order belief. For example, a person's commitment to *modus ponens* might be construed as a logical rule that they endorse, *or* as the belief that if a conditional and its antecedent are both true, its consequent must be true as well.

Various species of relativism support one another, although this support often falls short of entailment. Here we note just a few of the potential connections among various species of relativism.

Concepts, Beliefs, and Perception: Relativism about concepts or beliefs is connected, rather trivially, to other kinds of relativism because all of them involve concepts and beliefs. For example, groups with rather different ethical or epistemic concepts are likely to have somewhat different epistemic standards and values. More substantively, if certain empirical claims about the theory-ladenness of perception are true, relativism about concepts and beliefs leads to perceptual relativism.

Epistemic Relativism: Our epistemic standards and practices are interwoven with our concepts. Indeed, a central task of concepts is to mediate inferences. Furthermore, the concepts we project partially determine which ampliative inferences we sanction. These inferences can also depend on a background of general beliefs, for example the belief that the future will be pretty much like the past in ways we consider relevant or that if two types of events are correlated then either one causes the other or else they have a common cause.

Truth-Value Relativism: Normative relativism about epistemic standards does not entail normative relativism about truth or about reality. It can, however, be combined with other substantive principles in various ways in arguments designed to support the latter. First, if truth is explained in partially epistemic terms, e.g., as what would be warranted or justified under certain idealized conditions of inquiry, then relativism about standards of warrant or justification leads naturally to relativism about truth. But even on non-epistemic conceptions of truth, the view that an epistemic standard is legitimate only if it is *truth-conducive*, i.e., only if it tends to lead to true conclusions when applied to true premises, together with the view that epistemic standards are relative, can be deployed to argue for the relativity of truth. The argument can also be run in the opposite direction, from the claim that truth is relative and that good epistemic standards are truth conducive, to the conclusion that epistemic standards are relative.

Reality Relativism: Reality relativism supports relativism about many other things. A common argument for reality relativism, examined below, turns on the claim that our central concepts and beliefs somehow structure or shape the world as we know it and that any notion of an objective world that is entirely independent of the way we know it is empty and useless. If this is correct, it is tempting to conclude that the only notion of truth that is not empty and useless is truth about things with respect to our conceptual framework. On this picture, which involves a standard relativistic reconstrual, the sentence 'grass is green' is true because it corresponds to the facts or fits the world—but since the only world we can talk or think or know about is the world of our framework, we must (we are told) conclude that the sentence corresponds to the facts of that world. Truth makers are relative to frameworks, and so the only sort of truth we can hope to discover is truth in, or relative to, a framework.

Independent Variables: Relative to What?

In this section we examine the chief candidates for relativistic independent variables. As with the dependent variables, the chief candidates here are not all independent of one another—language and religion are important facets of culture, for example—but they are often singled out for separate treatment, and we begin by following suite.

- 3.1 Language
- 3.2 Culture
- 3.3 Historical Period
- 3.4 Innate Cognitive Architecture
- 3.5 Choice
- 3.6 Other Contenders
  - o 3.6.1 Scientific Frameworks
  - o 3.6.2 Religion
  - o 3.6.3 Gender, Race and Social Status
  - o 3.6.4 The Individual
- 3.7 Frameworks Revisited

While such things are concepts, logical principles, and truth are often relativized to conceptual frameworks, frameworks in turn are usually thought to be determined by something else. Issues involving descriptive relativism are often central in discussions of the independent variables, since one of the chief questions is whether (and, if so, how) something like language or culture *in fact* influences modes of thought or evaluation. But normative issues often surface as well.

Relativism as Social. Over two thousand years ago the Greek philosopher Protagoras declared that man is the measure of all things. Plato interpreted this as the claim that what is true is relative to each individual person's beliefs. But virtually all of the versions of relativism that have been defended in any detail since Plato's time treat it a *social* phenomenon, and almost no later writers take their inspiration from Protagoras. Instead, members of a group said to have their modes of thought as part of their social heritage, because of some common possession like culture or language, or as part of their shared biological endowment.

Language

Language (along with culture) is the most frequently discussed independent variable, the thing most commonly said to influence modes of thought. This can be generalized, as it has by Nelson Goodman (1978), to the claim that symbol systems—including computer languages, conventions for diagrams, even styles of painting—influence perception and thought.

The claim that one's language affects how she experiences and thinks about the world is known as the *linguistic relativity hypothesis* or *linguistic relativism* (it is also called, in deference to two prominent proponents, the *Whorf hypothesis* or the *Sapir-Whorf hypothesis*). It is typically a descriptive (rather than a normative) claim about the actual influence of human languages on human thought and experience.

Any serious discussion of linguistic relativism requires us to answer three questions:

1. *Which aspects* of language influence *which aspects* of thought in a systematic way?
2. What *form* does this influence take?
3. How *strong* is the influence?

For example, certain features of a language's syntax (e.g., whether there is a distinction between intransitive verbs and adjectives) or its lexicon (e.g., what colour words or numerical vocabulary it has) might be said to influence perception, classification, or memory in clearly specifiable ways.

As with relativistic claims about the other independent variables, linguistic relativity hypotheses are claims about *causal influence*: one or more aspects of language causally affect one or more aspects of thought. Such influences can vary in magnitude, so linguistic relativity hypotheses differ in the strength of the hypothesized influence. Finally, as with many other versions of relativism, the weakest versions of linguistic relativism are trivially true and the strongest versions are known to be false. The important question is whether interesting versions between these extremes are true. Current evidence suggests that a person's language does have some influence on her perception and thought, but that it is much less dramatic than the more extreme partisans of linguistic relativism have maintained.

Morals for Independent Variables in General

The greatest challenge for proponents of linguistic relativism is to adduce evidence to show that differences in language actually *lead* to differences in thought. This is a problem that arises for most of the independent variables we will consider, so linguistic relativism is a good case study for descriptive relativism in general. The points that emerge from an examination of linguistic relativism are defended in a supplement to this section; the discussion there suggests the following morals for a number of independent variables, including culture and history, as well as language.

1. Questions about the impact of an independent variable on cognition are empirical and causal questions.
2. Such questions can only be answered once we specify *which aspects* of an independent variable (e.g., the colour lexicon, religious practices) influence *which aspects* of thought (e.g., perception, causal reasoning) and what form the hypothesized influence takes.
3. Such hypotheses can vary greatly in specificity, strength, and scope.
4. Testing a specific version of a relativity hypothesis requires a combination of skills. Depending on the type of relativism involved in may require the expertise of an ethnographer, linguist, experimental psychologist, historian, or biologist.
5. A comparison of more than two groups (e.g., linguistic communities, cultures) is needed to draw any firm conclusions about a descriptive relativity hypothesis.
6. The truth of specific relativity hypotheses may turn on issues involving the modularity of mind and the degree of modular encapsulation. For example, if the mind is highly modular, finding an influence of one aspect of language or culture of some aspect of cognition (e.g., language comprehension) may tell us little about the influence of other aspects of language or culture on other aspects of cognition (e.g., long-term memory).

Culture

Culture is perhaps the most central theoretical concept in anthropology, and it is important in many of the other social sciences as well. The nature and role of culture are matters of controversy, but a quite general characterization will suffice here. Culture is socially transmitted from one generation to the next. It includes ideals about how one should live, customs, mores, taken-for-granted common knowledge, systems of production and exchange, ways of coping with illness, disease and death, legal institutions, religion, rituals, rites of passage, myths, taboos, technologies, social hierarchies and status, sexual practices, accepted ways of displaying emotions, marriage, kinship structures, power hierarchies, sports, games, art, architecture, language.

There are always differences in outlooks and beliefs within the same culture, especially in large and heterogeneous ones, and at some point the notion of a culture may begin to blur enough that we introduce notions of like that of a subculture. These also have a certain haziness (we will return to this below), but useful generalizations about particular cultures are still often possible.

Cultural relativism is the thesis that a person's culture strongly influences her modes of perception and thought. Many anthropologists, particularly in the earlier parts of the twentieth century, saw culture as a force that was nearly unlimited in its power to shape human beings. This passage, from the influential American anthropologist Ruth Benedict, is typical:

> No man ever looks at the world with pristine eyes. He sees it edited by a definite set of customs and institutions and ways of thinking. Even in his philosophical probings he cannot go behind these stereotypes ...The life-history of the individual is first and foremost an accommodation to the patterns and standards traditionally handed down in his community. From the moment of his birth the customs into which he is born shape his experience and behaviour. By the time he can talk, he is the little creature of his culture, and by the time he is grown and able to take part in its activities, its habits are his habits, its beliefs his beliefs, its impossibilities his impossibilities. Every child that is born into his group will share them with him, and no child born into one on the opposite side of the globe can ever achieve the thousandth part (1934, pp. 2-3).

Amorphous debates over pre-logical and pre-literate modes of thought that were once popular have now given way to more detailed and precise work in cross-cultural psychology and cognitive anthropology. The extent to which cultural forces can shape modes of thought is still not fully understood, but it appears that although there are some modest cognitive differences between cultures, nothing remotely as dramatic as the claims made in some of the earlier literature on cultural relativism have received much support.

Historical Period

Technology and art are products of their times. So are many concepts, standards, and beliefs. *Historical relativism* (or *historicism*, in one of its many meanings) is the view that groups from quite different historical epochs will have different modes of thought. The British philosopher and historian R. G. Collingwood (e.g., 1940, esp. ch. 6) particularly stressed the historical dimension of relativism, but many other thinkers agreed. Karl Mannheim, the founder of the sociology of knowledge, put it this way:

When we attribute to one historical epoch one intellectual world and to ourselves another one, or if a certain historically determined social stratum thinks in categories other than our own, we refer not to the isolated cases of thought content, but to fundamentally divergent thought systems and to widely differing modes of experience and interpretation (1929/1936, p. 57).

Historical differences are typically thought to stem from cultural and linguistic differences, so historical relativism does not add anything radically new to cultural and linguistic relativism. Introducing history as an independent variable makes a new range of cases relevant, however, and it means that historical texts and historiography can be used to study relativistic themes. History has also played a key role in discussions of more local types of relativism, particularly in science.

In his influential book, *The Whig Interpretation of History*, Herbert Butterfield (1931) made a strong case against the "Wiggish" view that history involves progressive evolution toward where we are now. This picture is often another form of ethnocentric projection, and in fact changes of many sorts occur for many reasons. Still, history sometimes allows us to see earlier modes of thought as precursors to our own, and this opens the door to studies of conceptual change. It also holds out the hope of a sort of self-understanding, some insight into how we came to be the way we are.

Innate Cognitive Architecture

Nature vs. Nurture: The *nature-nurture debate* is the perennial dispute over the relative strength of innate biological makeup (nature), on the one hand, and enculturation, socialization, and other forms of learning (nurture), on the other. Both are obviously necessary for normal human life, and the debate has often been confused or oversimplified, with inexact talk about a gene for this or being "wired up" to do that. Still, there *is* a genuine empirical question about the extent of the malleability vs. the constancy of human nature, about the boundaries of the biologically possible and the degree to which our biological makeup, especially the organization of our nervous systems and brains, underdetermines culture, language, and modes of thought.

Nurture: During the 1940s and 50s, when behaviourism was dominant in psychology, linguistics, and (perhaps to a lesser extent) the other social sciences, the pendulum had swung sharply to the empiricist (nurture) pole. Very little, save for general learning mechanisms, were thought to be built into the human mind, and so there was a good deal of scope for language and culture to shape modes of thought.

Nature: In recent decades the pendulum has swung sharply to the opposite (nature) pole. The pioneering linguist Noam Chomsky emphasized innate linguistic universals, which this led to a picture of deep commonality beneath surface differences in languages. And with the increasing popularity of nativist views in cognitive science, e.g., claims that the mind comes with a number of innate modules, talk of cognitive universals and pre-configured modules is now common. From this perspective, a rich cognitive architecture is "wired in," so there is less scope for culture or language to influence how we experience or think about the things.

In the last few years, however, even some of cognitive science's founders (e.g., Bruner, 1992) have reacted against what they see as its overemphasis emphasis on information processing and its relative neglect of culture. Culture is now being worked back into the picture, and people are once again asking just how much influence it can have on cognition. Still, although the issues here are difficult and far from settled, a good deal of empirical work does suggest that the human mind comes pre-wired in interesting and important ways (e.g., with predispositions to learn certain kinds of languages, or to recognize human faces). So it may well turn out that at an abstract, but still interesting level, people do in fact think in much the same ways. (We will return to some of these matters below).

Nativism Only Bears on Some Types of Relativism: Nativist views of cognition support many sorts of descriptive relativism with respect to human beings. But they raise the possibility that certain aspects of human cognition result from the contingent, often highly accidental, evolutionary history of our species, and if the similarities among human beings stem from contingent features of our brain and our sensory apparatus, creatures with quite different biological makeups might perceive and think in quite different ways. From this perspective, in fact, the contingent features of our cognitive architecture may begin to look like limitations.

Even if human nature is strikingly uniform beneath the veneer of cultural and historical differences, normative issues about objectivity, justification, and truth also remain. Indeed, nativist views can accentuate normative issues, since it is possible that human cognition is less than optimal in various ways; for example, evolutionary selection pressures may have favoured quick and tolerably accurate cognitive mechanisms over slower but more accurate ones.

Choice

If alternative frameworks of central concepts, beliefs, and standards are possible, can we simply decide which ones to adopt? On some accounts it is discretionary, a matter of choice or explicit convention, which categories and principles we employ; this is not to say that it is arbitrary or capricious, since there may be good reasons—e.g., simplicity, ease of use, comprehensiveness—for preferring some choices to others, but we do have some say in the matter. On other accounts, alternatives may be possible in some abstract sense, but they are not live options for us.

Voluntarism

At the voluntaristic end of the spectrum we find thinkers urging that there is a great deal of leeway for choice. For example, existentialists like Sartre hold that there are no objective facts about moral values and principles, and that we must select them for ourselves with an existential leap, a fateful existential choice. Many Anglo-American non-cognitivists about ethics, including Ayer, Stevenson, and the early Hare held less portentous versions of a similar view. Going a step further, some of Nietzsche's remarks in his posthumously edited and published *Will to Power* (1906/1967) (which he might not have endorsed) suggest that many other aspects of cognition are also matters of choice. And, to take a very different figure, Carnap (1950, §2) tells us that we can choose to speak the "thing language," in which physical objects are central, *or* a "phenomenalistic language," in which sense data are.

Coercion

Writers at the opposite end of the spectrum argue that it is difficult, or even impossible, to make substantial changes in our central concepts, beliefs, and evaluative standards. We cannot simply decide, for example, to begin thinking about the world in completely non-causal terms. Indeed, if our most fundamental concepts and beliefs are part of our biological endowment, it may not be biologically possible to dispense with then. There would be less scope for changing the way we experience and think about colours, for example, if certain aspects of colour cognition were determined by the neurophysiology of our visual system (as the opponent-processes theory suggests) than if they were determined by the colour lexicon of our native language (as some linguistic relativists supposed).

But many writers who stress nurture over nature also resist the picture of easy alteration. Some even invoke the language of coercion to emphasize the point. For example, some early champions of the linguistic relativity hypothesis employed phrases like 'linguistic determinism.' Thus Whorf tells us that "[n]o individual is free to describe nature with absolute impartiality but is constrained to certain modes of interpretation [determined by the language he speaks] even while he thinks himself most free" (1956, p. 214). Benedict makes similar claims for culture, as does Collingwood (1940) for history. Among other things, these writers urge that our central concepts and beliefs permeate our thought so thoroughly that it doesn't even occur to most of us that there could be alternatives.

Conversion

Between these extremes we find writers who hold that dramatic revisions of frameworks are occasionally possible, but only in exceptional circumstances. Speaking of a scientist's choice to embrace a new paradigm in its early stages, Kuhn tells us that "a decision of that kind can only be made on faith," and he frequently speaks on accepting a new paradigm in terms of faith and conversion (1970b, p. 158 and pp. 19, 148, 150). Polanyi (1958, pp. 152f) speaks of conversion in a similar context, and when imagining a confrontation between people with very difference cognitive practices. Collingwood (1940, p. 256) speaks of faith in a similar context. And Wittgenstein tells us that "at the end of reasons comes *persuasion*. (Think of what happens when missionaries convert natives.)" (1969, §612; cf. §92)

Piecemeal Modification

Probably the most popular view among current philosophers is that human beings can only modify their frameworks gradually and that some parts may be utterly immune to revision at any given time. Such claims are often accompanied by an invocation of Neurath's simile of rebuilding a ship at sea: we can change the ship bit-by-bit, relying on the unchanging parts for stability as we proceed, but we cannot rebuild the entire ship all at once.

Similarly, gradual and piecemeal changes in our conceptual framework are possible, but we cannot change large chunks of it all at once, since we would have no concepts or principles to use in working out the transition. For example, we would have no standards to judge whether two proposed modifications were consistent with one another.

Religion

The great French pioneer of sociology, Émile Durkheim, (1858-1917) argued (not terribly convincingly) for the formative power of religion in *The Elementary Forms of Religious Life* (1912/1995). He held that a great deal of our cognitive and social life is strongly influenced by religion and that concepts as fundamental as genus and species, and even logic itself, have their source in religious thoughts and practices. Durkheim himself thought that human religions were similar enough that these concepts would be the same across cultures, but if we combine his account with a more relativistic picture of actual cultures and religions, we would get a sort of relativism.

And the great German pioneer of sociology, Max Weber (1864-1920), argued that various features of protestantism had led to the an "iron cage" of instrumental rationality. This involves the "disenchantment" of the earlier world, with all its rules, regulations, and the whole dreary apparatus of quantification and everything-by-the-book bureaucracies.

The influence of religion on modes of thought will seem more plausible when we consider cultures where religion plays a more pervasive role than it does in many cultures and sub-cultures in the West. In more traditional cultures there is often no separation of church and state, a priest or shaman may be the ultimate authority on virtually everything, and morality, law, and religion are thoroughly entwined. If the religion is animistic, all of nature may seem alive and capable of causing harm. In such settings, the impact of religion on modes of experience and thought could be quite powerful.

Gender, Race, and Social Status

In many societies members of some ethnic groups, genders, or social classes are treated differently than members of other ethnic groups, genders, and classes. They are thus situated differently, and it is sometimes argued that this can lead to important differences in modes of thought and patterns of evaluation. Furthermore, the argument continues, those in power may, consciously or unconsciously, downplay or suppress the modes and patterns of those who are not, and having ones viewpoints recognized can often be a step toward achieving empowerment and equality.

Marx's account of *ideology* is one of the earliest views of this sort, but this theme has been developed in various ways in later thinkers. In some cases, e.g., Michel Foucault (1980), these ideas are linked quite intimately to themes of domination and power. A good discussion of many of the relevant issues can be found in the entry on feminist epistemology and philosophy of science.

Combinations

It is possible that various combinations of independent variables (e.g., language and religion) would lead to interesting outcomes, reinforcing one another, neutralizing one another, or interacting in complex and unexpected ways. It is also possible that some of the variables lead to relativistic effects only under certain conditions; this is, after all, how causes typically work.

Frameworks Revisited

Overlap: Everyone is a member of many different groups—tribes, linguistic communities, subcultures, social classes, religious groups, political parties, clans, families—with a variety of perspectives and allegiances. Which groups matter for relativism? The answer is that different species of relativism single out different groups as relevant. The claim that a certain sort of group (e.g., culture, linguistic community) is important for relativism, whereas other sorts of groups (e.g., soccer teams, bridge clubs) are not, is a substantive, descriptive, relativistic thesis that must be defended, or refuted, by empirical evidence.

Our Framework: Who are We?

Different philosophers use different terms for their versions of the more generic notion of a conceptual framework employed here. Terms that have been used in related ways include *worldview* (*Weltanschauung*) and *categorial scheme*. There are also similarities to Wittgenstein's *forms of life*, various phenomenologists' notions of the *life world* (*Lebenswelt*), R. G. Collingwood's sets of *absolute presuppositions* of a given culture and time, Thomas Kuhn's *paradigms*, Michel Foucault's *epistemes*, and Nelson Goodman's *world versions*. Some of these, e.g., a culture's entire form of life, are quite global, influencing almost all aspects of cognition. Others e.g., paradigms and many world versions, are typically more local; for example, the first involves just a particular style of science during a particular period, and second might involve something as local as a given style of painting.

It would illuminate the general notion of a framework if we were clearer about our own. Just what does it involve? And who are *we*? In large, heterogeneous, multicultural societies with many subcultures, talk of things like "our morality" involves considerable oversimplification (and often a bit of ethnocentric projection as well). Muslims, evangelical Christians, the Amish, secular humanists, and disaffected teenagers in the inner city doubtless share some moral outlooks, and if we describe their views at a sufficiently abstract level they may look similar.

But down at ground level, in the shadows and fog where human action and feeling actually take place, abstract principles at best tell part of the story. At this more elemental level the moral outlooks of such groups differ in ways that can matter a lot. At this level you don't have to go halfway around the world to find moral alternatives; if you live in a large city, you don't even have to go half way across town.

Something similar may be true, though perhaps to a lesser extent, of other relativistic dependent variables like rationality or evidential standards. For example, many members of modern Western societies believe in the existence of a supernatural being and view (what they take to be) its pronouncements as having strong epistemic force, others are more skeptical, and some simply dismiss such beliefs as superstitions.

Furthermore, even if we confine attention to relatively small and homogeneous groups, it is often difficult to say with any precision just what their concepts and evaluative standards amount to. Indeed, philosophers who have spent decades trying to say what "our" standards of rationality involve, what logic (if any) we use, or what such central concepts as causation, person, or justification boil down to are nowhere near a consensus. In fact, the general project of conceptual analysis that was supposed to answer some of these questions is now widely regarded as a failure.

Given the lack of clarity about our own case, caution is recommended when we hear astonishing claims about the Hopi conception of time, the Trobriand conception of causation, or the other exotic concepts or values or beliefs so often attributed to other groups in discussions of relativism.

Pyramid Relativism and Raft Relativism

On the simplest picture, sets of central beliefs and standards serve as principles that individuate frameworks. We might call this *pyramid relativism.* It may be tempting to view such principles as akin to the basic beliefs in foundationalist theories of knowledge.

This would not be completely wrong, but it may suggest a model of central beliefs as axioms that are used to justify further claims, where these on construed on the model of theorems, whereas the role of central beliefs is more to provide a structure within which experience and thought can occur. We will encounter this view briefly below.

But a rather different picture of the structure of frameworks is also possible, one in which the notion of centrality is a matter of degree and in which no single set of beliefs or principles serves to individuate a framework. This picture fits naturally with a more coherentist conception of justification in which each belief may receive support from others. We might call this *raft relativism*, since (as suggested by Neurath's boat) there are no essential framework principles and all beliefs can receive support from other beliefs, although some may be much more central than others.

Pyramid relativism suggests that our concepts, beliefs, and standards are more precise and well defined than they actually seem to be. Such accounts also fit most naturally with a foundationalist picture of justification, and this picture doesn't accurately depict many of our actual epistemic practices. Furthermore, features like centrality and depth come in degrees, and we would be hard pressed to name the foundational principles of our own framework. Raft relativism can accommodate these facts more easily than pyramid relativism can.

Raft frameworks are more difficult to individuate than pyramid frameworks, but this is not clearly a drawback, since there is no reason to think that there is always a clear fact of the matter as to whether two groups have the same culture, language or, more generally, framework. Often it is more enlightening to simply note the most salient similarities and differences between groups, without worrying about thresholds or sharp *yes*-or-*no* answers.

Arguments for Relativism

The various types of relativism are often assumed rather than argued for, and when they are defended the arguments on their behalf vary greatly in quality. We have touched on several arguments for various species of relativism above; in this section we consider the most common arguments in more detail.

- 4.1 Perception is Theory-Laden
- 4.2 Alternative Frameworks are Incommensurable
- 4.3 Normative Relativism as the Best Explanation [Not yet available]
- 4.4 Normative Relativism and the Nature of Justification [Not yet available]
- 4.5 The Master Argument for Normative Relativism [Not yet available]

Perception is Theory-Laden

We discussed perceptual relativism earlier, so here we only need to recall how arguments for it typically proceed. The basic claim is that perception is not, contrary to what have supposed, a neutral physiological process that leads all normal human beings to perceive the same thing in the same way when they gaze in the same direction. Instead what we see (hear, feel, etc.) in any particular situation is partially determined by the concepts, beliefs, and expectations we bring to the situation.

Claims about top-down processing and theory-ladenness are descriptive claims about the human perceptual system, and by themselves do not entail any normative conclusions. But, various writers add, the *way* that observations are coloured by our beliefs and expectations makes it difficult, perhaps even impossible, to adjudicate between competing scientific theories or paradigms, forms of life, or the like.

Many philosophers of science had believed that a theory-neutral observation language existed which could be used to frame theory-neutral descriptions of scientific observations. Others spoke of a given, non-conceptual, element in experience. If such claims were correct, then theory-neutral observations, a sort of perceptual Archimedean point, could be used to adjudicate competing claims in a way that would not beg the question in favour of one party and to the detriment of the other.

Such arguments were given a prominent role by philosophers of science like Norwood Russell Hanson (1958), Thomas Kuhn (1962), and Paul Feyerabend (1975/1993), who argue that scientific observation is theory-laden. Their claims were important because many philosophers of science had supposed that there is a observation language that could be used to describe experience in a neutral way, independent of any theories. The existence of such a language would weaken many relativistic claims, since it would provide a neutral, non-question begging perspective from which we adjudicate the claims of competing conceptions of the world. And many other writers, from anthropologists to art historians, make related points, urging that perception is influenced by various aspects of language or culture.

For example, in a much-cited thought experiment, Hanson (1958, Ch. 1) asks us to imagine Tycho Brahe (an advocate of a geocentric picture of the solar system) and Johannes Kepler (an advocate of a heliocentric view) as they gaze to the east at sunrise. Although they do see the same object, the sun, Hanson tells us they see it very differently. Tycho sees the sun rising, whereas Kepler sees the horizon dipping or falling away from the fixed and immobile sun. Hence there is no neutral observational framework that allows them to determine who is correct.

Such claims are sometimes used (often in conjunction with other premises) to support various species of normative relativism, especially normative epistemological relativism, by noting the fundamental role of observation in forming and justifying our beliefs. At the very least, such arguments would eliminate simple pictures of justification as based in perception which would, if correct, be a serious obstacle to relativism (responses to such arguments are discussed below in 5.2).

Alternative Frameworks are Incommensurable

In our discussion of incommensurability and semantic holism incommensurability and semantic holism we noted the view that the meanings of a person's words and sentences (or the contents of her concepts and beliefs) are determined by the overall role the words or concepts play in her culture, scientific framework, linguistic community, or the like. So, the argument continues, if two frameworks are *substantially* different from one another, the concepts and linguistic meanings of one will not *line up* well enough with those of the other for the members of the respective groups to even discuss the same things. For example, we may be told, earlier concepts of mass, or rights, even logical concepts can differ so much from ours that we cannot accurately interpret their users as having any phrases or concepts that are genuine counterparts of our words or concepts or, indeed, as having any beliefs about mass or about rights or logical consequence.

Such arguments turn on claims about the meanings of words and concepts, but they are sometimes buttressed by claims about perception.

For example, Feyerabend (1975/1993, p. 166) tells us that "[g]iven appropriate stimuli, but different systems of classification (different 'mental sets'), our perceptual apparatus may produce perceptual objects which cannot be easily compared."

If incommensurability arguments are sound, they support weak normative truth-value relativism, because they tell us that if the two groups' concepts and beliefs differ in fundamental ways, the subject matters they can discuss are so different that they cannot be compared (responses to such arguments are discussed in §5.4).

Arguments against Relativism

Different responses are appropriate to different versions of relativism. Although there are a few *a priori*, philosophical arguments designed to show that certain sorts of cognitive or evaluative differences are in fact impossible, most species of descriptive relativism are empirical claims that must be supported, or discredited, with empirical evidence. Most species of normative relativism, by contrast, require a more purely philosophical response.

The most damning objection to the more dramatic forms of normative relativism (like truth-value relativism) is that they are self-refuting, but other objections have been leveled against various versions of relativism, and in this section we consider some of the more compelling ones.

The first four responses on the list below are targeted primarily at various forms of descriptive relativism; the remaining responses are targeted primarily at various forms of normative relativism, although empirical considerations enter here and there.

- 5.1 No Facts of the Matter
- 5.2 Perception is not Hopelessly Theory-Laden
- 5.3 Cognitive Architecture and Cognitive Universals
- 5.4 Semantic Realism
- 5.5 Mediation: Concepts aren't Veils
- 5.6 Going off the Deep End: Extrapolation into Unintelligibility?
    - 5.6.1 Live Options
- 5.7 Transcendental Arguments
- 5.8 Understanding and Charitable Construal
- 5.9 Self-Refutation: Quicksand all the Way Down?
- 5.10 "Beyond Relativism"

No Facts of the Matter

If there are no concepts or beliefs, then groups cannot differ with respect to their concepts or beliefs and descriptive claims about the relativity of concepts or beliefs cannot get off the ground. In such cases it also makes little sense to ask normative questions about whether some concepts or beliefs are better or more correct than others.

Although he popularized phrases like 'ontological relativity', we saw above that Quine opposes relativism with respect to concepts, beliefs, and meanings precisely because he holds that there are no facts of the matter about such things. Much of Quine's skepticism about minds and meanings and mental representations is based on non-discredited behaviourist assumptions, but there are more current anti-realist views about the mind that would also nip many versions of relativism in the bud. The best-known example is eliminative materialism, the view that our everyday talk of concepts and beliefs and intentions is part of a defective theory that should disappear as science progresses. But the thoroughgoing anti-realism about concepts, beliefs, and other representations required to discredit most versions of relativism is very counterintuitive, and few philosophers find the existing arguments for such views very compelling.

Perception is not Hopelessly Theory-Laden

Descriptive perceptual relativism is an empirical claim about human beings, and a common response to it is that although human perception is somewhat theory-laden, it is not as theory-laden as more extreme relativists often maintain. Furthermore, the reply continues, to the extent that descriptive perceptual relativism has been used to support various types of normative relativism, the limits of theory-ladenness weakens the case for them.

Controversy persists among vision scientists over the extent to which our concepts and beliefs and expectations influence the content of our perceptions, but the cumulative force of a large number of examples and experiments leaves little doubt that they sometimes play an important role. Still, there are limits; we cannot, on pain of hallucination, see just anything we hope or expect or are primed to see. Once again, the question is whether there is room between two extremes for an interesting version of relativism.

Science and Observation

As noted above, various philosophers have argued that perception is theory-laden in a way that can make it difficult, perhaps even impossible, to use our observations to adjudicate between competing frameworks. For example, in a much-cited thought experiment, Hanson (1958, Ch. 1) asks us to imagine Tycho Brahe (an advocate of a geocentric picture of the solar system) and Johannes Kepler (an advocate of a heliocentric view) as they gaze to the east at sunrise. Although they do see the same object, the sun, Hanson tells us they see it very differently. Tycho sees the sun rising, whereas Kepler sees the horizon dipping or falling away from the fixed and immobile sun.

But Hanson's claims far outrun any historical evidence. Many people today think of the earth as moving and the sun as standing still, but almost four centuries after Kepler's work we still speak of the sun rising and setting, and it looks and feels that way to many of us even now. More importantly, by Kepler's time all responsible parties to this debate knew that things would look exactly the same to observers on the surface of the Earth, whether Tycho or Kepler (or Ptolemy or, we may now add, Einstein) was right about the layout of the cosmos.

Culture and Perception

It is also an empirical question just how much (if at all) the mechanisms involved in top-down perceptual processing lead members of different cultures to perceive the things differently. As with all cross-cultural work, especially with cultures that are very different from our own, experiments here are vulnerable to many mishaps, and so it is not surprising that much remains uncertain. Current evidence does suggest that culture and language can influence perception; for example, there is evidence that people tend to perceive things in ways that are influenced by the manner in which they have learned to think in order to function efficiently in their ecological setting. But large influences of culture or language or beliefs on perception have yet to be documented.

Upshot

A neutral, pure sense-datum language is indeed a myth, but most evidence suggests that the familiar world of physical objects is usually neutral enough to allow for tests of scientific theories and at least passable communication across cultural divides. Such empirical claims, which of course may require revision as new evidence is found, only bear on descriptive perceptual relativism in the case of human beings. They leave open the possibility that other intelligent creatures—particularly those with quite different sensory modalities like echolocation or delicate sensitivity to magnetic fields—might perceive the world in quite different ways. They also leave open many of the issues involving normative perceptual relativism.

Cognitive Architecture and Cognitive Universals

To the extent that predispositions to use certain central concepts (e.g., physical object, person, causation), hold certain central beliefs (e.g., at least some events have causes, human beings have intentions), or employ certain inference patterns (e.g., induction by enumeration) are innate, it tells against descriptive relativism with respect to those concepts, beliefs, or styles of reasoning. It is an empirical matter whether human infants come into the world with such predispositions, but there is emerging evidence that they do and, indeed, that there are at least some important linguistic, cognitive, and cultural universals.

The Evidence Comes from Several Fields.

Linguistics: Noam Chomsky's emphasis on innate linguistic universals led to a picture of deep commonality beneath surface differences in natural languages. Linguistics is particularly important, because universals were first defended here, and many languages have now been carefully studied from this point of view.

Developmental Psychology

In the last two or three decades developmental psychologists have devised several ingenious techniques for studying the perceptions and concepts of infants, and there is growing evidence that human neonates arrive in the world with strong propensities to perceive and think in certain ways. For example, they are strongly predisposed to think of the world in terms of physical objects that behave in predictable ways (e.g., their paths of motion are continuous, they do not disappear when people quit looking at them), persons with intension, and so on (e.g., Xu and Carey, 1996; Spelke and Newport, 1998; Chiang and Wynn, 2000).

Anthropology

Some workers in cognitive anthropology and cross-cultural psychology have argued for the existence of rather intricate cultural or human universals. Frequent candidates, often said to be found in all known cultures (though not necessarily in all individuals), include the use of tools, the differentiation of sex roles, having myths and legends, music and dance, and common facial expressions of certain emotions (e.g., smiling when happy). To the extent that there is a fairly rich and detailed set of human universals, a common core of human nature, it places important limits on descriptive relativism with respect to human beings.

Normative Mileage from Factual Consensus?

Claims about human universals bear most directly on descriptive relativism, and then only with respect to humans, but they can also arise in discussions of normative issues. One popular idea is that evolution weeded out genotypes that built people who got things badly wrong; the process favoured a cognitive architecture that implements normatively sound modes of perceiving and reasoning. Hence, the mere fact that certain concepts or beliefs survived in our species is reason to think that they are pretty close to being right. Thus the psychologist Donald Campbell speaks of natural selection as "validating the categories" (1974, p. 444).

Such claims have their critics. Some of the criticism is based on general critiques of certain kinds of adaptationist reasoning (e.g., Gould and Lewontin, 1979), but even many thinkers who do not object to adaptationism in principle have doubts about such claims. Thus, it is often pointed out that evolution rarely has an opportunity to design the best. It can only work with organisms as they already are, and kludges that are prone to certain kinds of errors may have been the best it could do under the circumstances. Furthermore, evolution might be willing to trade a propensity to certain kinds of error for other adaptations, e.g., for perceptual or conceptual mechanisms that are fast and automatic. It would probably be more adaptive to classify some nonpredators as predators, for example, than to take more time getting things right, since greater accuracy here might be purchased at the cost of an increased likelihood of being eaten.

Debate over these issues often has an all-or-nothing flavour, but more nuanced approaches are possible. In his program for the rational analysis of human cognition, the psychologist John R. Anderson (e.g., 1990) has made a detailed attempt to explain various aspects of human cognition on the assumption that they are well adapted to the environment, i.e., that they are optimized with respect to specific criteria of adaptive importance. And in a series of highly original papers, the cognitive psychologist Roger Shepard (e.g., 1994) has explored ways in which various perceptual and cognitive universals may be adaptive reflections of certain very general features of the world around us.

On a more philosophical note, Christopher Stephens (2001) has argued that under some conditions having reliable belief-forming mechanisms might confer a selective advantage, while under other conditions it might not, and he has developed a decision-theoretic model that tells us which to expect when. Of course, it is always important to bear in mind that evolution involves more forces than just natural selection, and it is possible that countervailing, non-selective evolutionary forces (e.g., genetic drift, migration) would swamp the effects of selection even in cases where it favoured having true beliefs or using extremely reliable patterns of inference.

Semantic Realism

Reference and Relativism

Reference or *denotation* is an especially important species of meaning. It is standardly viewed as a relation between linguistic expressions, on the one hand, and things and properties in the world, on the other. The thing or property that a linguistic expression (or, on more mentalistic accounts, concept) refers to is called its *referent* or *denotation.*

Reference is sometimes thought to provide a way to break out of a group's language and concepts and beliefs. Several early opponents of incommensurability theses in the philosophy of science argued that just as two witnesses in a courtroom could have different beliefs about a single person—the defendant—while still referring *to her*, two scientists could have rather different beliefs about mass or genes without the denotation of 'mass' or 'gene' changing at all. Moreover, some philosophers have argued, even in cases where terminology may change, scientists may use words that apply to one and the same physical magnitude; for example, Earman and Fine (1977) argue that Newton's word 'mass' has the same meaning as our phrase 'proper mass'.

Similarly, it may be argued, members of two cultures may have words or phrases that refer to the same kinds of things (e.g., rabbits) or to the same specific thing (e.g., that rabbit by the elm tree). And when this is so, the denotations of their words provide a common denominator that allows different groups to break out of their frameworks and to talk to each other about a common, objective world.

Partisans of incommensurability often responded by claiming that the denotation of a linguistic expression, and not just its meaning in some more amorphous sense, is determined by its place in an overall theory or web of beliefs. Such claims rely on what philosophers of language call *descriptivist theories of reference*, according to which a word's denotation is determined by the descriptions or the contents of the beliefs that constitute the word's meaning, intension, or sense. Descriptivist theories have come under withering attack from partisans of direct theories of reference, who argue that words and concepts are attached more directly to their denotations, without the mediation of a cluster of descriptions.

Hence, it may be prudent for the semantic relativist to grant that reference is more like the advocates of direct theories contend, but to hold that it refers to things in a world relativized to a framework (this is an instance of the second strategy below).

Semantic Externalism and Relativism

There is a more general picture about the meanings of words and (with minor adaptations) concepts that has a similar anti-relativistic flavour. About twenty-five years ago the American philosophy Hilary Putnam presented a thought experiments in which we were invited to imagine twin-earth, a planet as much like earth as possible except that every place there is water on earth the counterpart of that place on twin-earth has a liquid that seems very much like water, but which in fact has some complicated chemical makeup, call it *XYZ*.

Putnam argues that the word 'water' has a different meaning when used by citizens of twin-earth than it does here on earth and that the external, chemical composition of the liquid affects the word's meaning. The moral we are encouraged to draw from this, and related examples developed by Tyler Burge and others, is that *meanings just are not in the head*. At least not completely. Many philosophers found these examples intuitively compelling, and so they accepted one or another version of *semantic externalism*, according to which the meanings of many words (or the contents of many concepts and thoughts) are at least partially individuated by environmental and social factors (like the chemical structure of *XYZ*).

If such views are right, it seems natural to conclude that the meanings of words and the contents of concepts and thoughts often involve features (like the molecular constitution of a liquid) of an objective, mind-independent, non-relativistic world that play a vital role in determining the meanings of our words and the contents of our thoughts.

The issues here are complex, and we will just note two responses the relativist might make. First, although these thought experiments provide good support for their suggested conclusions, it is not conclusive, and the relativist could simply reject Putnam's intuitions about the roles of various external factors in determining linguistic meanings.

Second, the relativist could opt for a relativistic reconstrual, arguing that the meanings of many of our words and concepts *do* involve external factors, but that these are in turn shaped by, or relativized to, frameworks. On most accounts frameworks are shared, social things whose details are not always transparent to their users. So, the relativist might argue, once we adopt a framework in which things can be individuated in terms of chemical structure, there could be facts about chemical structure that we have yet to discover, and these could affect the meanings of our words and concepts. In short, the relativist can argue for a world-relative externalism.

Platonism and Relativism

Platonism is a family of views that get their name because they involve entities—propositions, properties, sets—which, like Plato's Forms, are held to be abstract, immutable things that exist outside space and time. On many platonistic approaches, concepts express abstract properties and beliefs are relations between people and abstract propositions. This suggests a way around some types of relativism, since people in quite different cultures could have many of the same beliefs (because they could believe the same abstract propositions), and a belief would be true just in case the immutable proposition it expresses is true.

The relativist may reply that platonistic accounts lead to severe difficulties in epistemology and semantics. The problem is that we are physical organisms living in a spatio-temporal world, and we cannot interact causally (or in any other discernible way) with abstract, causally inert things. Moreover, few people are aware of having any special cognitive faculty that puts them in touch with a timeless realm of abstract objects, neuroscientists have never found any part of the brain that subserves such an ability, such a view is not suggested by what is known about the ways children acquire concepts and beliefs, and nothing in physics suggests any way in which a physical system (the brain) can make any sort of contact with causally inert, non-physical objects. Moreover, if our minds cannot make epistemic contact with such things, it is difficult to see how our words and linguistic practices can make semantic contact with them.

None of this proves that abstract propositions don't exist, but it shows it isn't obvious that they do. There have been few debates between relativists and platonists over such matters, however, perhaps because the two views lie so far apart that their proponents cannot easily engage one another.

The Mediation Problem: Concepts aren't Veils

A common line of argument for several species of relativism, including truth-value relativism and reality relativism, turns on what we might call the *mediation problem.* This argument takes various forms, but the fundamental idea is that we are trapped in our concepts or beliefs or epistemic standards or, more generally, trapped in our frameworks in a way that precludes our checking to see if they match reality. And once we add that alternative frameworks of concepts, beliefs, or standards are possible, the relativist urges, we are well on our way to relativism. One especially common version of this argument focuses on concepts. We cannot think without concepts (or talk without words), and so we cannot get outside our concepts (and words) to assess their fidelity to the world as it really is, independent of language and thought.

Such arguments encourage the picture of concepts as intermediaries that stand *between* us and the world "out there." The model of mediation at work here is similar to representative realism, a position once commonly attributed to John Locke (1632-1704), in which ideas are always interposed *between* our experience and cognition, on the one hand, and the outside world, on the other. On this model there is indeed a problem of knowing whether our thoughts and ideas accurately represent external reality, and it is no accident that such views tend toward skepticism. I am trapped behind the veil of my ideas, and so I can never discover, even in principle, whether my ideas of dogs or chairs correspond to anything out there in the world.

But, the anti-relativist may respond, representational realism is the wrong model for conceptual mediation. In ordinary circumstances my concept of a dog allows me to individuate and reidentify dogs, to recognize and reason about them, but it does not stand between me and Rover. Under normal conditions I can just look and see that there is a dog in front of me.

To be sure, different frameworks of concepts are possible, at least to some degree, and of course we cannot talk without language or think without concepts. But, this response continues, *once* we have a battery of concepts, truth often is completely clear and perfectly objective. If we don't accept the view that there is just One True Story of the world told in terms of The One Right Lexicon of Concepts, we do not *need* to check to see if our concepts are the right ones. Rather, we need to check to see whether our *beliefs* or *sentences* (*framed* in terms of our concepts or words) *are true.* And it is not necessary to go to a "neutral cosmic exile," or to find an "Archimedean point" outside all language and thought, in order to do this. It is something we do all the time, right from where we are; once I have the concept of a dog, it is often obviously and unproblematically true that there is a dog in the corner.

As always, relativists have various rejoinders, e.g., that when we factor in the framework-relativity of central beliefs and epistemic standards, we may be trapped in our frameworks in more sinister ways. But there is no quick and simple argument from the necessity of some concepts (or other) for experience and thought, even together with the possibility (at least up to a point) of different frameworks of concepts, to the conclusion that we are ineluctably trapped in a way that leads to any of the more insidious versions of relativism.

Going off the Deep End: Extrapolation into Unintelligibility?

Relativistic conclusions are sometimes based on claims about the exotic beliefs and practices of distant cultures or on thought-experiments in which we are encouraged to imagine (putative) dramatic alternatives to our own modes of evaluation and thought. But the fact that we can coherently imagine beliefs and standards and practices that differ in small ways from our own does not mean that we can coherently imagine ones that differ in massive ways. Efforts to extrapolate from genuine, but modest, differences to vast differences may simply lead to incoherence.

We can, for example, imagine people who reject the law of excluded middle and people who do not, and we can probably imagine one group using intuitionistic logic where another uses classical logic. But we cannot easily make sense of the idea of a group that regards conjunction introduction and elimination as blatantly fallacious. And if attempts at dramatic extrapolation beyond our familiar modes of thought fail to reveal real possibilities, they do not support relativism after all.

Making Sense of Things

To doubt, to raise questions, to offer justification, to engage in *any* sort of rational activity requires the possession of some concepts and beliefs and epistemic standards that we use to perform the activity. Perhaps we can replace many, or most, or (some tell us) even all of our beliefs and epistemic standards, provided that we modify them bit-by-bit over a long stretch of time. But we cannot make drastic revisions in our entire corpus of beliefs and standards all at once. This would be like dismantling Neurath's ship all at once while at sea; among other things, it would leave us without any standards to judge whether two proposed modifications were consistent with one another, whether one provided evidence for another, whether one explained another.

Trying to understand vastly different norms and practices requires us to do something similar in imagination. To get a genuine feel for what it would be *like* to think in a vastly different way requires us to bracket more and more of our own cognitive resources, to jettison our very standards of understanding and intelligibility, and this leaves us bereft of resources for understanding anything at all. For example, a vital core of our reasoning involves the use of logical principles like modus ponens and conjunction elimination. These are very nearly constitutive of our ability to think, and attempts to imagine our way into forms of reasoning that constantly flout these principles leave us dumbfounded, rather than with an enriched sense of the possibilities. Such projects ask us to make sense of alternatives that require us to abandon our resources for making sense of anything whatsoever.

Partisans of more local versions of relativism may concede the point, urging that it leaves open the possibility that more limited thought experiments may be more successful. For example, trying to imagine a morality rather different from our own needn't deprive us of logic or some of our other standards of rationality, so the project is not obviously self-subverting.

When it comes to more global versions of relativism the more extreme relativist may reply that our inability to make sense of various alternatives now does little to show they are impossible or incoherent, because what we can make sense of or imagine is itself historically and culturally (and doubtless biologically) conditioned. The limits to conceivability depend partly on our current concepts, beliefs, and epistemic standards. Before the nineteenth century most people believed non-Euclidean geometries to be impossible, even incoherent, but this is no longer true.

Alternative Standards aren't All that Different

In some cases we *can* make sense of modes of thought and reasoning that are somewhat different from our own, but it is often easy to overestimate just how different they are. For example, even professional philosophers, economists, and mathematicians in our own culture champion somewhat different normative models that sometimes offer conflicting advice. Thus we find alternative logics (classical logic, intuitionistic logic, and many others), probability theories (e.g., the classical theory, Shafer's belief functions), schools of statistics (e.g.,

Fisher's, Neyman and Pearson's, the ill-motivated blend of the two often taught today), and decision theories (e.g., evidential decision theories, various causal decision theories, regret theory). And if the experts can't agree about which model is best, the relativist may ask, how can we expect to find any solid ground in the area?

But competing normative models they needn't be viewed as package deals to be accepted in all-or-none fashion. Usually some aspects of a model will be more compelling and defencible than others, and when it comes to this more solid core, many of the competing models agree. For example, classical and intuitionist logic disagree about whether the law of excluded middle is valid, but there is no logical system (with any adherents) in which *modus ponens* is invalid. Similarly, although there are alternative normative models of probability, none of them permits a conjunction to be more probable than either of its conjuncts.

Even when there is no uniquely correct answer to a problem, it doesn't follow that every possible answer is equally good. This is reflected in the fact that when competing models do not agree on a precise answer, they often agree that the answer falls within a certain range. We may overlook the large measure of overlap because it is so obvious it goes without saying, while the areas of difference seem much more interesting.

Live Options

Where we can go next depends on where we are now. The bare, abstract possibility of an alternative mode of evaluation or thought does not mean that it is a live option *for us*, here and now. Indeed, even if we can make sense of an alternative and would like to adopt it, it doesn't follow that we can. There are several reasons why this is so.

For one thing, as Bernard Williams (1986) notes, cultures provide contexts that make certain ways of life possible and others impossible. The social and cultural structure no longer exist anywhere today that would enable someone to live the life or think the thoughts of a Greek Bronze Age chief or a medieval samurai. Or, to take a rather different sort of case, some cognitive and evaluative options are probably too complex for human beings to even grasp; among other things, the rather severe limitations on human working memory and the fact that our neurons react rather slowly place some kinds of concepts and reasoning beyond our reach. You can't get there from here.

The fact that we cannot currently understand certain (putative) alternatives is sometimes taken to show that they are not really possible at all, but such arguments turn on a verificationism and anthropomorphism that are as implausible here as anywhere else. Arguments concerning conceivability and cognitive options are often inconclusive, however, partly because the limits to the humanly or biologically possible are difficult enough to chart, and the margins of absolute coherence or possibility are even more uncertain.

Should Merely Abstract Possibilities Matter?

When something isn't a live option for us we do not face practical worries about whether to adopt it, but it doesn't follow that learning about it shouldn't affect how we think about things. Realizing that if we had been born in a very different time and place many of the things that now seem obvious and important to us would have seemed implausible or trivial, while things that now seem implausible or trivial might have seemed obvious and important, can reinforce our sense of the contingency of our current forms of evaluation and thought.

This in turn can affect our normative views, because it can undermine our confidence, in our more reflective moments, that the (apparent) obviousiousness or inevitability of a principle or a belief ensures that it is right or true.

Transcendental Arguments

Transcendental arguments are often characterized as arguments designed to show that some obvious feature of experience or knowledge presupposes our having certain concepts and beliefs. The most famous transcendental arguments were developed by the German philosopher Immanuel Kant (1724-1804) in the *Critique of Pure Reason*. His aim was to justify our use of the twelve central concepts he called *categories* (e.g., causation, substance) and our belief in certain principles (e.g., that every event has a cause), which are framed in terms of the categories.

Kant's arguments are designed to do two things. First, they are intended to show that all finite creatures who experience things as being in space and time *must* think of the world in terms of central concepts like object and property, causation, reality, negation, possibility, and so on (although Kant doesn't always mean by these exactly what we would mean now). Furthermore, such creatures must regulate their thought by the principles associated with these concepts (e.g., they must assume that every event is caused).

In short, certain concepts and beliefs are necessary or indispensable for experience and knowledge.

Second, Kant's arguments are intended to show that we are *correct* or *justified* in using these concepts and holding these beliefs. Events really do have causes or, as Kant puts it, the concept of causation has "objective validity." Kant saw these two aspects of his arguments as inseparable, but it will be useful here to focus on them separately; we may call the first the *indispensability aspect* and the second the *justificatory aspect*.

Although Kant's one-time student (and one-time friend) Johann Gottfried Herder (1744-1803), and Kant's neighbour and friend Johann Georg Hamann (1730-88) were busy sowing the seeds of relativism in Königsberg, right in Kant's backyard, their claims would only later find a following, and Kant himself was not much concerned with such views. Still, if the indispensability aspects of Kant's arguments were sound, there would be a common core of thought that is indispensable, necessary, immune to revision, and invariant across all creatures remotely like us. This would provide a purely philosophical, *a priori* refutation of descriptive relativists' claims that different groups do—or even that different groups might—lack concepts like causation or get by without thinking that events have causes.

Furthermore, if the justificatory aspects of Kant's arguments were sound, they would answer the normative relativist by showing that the use of these concepts and principles is justified. Moreover, they would justify our modes of thought *from within*, without any yearning to escape to some mythical Archimedean point in a futile effort to justify them from the outside.

Kant's arguments are subject to an enormous scholarly dispute, but the basic claim is that finite creatures (like us) who experience things as being in space and time cannot have even a rudimentary *self*-consciousness or sense of a temporal history—cannot have any coherent experience at all—unless they are aware of an objective world. Dispensing with Kant's jargon, the general view is that coherent temporal experience is possible only if it is experience of a world of physical objects with determinate extensive and intensive properties, each of which has a definite location in a single, unified (Euclidean) space and a single unified time, and in which every event has a cause and each object causally interacts with all of the rest.

All of this sounds a little too good to be true. The most immediate difficulty is that many of the things Kant held to be necessarily true no longer seem true at all. It is no longer possible to maintain that it is necessarily true and knowable *a priori* that physical space is Euclidean. Furthermore, the special theory of relativity tells us that time is not unified in the strong sense that Kant supposed and that not all objects can causally interact with each other. And on the usual interpretations (most other than David Bohm's), quantum theory tells us that determinism fails and that objects need not always have determinate locations in space and time or determinate magnitudes (like a particular momentum or energy or spin).

The justificatory aspects of Kant's arguments depend on his doctrine of transcendental idealism, the claim that space and time and, hence, spatio-temporal objects and occurrences, do not exist in the world as it really is, independently of how we think about it. But Kant's defence of this thesis is almost universally agreed to be unsound. Indeed, the view that the world as it really is, independently of how we know and experience it, is not spatial or even temporal is very difficult to understand, much less believe.

Two Types of Retrenchment

Although few philosophers have endorsed all of the details of Kant's philosophy, many later thinkers tried to adapt various aspects of his approach to their own ends. We briefly note two general approaches here. The first, like Kant's own work, would tell against many versions of relativism. But when it comes to relativism Kantian themes are a double-edged sword, and the second approach has, ironically, often been used to support various relativistic theses.

Necessity without Construction

In *Individuals* Sir Peter Strawson (1959) attempts to salvage a scaled-down Kantianism that does not depend on transcendental idealism. Strawson believes his arguments show both the indispensability and justifiability of certain modes of thought, roughly that we employ a framework of physical objects and persons that exist in a single, unified space and time.

Barry Stroud (1968) makes a compelling case that without something very much like transcendental idealism Strawson's arguments at best show that certain modes of thought are inevitable for us. For example, we may not be able to help believing in the existence of objects in an external world, but it doesn't follow that this belief is correct.

If the indispensability aspects of Strawson's arguments worked they would still show that various sorts of descriptive relativism are untenable, but many philosophers now believe that although he shows that *certain ways* of dispensing with concepts like those of physical objects (as in his ingenious universe of sounds in ch. 2), he fails to show that *no ways* of dispensing with them could work. Hence, he doesn't even show these concepts to be indispensable.

Construction without Necessity

Strawson tries to retain some of the indispensability aspects of Kant's arguments while abandoning Kant's transcendental idealism. Other philosophers tried the reverse, agreeing with Kant that the mind does play an essential role in shaping the structure of experience and knowledge (although few philosophers go so far as to hold that the mind literally contributes all aspects of space and time), while abandoning the indispensability aspects of Kant's work.

The basic idea here is to endorse Kant's claim that a person's central concepts and beliefs play a large role in structuring the world as they know it, but to argue that rather different frameworks of concepts and beliefs can be used for this task. Different historical periods or cultures may have rather different central concepts and beliefs and standards, i.e., different frameworks, and when they do, this will lead their members to construct their worlds in rather different ways. Views of this sort, which still have their proponents, were developed by thinkers as diverse as William James (e.g., 1907, esp. Lecture 5), C. I. Lewis (1923, 1929), Hans Reichenbach (1920), Ernst Cassirer (e.g., 1923), R. G. Collingwood (e.g., 1940), Rudolf Carnap (e.g., 1950) and to some extent the Wittgenstein of *On Certainty* (1969).

In most cases the debt to Kant was quite explicit, and one Kantian theme running through many of these discussions is that a group's central principles and concepts provide something like conditions for the possibility of knowledge; the unKantian part is that the principles and concepts are not fixed and immutable.

It is a great irony that Kant, a supreme objectivist and champion of the Enlightenment who would have been repelled by virtually any form of relativism, introduced an idea that came to play a pivotal role in many relativistic arguments, including arguments for reality relativism, the strongest version of relativism that there is.

Understanding and Charitable Construal

A number of philosophers and social scientists, including W. V. O. Quine (1960, ch. 2), Donald T. Campbell (1964), Martin Hollis (1967), and Donald Davidson (e.g., 1974), have argued that we can only understand or interpret others if they largely agree with us about what is true, reasonable, justified or the like.

Davidson's discussion is the most detailed and the most well-known. He argues that we must employ a *principle of charity* if we are to interpret or understand the members of a newly-discovered alien culture (or anyone else, for that matter). Without worrying about detailed formulations for a moment, the principle counsels us to interpret others in a way that makes as many of their beliefs true as we can.

The point is not merely philosophical. In a methodological discussion of his cross-cultural work on visual illusions (Segal, Campbell, and Herskovits, 1966), Campbell (1964) stresses the need for comprehension checks. He and his coworkers used pictures of lines of various colours, lengths, and orientations, and it was only after their informants correctly identified which of two lines were longer, which more slanted, and so on that the experiment could begin. Without such agreement, it would be impossible to go on to test for susceptibility to illusions, because the results could not be interpreted as showing that the subject was talking about the same things that the experimenter was asking about. As Campbell puts it:

It turns out that the anthropologist's main cue for achieved communication is similarity between the response of the other to a stimulus and the response which he himself would make. Disagreement turns out to be a sign of communication failure (1964, p. 37).

Although many writers agree that something like a principle of charity is right, they disagree about the details. A recurring criticism is that some kinds of agreement (e.g., agreement about physical objects in the immediate environment) matter more than others (e.g., agreement about the more subtle aspects of religion), so simply aiming to maximize or optimize the degree to which others agree with us is insufficiently discriminating. Still, in retrospect it appears that many writers had the same general point in mind: in order to understand others we must assume that many of their beliefs about most obvious things (e.g., that there is a rabbit in front of them) are true or at least sensible (by our lights), that they hold many beliefs that we would hold if we were in their circumstances, and that they reason in ways not too different from the ways that we reason.

But how could we possibly know, without actual empirical investigation, that others will agree with much of what we think? Well, the response goes, suppose that I point to a rabbit and my informant says 'Gavagai'. Unless I assume that she sees what I see, takes me to be asking a question about it, and intends her answer to be relevant and true, I have no reason to interpret any of her behaviour *as evidence* that 'Gavagai' means 'Rabbit'. And if I can't get a line on her beliefs about salient objects right there in front of us, how can I ever come to understand her when we turn to more abstruse matters like ethics or religion? Or consider a few of the agreements involved with Campbell's comprehension checks: we require agreement about what lines are, which figure the experimenter is pointing to, that the experimenter is asking a question and hopes for an answer, and a host of other things that are so obvious they are easily overlooked.

In short, the argument concludes, it is not that successful translation and interpretation just often happen to disclose a good measure of agreement. A good measure of agreement is a *precondition* for successful translation and interpretation.

Morals for Relativism

If something like the principle of charity is right, it would place rough limits on the amount of conceptual or epistemic diversity that translation or interpretation could reveal. But the argument from charity does not show that there couldn't be groups with concepts and beliefs very different from our own, so different, perhaps, that we couldn't even understand or express one another's views. The fact that we cannot translate what we think might be a group's language or understand what we think might be their mental life only tells against the claims that they have a language and a mental life if some dubious version of verificationism, according to which there could only be conceptual differences if we could discover them, is right.

Davidson has also used the principle of charity to defend the normative thesis that any creature capable of having beliefs at all must have mostly true beliefs. But even if this is so, it leaves open the possibility of a weak version of a truth-value relativism in which the sets of beliefs of two groups are so different that there is very little overlap between them.

Finally, the principle of charity precludes the discovery of dramatic and disquieting differences between groups only if we have very exacting standards for what counts as dramatic or disquieting. After all, vast differences—e.g., those between Hitler and Mother Teresa—actually do exist. Indeed, at least many real differences, genuine clashes, can only take place against the background of a certain amount of agreement that allows for a shared subject matter; if two groups are to disagree about whether most events have causes or whether murder is wrong, they must share the concepts of an event and causation, of murder and being wrong.

Self-Refutation: Quicksand All the Way Down?

Truth is the Achilles' heel of relativism. According to the normative thesis of strong truth-value relativism one and the same thing can be *true relative to one framework* and *false relative to another*, *true for* some groups and *false for* others, and ever since Plato's argument against this form of relativism in the *Theatetus* many philosophers have agreed that the view is self-contradictory or self-refuting. Plato's argument is sometimes known as the *peritrope*; it's a turning the tables, turning the relativist's line of reasoning back against itself to show that his thesis succumbs to the very relativity he defends. Relativists always face the occupational hazard of sawing off the limb they are sitting on, but with strong truth-value relativism they seem to cut down the whole tree.

The Problem is General

The problem of self-refutation is quite general. It arises when truth is relativized to a framework of concepts, beliefs, standards, or practices. It also arises for many of the more sweeping claims that central epistemic notions are somehow relative. If the epistemic relativist argues that all justification or rationality is framework relative, he lays himself open to the reply that his very claim is at best justified relative to his framework, only rational by his own standards, only defencible by his own guidelines, just as much a social construction as he insists everything else is.

Plato's argument against strong truth-value relativism is typically said to go like this: either the claim that truth is relative is true absolutely (i.e., true in a non-relative sense) or else it is only true relative to some framework. If it is true absolutely, all across the board, then at least one truth is not merely true relative to a framework, so this version of the claim is inconsistent. Furthermore, if we make an exception for the relativist's thesis, it is difficult to find a principled way to rule out other exceptions; what justifies stopping here? On the other hand, if the relativist's claim that truth is relative is only true relative to *his* framework, then it can be false in other, perhaps equally good, frameworks. And why should we care about that the relativist's (perhaps rather idiosyncratic or parochial) framework?

Complete Metastasis

Weak truth-value relativism escapes many of the dangers of self-refutation, since it does not allow one and the same thing to be true in one framework and false in another. But if normative truth-value relativism is intended as a view that is true simpliciter, it metastasizes very quickly. Suppose, for the sake of argument, that truth *is* relative to a person's (or group's) conceptual framework (for ease of exposition we consider individuals, but the point generalizes easily). Then, the relativist tells us, the very same belief (or sentence), call it *p*, can be true in Wilbur's framework, *W*, but false in Sam's framework, *S*. But if truth is relative in the strong sense, it can also be true in Wilbur's framework *W* that *p* is true in *W* and false in Sam's framework *S* that *p* is true in *Wilbur's* framework *W*. There is not even any objective fact about what is true in any given framework.

Worse is in store. There could be frameworks in which it is true that Wilbur's current belief has the content that grass is green and other frameworks in which his belief has the content that snow is white. There could be frameworks in which it is true that Wilbur's framework is *W* and other frameworks in which it is false that Wilbur's framework is *W*, and so there is no objective fact about what framework anyone has. Furthermore, it may be true in Wilbur's framework that the frameworks *W* and *S* are identical ($W = S$) but true in Sam's framework that *W* and *S* are distinct ($W \neq S$). It may also be true in Wilbur's framework that *W* itself is a framework and true in Sam's that *W* is not a framework. It may be true in Sam's framework that there are no frameworks, or that everything is true in every framework, or that nothing is true in any. It may also be true in some frameworks (e.g., ones without concepts of physical objects or persons) that Wilbur and Sam do not exist. In short, there is no fact about whether there are frameworks, about what frameworks are, about what is true in any particular framework, about what framework anyone has, about what anyone even thinks his own framework is like, or about anything else. It is quicksand all the way down. The metastasis is total. The meltdown is complete.

Damage Control

There seem to be only three hopes for escape.

Exemptions?

Champions of relative truth often find it tempting to suppose that their thesis of strong truth-value relativism (perhaps along with a few other things that go along with it) is true in some absolute sense. The doctrine of relative truth is somehow *exempt*. But why go just *this* far and no further? No one has ever given any argument that would begin to support the case for such exemptions, and the prospects are dim, because such a strategy is in considerable tension with the general pictures that lead to strong truth-value relativism in the first place.

Other Defences of the Relativist's Framework

The relativist might urge that frameworks in which truth is relative are superior in some way to frameworks in which it is not, then urge that this difference gives us a reason to accept his framework, and with it the thesis of strong truth-value relativism. But the relativist's framework cannot be superior by virtue of containing *the* truth about relativism (or about anything else) since, according to his view, all truth is relative. Nor is it clear how the relativist's framework could be better justified than the non-relativist's. Among other things, justified beliefs are ones that track truth in some way, and if truth is relative, justification is likely to turn out relative as well. Indeed, the arguments to support the claim that truth is relative in the strong sense are very likely to support the claim that justification is relative as well. The problem is that no one has yet found any good reasons why the relativist's framework should command our allegiance, while his opponent's framework should not.

Taking a Stand

The relativist's best hope is to admit that he inhabits a framework and can only speak from within it. He can even acknowledge that his claims are only true relative to it. Still, it's his and his claim is important in it.

It's us, not Just Me

This strategy will be more compelling if the relativist can convince his interlocutors that *their*—seemingly objective—concepts and beliefs in fact presuppose the same framework as the relativist's and that the doctrine of relative truth is true in the framework they all share. It's not just that his claim is true in his idiosyncratic framework, but that it's true in the framework that we also inhabit. If the relativist could make such a view plausible, he could then add that his claims are no worse off than most of the other things *we* hold to be true. In short, The realist's or objectivist's seemingly objective concepts and beliefs presuppose the same framework as the relativist's, and truth is relative *in it*. And if relativism's claims are as secure as the myriad claims that are on solid ground for us normally, what more can we say? Indeed, the relativist might even attempt to expropriate one response to relativism and argue that frameworks in which his thesis is false are not live options for us.

The project of showing the objectivist that her beliefs depend on a common framework of concepts, standards, and beliefs and that relativism is reasonable according to them would not be easy; in effect it would involve the various sorts of arguments and counterarguments that have surfaced throughout this entry. Furthermore, even if the relativist succeeded, his view would still be at best relatively true. Whether such a position is at all defencible is a matter of debate, but at this juncture things have become more complicated than the simpler versions of Plato's refutation might suggest.

Culture Shock: Non-Trivial Differences

The claim that truth is relative in the strong sense does indeed subvert itself, but this doesn't mean that there couldn't be genuine and interesting differences among groups that could quite reasonably be called relativistic. What it does mean is that if these views are to be developed in an interesting way, we must find a way to dissociate them from the strong version of truth-value relativism.

"Beyond Relativism"

It is difficult to deny some of the key premises relativists employ in defending their views. We *are* historically and culturally situated creatures who cannot step outside our concepts and standards and beliefs to appraise their fit with some mind-independent reality of "things-in-themselves." Furthermore, although we can justify many of our more central beliefs and epistemic standards in a piecemeal way, we cannot justify all of them at once, and perhaps we cannot justify some of them, like induction, at all.

The challenge is to do justice to such facts without ending up in the quicksand of extreme relativism, and many writers now advise moving "beyond relativism" (many books, chapters, and articles bear this phrase in the title), counselling us to steer a course between the Scylla of relativism, on the one side, and the Charybdis of an over-simplified absolutism, on the other. Finding such a course is easier said than done, however, and there is more agreement on the desirability of such a project than on how to carry it out. Still, various proposals recur in the literature.

Not Just Anything Goes

Relativistic claims often sound better in the abstract than they do when we get down to cases (a point that made an unusual appearance in the public press in 1996 with the Sokal hoax). When we turn to concrete examples, extreme relativistic claims are often not at all true to experience. No one really supposes that a postmodernist witness can justify his testimony, come what may, that he saw Jones commit the murder on the grounds that everything is a social construction and this is just how he constructs things. Indeed, our belief that such practices are unacceptable is much stronger than our beliefs in most of the premises used in arguments for stronger versions of relativism.

Once a framework is up and running, there are many obvious facts about what is right or wrong, probable or improbable, true or false. Furthermore, coherent and workable frameworks cannot be created by simple fiat. It took several millennia of extraordinary imagination and labour on the parts of thousands and thousands of people to produce the frameworks of modern science. It just isn't true that "anything goes."

Rational Change Does Occur

Conceptual and epistemic changes do occur, and talk of being trapped in our current beliefs and standards can be overstated. Children learn radically new things, adults sometimes acquire jarringly new values and beliefs, scientists occasionally embrace dramatically new theories. Moreover, people often view things after the change as great improvements over what went before (although this is tempered by the fact that the new convert to Nazism or to mystical anti-rationalism may feel a sense of improvement just as keenly as those who move in the opposite directions).

Reconciling Rationality and Contingency

Perhaps the most promising strategy for finding a middle way between extreme relativism, on the one hand, and an over-simplified objectivism, on the other, is to try to reconcile the contingent, historical, culture-bound nature of our thought with what seems to be our ability to come to think in *better*—and not simply *different*—ways.

Thinkers who attempt this often begin by observing that we must start from where we are, warts and all, with our current concepts and beliefs and standards and limitations (we could, after all, scarcely begin from anywhere else). Furthermore, they often continue, our beliefs and standards do not require justification unless they are challenged in some relevant way. This is not to say that we are forever stuck with our current views, however, because various pressures can lead us to make improvements. This possibility of improvement is often overlooked, however, because we are in the grip of some overly-ambitious model of rationality or justification that refuses to count something as an improvement unless we can give something like a formal demonstration that it is better than what went before.

These lofty conceptions of rationality and justification often go hand in hand with the view that rationality is powerful enough, in principle, to settle all difficult cases or to bring all rational people into agreement. But this overlooks the possibility of less-exalted conceptions of rationality which, although they cannot guarantee convergence or agreement, can still lead to various sorts of epistemic improvements in a person's or group's standards and beliefs. What we need are not completely framework-independent epistemic standards, but a diligent attempt to do the best with what we have; to forthrightly acknowledge that we have preconceptions and biases of various sorts, but to strive to pinpoint such limitations and to discount for them when we can.

Various philosophers have suggested ways in which our beliefs and standards could improve over time in spite of the fact that we are historically and culturally situated creatures. For example, John Dewey and others argue that our epistemic standards evolve in trial-and-error process of inquiry itself. Others suggest that the criteria for rational change, even in science, sometimes involve things like problem-solving ability, rather than getting closer to the truth about some reality that is independent of our language and thought. Again, the method of reflective equilibrium may allow us to improve both our general standards and our particular beliefs from the inside, without having to employ some timeless and immutable standards. Although this method cannot guarantee that groups that begin with different standards and beliefs will converge, it may nevertheless lead both groups to better-justified overall sets of standards and beliefs.

A Residual Sense of Contingency?

Even if we scale back our demands of rationality and justification, however, an uncomfortable sense of the contingency of our own modes of thought and evaluation may remain. The increasing salience of historical and cultural diversity highlights modes of thinking and acting that differ in interesting, and sometimes disquieting, ways from our own. Had we been raised in a very different time or place, we could easily have wound up with very different styles of thought, standards of evaluation, and intuitions about what is obvious. Moreover, some of these alternatives do not involve any obvious failure of rationality or any violation of epistemic norms.

All of this can be unsettling, because the recognition of such differences, especially differences that seem difficult to settle in a nonquestion-begging way, is in tension with the fact that in practice it is virtually impossible to view our most central concepts and beliefs and principles as just one set among many equally good ones. We want to be able to say more than "Well, this is how we do things where *I* come from," or "You are wrong because you aren't measuring up to *my* standards." It would be gratifying to find a way to avoid the tension this sense of contingency can generate, but it is not altogether obvious there is one to be found.

Ideology

An ideology is a set of conscious and unconscious ideas that constitute one's goals, expectations, and actions. An ideology is a comprehensive vision, a way of looking at things (compare worldview) as in several philosophical tendencies, or a set of ideas proposed by the dominant class of a society to all members of this society (a "received consciousness" or product of socialization).

Ideologies are systems of abstract thought applied to public matters and thus make this concept central to politics. Implicitly every political or economic tendency entails an ideology whether or not it is propounded as an explicit system of thought.

History

The term "ideology" was born in the highly controversial philosophical and political debates and fights of the French Revolution and acquired several other meanings from the early days of the First French Empire to the present. The word was coined by Antoine Destutt de Tracy in 1796, assembling the parts *idea* (near to the Lockean sense) and *-logy*. He used it to refer to one aspect of his "science of ideas" (to the study itself, not the subject of the study). He separated three aspects, namely: ideology, general grammar, and logic, considering respectively the subject, the means, and the reason of this science. He argues that among these aspects ideology is the most generic term, because the science of ideas also contains the study of their expression and deduction.

According to Karl Mannheim's historical reconstruction of the shifts in the meaning of ideology, the modern meaning of the word was born when Napoleon Bonaparte (as a politician) used it in an abusive way against "the ideologues" (a group which included Cabanis, Condorcet, Constant, Daunou, Say, Madame de Staël, and Destutt de Tracy), to express the pettiness of his (liberal republican) political opponents.

Perhaps the most accessible source for the near-original meaning of *ideology* is Hippolyte Taine's work on the Ancien Regime (the first volume of "Origins of Contemporary France"). He describes ideology as rather like teaching philosophy by the Socratic method, but without extending the vocabulary beyond what the general reader already possessed, and without the examples from observation that practical science would require. Taine identifies it not just with Destutt De Tracy, but also with his milieu, and includes Condillac as one of its precursors. (Destutt de Tracy read the works of Locke and Condillac while he was imprisoned during the Reign of Terror.)

The word "ideology" was coined long before the Russians coined "intelligentsia", or before the adjective "intellectual" referred to a sort of person, i.e. an intellectual. Thus these words were not around when Napoleon Bonaparte took the word "ideologues" to ridicule his intellectual opponents. Gradually, however, the term "ideology" has dropped some of its pejorative sting, and has become a neutral term in the analysis of differing political opinions and views of social groups. While Karl Marx situated the term within class struggle and domination, others believed it was a necessary part of institutional functioning and social integration.

Analysis

Meta-ideology is the study of the structure, form, and manifestation of ideologies. Meta-ideology posits that ideology is a *coherent system of ideas*, relying upon a few basic assumptions about reality that may or may not have any factual basis, but are subjective choices that serve as the seed around which further thought grows. According to this perspective, ideologies are neither right nor wrong, but only a relativistic intellectual strategy for categorizing the world. The pluses and minuses of ideology range from the vigor and fervor of true believers to ideological infallibility. Excessive need for certitude lurks at fundamentalist levels in politics and religions.

The works of George Walford and Harold Walsby, done under the heading of systematic ideology, are attempts to explore the relationships between ideology and social systems. Charles Blattberg has offered an account which distinguishes political ideologies from political philosophies.

David W. Minar describes six different ways in which the word "ideology" has been used:

1. As a collection of certain ideas with certain kinds of *content*, usually normative;
2. As the *form or internal logical structure* that ideas have within a set;
3. By the role in which ideas play in *human-social interaction*;
4. By the role that ideas play in the *structure of an organization*;

5. As meaning, whose purpose is *persuasion*; and
6. As the *locus* of social interaction, possibly.

For Willard A. Mullins, an ideology is composed of four basic characteristics:

1. it must have power over cognition
2. it must be capable of guiding one's evaluations;
3. it must provide guidance towards action;
4. and, as stated above, it must be logically coherent.

Mullins emphasizes that an ideology should be contrasted with the related (but different) issues of *utopia* and *historical myth.*

The German philosopher Christian Duncker called for a "critical reflection of the ideology concept" (2006). In his work, he strove to bring the concept of ideology into the foreground, as well as the closely connected concerns of epistemology and history. In this work, the term ideology is defined in terms of a system of presentations that explicitly or implicitly claim to absolute truth.

Though the word "ideology" is most often found in political discourse, there are many different kinds of ideology: political, social, epistemological, ethical, etc.

Marxist View

In the Marxist economic base and superstructure model of society, *base* denotes the relations of production and modes of production, and *superstructure* denotes the dominant ideology (religious, legal, political systems). The economic base of production determines the political superstructure of a society. Ruling class-interests determine the superstructure and the nature of the justifying ideology—actions feasible because the ruling class control the means of production. For example, in a feudalmode of production, religious ideology is the most prominent aspect of the superstructure, while in capitalist formations, ideologies such as liberalism and social democracy dominate. Hence the great importance of the ideology justifying a society; it politically confuses the alienated groups of society via false consciousness, such as in the case of commodity fetishism—the belief that value is inherent to a commodity, rather than external, added to it via labour.

The ruling class affect their social reproduction by the dominant ideology's representing—to every social-economic class—that the economic interests of the ruling class are the economic interests of the entire society. Some explanations have been presented. György Lukács proposes ideology as a projection of the class consciousness of the ruling class. Antonio Gramsci uses cultural hegemony to explain why the working-class have a false ideological conception of what are their best interests. Marx observed, "The class which has the means of material production at its disposal has control at the same time over the means of mental production."

Chronologically, the dominant ideologies in Capitalism are:

1. classical liberalism
2. modern liberalism
3. social democracy
4. neo-liberalism corresponding to these three capitalist stages of development:
    1. extensive stage
    2. intensive stage
    3. contemporary capitalism (late capitalism)

The Marxist formulation of "ideology as an instrument of social reproduction" is conceptually important to the sociology of knowledge, viz. Karl Mannheim, Daniel Bell, and Jürgen Habermas et al. Moreover, Mannheim has developed, and progressed, from the "total" but "special" Marxist conception of ideology to a "general" and "total" ideological conception acknowledging that all ideology (including Marxism) resulted from social life, an idea developed by the sociologist Pierre Bourdieu. Slavoj Žižek and the earlier Frankfurt School added to the "general theory" of ideology a psychoanalytic insight that ideologies do not include only conscious, but also unconscious ideas.

Louis Althusser's Ideological State Apparatuses

Louis Althusser proposed a materialistic conception of ideology, which made use of a special type of discourse: the lacunar discourse. A number of propositions, which are never untrue, suggest a number of other propositions, which are. In this way, the essence of the lacunar discourse is what is *not* told (but is suggested).

For example, the statement "All are equal before the law", which is a theoretical groundwork of current legal systems, suggests that all people may be of equal worth or have equal "opportunities". This is not true, for the concept of private property and power over the means of production results in some people being able to own more (*much* more) than others. This power disparity contradicts the claim that all share both practical worth and future opportunity equally; for example, the rich can afford better legal representation, which practically privileges them before the law.

Althusser also proffered the concept of the Ideological State Apparatus to explain his theory of ideology. His first thesis was "*ideology has no history*": while individual ideolog*ies* have histories, interleaved with the general class struggle of society, the general form of ideology is external to history.

For Althusser, beliefs and ideas are the products of social practices, not the reverse. His thesis that "*ideas are material*" is illustrated by the "scandalous advice" of Pascal toward unbelievers: "kneel and pray, and then you will believe". What is ultimately ideological for Althusser are not the subjective beliefs held in the conscious "minds" of human individuals, but rather discourses that produce these beliefs, the material institutions and rituals that individuals take part in without submitting it to conscious examination and critical thinking.

Silvio Vietta: Ideology and Rationality

The German cultural historian Silvio Vietta described how the development and expansion of Western rationality from ancient times onwards was often accompanied by and shaped by ideologies like that of the "just war", the "true religion", the ideology of racism, nationalism, or the eschatological vision of future history as a kind of heaven on earth in communism. Ideas like these became ideologies by giving hegemonic political actions an idealistic veneer and equipping their leaders with a higher and, in the "political religions" (Eric Voegelin), nearly God-like power, so that they became masters over the lives (and the deaths) of millions of people. Ideologies therefore contributed to power politics irrational shields of ideas beneath which they could operate as manifestations of idealism.

Political Ideologies

Many political parties base their political action and program on an ideology. In social studies, a political *ideology* is a certain ethical set of ideals, principles, doctrines, myths, or symbols of a social movement, institution, class, or large group that explains how society should work, and offers some political and cultural blueprint for a certain social order. A political ideology largely concerns itself with how to allocate power and to what ends it should be used. Some parties follow a certain ideology very closely, while others may take broad inspiration from a group of related ideologies without specifically embracing any one of them. Political ideologies have two dimensions:

1. *Goals*: how society should work
2. *Methods*: the most appropriate ways to achieve the ideal arrangement

An ideology is a collection of ideas. Typically, each ideology contains certain ideas on what it considers to be the best form of government (e.g. democracy, theocracy, caliphate etc.), and the best economic system (e.g. capitalism, socialism, etc.). Sometimes the same word is used to identify both an ideology and one of its main ideas. For instance, "socialism" may refer to an economic system, or it may refer to an ideology which supports that economic system.

Ideologies also identify themselves by their position on the political spectrum (such as the left, the centre or the right), though this is very often controversial. Finally, ideologies can be distinguished from political strategies (e.g. populism) and from single issues that a party may be built around (e.g. legalization of marijuana). Philosopher Michael Oakeshott provides a good definition of ideology as "the formalized abridgment of the supposed sub-stratum of the rational truth contained in the tradition".

Studies of the concept of ideology itself (rather than specific ideologies) have been carried out under the name of systematic ideology.

Political ideologies are concerned with many different aspects of a society, some of which are: the economy, education, health care, labour law, criminal law, the justice system, the provision of social security and social welfare, trade, the environment, minors, immigration, race, use of the military, patriotism, and established religion.

There are many proposed methods for the classification of political ideologies, each of these different methods generate a specific political spectrum. Today, many commentators claim that we are living in a post-ideological age, in which redemptive, all-encompassing ideologies have failed, and this is often associated with Francis Fukuyama's writings on "the end of history".

Government Ideology

When a political ideology becomes a dominantly pervasive component within a government, it can be considered an ideocracy. Different forms of government utilize ideology in various ways, not always restricted to politics and society. Certain ideas and schools of thought become favoured, or rejected, over others, depending on their compatibility with or use for the reigning social order.

Epistemological Ideologies

Even when the challenging of existing beliefs is encouraged, as in scientific theories, the dominant paradigm or mindset can prevent certain challenges, theories, or experiments from being advanced. A special case of science adopted as ideology is that of ecology, which studies the relationships among living things on Earth. Perceptual psychologist James J. Gibson believed that human perception of ecological relationships was the basis of self-awareness and cognition itself. Linguist George Lakoff has proposed a cognitive science of mathematics wherein even the most fundamental ideas of arithmetic would be seen as consequences or products of human perception—which is itself necessarily evolved within an ecology.

Deep ecology and the modern ecology movement (and, to a lesser degree, Green parties) appear to have adopted ecological sciences as a positive ideology.

Some accuse ecological economics of likewise turning scientific theory into political economy, although theses in that science can often be tested. The modern practice of green economics fuses both approaches and seems to be part science, part ideology.

This is far from the only theory of economics to be raised to ideology status—some notable economically based ideologies include neoliberalism, monetarism, mercantilism, mixed economy, social Darwinism, communism, laissez-faire economics, and free trade. There are also current theories of safe trade and fair trade which can be seen as ideologies.

Psychological Research

Psychological research increasingly suggests that ideologies reflect (unconscious) motivational processes, as opposed to the view that political convictions always reflect independent and unbiased thinking. Research in 2008 proposed that ideologies may function as prepackaged units of interpretation that spread because of basic human motives to understand the world, avoid existential threat, and maintain valued interpersonal relationships. The authors conclude that such motives may lead disproportionately to the adoption of system-justifying worldviews. Psychologists have generally found that personality traits, individual difference variables, needs, and ideological beliefs seem to have a common thread.

Ideology and Semiotic Theory

According to the semiotician Bob Hodge, ideology "identifies a unitary object that incorporates complex sets of meanings with the social agents and processes that produced them. No other term captures this object as well as 'ideology'. Foucault's 'episteme' is too narrow and abstract, not social enough. His 'discourse', popular because it covers some of ideology's terrain with less baggage, is too confined to verbal systems. 'Worldview' is too metaphysical, 'propaganda' too loaded. Despite or because of its contradictions, 'ideology' still plays a key role in semiotics oriented to social, political life.

Is Science an Ideology?

To defenders of science, like Karl Popper, the claim that science itself might be prey to distortion, prejudice and ideology is anathema. To people who believe like Paul Feyerabend that science is "just another ideology", the common belief that science is a neutral and objective body of knowledge is an indication of just how great an ideological grip it has on people's minds.

Science and Pseudo-Science

Popper's famous distinction between science and pseudo-science (or ideology) depends on his equally famous principle of falsification. Quite simply, he argues that if a theory is in principle open to being disproved or 'falsified' by the facts of the world, then it is scientific. If it is not open to being falsified by the facts of the world, then it is pseudo-science, ideology. For example, the claim "Nothing can travel faster than the speed of light", on which the Special Theory of Relativity crucially depends, can in principle be falsified by observing something in the actual world that *does* travel faster than the speed of light. But the statement "God's in His Heaven" *cannot* be scientific, because it's unclear what sort of evidence in the world would count as falsifying it. Therefore it must be pseudo-science or ideology.

More insidiously, some pseudo-sciences or ideologies which do, on the face of it, seem capable of having the facts of the world cited against them as contrary evidence, resort to a more devious tactic. Such is the case, thinks Popper, with Marxism and Psychoanalysis. What he objects to is that both Marxism and Psychoanalysis *call* themselves 'scientific' while their procedure is thoroughly pseudo-scientific. How so? Because, for example, if you say to a Marxist: "Look, Communist regimes have collapsed all over the world and global Capitalism seems stronger than ever. Doesn't that falsify your claim that Marxism is the 'inevitable lesson of history'?", the Marxist can always reply: "Not at all. It's just another twist in the materialist dialectic of history. Communism will win in the end." And so on for every bit of contrary evidence that you might try to cite as falsifying Marxism. It will always, says Popper, be 'explained away' by the Marxist.

So, for Popper, the mark of pseudo-science or ideology is *that it will never allow itself to be falsified by any evidence. It will always reinterpret what is proposed as evidence against it by interpreting that evidence in its own favour*, as in the Marxist example given above.

So far so good. But the trouble is that it has been persuasively argued that science can and does behave in just the same way as Popper claims that pseudo-science or ideology behaves.

Defenders of a scientific theory may either ignore anomalies – awkward facts that don't behave as the scientific theory says they should – or they may try to explain them away by inventing auxiliary hypotheses to try and make the anomalies consistent with the theory. In other words, they may and do try to *reinterpret contrary evidence in their own favour*. Some people have accused supporters of the Theory of Evolution of doing just this. And it has been argued that it is a perfectly sensible thing to do, especially if there is no better theory available at present and if the existing theory is fruitful in other respects.

But the price of defending any theory – scientific or not – against an increasing body of factual evidence that seems to cast doubt on its truth is that your theory becomes more and more difficult to defend, more and more cumbersome to work with, and less and less persuasive. So you can defend any theory indefinitely, *but only at the price of sounding less and less convincing*. But exactly the same thing applies to what Popper calls 'pseudo-science' as applies to what Popper calls 'science'. Just as the Theory of Evolution will look less and less convincing if contrary evidence mounts against it, so too will the theory of Marxism. But it is bound to be a messy and imprecise decision at what point any theory is so riddled with anomalies, so weighed down with auxiliary hypotheses, and, in general, flies so much against the facts of the world that it can be said to be decisively falsified.

The upshot of this is that the apparently nice and clear distinction between science and pseudo-science made by Popper turns out, on inspection, to be rather unclear. We might say that his distinction itself, while not being decisively falsified, does look a bit unconvincing in the light of the facts.

Progress in Science: Kuhn and Feyerabend

Kuhn and Feyerabend are so often cited as examples of people who don't believe in progress in scientific truth that I think it is worth assembling some reminders of the extent to which they both *do* believe in it. Kuhn, for instance, believes in progress in scientific truth not just within a paradigm ('normal science') but also *between* paradigms ('revolutionary science'). It is just that he thinks we have a false picture of what 'progress in scientific truth' actually is. He says:

"Later scientific theories are better than early ones for solving puzzles in the often quite different environments to which they are applied. This is not a relativist position, and it displays the sense in which I am a convinced believer in scientific progress.

"Compared with the notion of progress most prevalent among both philosophers of science and laymen, however, this position lacks an essential element. A scientific theory is usually felt to be better than its predecessors not only in the sense that it is a better instrument for discovering and solving puzzles but also because it is somehow a better representation of what nature is really like...

"I do not doubt ... that Newton's mechanics improves on Aristotle's and that Einstein's improves on Newton's as instruments for puzzle solving. But I can see in their succession no coherent direction of ontological development. On the contrary, in some important respects, though by no means in all, Einstein's general theory of relativity is closer to Aristotle's than either of them is to Newton's. Though the temptation to describe that position as relativistic is understandable, the description seems to me wrong. Conversely, if the position be relativism, I cannot see that the relativist loses anything needed to account for the nature and development of the sciences." (T.S. Kuhn, *The Structure of Scientific Revolutions*, Univ. of Chicago Press 1970, pp.206-207).

Feyerabend argues for a qualified idea of progress in scientific truth in the following way:

"There is only *one* task we can legitimately demand of a theory, and it is that it should give us a correct account of the world, i.e., of the totality of facts *as constituted by its own basic concepts...* Is it not reasonable to assume that a point of view, such as the point of view of classical mechanics, that has been found wanting in various respects and that gets into difficulty *with its own facts...* cannot have entirely adequate concepts? Is it not equally reasonable to try to replace its concepts by those of a more successful cosmology?...

"Incommensurable theories, then, can be refuted by reference to their own respective kinds of experience; i.e., by discovering the *internal contradictions* from which they are suffering. (In the absence of commensurable alternatives these refutations are quite weak, however, as can be seen from the arguments for proliferation in chapters 2 and 3)." (P. Feyerabend, *Against Method*, London, NLB 1975, p.284).

Science and Non-Science

Such qualified views of scientific progress as those expressed above need to be integrated into a wider picture in which the status of scientific truth is compared with the status of truth in other types of human activity. I am thinking of Feyerabend's provocative remarks about voodoo being as legitimate a form of inquiry as particle physics (and, even stronger, Heidegger's Romantic-style views that poetry gives us a *deeper* understanding of the world than science). Such views, I think, point to the following general line of criticism.

Most contemporary defences of scientific realism are *pragmatic* in nature. They follow the lines laid down by philosophers like C.S. Peirce and Karl Popper. The fact that our technologies *work*, they say, is strong evidence that the scientific theories on which they are based are *true* or at least getting ever closer to the truth. What they mean by 'truth' here is correspondence truth - that is, our theories correspond to the way the world really is. Few serious critics would be so irrational as to deny this, but some would want to modify such claims by adding that scientific vocabularies work and provide 'an accurate description of reality' *relative to a certain purpose.* Change the human purposes and you simultaneously change the idea of 'what works' and of what provides 'an accurate description of reality' relative to this different purpose.

This is what enables Richard Rorty to say that for certain purposes a literary vocabulary works better than a scientific one and therefore, relative to those purposes, provides a 'truer description of reality'. In other words, Heidegger was halfright: poetry may be truer than science - for certain purposes.

It is also what enables Paul Feyerabend to engage quite consistently in some of his more bizarre-sounding proposals, such as that we should, if we don't much care for the Theory of Evolution, decide on whether it is true or false by democratic majority vote. Or which leads him to engage in the following classic fulmination against science:

"Our well-conditioned materialistic contemporaries are liable to burst with excitement over events such as the moonshots, the double helix, nonequilibrium thermodynamics. But let us look at the matter from a different point of view, and it becomes a ridiculous exercise in futility. It needed millions of dollars, thousands of well-trained assistants, years of hard work to enable some inarticulate and rather limited contemporaries to perform a few graceless hops in a place nobody in his right mind would think of visiting – a dried out, airless, hot stone.

But mystics, using only their minds, travelled across the celestial spheres to God himself whom they viewed in his splendour receiving strength for continuing their lives and enlightenment for themselves and their fellow men. It is only the illiteracy of the general public and of their stern trainers that makes them reject such comparisons without further ado. A free society does not object to such an attitude but it will not permit it to become a basic ideology either." (P. Feyerabend, Science *In A Free Society*, Verso/NLB 1982, p.31).

It seems to me that what is going on here is a perfectly consistent drawing out of the implications of a pragmatist theory of truth. If truth is defined as what works relative to human purposes, then the phrase 'true description of reality' must logically be dependent on the phrase 'what works best for a certain purpose'. In short: "The vocabulary that works best for a certain purpose can legitimately be regarded as the truest description of reality for that purpose." And, as Feyerabend suggests, which purposes are best, and therefore which descriptions are to be deemed truest, should, in a free society, be open to debate.

'Making' and 'Finding', 'Scheme' and 'Content', 'Language' and 'World'

Linked to the view above are the arguments variously put forward by Donald Davidson, Richard Rorty, and Hilary Putnam (and, some would say, also by Continental thinkers like Nietzsche, Heidegger, Gadamer, Foucault, Derrida) that it is systematically impossible to state where language ends and the world begins, or to separate 'interpretation' from 'text', or to isolate the timeless, universal facts or 'content' from the changing, particular vocabulary or 'scheme'. As Rorty puts it:

"It is no truer that 'atoms are what they are because we use 'atom' as we do' than that 'we use 'atom' as we do because atoms are as they are'. *Both* of these claims... are entirely empty, both are pseudo-explanations.

"[On the realist account] the reason why physicists have come to use 'atom' as we do is that there really are atoms out there which caused them to be represented more or less accurately... The reason why such explanation meets with more success than, say, astrological explanation, is that there are no planetary influences out there, whereas there really *are* atoms out there...

"[But] the representationalist's attempt to explain the success of astrophysics and the failure of astrology is... bound to be an empty compliment unless we can attain to... a God's eye standpoint – one which has somehow broken out of our language and beliefs and tested them against something known without their aid.

But we have no idea of what it would be like to be at that standpoint. As Davidson puts it, 'there is no chance that someone can take up a vantage point for comparing conceptual schemes [e.g., the astrologer's and the astrophysicist's] by temporarily shedding their own.' " (R. Rorty, *Objectivity, Relativism and Truth, Cambridge University* Press 1991, pp.5 - 6).

Perhaps a still clearer statement of the point Rorty is making is provided by the following:

"For example, someone says 'There is a chair' (for a scientific example replace 'chair' with 'electron') - what makes this statement true? Is it not an appeal to our conventions about what we call chairs? As Quine made clear - that there is a chair present would not be true in a culture which defined chairs differently or had no conception of chairs at all.

"What does the truth of the statement depend on, then? For one thing it depends on a certain agreement on how we use our language. But is that all? It must also depend on the way the world is. There has to be something that allows us to agree or disagree about the presence of the chair.

What is important to the truth or falsity of the statement is both the way in which we use our language and the way the world is - but neither element can be separated from the other. What makes something true or false, there or not there, and this includes scientific discoveries, is how things stand from our human (not an impersonal) perspective." (D. Hutto, 'A Job For Philosophy', *Philosophy Now*, Autumn 1992, p.22).

The overall conclusion seems to be that all forms of knowledge, including scientific knowledge, are 'ideological' in the sense that there is no neutral, objective body of knowledge that is not infected by the purpose-relative concepts of a group of inquirers.

This is a meaning of 'ideology' that still retains some vestiges of the original Marxist meaning of 'ideology' as a mask and cover for vested interests.

Science and Non-Science

The modern world has seen technological wonders multiply rapidly, made possible through an accumulation of scientific discoveries about the natural world applied in practical ways. Because of the successes of its applications, science has become humanity's preferred means of collecting, evaluating, and organizing knowledge. This is possibly why the mantle of 'scientific' can confer a measure of certainty to any postulate or undertaking. Yet there remain conflicts, competing visions of truth, between those ideas fielded by the practitioners of science and, for example, its theological competitors. A question to be answered then is, *What is science?* – and by opposition, *What is non-science?*

Scientific Methods

In earlier eras, the human desire to explain natural phenomena linked what was observed with preconceived notions of the world taken from mythology, religion, and philosophy. Modern science developed as an alternative way to explain those phenomena, through systematically observing them, and testing ideas about them.

The scientific method proceeds from data collected by observing phenomena. Based on the observations, the inquirer crafts a *hypothesis* – an idea that hopes to explain the observations. Ideally, a scientific experiment to test a hypothesis seeks to control the variables thought to effect the experiment's outcome, varying only a single element of the experimental situation at a time so that the effect of this single variable on the results can be measured or otherwise observed. Analysis of experimental results might then show the original hypothesis to be mistaken, in which case it is discarded, and an alternative hypothesis developed and tested. In the event that a hypothesis is not disproved by experimental results, it might form the basis for a *theory* explaining the phenomenon. Science also places importance on the publication of experiments, that they might be recreated by other researchers, demonstrating the consistency of claimed observations, and so that they may possibly further refine the process.

Early in the rift between scientists and (say) theologians, an *empiricist* view emerged in philosophy (*cf*, for example, John Locke, *An Essay Concerning Human Understanding*, 1689). On this view, only that which can be observed or measured in some way is a reliable source of truth. Religious authoritarianism, mysticism, and metaphysics were ruled out by this process. Indeed, evidence is essential in the scientific process. The scientist's prime role is that of measuring and collecting data about the natural processes of interest. However, observations can be influenced by a bias towards the hypothesis the experimenter seeks to test, or by the paradigm the scientist is working within.

Although in practice the ideal of having a purely objective or disinterested approach to the collection of data is rarely (if ever) achieved, science could not advance without some adherence to the empirical principle. Few examples exist of scientific theories not formed primarily from directly reacting to empirical data: the best-known is Einstein's Theory of Special Relativity. Einstein developed this theory from thought experiments and mathematics, although observations of natural phenomena later confirmed his concepts. Or as Einstein said, "Physics constitutes a logical system of thought which is in a state of evolution, whose basis cannot be distilled, as it were, from experience by an inductive method, but can only be arrived at by free invention. The justification of the system rests in the verification of the derived propositions by sense experiences." (Albert Einstein, from *Ideas and Opinions*, 1954.)

To be scientific, the observations upon which a theory is based must be repeatable. Originally it was thought by philosophers of science that theories must be verifiable. This approach, known as verificationism, was inverted by Karl Popper in his book *Conjectures and Refutations* (1963), where he pointed out that no amount of observation agreeing with a hypothesis will ever prove that hypothesis, whereas a single contrary observation will disprove it. He therefore proposed that *falsifiability* provided the demarcation between scientific and non-scientific hypotheses. So, rather than by demonstrably being proven correct by empirical means, to be scientific, propositions should be capable of being disproved, either by observation or in theoretical principle. Generally, whether through verification or falsification, *testability* is essential to an idea being a scientific hypothesis.

Figure: *"Some of us are looking at the stars" – Oscar Wilde*

One problem here is that when observed data seems to refute a theory, one may not know with certainty which aspect of the theory to reject. Observations may in fact support several competing theories, and may not of themselves be neutral arbitrators between opposing claims. Thomas Kuhn suggested in *The Structure of Scientific Revolutions* (1962) that scientific observations are made in an established theoretical context called a *paradigm*, and that for any given discipline an accepted paradigm of scientific thought suggests the course for continued experimentation. A paradigm is modified or abandoned when a replacement paradigm is found by the discipline's community of scientists to be more useful, that is, it produces results which explain more phenomena. This also illustrates another characteristic of science – that its theories are tentative, and always subject to revision, correction or abandonment when incontrovertibly challenged by the data.

Scientific theories are often predictive. If a theory correctly models a natural phenomenon, then one should be able to use that model to make predictions about further related phenomena. Failure of the prediction might indicate that the underlying theoretical assumptions are incorrect, and the theory needs to be re-evaluated.

Non-Scientific Methods

'Non-science' means more than that which is antithetical to science. As sources of human knowledge, non-scientific approaches such as philosophy, theology, and art have usefully guided visions of the 'why' of our existence, our interactions with one another, or defined morality/ ethics. By contrast, the label 'pseudo-science' encompasses attempts at claiming a mantle of truth by endeavours that, although to the layman might seem scientific, lack testability and the vigorous peer-review inherent in the scientific process. Astrology, for example, has a set of rules and underlying concepts which cannot be tested. The vagueness of its predictions avoid falsification precisely because they are ambiguous.

A common thread unifying non-scientific theories of the world is the reliance upon unseen (ie, unmeasurable by any known instrumentation) forces to form their explanations. There being no objective means by which to quantify or qualify these unknown variables, there can be no independent test of their validity, and there is also no consistency of experience among practitioners. Theological arguments such as the existence and nature of God are beyond the scope of evaluation by science because the subject transcends the natural world and is not testable by any empirical means. Science cannot develop means of either verifying or falsifying this religious construct. Creation science attempts to use observation of the natural world to support its theorem that the world was designed by God. In 'Intelligent Design is Empirically Testable and Makes Predictions' (available from *evolutionnews.org/2006/01*), J. Richards and J. Witt, proponents of creation science, suggest the bacterial flagellum [a 'tail'] as a clear example of design. The 'irreducible complexity' of this structure is offered as proof that it was designed. Yet 'irreducible complexity' is a value judgment without an objective basis, and so is not a scientific hypothesis. It is pseudo-science. (The potential for falsification they offer is in that evolutionary precursors to the flagellum have not been identified. Finding such an evolutionary path, they argue, would render their hypothesis false; thus to them their theory is scientific because it is empirically testable.)

Conclusions

The philosophy of science offers several points of demarcation of science from non-science. Science hopes to find truth by observation. Those things that cannot be measured cannot be evaluated by science, and are irrelevant to it. Scientific observations must exhibit consistency across repeated experiments. Where there is an instance of relevant data to which the theory cannot apply, it must be modified. Science is open to constant revision as new facts are discovered and integrated into the emerging picture of the world it seeks to formulate. By contrast, non-scientific theories tend to be more dogmatic. Rather than modify an outdated premise when it finds new observations, in a non-scientific theory the data may itself be ignored or denied.

Science has been the force behind humanity's push forward. It defines new directions and possibilities and redefines old beliefs. It has helped cure diseases and saved millions from misery and hunger, yet it has also helped to develop weapons that have threatened humanity's very existence. At its best, non-science roots us to traditions and helps us find ethical paths, yet it has also at times been a force against human progress. Mankind needs the best of both ways of thinking.

9

In Praise of Intolerance Toward Academic Charlatanism

Antiscience

Antiscience is a position that rejects science and the scientific method. People holding antiscientific views do not accept that science is an objective method, as it purports to be, or that it generates universal knowledge. They also contend that scientific reductionism in particular is an inherently limited means to reach understanding of the complex world we live in. Antiscience proponents also criticize what they perceive as the unquestioned privilege, power and influence science seems to wield in society, industry and politics; they object to what they regard as an arrogant or closed-minded attitude amongst scientists.

History

In the beginnings of the scientific revolution, scientists such as Robert Boyle found themselves in conflict with those such as Thomas Hobbes, who were skeptical of whether science was a satisfactory way to obtain genuine knowledge about the world.

Hobbes' Stance is Sometimes Regarded as an Antiscience Position: In his *Six Lessons to the Professors of Mathematics,...* [published in 1656, Hobbes] distinguished 'demonstrable' fields, as 'those the construction of the subject whereof is in the power of the artist himself,' from 'indemonstrable' ones 'where the causes are to seek for.' We can only know the causes of what we make. So geometry is demonstrable, because 'the lines and figures from which we reason are drawn and described by ourselves' and 'civil philosophy is demonstrable, because we make the commonwealth ourselves.' But we can only speculate about the natural world, because 'we know not the construction, but seek it from the effects.'

It was also Hobbes who "put forth the idea of the significance of the nonrational in human behaviour." Jones goes on to group Hobbes along with others he classes as 'antireductionists' and 'individualists,' such as Wilhelm Dilthey, Karl Marx, Jeremy Bentham and J S Mill, and then he adds Karl Popper, John Rawls and E. O. Wilson.

Jean-Jacques Rousseau, in his *Discourse on the Arts and Sciences,* claimed that science can lead to immorality. "Rousseau argues that the progression of the sciences and arts has caused the corruption of virtue and morality" and his "critique of science has much to teach us about the dangers involved in our political commitment to scientific progress, and about the ways in which the future happiness of mankind might be secured". Nevertheless, Rousseau does not state in his Discourses that sciences are *necessarily* bad, and states that figures like René Descartes, Francis Bacon, and Isaac Newton should be held in high regard. In the conclusion to the Discourses, he says that these (aforementioned) can cultivate sciences to great benefit, and that morality's corruption is mostly because of society's bad influence on scientists.

William Blake reacted strongly against the work of Isaac Newton in his paintings and writings, and is seen as being perhaps the earliest (and almost certainly the most prominent and enduring) example of what is seen by historians as the aesthetic or romantic antiscience response. For example, in his 1795 poem Auguries of Innocence, Blake describes the beautiful and natural robin red-breast imprisoned by the materialistic cage of Newtonian mathematics and science. In Blake's painting of Newton, he is depicted "as a misguided hero whose gaze was directed only at sterile geometrical diagrams drawn on the ground". Blake thought that "Newton, Bacon, and Locke with their emphasis on reason were nothing more than 'the three great teachers of atheism, or Satan's Doctrine'...the picture progresses from exuberance and colour on the left, to sterility and blackness on the right. In Blake's view Newton brings not light, but night". In a poem, W.H. Auden summarises Blake's anti-scientific views by saying that he "[broke] off relations in a curse, with the Newtonian Universe".

One recent biographer of Newton considers him more as a renaissancealchemist, natural philosopher, and magician rather than a true representative of scientific illuminism, as popularized by Voltaire and other illuminist Newtonians.

Antiscience issues are seen as a fundamental consideration in the transition from 'pre-science' or 'protoscience' such as that evident in alchemy. Many disciplines which pre-date the widespread adoption and acceptance of the scientific method, such as geometry and astronomy, are not seen as anti-science. However, some of the orthodoxies within those disciplines which predate a scientific approach (such as those orthodoxies repudiated by the discoveries of Galileo) are seen as being a product of an anti-scientific stance.

The term 'scientism' derives from science studies and is a term spawned and used by sociologists and philosophers of science to describe the views, beliefs and behaviour of strong supporters of science. It is commonly used in a pejorative sense, for individuals who seem to be treating science in a similar way to a religion. The term reductionism is occasionally used in a similarly pejorative way (as a more subtle attack on scientists). However, some scientists feel comfortable being labelled as reductionists, while agreeing that there might be conceptual and philosophical shortcomings of reductionism.

However, non-reductionist views of science have been formulated in varied forms in several scientific fields like statistical physics, chaos theory, complexity theory, cybernetics, systems theory, systems biology, ecology, information theory, etc. Such fields tend to assume that strong interaction between units produce new phenomena in higher levels that cannot be accounted for solely by reductionism. For example, it is not valuable (or currently possible) to describe a chess game or gene networks using quantum mechanics. The emergentist view of science ("More is Different", in the words of Nobel physicist Philip W. Anderson) has been inspired in its methodology by the European social sciences (Durkheim, Marx) which tend to reject methodological individualism.

Political Antiscience

Left-Wing Antiscience: One expression of antiscience is the "denial of universality and... legitimisation of alternatives", and that the results of scientific findings do not always represent any underlying reality, but can merely reflect the ideology of dominant groups within society. In this view, science is associated with the political Right and is seen as a belief system that is conservative and conformist, that suppresses innovation, that resists change and that acts dictatorially. This includes the view, for example, that science has a "bourgeois and/or Eurocentric and/or masculinist world-view."

The anti-nuclear movement, often associated with the left, has been criticized for overstating the negative effects of nuclear power, and understating the environmental costs of non-nuclear sources that can be prevented through nuclear energy.

Right-Wing Antiscience

The origin of antiscience thinking may be traced back to the reaction of Romanticism to the Enlightenment, French Revolution and the Industrial Revolution. This movement is often referred to as the 'counter-enlightenment'. Romanticism emphasizes that intuition, passion and organic links to Nature are primal values and that rational thinking is secondary to human life. There are many modern examples of conservative antiscience polemics. Primary among the latter are the polemics about evolutionary theory and modern cosmology teaching in high schools, and environmental issues related to global warming and energy crisis.

Characteristics of antiscience associated with the right include the appeal to conspiracy theories to explain why scientists believe what they believe, in an attempt to undermine the confidence or power usually associated to science (e.g. in global warming conspiracy theories). Another feature of "conservative antiscience" discourse is the widespread use of informal fallacies, in particular the false dilemma, appeal to consequences, appeal to fear, and the appeal to probability fallacies.

Religious Antiscience

In this context, antiscience may be considered dependent on religious, moral and cultural arguments. For this kind of religious antiscience philosophy, science is an anti-spiritual and materialistic force that undermines traditional values, ethnic identity and accumulated historical wisdom in favour of reason and cosmopolitanism. In particular, the traditional and ethnic values emphasized are similar to those of white supremacist Christian Identity theology, but similar right-wing views have been developed by radically conservative sects of Islam, Judaism, Hinduism, and Buddhism. New religious movements such as New Age thinking also criticize the scientific worldview as favouring a reductionist, atheist, or materialist philosophy.

A frequent basis of antiscientific sentiment is religious theism with literal interpretations of sacred text. Here, scientific theories that conflict with what is considered divinely-inspired knowledge are regarded as flawed. Over the centuries religious institutions have been hesitant to embrace such ideas as heliocentrism and planetary motion because they contradicted the dominant understanding of various passages of scripture. More recently the body of creation theologies known collectively as creationism, including the teleological theory of intelligent design, have been promoted by religious theists in response to the process of evolution by natural selection.

Three Areas of Antiscience

Historically, antiscience first arose as a reaction against scientific materialism. The 18th century Enlightenment had ushered in "the ideal of a unified system of all the sciences", but there were those fearful of this notion, who "felt that constrictions of reason and science, of a single all-embracing system... were in some way constricting, an obstacle to their vision of the world, chains on their imagination or feeling". Antiscience then is a rejection of "the scientific model [or paradigm]... with its strong implication that only that which was quantifiable, or at any rate, measurable... was real". In this sense, it comprises a "critical attack upon the total claim of the new scientific method to dominate the entire field of human knowledge". However, scientific positivism (logical positivism) does not deny the reality of non-measurable phenomena, only that those phenomena should not be adequate to scientific investigation. Moreover, positivism, as a philosophical basis for the scientific method, is not consensual or even dominant in the scientific community.

Three major areas of antiscience can be seen in philosophy, sociology, and ecology. The following quotes explore this aspect of the subject.

Ecology and Health Sphere

Within the ecological and health spheres, Levins identifies a conflict "not between science and antiscience, but rather between different pathways for science and technology; between a commodified science-for-profit and a gentle science for humane goals; between the sciences of the smallest parts and the sciences of dynamic wholes... [he] offers proposals for a more holistic, integral approach to understanding and addressing environmental issues". These beliefs are also common within the scientific community, with for example, scientists being prominent in environmental campaigns warning of environmental dangers such as ozone depletion and the greenhouse effect. It can also be argued that this version of antiscience comes close to that found in the medical sphere, where patients and practitioners may choose to reject science and adopt a pseudoscientific approach to health problems. This can be both a practical and a conceptual shift and has attracted strong criticism: "therapeutic touch, a healing technique based upon the laying-on of hands, has found wide acceptance in the nursing profession despite its lack of scientific plausibility. Its acceptance is indicative of a broad antiscientific trend in nursing".

Glazer also criticises the therapists and patients, "for abandoning the biological underpinnings of nursing and for misreading philosophy in the service of an antiscientific world-view". In contrast, Brian Martin criticized Gross and Levitt by saying that "[their] basic approach is to attack constructivists for not being positivists," and that science is "presented as a unitary object, usually identified with scientific knowledge.

It is portrayed as neutral and objective. Second, science is claimed to be under attack by 'antiscience' which is composed essentially of ideologues who are threats to the neutrality and objectivity that are fundamental to science.

Third, a highly selective attack is made on the arguments of 'antiscience'". Such people allegedly then "routinely equate critique of scientific knowledge with hostility to science, a jump that is logically unsupportable and empirically dubious". Having then "constructed two artificial entities, a unitary 'science' and a unitary 'academic left', each reduced to epistemological essences, Gross and Levitt proceed to attack. They pick out figures in each of several areas — science studies, postmodernism, feminism, environmentalism, AIDS activism — and criticise their critiques of science".

The writings of Young serve to illustrate more antiscientific views: "The strength of the antiscience movement and of alternative technology is that their advocates have managed to retain Utopian vision while still trying to create concrete instances of it". "The real social, ideological and economic forces shaping science...[have] been opposed to the point of suppression in many quarters. Most scientists hate it and label it 'antiscience'. But it is urgently needed, because it makes science self-conscious and hopefully self-critical and accountable with respect to the forces which shape research priorities, criteria, goals".

Genetically modified foods also bring about antiscience sentiment. The general public has recently become more aware of the dangers of a poor diet, as there have been numerous studies that show that the two are inextricably linked. Anti-science dictates that science is untrustworthy, because it is never complete and always being revised, which would be a probable cause for the fear that the general public has of genetically modified foods despite scientific reassurance.

Antivacinationists rely on whatever comes to hand presenting some of their arguments as if scientific, however a strain of antiscience is part of their approach.

Opposition to Reductionism and Positivism

On the Limitations of Models: A common antiscientific point of contention arises from the fact that mathematical models do not capture the full reality of existence, as can see in this quote:

The formulas of mathematical models are "artificial constructions, logical figments with no necessary relation to the outside world". These models always "leave out the richest and most important part of human experience...daily life, history, human laws and institutions, the modes of human self- expression". A failure to appreciate the subtle complexity of social worlds, means they get excluded from the formulas, even though, "no easy reductionism will do justice to the material". This approach often fails to concentrate "on social structures, processes, and actions in a specific sense (inequality, mobility, classes, strata, ethnicity, gender relations, urbanization, work and life of different types of people, not just elites)", and so tends to generate mostly meaningless oversimplifications.

It is also a common antiscientific point to state that *verbal* (say, literary and non-mathematical) models are poor representations of reality. If it is clear that a particular statistical or psychological study about romantic love or religious ecstasy, captures only a tiny fraction of such human experiences, literary accounts and simplified verbal models also cannot adequately convey their full complexity. Both verbal and mathematical models are (partial) maps of reality, providing different points of view, but inherently incomplete descriptions of the territory of human and universe existence.

Pseudoscience

Pseudoscience is a claim, belief or practice which is presented as scientific, but does not adhere to a validscientific method, lacks supporting evidence or plausibility, cannot be reliably tested, or otherwise lacks scientific status. Pseudoscience is often characterized by the use of vague, contradictory, exaggerated or unprovable claims, an over-reliance on confirmation rather than rigorous attempts at refutation, a lack of openness to evaluation by other experts, and a general absence of systematic processes to rationally develop theories.

A field, practice, or body of knowledge can reasonably be called pseudoscientific when it is presented as consistent with the norms of scientific research, but it demonstrably fails to meet these norms. Science is also distinguishable from revelation, theology, or spirituality in that it offers insight into the physical world obtained by empirical research and testing. Commonly held beliefs in popular science may not meet the criteria of science. "Pop science" may blur the divide between science and pseudoscience among the general public, and may also involve science fiction. Pseudoscientific beliefs are widespread, even among public school science teachers and newspaper reporters.

The demarcation problem between science and pseudoscience has ethical political implications, as well as philosophical and scientific issues. Differentiating science from pseudoscience has practical implications in the case of health care, expert testimony, environmental policies, and science education. Distinguishing scientific facts and theories from pseudoscientific beliefs such as those found in astrology, medical quackery, and occult beliefs combined with scientific concepts, is part of science education and scientific literacy.

The term *pseudoscience* is often considered inherently pejorative, because it suggests something is being inaccurately or even deceptively portrayed as science. Accordingly, those labelled as practicing or advocating pseudoscience usually dispute the characterization.

Overview

Scientific methodology: While the standards for determining whether a body of knowledge, methodology, or practice is scientific can vary from field to field, a number of basic principles are widely agreed upon by scientists. The basic notion is that all experimental results should be reproducible, and able to be verified by other individuals.

These principles aim to ensure experiments can be measurably reproduced under the same conditions, allowing further investigation to determine whether a hypothesis or theory related to given phenomena is both valid and reliable. Standards require the scientific method to be applied throughout, and bias will be controlled for or eliminated through randomization, fair sampling procedures, blinding of studies, and other methods.

All gathered data, including the experimental or environmental conditions, are expected to be documented for scrutiny and made available for peer review, allowing further experiments or studies to be conducted to confirm or falsify results. Statistical quantification of significance, confidence, and error are also important tools for the scientific method.

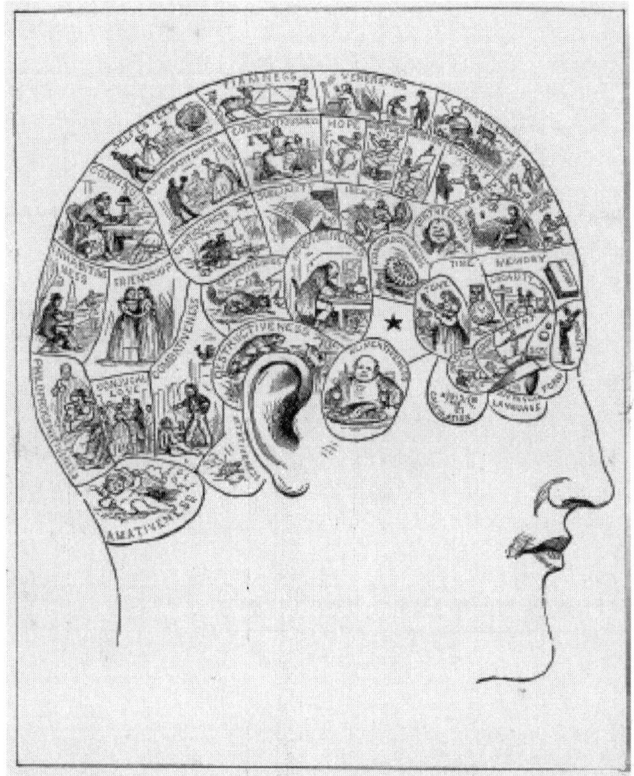

Figure: *A typical 19th century phrenology chart: In the 1820s, phrenologists claimed the mind was located in areas of the brain, and were attacked for doubting that mind came from the nonmaterial soul. Their idea of reading "bumps" in the skull to predict personality traits was later discredited. Phrenology was first called a pseudoscience in 1843 and continues to be considered so.*

Falsifiability

In the mid-20th century, Karl Popper put forth the criterion of falsifiability to distinguish science from nonscience. Falsifiability means a result can be disproved. For example, a statement such as "God created the universe" may be true or false, but no tests can be devised that could prove it either way; it simply lies outside the reach of science. Popper used astrology and psychoanalysis as examples of pseudoscience and Einstein's theory of relativity as an example of science. He subdivided nonscience into philosophical, mathematical, mythological, religious and/or metaphysical formulations on one hand, and pseudoscientific formulations on the other, though he did not provide clear criteria for the differences.

Merton's Norms

In 1942, Robert K. Merton identified a small set of "norms" which characterized what makes a "real" science. If any of the norms were violated, Merton considered the enterprise to be nonscience. These are not broadly accepted in the scientific community. His norms were:

- Originality: The tests and research done must present something new to the scientific community.
- Detachment: The scientists' reasons for practicing this science must be simply for the expansion of their knowledge. The scientists should not have personal reasons to expect certain results.
- Universality: No person should be able to more easily obtain the information of a test than another person. Social class, religion, ethnicity, or any other personal factors should not be factors in someone's ability to receive or perform a type of science.
- Skepticism: Scientific facts must not be based on faith. One should always question every case and argument and constantly check for errors or invalid claims.
- Public accessibility: Any scientific knowledge one obtains should be made available to everyone. The results of any research should be openly published and shared with the scientific community.

Refusal to Acknowledge Problems

In 1978, Paul Thagard proposed that pseudoscience is primarily distinguishable from science when it is less progressive than alternative theories over a long period of time, and its proponents fail to acknowledge or address problems with the theory. In 1983, Mario Bunge has suggested the categories of "belief fields" and "research fields" to help distinguish between pseudoscience and science, where the first is primarily personal and subjective and the latter involves a certain systematic approach.

Criticism of the Term

Philosophers of science, such as Paul Feyerabend, argued that a distinction between science and nonscience is neither possible nor desirable. Among the issues which can make the distinction difficult is variable rates of evolution among the theories and methodologies of science in response to new data. In addition, specific standards applicable to one field of science may not be applicable in other fields.

Larry Laudan has suggested pseudoscience has no scientific meaning and is mostly used to describe our emotions: "If we would stand up and be counted on the side of reason, we ought to drop terms like 'pseudo-science' and 'unscientific' from our vocabulary; they are just hollow phrases which do only emotive work for us". Likewise, Richard McNally states, "The term 'pseudoscience' has become little more than an inflammatory buzzword for quickly dismissing one's opponents in media sound-bites" and "When therapeutic entrepreneurs make claims on behalf of their interventions, we should not waste our time trying to determine whether their interventions qualify as pseudoscientific. Rather, we should ask them: How do you know that your intervention works? What is your evidence?"

History

The history of pseudoscience is the study of pseudoscientific theories over time. A pseudoscience is a set of ideas that presents itself as science, while it does not meet the criteria to properly be called such.

Distinguishing between proper science and pseudoscience is sometimes difficult. One proposal for demarcation between the two is the falsification criterion, most notably attributed to the philosopher Karl Popper. In the history of science and "history of pseudoscience" it can be especially hard to separate the two, because some sciences developed from pseudosciences. An example of this is the science chemistry, which traces its origins to pseudoscientific alchemy.

The vast diversity in pseudosciences further complicates the history of science. Some modern pseudosciences, such as astrology and acupuncture, originated before the scientific era. Others developed as part of an ideology, such as Lysenkoism, or as a response to perceived threats to an ideology. Examples are creation science and intelligent design, which were developed in response to the scientific theory of evolution.

Despite failing to meet proper scientific standards, many pseudosciences survive. This is usually due to a persistent core of devotees who refuse to accept scientific criticism of their beliefs, or due to popular misconceptions. Sheer popularity is also a factor, as is attested by astrology, which remains popular despite being rejected by a large majority of scientists.

Identifying Pseudoscience

A field, practice, or body of knowledge might reasonably be called pseudoscientific when it is presented as consistent with the norms of scientific research, but it demonstrably fails to meet these norms. Karl Popper stated it is insufficient to distinguish science from pseudoscience, or from metaphysics, by the criterion of rigorous adherence to the empirical method, which is essentially inductive, based on observation or experimentation. He proposed a method to distinguish between genuine empirical, nonempirical or even pseudoempirical methods. The latter case was exemplified by astrology, which appeals to observation and experimentation. While it had astonishing empirical evidence based on observation, on horoscopes and biographies, it crucially failed to adhere to acceptable scientific standards. Popper proposed falsifiability as an important criterion in distinguishing science from pseudoscience.

To demonstrate this point, Popper gave two cases of human behaviour and typical explanations from Freud and Adler's theories: "that of a man who pushes a child into the water with the intention of drowning it; and that of a man who sacrifices his life in an attempt to save the child." From Freud's perspective, the first man would have suffered from psychological repression, probably originating from an Oedipus complex, whereas the second had attained sublimation. From Adler's perspective, the first and second man suffered from feelings of inferiority and had to prove himself which drove him to commit the crime or, in the second case, rescue the child. Popper was not able to find any counterexamples of human behaviour in which the behaviour could not be explained in the terms of Adler's or Freud's theory. Popper argued it was that the observation always fitted or confirmed the theory which, rather than being its strength, was actually its weakness.

In contrast, Popper gave the example of Einstein's gravitational theory, which predicted "light must be attracted by heavy bodies (such as the sun), precisely as material bodies were attracted." Following from this, stars closer to the sun would appear to have moved a small distance away from the sun, and away from each other. This prediction was particularly striking to Popper because it involved considerable risk.

The brightness of the sun prevented this effect from being observed under normal circumstances, so photographs had to be taken during an eclipse and compared to photographs taken at night. Popper states, "If observation shows that the predicted effect is definitely absent, then the theory is simply refuted." Popper summed up his criterion for the scientific status of a theory as depending on its falsifiability, refutability, or testability.

Paul R. Thagard used astrology as a case study to distinguish science from pseudoscience and proposed principles and criteria to delineate them. First, astrology has not progressed in that it has not been updated nor added any explanatory power since Ptolemy. Second, it has ignored outstanding problems such as the precession of equinoxes in astronomy. Third, alternative theories of personality and behaviour have grown progressively to encompass explanations of phenomena which astrology statically attributes to heavenly forces. Fourth, astrologers have remained uninterested in furthering the theory to deal with outstanding problems or in critically evaluating the theory in relation to other theories. Thagard intended this criterion to be extended to areas other than astrology. He believed it would delineate as pseudoscientific such practices as witchcraft and pyramidology, while leaving physics, chemistry and biology in the realm of science. Biorhythms, which like astrology relied uncritically on birth dates, did not meet the criterion of pseudoscience at the time because there were no alternative explanations for the same observations. The use of this criterion has the consequence that a theory can at one time be scientific and at another pseudoscientific.

Science is also distinguishable from revelation, theology, or spirituality in that it offers insight into the physical world obtained by empirical research and testing. For this reason, the teaching of creation science and intelligent design has been strongly condemned in position statements from scientific organisations. The most notable disputes concern the evolution of living organisms, the idea of common descent, the geologic history of the Earth, the formation of the solar system, and the origin of the universe. Systems of belief that derive from divine or inspired knowledge are not considered pseudoscience if they do not claim either to be scientific or to overturn well-established science. Moreover, some specific religious claims, such as the power of intercessory prayer to heal the sickcan be tested by the scientific method, though they may be based on untestable beliefs.

Some statements and commonly held beliefs in popular science may not meet the criteria of science. "Pop" science may blur the divide between science and pseudoscience among the general public, and may also involve science fiction. Indeed, pop science is disseminated to, and can also easily emanate from, persons not accountable to scientific methodology and expert peer review.

If the claims of a given field can be experimentally tested and methodological standards are upheld, it is not "pseudoscience", however odd, astonishing, or counterintuitive. If claims made are inconsistent with existing experimental results or established theory, but the methodology is sound, caution should be used; science consists of testing hypotheses which may turn out to be false. In such a case, the work may be better described as ideas that are "not yet generally accepted". Protoscience is a term sometimes used to describe a hypothesis that has not yet been adequately tested by the scientific method, but which is otherwise consistent with existing science or which, where inconsistent, offers reasonable account of the inconsistency. It may also describe the transition from a body of practical knowledge into a scientific field.

Pseudoscientific Concepts

Examples of pseudoscience concepts, proposed as scientific when they are not scientific, include acupuncture, alchemy, ancient astronauts, applied kinesiology, astrology, Ayurvedic medicine, biorhythms, cellular memory, cold fusion, craniometry, creation science, Scientology founder L. Ron Hubbard's engram theory, enneagrams, eugenics,extrasensory perception (ESP), facilitated communication, graphology, homeopathy, intelligent design, iridology, *kundalini*, Lysenkoism, metoposcopy, N-rays, naturopathy, orgone energy, paranormal plant perception, phrenology, physiognomy, qi, New Age psychotherapies (e.g., rebirthing therapy), reflexology, remote viewing, neuro-linguistic programming (NLP), reiki, Rolfing, therapeutic touch, and the revised history of the solar system proposed by Immanuel Velikovsky.

Robert T. Carroll stated, in part, "Pseudoscientists claim to base their theories on empirical evidence, and they may even use some scientific methods, though often their understanding of a controlled experiment is inadequate. Many pseudoscientists relish being able to point out the consistency of their ideas with known facts or with predicted consequences, but they do not recognize that such consistency is not proof of anything. It is a necessary condition but not a sufficient condition that a good scientific theory be consistent with the facts."

In 2006, the U.S. National Science Foundation (NSF) issued an executive summary of a paper on science and engineering which briefly discussed the prevalence of pseudoscience in modern times. It said, "belief in pseudoscience is widespread" and, referencing a Gallup Poll, stated that belief in the 10 commonly believed examples of paranormal phenomena listed in the poll were "pseudoscientific beliefs". The items were "extrasensory perception (ESP), that houses can be haunted, ghosts, telepathy, clairvoyance, astrology, that people can communicate mentally with someone who has died, witches, reincarnation, and channelling". Such beliefs in pseudoscience reflect a lack of knowledge of how science works. The scientific community may aim to communicate information about science out of concern for the public's susceptibility to unproven claims.

The following are some of the indicators of the possible presence of pseudoscience.

Use of Vague, Exaggerated or Untestable Claims

- Assertion of scientific claims that are vague rather than precise, and that lack specific measurements
- Failure to make use of operational definitions (i.e. publicly accessible definitions of the variables, terms, or objects of interest so that persons other than the definer can independently measure or test them)
- Failure to make reasonable use of the principle of parsimony, i.e. failing to seek an explanation that requires the fewest possible additional assumptions when multiple viable explanations are possible
- Use of obscurantist language, and use of apparently technical jargon in an effort to give claims the superficial trappings of science
- Lack of boundary conditions: Most well-supported scientific theories possess well-articulated limitations under which the predicted phenomena do and do not apply.
- Lack of effective controls, such as placebo and double-blind, in experimental design
- Lack of understanding of basic and established principles of physics and engineering

Over-Reliance on Confirmation rather than Refutation

- Assertions that do not allow the logical possibility that they can be shown to be false by observation or physical experiment
- Assertion of claims that a theory predicts something that it has not been shown to predict Scientific claims that do not confer any predictive power are considered at best "conjectures", or at worst "pseudoscience" (e.g. *Ignoratio elenchi*)
- Assertion that claims which have not been proven false must be true, and vice versa (*see*: Argument from ignorance)
- Over-reliance on testimonial, anecdotal evidence, or personal experience: This evidence may be useful for the context of discovery (i.e. hypothesis generation), but should not be used in the context of justification (e.g. Statistical hypothesis testing).

- Presentation of data that seems to support its claims while suppressing or refusing to consider data that conflict with its claims This is an example of selection bias, a distortion of evidence or data that arises from the way that the data are collected. It is sometimes referred to as the selection effect.
- Promulgating to the status of facts excessive or untested claims that have been previously published elsewhere; an accumulation of such uncritical secondary reports, which do not otherwise contribute their own empirical investigation, is called the Woozle effect.
- Reversed burden of proof: In science, the burden of proof rests on those making a claim, not on the critic. "Pseudoscientific" arguments may neglect this principle and demand that skeptics demonstrate beyond a reasonable doubt that a claim (e.g. an assertion regarding the efficacy of a novel therapeutic technique) is false. It is essentially impossible to prove a universal negative, so this tactic incorrectly places the burden of proof on the skeptic rather than the claimant.
- Appeals to holism as opposed to reductionism: Proponents of pseudoscientific claims, especially in organic medicine, alternative medicine, naturopathy and mental health, often resort to the "mantra of holism" to dismiss negative findings.

Lack of Openness to Testing by Other Experts

- Evasion of peer review before publicizing results (called "science by press conference"): Some proponents of ideas that contradict accepted scientific theories avoid subjecting their ideas to peer review, sometimes on the grounds that peer review is biased towards established paradigms, and sometimes on the grounds that assertions cannot be evaluated adequately using standard scientific methods. By remaining insulated from the peer review process, these proponents forgo the opportunity of corrective feedback from informed colleagues.
- Some agencies, institutions, and publications that fund scientific research require authors to share data so others can evaluate a paper independently. Failure to provide adequate information for other researchers to reproduce the claims contributes to a lack of openness.
- Appealing to the need for secrecy or proprietary knowledge when an independent review of data or methodology is requested.

Absence of Progress

- Failure to progress towards additional evidence of its claim. Terence Hines has identified astrology as a subject that has changed very little in the past two millennia.
- Lack of self-correction: scientific research programmes make mistakes, but they tend to eliminate these errors over time. By contrast, ideas may be regarded as pseudoscientific because they have remained unaltered despite contradictory evidence. The work *Scientists Confront Velikovsky* (1976) Cornell University, also delves into these features in some detail, as does the work of Thomas Kuhn, e.g. *The Structure of Scientific Revolutions* (1962) which also discusses some of the items on the list of characteristics of pseudoscience.
- Statistical significance of supporting experimental results does not improve over time and are usually close to the cutoff for statistical significance. Normally, experimental techniques improve or the experiments are repeated, and this gives ever stronger evidence. If statistical significance does not improve, this typically shows the experiments have just been repeated until a success occurs due to chance variations.

Personalization of Issues

- Tight social groups and authoritarian personality, suppression of dissent, and groupthink can enhance the adoption of beliefs that have no rational basis. In attempting to confirm their beliefs, the group tends to identify their critics as enemies.
- Assertion of claims of a conspiracy on the part of the scientific community to suppress the results
- Attacking the motives or character of anyone who questions the claims

Use of Misleading Language

- Creating scientific-sounding terms to add weight to claims and persuade nonexperts to believe statements that may be false or meaningless: For example, a long-standing hoax refers to water by the rarely used formal name "dihydrogen monoxide" and describes it as the main constituent in most poisonous solutions to show how easily the general public can be misled.
- Using established terms in idiosyncratic ways, thereby demonstrating unfamiliarity with mainstream work in the discipline

Demographics

In his book *The Demon-Haunted World*Carl Sagan discusses the government of China and the Chinese Communist Party concern about Western pseudoscience developments and certain ancient Chinese practices in China. He sees pseudoscience occurring in the U.S. as part of a worldwide trend and suggests its causes, dangers, diagnosis and treatment may be universal. In Spain, another science writer Luis Alfonso Gámez was sued after he notified the public about the lack of efficacy to support the claims of a popular pseudoscientist. In the US, 54% of the population believe in psychic healing and 35% believe in telepathy. In Europe, the statistics are not that much different. A significant percentage of Europeans consider homeopathy (34%) and horoscopes (13%) to be reliable science. Over the past decade, consumer interest in the use of complementary and alternative medicine (CAM) practices and/or products has increased. Surveys demonstrate that the people with the most serious medical conditions, such as cancer, chronic pain, and HIV, are the most routine consumers of CAM.

The National Science Foundation stated that pseudoscientific beliefs in the U.S. became more widespread during the 1990s, peaked near 2001, and declined slightly since with pseudoscientific beliefs remaining common. According to the NSF report, there is a lack of knowledge of pseudoscientific issues in society and pseudoscientific practices are commonly followed. Surveys indicate about a third of all adult Americans consider astrology to be scientific.

In the Journal of College Science Teaching, Art Hobson writes, "Pseudoscientific beliefs are surprisingly widespread in our culture even among public school science teachers and newspaper editors, and are closely related to scientific illiteracy."

Explanations

In a report Singer and Benassi (1981) wrote that pseudoscientific beliefs have their origin from at least four sources.

- Common cognitive errors from personal experience
- Erroneous sensationalistic mass media coverage
- Sociocultural factors
- Poor or erroneous science education

Another American study (Eve and Dunn, 1990) supported the findings of Singer and Benassi and found sufficient levels of pseudoscientific belief being promoted by high school life science and biology teachers.

Psychology

Pseudoscientific thinking has been explained in terms of psychology and social psychology. The human proclivity for seeking confirmation rather than refutation (confirmation bias), the tendency to hold comforting beliefs, and the tendency to overgeneralize have been proposed as reasons for the common adherence to pseudoscientific thinking. According to Beyerstein (1991), humans are prone to associations based on resemblances only, and often prone to misattribution in cause-effect thinking.

Lindeman states that social motives (i.e., "to comprehend self and the world, to have a sense of control over outcomes, to belong, to find the world benevolent and to maintain one's self-esteem") are often "more easily" fulfilled by pseudoscience than by scientific information. Furthermore, pseudoscientific explanations are generally not analyzed rationally, but instead experientially. Operating within a different set of rules compared to rational thinking, experiential thinking regards an explanation as valid if the explanation is "personally functional, satisfying and sufficient", offering a description of the world that may be more personal than can be provided by science and reducing the amount of potential work involved in understanding complex events and outcomes.

In our culture and thinking, people appear to have trouble distinguishing science from pseuodoscience. The prime reason people believe in wishful things is because they want to, it feels good and it is consoling. Many weird beliefs give immediate gratification. Immediate gratification of a person's belief is made a lot easier by simple explanations for an often complicated and contingent world. The scientific and secular systems of morality and meaning are generally unsatisfying to most people. Humans are, by nature, a forward-minded species pursuing greater avenues of happiness and satisfaction, but we are all too frequently willing to grasp at unrealistic promises of a better life.

Psychology has much to discuss about pseudoscience thinking, as it is the illusory perceptions of causality and effectiveness of numerous individuals that needs to be illuminated. Research suggests that illusionary thinking happens in most people when exposed to certain circumstances such as reading a book, an advertisement or the testimony of others are the basis of pseudoscience beliefs. It is assumed that illusions are not unusual, and given the right conditions, illusions are able to occur systematically even in normal emotional situations. One of the things pseudoscience believers quibble most about is that academic science usually treats them as fools. Minimizing these illusions in the real world is not simple. To this aim, designing evidence-based educational programs can be effective to help people identify and reduce their own illusions.

Boundaries between Science and Pseudoscience

In the philosophy and history of science, Imre Lakatos stresses the social and political importance of the demarcation problem, the normative methodological problem of distinguishing between science and pseudoscience. His distinctive historical analysis of scientific methodology based on research programmes suggests: "scientists regard the successful theoretical prediction of stunning novel facts – such as the return of Halley's comet or the gravitational bending of light rays – as what demarcates good scientific theories from pseudo-scientific and degenerate theories, and in spite of all scientific theories being forever confronted by 'an ocean of counterexamples'". Lakatos offers a "novel fallibilist analysis of the development of Newton's celestial dynamics, [his] favourite historical example of his methodology" and argues in light of this historical turn, that his account answers for certain inadequacies in those of Sir Karl Popper and Thomas Kuhn. "Nonetheless, Lakatos did recognize the force of Kuhn's historical criticism of Popper – all important theories have been surrounded by an 'ocean of anomalies', which on a falsificationist view would require the rejection of the theory outright... Lakatos sought to reconcile the rationalism of Popperian falsificationism with what seemed to be its own refutation by history".

Many philosophers have tried to solve the problem of demarcation in the following terms: a statement constitutes knowledge if sufficiently many people believe it sufficiently strongly. But the history of thought shows us that many people were totally committed to absurd beliefs. If the strengths of beliefs were a hallmark of knowledge, we should have to rank some tales about demons, angels, devils, and of heaven and hell as knowledge. Scientists, on the other hand, are very sceptical even of their best theories. Newton's is the most powerful theory science has yet produced, but Newton himself never believed that bodies attract each other at a distance. So no degree of commitment to beliefs makes them knowledge. Indeed, the hallmark of scientific behaviour is a certain scepticism even towards one's most cherished theories. Blind commitment to a theory is not an intellectual virtue: it is an intellectual crime.

Thus a statement may be pseudoscientific even if it is eminently 'plausible' and everybody believes in it, and it may be scientifically valuable even if it is unbelievable and nobody believes in it. A theory may even be of supreme scientific value even if no one understands it, let alone believes in it.

—Imre Lakatos, *Science and Pseudoscience*

The boundary lines between science and pseudoscience are disputed and difficult to determine analytically, even after more than a century of dialogue among philosophers of science and scientists in varied fields, and despite some basic agreements on the fundaments of scientific methodology.

The concept of pseudoscience rests on an understanding that scientific methodology has been misrepresented or misapplied with respect to a given theory, but many philosophers of science maintain that different kinds of methods are held as appropriate across different fields and different eras of human history.

According to Lakatos, the typical descriptive unit of great scientific achievements is not an isolated hypothesis but "a powerful problem-solving machinery, which, with the help of sophisticated mathematical techniques, digests anomalies and even turns them into positive evidence."

To Popper, pseudoscience uses induction to generate theories, and only performs experiments to seek to verify them. To Popper, falsifiability is what determines the scientific status of a theory. Taking a historical approach, Kuhn observed that scientists did not follow Popper's rule, and might ignore falsifying data, unless overwhelming.

To Kuhn, puzzle-solving within a paradigm is science. Lakatos attempted to resolve this debate, by suggesting history shows that science occurs in research programmes, competing according to how progressive they are. The leading idea of a programme could evolve, driven by its heuristic to make predictions that can be supported by evidence. Feyerabend claimed that Lakatos was selective in his examples, and the whole history of science shows there is no universal rule of scientific method, and imposing one on the scientific community impedes progress.

—David Newbold and Julia Roberts, *"An analysis of the demarcation problem in science and its application to therapeutic touch theory" in International Journal of Nursing Practice, Vol. 13*

Laudan maintained that the demarcation between science and non-science was a pseudo-problem, preferring to focus on the more general distinction between reliable and unreliable knowledge.

[Feyerabend] regards Lakatos's view as being closet anarchism disguised as methodological rationalism. It should be noted that Feyerabend's claim was not that standard methodological rules should never be obeyed, but rather that sometimes progress is made by abandoning them. In the absence of a generally accepted rule, there is a need for alternative methods of persuasion. According to Feyerabend, Galileo employed stylistic and rhetorical techniques to convince his reader, while he also wrote in Italian rather than Latin and directed his arguments to those already temperamentally inclined to accept them.

—Alexander Bird, *"The Historical Turn in the Philosophy of Science" in Routledge Companion to the Philosophy of Science*

Politics, Health, and Education

Political Implications: The demarcation problem between science and pseudoscience brings up debate in the realms of science, philosophy and politics. Imre Lakatos, for instance, points out that the Communist Party of the Soviet Union at one point declared that Mendelian genetics was pseudoscientific and had its advocates, including well-established scientists such as Nikolai Vavilov, sent to a Gulag and that the "liberal Establishment of the West" denies freedom of speech to topics it regards as pseudoscience, particularly where they run up against social mores.

Pseudoscience is used recurrently in political, policy-making discourse in allegations of distortion or fabrication of scientific findings to support a political position.

The Prince of Wales has accused climate change skeptics of using pseudoscience and persuasion to hinder the world from adopting precautionary principles to avert the negative effects of global warming. People have given attention to the climate skeptics and have tried to understand the kind of pseudoscience they are canvassing. But he insisted the "environmental collapse" evidence is already here, not only in climbing temperatures but the imprint on particular species like honey bees.

It becomes pseudoscientific when science cannot be separated from ideology, scientists misrepresent scientific findings to promote or draw attention for publicity, when politicians, journalists and a nation's intellectual elite distort the facts of science for short-term political gain, when powerful individuals in the public conflate causation and cofactors (for example, in the causes of HIV/AIDS) through a mixture of clever wordplay, or when science is being used by the powerful to promote ignorance rather than tackle ignorance. These ideas reduce the authority, value, integrity and independence of science in society.

A large percentage of the United States population lacks scientific literacy, not adequately understanding scientific principles and methodology.

Health and Education Implications

Distinguishing science from pseudoscience has practical implications in the case of health care, expert testimony, environmental policies, and science education. Treatments with a patina of scientific authority which have not actually been subjected to actual scientific testing may be ineffective, expensive, and dangerous to patients, and confuse health providers, insurers, government decision makers, and the public as to what treatments are appropriate. Claims advanced by pseudoscience may result in government officials and educators making poor decisions in selecting curricula; for example, creation science may replace evolution in studies of biology.

The extent to which students acquire a range of social and cognitive thinking skills related to the proper usage of science and technology determines whether they are scientifically literate. Education in the sciences encounters new dimensions with the changing landscape of science and technology, a fast-changing culture, and a knowledge-driven era. A reinvention of the school science curriculum is one that shapes students to contend with its changing influence on human welfare. Scientific literacy, which allows a person to distinguish science from pseudosciences such as astrology, is among the attributes that enable students to adapt to the changing world. Its characteristics are embedded in a curriculum where students are engaged in resolving problems, conductung investigations, or developing projects.

Scientists do not want to get involved to counter pseudoscience for various reasons. For example, pseudoscientific beliefs are irrational and impossible to combat with rational arguments, and even agreeing to talk about pseudoscience indicates acceptance as a credible discipline. Pseudoscience harbors a continuous and an increasing threat to our society.

It is impossible to determine the irreversible harm that will happen in the long term. In a time when the public science literacy has declined and the danger of pseudoscience has increased, revising the conventional science course to address current science through the prism of pseudoscience could help improve science literacy and help society to eliminate misconceptions and assault growing trends (remote viewing, psychic readings, etc.) that may harm (financially or otherwise) trusting citizens.

Pseudosciences such as homeopathy, even if generally benign, are magnets for charlatans. This poses a serious issue because incompetent practitioners should not be given the right of administering health care. True-believing zealots may pose a more serious threat than typical con men because of their affection to homeopathy's ideology. Irrational health care is not harmless, and it is careless to create patient confidence in pseudomedicine.

Bibliography

Ajit, M.: *Kundalini: The Arousal of the Inner Energy*, Destiny Books, New York, 1986.

Anant, S. S.: *Changing Caste Hindu Attitudes Towards Harijans: A Follow Up After Four Years*, New Delhi, Vikas, 1979.

Austin, B.: *Guide to Indian Philosophy*, G. K. Hall, Boston, 1988.

Baba, Pagal: *Temple of the Phallic King: The Mind of India*, Simon and Schuster, New York, 1973.

Benoytosh, B.: *Two Vajrayana Works*, Gaekwad's Oriental Series, Baroda, 1956.

Bhatia, S.C.: *Education and Social Cultural Disadvance,* Delhi Xeres Publication, 1982.

Burgess, J.: *The Chronology of Modern India*, MacMillan, London, 1984.

Chakravarti, C. : *The Tantras: Studies on their Religion and Literature*, Punthi Pustak, Calcutta, 1963.

David, J.: *Shiva's Other Children: Religion and Social Identity amongst Overseas Indians,* Sage, Walnut Creek, 1998.

Devi, Kamala : *Indian Women's Battle for Freedom,* New Delhi, Abhinav Publications, 1983.

Engineer, Asghar Ali: *Mandal Commission Controversy*, Delhi, Ajanta Publications, 1991.

Feuerstein, Georg : *The Philosophy of Classical Yoga,* Inner Traditions, Rochester, 1996.

Flood, L.: *The Origins and Developments of Classical Hinduism,* Beacon Press, Boston, 1998.

Goldman, Robert : *The Ramayana of Valmiki,* Princeton UP, 1984.

Gorhe, Neelam: *Social Development and Dalit Women*, Gyan Pub. House, New Delhi, 1995.

Harman, William: *The Sacred Marriage of a Hindu Goddess*, Indiana University Press, Bloomington, 1998.

Hashemi, Syed M.: *Defining and Studying Empowerment of Women: A Research Note from Bangladesh,* Washington, John Snow, 1993.

Jahan, Rounaq: *The Elusive Agenda: Mainstreaming Women in Development*, Atlantic Highlands, Zed Books Ltd, 1995.

Kamble, J. R.: *Rise and Awakening of Depressed Classes in India*, New Delhi, National Publishers, 1979.

Khan, Mumtaz Ali: *Identity Formation and Self Identity Among Harijan Elite*, New Delhi, Uppal Publishing House, 1994.

Lessing, Ferdinand : *Introduction to the Buddhist Tantric Systems*, Motilal Banarsidass, Delhi, 1993.

Malkani, G.R.: *A Study of Reality*, The Modern Book Stall, Bombay, 1952.

Moody, H.: *Working Women: The Subterranean World of Street Prostitution*, New York, Harper & Row, 1985.

Narayan, Deepa : *Empowerment and Poverty Reduction,* Washington, World Bank, 2002.

Omar, G.: *Tantra: The Yoga of Sex*, Avon Books, New York, 1996.

Patwardhan, Sunanda: *Change Among India's Harijans: Maharashtra a Case Study*, New Delhi, Orient Longmans, 1973.

Payne, E. : *The Shaktas: An Introduction and Comparative Study*, Calcutta, 1933.

Pramathanath, M.: *Introduction to Vedanta Philosophy,* Basu Mallik Press, Calcutta: 1975.

Pushpendra, K.: *Hindu Religion and Ethics,* Asian Publication Services, Delhi, 2002.

Ramanujan, A. K. : *Hymns for Visnu by Nammalvar,* Princeton, 1981.

Rao, M. S. A.: *Social Movement and Social Transformation: A Study of Backward Class Movement*, New Delhi, Macmillian Press, 1978.

Sen, Amartya: *Development as Freedom of Women*, Oxford, Oxford University Press, 1999.

Stein, Burton: *Vijayanagara*, Cambridge University Press, Cambridge, 1989.

Tarkalankara, C.: *Hindu Philosophy,* Basu Mallik Press, Calcutta, 1922.

Vivekananda, S.: *Raja Yoga,* Chinmaya Publications, Piercy, 1993.

Walters, D.: *The Path: Autobiography of a Western Yogi (Swami Kriyananda),* Ananda Publications, Nevada City, 1977.

Winternitz, M. : *Notes on the Guhyasamaja Tantra and the Age of the Tantras*, IHQ, Calcutta, 1933.

Index

❑❑❑